National Association of Latino Independent Producers

the
latino
media
resource
guide
2005

National Association of Latino Independent Producers (NALIP)
P. O. Box 1247
Santa Monica, CA 90406
Phone 310.395.8880
Phone 310.457.4445
www.nalip.org

Published in cooperation with the
Hollywood Creative Directory
5055 Wilshire Blvd.
Los Angeles, CA 90036
Phone 323.525.2369
Toll-free 800.815.0503
www.hcdonline.com

Printed in the United States of America

Cover design by Jesus Garcia
Book design by Carla Green

National Association of Latino Independent Producers

The Corporation for Public Broadcasting
is proud to partner with NALIP
in addressing the needs
of the Latino Filmmaking Community.

A private corporation funded by the American people. CPB.ORG

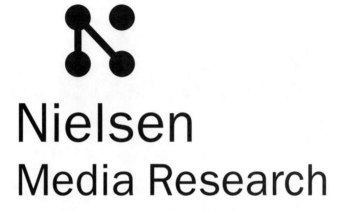

National Association of Latino Independent Producers

the latino media resource guide 2005

contents

DISCLAIMER
The information contained in this book is provided directly by the individuals, production companies, and all other resources listed. NALIP does not engage in editorializing and cannot be held responsible for the veracity of a particular listing or misrepresentation by a listee. NALIP is not responsible for information that has changed after the book has gone to press.

SíTV

proudly supports the

National Association

of

Latino Independent

Producers

Sítv
www.sitv.com

welcome from the NALIP Board Chair

Dear NALIP members, supporters and readers:

Welcome to the second edition of the National Association of Latino Independent Producers' **Latino Media Resource Guide**™.

It is not an exaggeration to say that the guide's first edition exceeded even our wildest expectations. Hundreds of people have been hired or found a key piece of information simply because they owned a copy of "the book," as we affectionately call the guide at NALIP. As a result, all we could think to build on this great achievement is…print another edition.

For those of you who are new to the Latino Media Resource Guide™, connecting to our community is as simple as picking up this book. By consulting this Guide you will be able to identify Latino talent working in all aspects of media-making, in every part of the country. To facilitate access, the Guide is available at no expense in hard copy and will be complemented with a web-based database that will provide continuous updated information starting in 2005.

The current Guide is also bigger and better. It includes over 400 additional names, updated credits, and two new sections: a sampling of contemporary Latino films and a list of independent distributors. These last two sections are designed to answer frequently asked questions to the staff concerning possible partners for distribution and about the success of Latino films in the United States and around the world.

By issuing the second edition of the Latino Media Resource Guide™, NALIP is once more not alone in our belief in the power of information to build community. The project's funders, including CBS, Coca Cola Co., CPB, the Ford Foundation, Fox Broadcasting, LA County Arts, Latino Public Broadcasting, Los Angeles Cultural Affairs Department, the MacArthur Foundation, NCLR, NEA, Nielsen Media Research, Packair, P.O.V., the Rockefeller Foundation, SiTV, Univision, Walt Disney Studios and Workplace Hollywood, have each contributed to the success of the guide and we are grateful for their support.

Again, we hope that you use the Latino Media Resource Guide™ until it falls apart and you need a new one.

Warmly,
Frances Negrón-Muntaner, Chair

CBS, Committed to Diversity.

CBS

For information, please visit our Web site: www.cbsdiversity.com.

acknowledgments

We would like to acknowledge and extend our deepest appreciation to all the wonderful people who embraced this project, saw its impact and tremendous potential, and then contributed to making our Second Edition a reality.

First, the NALIP Board of Directors: Eddie Borges, Moctesuma Esparza, Evy Ledesma Galán, Sonia González, Evangeline Griego, Lorena Hernandez, Cynthia López, Bienvenida Matias, Frances Negrón-Muntaner, David Ortiz, Edwin Pagán, and Alex Rodriguez.

Second, our Board of Trustees: Eddie Arnold, Rudy Beserra, Dennis Leoni, Lisa Navarrete, David Valdés and Jeff Valdez. Also, our research manager, Ismael Barrios Prado, for his dedication and superb work, and our fearless research team and staff, Mariana Garbagnati, Erick Garcia, Melissa Levin, Stephanie Martin, Jose Carlos Mangual, Jaime Pelayo, Ramiro Segovia and Jose Murillo. Plus our key art designer, Jesus Garcia, and our online database visionary, Samantha Smith.

In addition, our partners and friends at Hollywood Creative Directory: Jeff Black and production manager Carla Green.

And last but not least, our funders and supporters: The Rockefeller Foundation. The Ford Foundation. The John D. and Catherine T. MacArthur Foundation. Los Angeles Cultural Affairs Department. LA County Arts Commission. The Walt Disney Studios. Univision. Fox Broadcasting. CBS. The Corporation for Public Broadcasting. The NEA. Nielsen Media Research. NCLR. Latino Public Broadcasting. P.O.V.. The Coca Cola Company. SíTV. Workplace Hollywood. Southwest Airlines. Kinko's Westwood Village. Packair. We appreciate your vision, and your commitment to this resource, and we appreciate your sharing our dedication to the advancement of the professional and creative endeavors of so many.

Your generous participation is making a difference.

Finally, to the NALIP membership and many others who have so graciously supported our efforts, thank you.

Kathryn F. Galán
Executive Director

Octavio Marin
Signature Programs Director

National Association of Latino Independent Producers

our mission

The National Association of Latino Independent Producers (NALIP) address-es the professional needs of Latino/Latina independent filmmakers. Our mission: to promote the advancement, development and funding of Latino/Latina film and media arts in ALL genres. Since our founding in 1999, NALIP has developed four National Initiatives: our annual Conference, the Latino Writers Lab™, the Latino Producers Academy™, and this published/on-line Latino Media Resource Guide™ — our member directory plus so much more.

In addition, we have developed local chapters, and hosted many regional workshops and networking events that develop the professional skills of film, television, documentary and new media makers. NALIP is the only national organization committed to supporting both grassroots and community-based producers/media makers along with publicly funded and industry based producers. We aim to support a higher quality and quantity of projects by and about Latino/as. NALIP's values are:

- Commitment to Latino/a media and Filmmakers, regardless of the form or content of their work
- Commitment with respect for diversity based on a code of ethics open to and respectful of differences, including gender, geography, color, class, age, ethnicity, language, sexuality, religion, genre or physical abilities
- Commitment to solidarity and accountability, applying our code of ethics to the selection, funding, and mentoring process
- Commitment to raise the question of historical and cultural relevance and awareness of Latinos and Latinas
- Commitment to solidarity, alliance building and multiple visions of Latina/Latino experiences within the local, national, international and global context

MEMBERSHIP BENEFITS

- Participation in the National Latino/a Media Agenda
- Discounts and scholarships to NALIP National Conferences, LWL, LPA and workshops
- Trade discounts with Staples, Duart, LatPro Job Board and other vendors
- Affiliate membership programs with AIVF, the IDA and other organizations
- Web-based resource database and grants/events calendar at http://my.nalip.info
- Quarterly Board of Directors Minutes & annual NALIP financial report
- Copy of Latino Media Resource Guide™

ANNUAL MEMBERSHIP RATES

Student Membership (w/valid ID)	$20
Individual Filmmaker Membership	$50
Professional/Executive Producer Membership	$150
Organizational/Non-profit Membership	$200
Supporter	$500
Benefactor	$1,000
Patron	$5,000
Trustee	$10,000

Make checks payable to NALIP and mail to:
NALIP Membership
P.O. Box 1247
Santa Monica, CA 90406
Tel: 310.395.8880
Fax: 310.395.8811
Email: membership@nalip.info
Or join online at www.nalip.org

continued on page xiii

P.O.V. *salutes* Lourdes Portillo

NALIP 2005 Recipient
Pioneer Achievement In Producing Award

Las Madres: The Mothers of Plaza de Mayo (1988)

Corpus: A Home Movie For Selena (1999)

Señorita Extraviada (2002)

Congratulations Lourdes!
P.O.V. is honored to present your extraordinary work!
¡Felicitaciones!

Independent Television Service (ITVS) and
Latino Public Broadcasting (LPB) co-presentations

continued from page xi

NALIP CHAPTERS/CHAPTERS-IN-FORMATION

AUSTIN
Rupert Reyes
RupertReyes@yahoo.com

BOSTON
Maria Agui Carter
IguanaFilms@earthlink.net

CHICAGO
Juan Lopez
J_Lopez@nothwestern.edu

FLORIDA
Maritza Guimet
Maritza@nalip.info

NEW MEXICO
Marisa Casteneda
mcastan@unm.edu

NEW YORK
Edwin Pagan
PaganImage@aol.com

PHILADELPHIA
Juvencio Gonzalez
JGonzalez001@comcast.net

PUERTO RICO
Frances Lausell
IslaDigital@aol.com

SAN ANTONIO
Dora Peña
DoraLPena@hotmail.com

SAN FRANCISCO
Monica Nañez
Monanez@sbcglobal.net

TUCSON
Ben Lopez
BenLopez@email.arizona.edu

Latino Producers Academy™

AUGUST 2005

NALIP's signature program, the Latino Producers Academy™, will accept applications for our Third Year program starting in May 2005. This week-long intensive invites Latino feature and documentary producer/director teams in advanced states of development and packaging to a seven-day immersion program that provides each project team with the support needed to bring their film or documentary to production.

The program is not for beginners; it is designed as advanced training through practicums and mentoring with industry professionals. Only select projects are invited to participate, and each team attends on full scholarship, so the application is competitive. Curriculum is developed with UCLA's TFT Professional Certificate Program along with other post-graduate programs committed to the success of emerging creative Latino talent.

Applications available at www.nalip.org by **May 15, 2005.**

For more information, please contact:
Octavio Marin, NALIP Signature Programs Director
310.395.8880 / octavio@nalip.org

WE REALLY COVER A LOT OF GROUND.
IN THE AIR, THAT IS.

It's amazing where you can go by traveling Southwest. With Southwest Airlines' everyday low fares, convenient flights, and superb Customer Service, we can fly you to all of these cities. For details on the cities we serve and available flight connections, call your travel agent or Southwest Airlines and start exercising your freedom to fly.

SOUTHWEST®

OFFICIAL AIRLINE OF THE LATINO PRODUCERS ACADEMY

En Español
1-800-VAMONOS
(1-800-826-6667)

1-800-I-FLY-SWA
(1-800-435-9792)

Latino Writers Lab™

SPRING 2005 – NEW YORK, NY • FALL 2005 – SANTA MONICA, CA

NALIP's **Signature Program, the Latino Writers Lab™**, expands its format in 2005 in order to better support NALIP members who aspire to work as professional writers, or who desire to develop a strong, viable screenplay for production or sale. Only 12-15 writers will be selected to participate in this 8-day intensive workshop. The first four-day seminar will be conducted in New York City in May, 2005. The second four-day seminar will be held in Santa Monica, California, after each participant has written either a first draft from his/her proposed treatment, or a polished script based on a rough draft.

The New York seminar will examine storytelling techniques, and skills to align reader reactions with a writer's intention. It will include intensive mentoring on each writer's specific treatment or draft screenplay. **A complete first draft or rewrite must be completed by August 26 in order to gain admittance to the Fall workshop.**

The California seminar will examine scene writing and rewrite techniques, while using Lab writers' work as examples. Further mentor and peer review of each screenplay will be included in the second workshop, as well.

Applications available at www.nalip.org. **Deadline**: March 23, 2005.

For more information, please contact:
Octavio Marin, NALIP Signature Programs Director
310.395.8880 / octavio@nalip.org

The National Council of La Raza

Congratulates

NALIP

on their 2005
Annual Conference,
the Latino Media
Resource Guide, and
six years of service to
the Latino/Latina
media field

National Association of Latino Independent Producers

production
companies

4 Elements Entertainment

P.O. Box 341784
Los Angeles, CA 90034
Tel 310-980-8906
Email ....shawnabaca@hotmail.com
Web ....www.shawnabaca.com

Shawna Baca, Writer/Director/Producer

Credits
Rose's Garden, Impersonal Impression, Man,
Where's my Shoe?, De La Rosa,

In Development
3:52

Project Types
Short Films

About Time Productions

1918 Chicakasaw Ave.
Los Angeles, CA 90041
Tel 323-493-2790
Fax 323-982-1635
Email......................abouttyme@aol.com

Evangeline Griego, Producer

Credits
Border Visions/Visiones Fronterizos, Paño
Arte: Images from Inside

In Development
God Willing

Project Types
Documentaries

Accent Media Productions, Inc.

1350 Beverly Rd., #213
McLean, Virginia 22101
Tel ....703-356-9427 Ext. 26
Cell 703-477-0035
Fax 703-506-0643
Email ..jackjorgens@accentmediainc.com
Web ....www.accentmediainc.com

Cecilia Domeyko,President
Dr. Jack Jorgens, VP/Senior Producer

Credits
Magic Wool (Discovery), Portrait of Ana Maria
Vera (PBS), Uganda: Education for All,
Chilean Educational Reform, Cuba Mia:
Portrait of An All Woman Orchestra (American
Public Television), Code Name: Butterflies

In Development
La Familia Unida Esperanza de la Vida

Project Types
Documentaries, Training, Promotions

Alpha Studios

3540 N. Southport, #157
Chicago, IL 60657
Tel 773-610-5407
Studio Tel......................312-906-8888
Email..................rislas@alphaflicks.com
Email..................alphilms@hotmail.com
Web ....www.alphaflicks.com

Ricardo Islas, Producer/Director

Credits
Haciendo El Amor...Brujo

Project Types
Tele-Films, TV, Mini-Series, Features

Alta Vista Films

6121 Santa Monica Blvd., #102
Hollywood, CA 90038
Tel 323-461-0101
Fax 323-461-8181
Email ....altavista@altavistafilms.com
Web ....www.altavistafilms.com

David Lozano, Executive Producer

Credits
Amapola, Herod's Law

Project Types
Features

American View Productions

586 Clinton Ave.
Bridgeport, CT 06605
Tel 203-366-5033
Fax 203-366-5044
Email......................americanv@snet.net
Web ..www.americanviewproductions.com

Frank Borres, President
Robert Alvarado, Creative Director

Credits
Celia Cruz and Friends, Puerto Rican
Messages, LottoMundo

Project Types
TV Commercials, Documentaries,
Entertainment Segments

Anteros Films

P.O. Box 7083
Austin, TX 78713
Tel 512-576-9716
Email ....keiser_lupe@yahoo.com

Lupe Valdez, President and CEO

Credits
One Wish, Anteros, Delirium

Project Types
Features

Andale Pictures

12121 Wilshire Blvd., Suite 1400
Los Angeles, CA 90024
Tel 310-820-2111
Fax 310-207-6308
Email ....saguero@3monkeysla.com

Sergio Aguero, Producer

Credits
Y Tu Mamá También, Let the Devil Wear
Black

Project Types
Features

Arenas Entertainment

100 N. Crescent Dr., Garden Level
Beverly Hills, CA 90210
Tel 310-385-4401
Fax 310-385-4402
Email ....info@arenasgroup.com
Web ....www.arenasgroup.com

Santiago Pozo, CEO
Diana Lesmez, VP of Development,
    Production & Acquisitions

Credits
Imagining Argentina, Nicotina, Culture Clash
in America, Empire

Project Types
Features

Blind Ambition Films

P.O. Box 1513
Venice, CA 90294-1513
Tel 323-460-2846
Email ....yazzie@filmfestivals.net
Web ....http://members.tripod.com/
                    baf2005ca/index.htm

Yazmin Ortiz, CEO/President

Credits
A Mother's Cry, El Baile, Jamaican Market
Woman, The Road to the Oscars, Just
Another Skateboarder, My Encounter, The
Joke, The Corporation, Calling God, L.A.
Poverty Department, Global Children
Organization, Seeing Sarah

In Development
American Contra, Redemption, La Ola,
Doradillo, Abigail, 1041, Dead Air, On The
Air, Super Mambo, PRAP, Cell

Project Types
Features, TV, Theater, Documentaries

Boricua Films

Warner Hollywood Studios
1041 N. Formosa Ave.
Formosa Bldg., Suite 5
West Hollywood, CA 90046
Tel 323-850-2650
Fax 323-850-2638
Email ....bros@boricuafilms.com
Web ....www.boricuafilms.com

David and Erik Llauger-Maiselman,
  Executive Producers
Henry K. Priest, Producer

Credits
Urban Graffiti, Paris Falls, Ride the Spot,
Teva, TNK-Tomorrow Never Knows, The
Saving of Jesse O, The Bay School, L.A. River
Stories, Art Works

In Development
Development Hell, His Name Was Peres, Oh,
Mother Yemaña, El Matadero

Project Types
Features, TV, Shorts

Burning Bright Features

417 Canal St., 4th Fl.
New York, NY 10012
Tel 212-274-0856
Fax 212-601-5916
Email ....bmorley@monsoon-ent.com

Alfonso Cuaron
Carlos Cuaron
Jorge Vergara, Producer

Credits
Crónicas, The Assasination of Richard Nixon,
Tokyo Boogie, Y Tu Mamá Tambien, The
Devil's Backbone

In Development
Toto, Juego de Ajedrez, Las Mujeres de
Juarez, The Man on the Other Side of the
Street, Mexico 68, The Pan's Labyrinth

Project Types
Features

Caldera/De Fanti Entertainment

P.O. Box 402
Los Feliz, CA 90027
Tel 323-906-9500
Fax 323-906-9555

Carolyn Caldera, Partner
Jean-Luc DeFanti, Partner

Credits
Three Blind Mice

In Development
Diego

Project Types
Features, TV

Calla Productions

2301 Ocean Ave., Suite 107
Santa Monica, CA 90405
Tel 310-392-3775
Fax 310-399-5594
Email ....debcalla@callaproductions.com
Web ....www.callaproductions.com

Deborah Calla, Producer

Credits
Carnival In Rio-2003 Chicano Artists (HBO
Latino), 500th Anniversary of Brazil (TNT
Latin America), Ushi Goes USA (TV
Endemol), Dream House, Lost Zweig, Dream
House, Lehi's Wife, Carnival In Rio-2004,
Fox Kids Club

In Development
Miss Zacatecas, River City 106, Ted and
Michael, Rio de Janeiro, Everlasting

Project Types
Features, TV, Documentaries, Commercials

Carmona Entertainment

5400 E. Olympic Blvd., #227
Los Angeles, CA 90022
Tel 323-721-3456
Fax 323-728-4045
Email ..info@carmona-entertainment.com
Web ....www.carmona-entertainment.com

Gabriel Barbarena, CEO
Gabriel Carmona, President
Alfonso Espinosa, VP Production
Miguel Torres, VP Production Supervisor

Credits
Symbol of the Heart, In Search of Aztlan: a
Docu-Comedy, Behind-The-Scenes, Eva,
Latinos: Lost In Translation (PBS)

In Development
Mexican in American Sports, God's
Penitentiary, America's Hero

Project Types
Documentaries, TV

CineSon

Sherman Oaks, CA 91423
Tel 818-501-8246
Tel 818-501-3647
Email ....goncaproductions@mail.com
Web ....www.cineson.com

Andy Garcia, Producer

Credits
The Lost City, The Man From Elysian Fields,
The Ties That Bind, Just the Ticket, The
Arturo Sandoval Story, Cachao...For Love or
Country: Como Su Ritmo No Hay Dos

Project Types
Features, Documentaries

Concrete Images

P.O. Box 689, 647 Washington Blvd.
Venice, CA 90294
Tel 310-827-3573
Fax 310-827-9623
Email ..production@concreteimages.com
Web ....www.concreteimages.com

Thomas Lamelza, Producer
Hani Selim, Producer

Cris Franco Entertainment (CFE)

5324 Kester Ave., #1
Sherman Oaks, CA 91411-4060
Tel 818-642-0935
Email ....me@crisfranco.com
Email ....crisfrancoshow@aol.com
Web ....www.crisfranco.com

Cris Franco, Producer

Credits
The Cris Franco Show, Café California
Classics

In Development
Cris Cross Town

Project Types
Talk Shows, Sketch Comedy

Cuentos del Pueblo Productions

P.O. Box 10746
Beverly Hills, CA 90213
Email ....Cuentosdelpueblo@
cuentosdelpueblo.com
Web ....www.cuentosdelpueblo.com

Alejandro J. Diaz, Writer/Director
Adriana E. Padilla, Producer

Credits
Pan Dulce y Chocolate

In Development
Cuentos del Pueblo TV Series, Open Swim,
By the Light of the Moon

Project Types
Features, Suspense, Thriller, Horror, Drama,
TV Series

Cutting Edge Entertainment

695 W. 7th St.
Plainfield, NJ 07060
Tel 908-769-3250
Tel 732-669-0112
Fax 908-769-3252
Email ....info@ceetv.com
Web ....www.ceetv.com

Rey Blanco, CEO/Executive Producer

Credits
Gloria and Emilio Estefan: Made For Each
Other (A&E), Oscar de la Hoya: Body and
Soul (A&E), Broadway's Best (Tribune),
America Eats (Tribune), Viva! (SYN) Black
and White in Exile (PBS), Orozco in
Gringoland (PBS)

In Development
Wifredo and Me (PBS), Star Models: The
Audition, Opening Night, The Other Side of
Fame (TBA), Testimony: Death of a
Guatemalan Village (TBA), Cookin' With Salsa

Project Types
Documentaries, TV

Daniel Hernandez Productions

P.O. Box 90
Montebello, CA 90640
Tel 562-221-1278
Tel 562-634-3448
Fax 562-221-1278
Email ....Dan@sportfishing.com
Web ....www.sport-fishing.com

Daniel Hernandez, Executive Producer

Credits
Sport Fishing with Dan Hernandez, Angler's
Journal, Life of a Mariachi

Project Types
Features, TV

Diva Digital Pictures

2801 SW 31st Ave.
Coconut Grove, FL 33133
Tel 305-546-9320
Fax 305-445-1557
Email ......admin@divadigitalpictures.com
Web ....www.divadigitalpictures.com

Mayte Prida, President
Jorge Martinez, Executive Director

Credits
Soccer with Mayte, Solo en Miami,
Informalmente Formal, El Libro Mágico, Una
Noche Con...Las Estrellas, Un Mundo Con
Mayte, Finalmente A Solas, En Casa Con
Chabeli, Uno A Uno, Singing Bilingual

Project Types
TV, Corporate Videos, Commercials,
Documentaries

El Deséo S.A. (Spain)

c/o Francisco Navacerrada 24
Madrid, Spain 28028
Tel 34 91 724 81 99
Fax 34 91 355 74 67
Email ....eldeseo@eldeseo.es
Web ....www.eldeseo.com.es

Pedro Almodóvar, Producer

Credits
La Mala Educación, Descongélate, Mi Vida
Sin Mí, Hablé con Ella, El Espinazo del
Diablo, La Fiebre del Loco, Todo Sobre Mi
Madre, A Trabajar!, Carne Tremula, Pasajes,
Tengo una Casa, La Flor de Mi Secreto, Kika,
Acción Mutante, Tacones Lejanos, Atame!,
Mujeres al Borde de un Ataque de Nervios,
La Ley del Deséo, Que he Hecho Yo Para
Merecer Esto?, Entre Tinieblas, Matador

In Development
The Secret Life of Words

Project Types
Features

El Norte Productions

10202 W. Washington Blvd.
Barrymore Bldg., #302
Culver City, CA 90232
Tel 310-244-2518
Email ....bmjelnorte@hotmail.com

Gregory Nava, Producer/Director
Barbara Martinez-Jitner, Producer

Credits
Bordertown, American Family, Killing Pablo,
The 20th Century: American Tapestry

Project Types
Features, TV, Documentaries

Empire Pictures

595 Madison Ave., 39th Fl.
New York, NY 10022
Tel 212-629-3097
Fax 212-629-3629
Email ....webmaster@
empirepictures.usa.com
Web............www.empirepicturesusa.com

Armando Schwartz, CEO

Credits
Las Tres Marias, Tan De Repente

Project Types
Features

Encantado Films

P.O. Box 7000-55
Redondo Beach, CA 90277
Tel 310-373-0324
Fax 310-373-3749
Web ....www.encantadofilms.com

Don Henry
Lisa Henry
Candice Rosales
Cris Rosales

In Development
Desert of Blood, Something to Believe

Project Types
Features

Esperanza Films

1448 15th St., Suite 103
Santa Monica, CA 90404
Tel 310-899-9336
Fax 310-899-9007
Email ....renecruz@esperanza.com
Web.......................www.esperanza.com

Rene Simon Cruz, Jr., President

Credits
They Speak of Hope: the Church in El
Salvador, Beyond Borders: John Sayles in
Mexico, HBO: America Undercover/Battered,
Independent Focus, Cross the Line

In Development
The Salted Earth, Border Wars, The Love,
Thug Angels, By Any Means Necessary

Project Types
Features, TV, Documentary, Music
Productions

Espinosa Productions

P.O. Box 1925
Scottsdale, AZ 85252
Tel 480-965-5120
Fax 480-965-7165
Email ....espinosa@electriciti.com
Web ....www.espinosaproductions.com

Paul Espinosa, President

Credits
The Border, The U.S.-Mexican War 1846-
1848, ...And the Earth Did Not Swallow Him,
The Hunt for Pancho Villa, The Lemon Grove
Incident, Uneasy Neighbors, Ballad of an
Unsung Hero

In Development
Beyond the Dream: California and the
Rediscovery of America (PBS)

Project Types
Features, Documentaries

Ex-Bo Productions, Inc.
580 8th Ave., 8th Fl.
New York, NY 10018
Tel 646-366-0018
Fax 212-921-0456
Email.......................exboprod@aol.com

Joseph La Morte, Director/Executive
 Producer
Gloria La Morte, Executive Producer

Credits
Washington Heights, Details (HBO), What's
for Dinner

Project Types
Features

Eye On the Ball Films, Inc.
P.O. Box 46877
Los Angeles, CA 90046
Tel 323-935-0634
Fax 323-935-4188
Email.......................sergioarau.aol.com
Web ....www.sergioarau.com
Web ......www.adaywithoutamexican.com

Sergio Arau, Writer/Producer/Director
Yareli Arizmendi, Writer/Actress

Credits
A Day Without A Mexican, El Muro, Café
Tacuba, El Preso

Project Types
Features, Music Videos

Filmax International
Miguel Hernandez, 81-87
Distrito Economico L' Hopitalet
L' Hopitalet de Llobregat
08908 Barcelona Spain
Tel 34 9 33 36 85 55
Fax 34 9 32 63 08 24
Email ....m.yebra@filmax.com
Web ....www.filmaxinternational.com

Antonia Nava, SVP of Sales and
 Co-Production

Credits
The Machinist, Romasanta, Deadly Cargo,
Hypnos, El Cid the Legend, El Lobo, Beyond
Re-Animator, Killing Words, Darkness,
Second Name, Don't Breathe, Photos, The
Lighthouse, Subjudice, The City of Marvels,
The Domain of the Senses, A Body in the
Senses, In a Glass Cage, Threesome, Said

Project Types
Features

Flip Films
1617 Broadway Ave.
Santa Monica, CA 90404
Tel 310-401-6140
Fax 310-401-6149
Email ....info@flipfilms.com
Web ....www.flipfilms.com

Adrian Castagna, Executive Producer

Project Types
TV Commercials, Production, Post-production

Galán Entertainment
523 Victoria Ave.
Venice, CA 90291
Tel 310-823-2822
Fax 310-823-7361
Email ....info@galanent.com
Web ....www.galanent.com

Nely Galán, CEO
Diana R. Mogollon, Director of
 Development

Credits
The Swan, La Cenicienta, True Love Stories,
Padre Alberto, Los Beltran, Viva Vegas

In Development
Swan 2

Project Types
TV, Cable

Galán Productions

5524 Bee Caves Rd., Suite B-5
Austin, TX 78746
Tel 512-327-1333
Email ....galan@galaninc.com
Web ....www.galaninc.com

Hector Galán, Producer/Director
Evy Ledesma Galan

Credits
Visiones: Latino Art & Culture, Accordion
Dreams, The Forgotten Americans, Chicano!
The History of the Mexican/American Civil
Rights Movement, Numerous Frontline and
American Experience Documentaries, Cinco
de Mayo, Songs of The Homeland, Vaquero:
The Forgotten Cowboy, Cuba: A Personal
Journey, Cinco de Mayo: The Battle at Puebla

In Development
Los Lonely Boys, Cottonfields, Crossroads,
Tish, Hinojosa: My Heart, My Life, El Corrido
de 911, Avenida Latina

Project Types
Documentaries, CD-ROM Production, TV

Garcia Weiss Productions

118 Broadway, #525
San Antonio, TX 78205
Tel 210-224-2400
Fax 210-224-9618
Email ....garcia9@juno.com

David Garcia, Partner
Fred A. Weiss, Partner

Credits
The Last Carpa, Salt and Earth

In Development
Fausto-A Dark Comedy, Wifey Dearest, Latin
Hip Hop Awards

Project Types
Features, TV

Gaucho Productions

920 W. 25th St.
Houston, TX 77008
Tel 281-620-9696
Fax 713-937-9309
Email ....martin@gauchop.com
Web ....www.gauchop.com

Martin Delon
Andrea Elustondo-Sanchez

Credits
La Taqueria

In Development
Pizza Boy, La Loteria, Luchador Inmigrante

Project Types
Features, TV

Gonca Entertainment Productions

833 Deerflats Dr.
San Dimas, CA 91773
Tel 951-233-1828
Fax 909-394-5964

Jackie Gonzalez-Carlos, Executive
   Producer

Credits
Inner Heart, Morning Show, The Complainer,
United We Stand

Project Types
Features

Green Moon Productions

11718 Barrington Ct., #827
Los Angeles, CA 90041
Tel 310-471-8800
Fax 310-471-8022
Email ....catherine@greenmoon.com

Antonio Banderas
Melanie Griffith
Diane Sellan Isaacs

Credits
Imagining Argentina (Arenas Entertainment),
Tart (Lions Gate Films), Forever Lulu (Starz!
Movie Channel), Crazy in Alabama (Columbia
Tri Star), Killing Pablo, The Body, And
Starring Pancho Villa as Himself (HBO)

Project Types
Features

Ground Zero Latino
6701 Center Dr. W., Suite 655
Los Angeles, CA 90045
Tel 310-410-3030
Fax 310-410-3003
Email ....tony@groundzeroent.com
Web.................www.groundzeroent.com

Anthony Perez, Executive Producer
Nestor Miranda, Producer/Director

Credits
Destination Unknown

In Development
Shiver

Project Types
Features, Marketing, Distribution

Hispanic Information & Telecommunications Network, Inc
449 Broadway, 3rd Fl.
New York, NY 10013
Tel 212-966-5660
Fax 212-966-5725
Email ....info@hitn.org
Web ....www.hitn.org

Jose Luis Rodríguez, Founder

Credits
Noticias, El Journal, Prisma, Matematicas,
Lecturas, Ciencias, Contacto, TV Educativa la
Aventura del Saber, Historias del Rock,
Baratarias, El Autor y su Obra

Project Types
TV

Hope Street Productions, LLC
1800 E. Ft. Lowell Rd., #126-186
Tucson, AZ 85719
Tel ....520-319-2613 (Arizona)
Tel ....310-754-9725 (California)
Email..................hsp2@mindspring.com
Email ....ptoledo1@mac.com
Web ....www.runninatmidnite.com

Pablo Toledo, Director/Writer
Lawrence R. Toledo, Executive Producer

Credits
Runnin' at Midnite

In Development
Crossover, Libertad

Project Types
Commercials, PSA, Music Videos, Features

Humo Films
3640 Monon St., #205
Los Angeles, CA 90027
Tel 323-481-5914
Email ....humo@sbcglobal.net
Web ....www.humofilms.com

Gustavo Hernandez Perez,
   Director/Writer
Adam Schlachter, Writer/Producer

Credits
The Mexican Dream (AFI), Gentleman, Solo,
Coming Undone, Beware of You, Zero Miles,
XZC637

In Development
Stray Bullet, Ajileo The Greatest

Project Types
Features, Shorts

Iglos
850 2nd St., Suite 108
Santa Monica, CA 90403
Tel 310-428-9515
Email ....jadlands@msn.com
Email ....mangual1@msn.com

Jadit De Brito, Director
José Carlos Mangual, Producer

In Development
Iluminada, La Gran Batalla de Aimee

Project Types
Features

Imagentertainment

2706 W. Burbank Blvd.
Burbank, CA 91505
Tel 818-845-1524
Fax 818-845-1113
Email............info@imagentertainment.tv
Web ....www.imagentertainment.tv

Walter Carasco, Founder/CEO
Marvin Acuna, Producer
Jacob Mosler, Producer
Daniel Faraldo, Writer/Director

Credits
Te Amare en Silencio (Univision), How Did It
Feel

Project Types
Features, TV, Management

Impacto Films

3300 Marathon St., #5
Los Angeles, CA 90026
Tel 323-251-7787
Email ..info@MaidInAmericaTheDoc.com
Web ....www.impactofilms.com

Anayansi Prado, Director/Producer/Writer

Credits
Maid in America, Letter from the Other Side,
Immigrant Workers Freedom Ride, Beyond
the Dream: Rediscovering California

Project Types
Documentary

Isla Films

P. O. Box 6813
San Juan, PR 00913
Tel 787-268-0063
Fax 787-268-4379
Email ....islafilms@coqui.net
Web ....www.islafilms.com

Frances Lausell, Producer

Credits
The Kiss, Una Historia Comun, The American
Dream, The Lovely Faces of Tite Curet,
Caribbean Carnivals, Tibes Ceremonial Park,
Arecibo Ayer y Hoy

In Development
Different, Citizen Padilla

Project Types
Documentary, Features, Commercials

Jacobi Entertainment

P.O. Box 4493
Valley Village, CA 91617
Tel 818-744-8844
Email ....gigifilms@aol.com
Web ....www.gigierneta.com

Gigi Erneta, Actress/Producer/Writer

Credits
Crossed, The Chat Room, Raptor, Cheerleader
Masacre, El Chupacabras, Lost Treasure,
Strong Medicine, Hidden Hills, The
Misadventures of Maya and Miguel

Project Types
Features, TV

Jakmar Entertainment

P.O. Box 2771
Toluca Lake, CA 91610
Tel 818-761-5725
Fax 818-761-5725
Email ....jakmar@jackietorres.com
Email ....jakmar@marioramirez.com
Web.....................www.jackietorres.com
Web ....www.marioramirez.com

Jackie Torres, Director/Writer/Producer
Mario Ramirez, Director/Writer/Producer
Janet Torres, Marketing Director

Credits
The Price of the American Dream, La Hora
Lunatica, Atrapamos Bin Laden, Crossing
Frontiers

In Development
King of East L.A., Afterlife, The Fourth
Dimension, Sergio's True Story

Project Types
Features, TV, Theater

Joey Medina Productions

2758 Orange Ave., Suite 10
Torrance, CA 90501-4338
Tel 818-415-4434
Fax 626-797-5539
Email .... joeymedina@aol.com
Web......................www.joeymedina.com

Joey Medina, Writer/Director/Executive
  Producer
Jason Rohr Backer, Executive Producer
Randy Warner, Partner

Credits
El Matador, L.A. Limo, Below the Belt,
Circumcised Cinema (SiTV), Loco Comedy
Jam

In Development
Grand Opening, And Then There Were None

Project Types
Features, TV

Kinetic Arts, LLC

2973 Harbor Blvd., #461
Costa Mesa, CA 92626
Tel 714-343-3225

Antonio Solis, Creative Director

Credits
Forever Yours, Travel Videos

In Development
December 32nd

Project Types
Features, TV

La Banda Films

329 N. Wetherly Dr., #205
Beverly Hills, CA 90211
Tel 310-858-7204
Fax 310-858-7206
Email ....labanda@labandafilms.com
Web....................www.labandafilms.com

Roberto Sneider, President/Director
Francisco Cossio/Emilia Arau/David
  Phillips, Executive Producers

Project Types
TV Commercials, Production Services in U.S.,
Mexico and Argentina

La Negrita Productions, LLC

P.O. Box 1888
New York, NY 10021
Tel 347-739-1720
Tel 347-502-0316
Fax 212-772-1506
Email ..lanegritaproductions@yahoo.com
Web ....www.lanegritaproductions.com

Sandra Duque, Producer

Credits
Dear Abigail, Shattered Dream, Americanized
Latino

Project Types
Short Films, TV

Latin Hollywood Films

Email ....latinafilm@aol.com
Web............................www.kikikiss.com

Christian "Kiki" Melendez, CEO
Eva Longoria, Producer
David Baum, Vice President
Anthony Lopez, Head Writer

Credits
Salsa desde Hollywood, Kiki desde
Hollywood, Hot Tamales Live!

In Development
Hot Tamales Live! Television Show

Project Types
Features, TV

LatinPointe, Inc.

17563 W. 158th Terr.
Olathe, KS 66062
Tel 913-397-8850
Fax 913-397-0890
Email ....dchavez@latinpointe.com
Web ....www.latinpointe.com

David V. Chavez, Producer

Credits
The 2002 ALMA Awards, The 2005 ALMA
Awards, Paul Rodriguez All-Star Comedy
Tribute

Project Types
Specials, Concert/Entertainment

Latino Flavored Productions Inc.

P.O. Box 40728
Staten Island, NY 10314
Tel 212-971-1954
Fax 509-693-1758
Email ....latinoflavored@aol.com
Web ....www.latinoflavored.com

Linda Nieves-Powell

Credits
HBO New Writers Project, Yo Soy Latina!,
Soul Latina!

In Development
Jose Can Speak, The Latina Sex Project

Project Types
Features, TV, Theater

Latino Public Broadcasting

677 Hollywood Blvd., #512
Los Angeles, CA 90028
Tel 323-466-7110
Fax 323-466-7521
Email ....nfo@lpbp.org
Web ....www.lpbp.org

Luca Bentivoglio, Executive Director
Luis Ortiz, Program Manager

Credits
Farmingville, Every Child is Born a Poet,
Discovering Dominga, Visiones, The Life and
Times of Frida Kahlo, L.A Now., My Journey
Home, The New Americans, Valley of Tears,
Limon, Soundmix

In Development
La Lupe, Rebel, Race is the Place, Orozco:
Man on Fire, The Last Conquistador, God
Willing, Somos, Revolucion, The Head of
Joaquin Murrieta

Project Types
TV

Light Body Music

5 Marisa Ct.
Montrose, NY 10548
Tel 914-739-9410
Email..............info@lightbodymusic.com
Web ....www.lightbodymusic.com

Richard Martinez

Credits
S.W.A.T., Bossa Nova, The Daytrippers, Frida,
Titus, Final Fantasy, Batman and Robin, The
Butcher Boy, Interview with the Vampire,
Juan Darien

Project Types
Music Production

LisaLeine Productions, Inc.

c/o Elizabeth Iglesias
University Miami School of Law
Coral Gables, FL 33124
Tel 305-519-1289
Fax 305-284-1588
Email ....lisaleine@lisaleine.com

Elizabeth Iglesias, Co-Director and
  Owner
Madelene Plasencia, Co-Director and
  Owner

Mas and More Entertainment

674 Echo Park Ave.
Los Angeles, CA 90026
Tel 213-250-9162
Tel 323-365-5610
Fax 213-250-9162
Email ....mas@masandmore.com
Email ....mimas@prodigy.net
Web www.2plus2equals5equals1.com
Web ....www.masandmore.com

Miguel Mas,
  Producer/Director/Writer/Actor

Credits
2+2=5=1

In Development
Trickle, Metro Ruben Dario, Circulos

Project Types
Features

Material

73 Market St.
Venice, CA 90291
Tel 310-396-5937
Fax 310-450-4988
Email.............................material@gt.net

Jorge Saralegui, Producer

Credits
Queen of the Damned (Warner Bros.), The
Time Machine (Warner Bros.), Showtime
(Warner Bros.), The Big Bounce (Warner
Bros.), Red Planet

Project Types
Features

Maverick Entertainment

1191 E. Newport Center Dr., Suite 210
Ft. Lauderdale, FL 33442
Tel 954-422-8811
Fax 954-429-0565
Email ....ap@maverickentertainment.com
Web ....www.maverickentertainment.com

Doug Schwab, President
Alberto Perez de la Mesa, Director of
   Latin Product

Maya Media

70 La Salle, #14G
New York, NY 10027
Tel 212-866-5332
Fax 212-665-4779
Email ....luis@mayamediacorp.com

Luis Argueta, Producer/Director

Credits
Collect Call, El Silencio de Neto, Guatemala
9.11.03-El Rostro Humano de una Fiesta
Cívica

Project Types
Feature, Documentaries

Maya Pictures

1201 W. 5th St., Suite F-520
Los Angeles, CA 90017
Tel 310-281-3770
Fax 310-281-3777
Email ....luisg@mayapictures.com
Web ....www.maya-pictures.com

Moctesuma Esparza, Executive Producer
Kim Meyers, Director of Development
Tonantzin Esparza, Creative Development
Greg Gomez, Creative Development
Tery Lopez, Creative Development
Andre Orci, Creative Development
Luis Guerrero, Executive Assistant

Credits
Selena, Introducing Dorothy Dandridge, Price
of Glory

Project Types
Features, TV

Midcoast Pictures

12948 N. 131 E. Ave.
Collinsville, OK 74021
Tel 918-527-8796
Fax 918-573-1453
Email ....pppfilms@hotmail.com

Mario Avila, Producer/Director

Credits
Choices, The Cabin, Ghost of Red Rose, She
Still Stands Tall

In Development
Down the Road

Project Types
Features, Music Videos

production companies

15

Narrow Bridge Films

Studio City, CA
Tel 818-766-1582
Fax 818-766-1882
Email ..narrowbridgefilms@sbcglobal.net

Roni Eguia Menendez, Producer

Credits
Hunting Of Man, The Impostor, Lords of The Barrio

Project Types
Feature

Nuyorican Productions

1100 Glendon Ave., Suite 920
Los Angeles, CA 90024
Tel 310-943-6600
Fax 310-943-6609

Simon Fields, Partner
Jennifer Lopez, Producer/Singer/Actress
David Shaye
Gregg Martin
Gina Rizzo
Bianca Dohmen
Aida Bernal

Credits
Carmen, Monster-in-Law

Olmos Productions

500 S. Buena Vista St.
Old Animation Bldg., 1G2, Code 1675
Burbank, CA 91521-1675
Tel 818-560-8651
Fax 818-560-8655
Email ....olmosonline@earthlink.net

Edward James Olmos, Chairman
Lea Ybarra, Executive VP, Publishing Div.
Nick Athas, Producer
Javier Varon, Dir. Development
Martha Hernandez, Office Manager

Credits
American Family, Stand and Deliver, Lives in Hazard, Americanos, American Me

Project Types
Features, TV, MOWs

Open City Films

145 Avenue of the Americas, 7th Fl.
New York, NY 10013
Tel 212-255-0500
Fax 212-255-0455

Joana Vicente, Founder
Jason Cliot, Founder
Tory Tunnell, Vice President

Credits
The Guys, Site, Love in the Time of Money, Love the Hard Way, Little Senegal, Series 7: The Contenders, Down to You, Promise Her Anything, Return to Paradise Lost, Three Seasons, Chocolate Babies, A, B, C...Manhattan, Childhood's End, Too Much Sleep, Black Kites, Alkali, Iowa, Blixa Bargeld Stole My Cowboy Boots, Late Fall, Touch Base, Games & Private Life

In Development
Awake

Project Types
Features, Shorts

Palmarejo Films

3270 Oakshire Dr., #14
Los Angeles, CA 90068
Tel 323-708-1452
Email................adimafilm@hotmail.com
Web ....www.palmarejo.com

Adam Schlachter,
  Writer/Director/Producer

Credits
Palmarejo: My Backyard Was a Mountain, Caution To The Wind, Soledad, Facing The Ocean

In Development
The Facade, Top Ten, Deep Breath, The First Hit, The Extra, Nebraska

Project Types
Features, Shorts

Paradigm Productions, Inc.
Berkeley, CA 94702
Tel 510-653-1250
Email ......grtf@paradigmproductions.org
Web..........www.paradigmproductions.org

Ray Telles, Director/Producer/Writer
Rick Tejada-Flores, Director/Producer/Writer

Credits
Race is the Place, The Fight in the Fields:
Cesar Chavez and the Farmworker's Struggle,
The Best Little Towns in America, The Good
War and Those who Refused to Fight It

Project Types
Features, TV, Documentary

Patagonia House
P.O. Box 55007
Valencia, CA 91385
Tel 661-254-0979
Fax 661-253-1763
Email ....patagoniahouse@aol.com

Dennis Leoni, Writer/Producer/Director

Credits
Resurrection Blvd. (Showtime)

In Development
Black and White (Showtime), Get a Life
(Discovery Networks), One Love (Touchstone
Television)

Project Types
TV, Features

Payaso Entertainment
Email ....payaso90210@yahoo.com
Web ....www.payasoentertainment.com

Paul Rodriguez, President/Producer
Scott Montoya, Producer

Credits
Live in San Quentin, Latin Nights, Latino
Comedy Shocase, Deme con quien Andes, The
Original Latin Kings of Comedy, The Latin
Divas of Comedy, Shrinking Santa Fe,
Soulcatcher, Robin Hoodz, Dead Warrior's
Song, Three Days in Delano

Project Types
TV, Features

Perro Negro Productions
6525 Sunset Blvd., Suite 202
Los Angeles, CA 90028
Tel 323-856-4322

Gerardo Naranjo

Credits
Malachance, Perro Negro

Project Types
Features

Phil Roman Entertainment
4450 W. Lakeside Dr., #250
Burbank, CA 91505
Tel 818-985-1200
Fax 818-985-2668
Email ....sales@romanent.com
Web ....www.philromanent.com

Phil Roman, President/CEO

Credits
Tom & Jerry Movie, Garfield, Grandma Got
Run Over By a Reindeer

Project Types
Animation, TV, Features

Pigeon Productions
1267 Coral Way
Miami, FL 33145
Tel 305-856-2929
Fax 305-858-0357
Email ....info@pigeonprod.com
Web ....www.pigeonprod.com

Mercedes Palomo, President/Executive
   Producer
Angela Taro, Producer/Sales Director
Maria Burés, Executive Producer/Pigeon
   TV
John Hamlet, Controller
Luis Palomo, Director

Project Types
Film, TV, Commercials, Production Services,
Documentaries

Producciones Copelar

313 Calle Eleonor Roosevelt
San Juan, PR 00918
Fax 787-754-2809
Web............................www.copelar.com

Sonia Valentin, President
Alba Nydia Diaz, Producer

Credits
Sudor Amargo, Psychosis, Plaza Vacante, Y Si
Cristobal Despierta, Las Combatientes

Project Types
Features, TV, Commercials

Purple Velvet Productions

New York/Los Angeles
Email ....pepperphotography@yahoo.com
Web ....www.purplevt.com

Pepper Negrón, Director/Writer/Producer
Aldo Aguilar, Producer/Executive
    Producer
William Gonzalez, Producer/Executive
    Producer
Corina Katt Ayala, Writer/Songwriter/
    Singer/Recording Artist/Set Designer

Credits
Fear and All for Me (One Woman Show
Theater), Beauty, Empire

In Development
A Block From Last Monday

Project Types
Shorts, Features, Music Videos, Theater

Rain Forest Films, Inc.

45 N. Station Plaza, #313
Great Neck, NY 11021
Tel 718-279-0273
Fax 718-423-1157
Email..........rainforestfilms@netzero.com

Maria Escobedo, Writer/Director
Charles Gherarde, Producer

Credits
Rum and Coke, La Cocina

Project Types
Features, TV, Commercials

Raven's Call Productions

P.O. Box 410772
San Francisco, CA 94141-0772
Tel 415-821-7012
Email ....info@hiddeninplainsight.org
Web ....www.hiddeninplainsight.org

John H. Smihula, Director
Vivi Letsou, Producer

Credits
Hidden in Plain Sight, Skeleton Woman

Project Types
Features, Documentaries

Rebel Films

1 Worth St., 2nd Fl.
New York, NY 10013
Tel 646-613-8927
Fax 212-966-1125

Kathy DeMarco, Producer Executive
John Leguizamo, Producer Executive

Credits
Piñero, Undefeated, Joe the King, Sisters of
St. John of God

In Development
Big Shorty, Del Zero

Project Types
Features, TV, Documentary

Republica Trading Company

51 MacDougal St., #405
New York, NY 10012
Tel 212-795-1067
Email............info@republicatrading.com
Web ....www.republicatrading.com

Rafael Jimenez, Founder
Renzo Devia, Director of Production

Credits
Teen People's Top 25 Under 25, Ricky
Martin, Loaded Live (Sony
International/MTV), The Blaze, Battle World
Championship (HBO), MTV's Smokin' Grooves
Countdown

Project Types
Music Videos, Commercials, Industrial
Videos, Features

Safada y Sano Productions, LLC

P.O. Box 573
La Puente, CA 91747
Tel 323-445-0939
Email..................info@safadaysano.com
Web ....www.safadaysano.com
Web ....www.passthemic.net

Richard Montes,
   Writer/Director/Producer/Editor
Jessica Martinez, Writer/Producer/Actor

Credits
Pass the Mic!, Toci: A Mexican Tale

Project Types
Features, Documentaries, Shorts, Music Videos

Salvastian Pictures Inc.

Tel 310-576-6785
Email ....salvastianpics@aol.com
Web ....www.theotherconquest.com

Salvador Carrasco, Director/Producer

Credits
The Brothers Garcia, The Other Conquest

Project Types
Features

Silver Lion Films

701 Santa Monica Blvd.
Santa Monica, CA 90401
Tel 310-393-9177
Fax 310-458-9372
Email ....slf@silverlionfilms.com
Web ....www.silverlionfilms.com

Lance Hool, President/Producer
Conrad Hool Vice President/Producer

Credits
Man on Fire, Broken Lizard's Club Dread,
Crocodile Dundee in Los Angeles, One Man's
Hero, McHale's Navy, Flipper, The Air Up
There, Pure Luck, Missing in Action

In Development
Two Men and a Moving Truck, The Caretakers,
A Call from L.A., Storm Warning, Sunstroke,
Freeze Frame

Project Types
TV, Features, Production Services in Mexico

SíTV

3030 Andrita St., Bldg. D, Fl. 2
Los Angeles, CA 90065
Tel 323-256-8900
Fax 323-256-9888
Email ....dollyjosette@SiTV.com
Web...............................www.SiTV.com

Jeff Valdez, Co-Chairman
Leo Perez, COO
Ed Leon, VP of Production
Dolly Espinal, Manager of Development

Credits
Comedy Compadres, Café Ole with Gisele
Fernandez, The Brothers Garcia, The Drop,
The Rub, Latino Laugh Festival, Styleyes,
Urban Jungle, Inside Joke, Across the Hall,
Circumcised Cinema

Project Types
Cable, Network, Unscripted Series

Sleeping Giant Productions

1635 Angelus Ave.
Los Angeles, CA 90026
Tel 323-667-3390
Fax 323-887-9600
Email............SleepingGiantPro@aol.com
Web ....www.sleepinggiantpro.com

Evelina Fernandez, Partner/Writer
Sal Lopez, Partner/Producer
Jose Luis Valenzuela, Partner/Director

Credits
Luminarias, Gang of Roses

In Development
Dementia

Project Types
Features, TV, Theatre

Three Moons Entertainment, Inc.

7040-F W. Sunset Blvd., #206
Los Angeles, CA 90028
Tel 323-890-1969
Email......................treslunas3@aol.com

Xavier C. Salinas, Manager/Producer

Credits
The Making of a Calendar Girl Volumes 1 & 2,
Angels on the Fairway Sunset Park, Asthma:
Fighting to Breathe, Un Titan, Hot Babes, Hot
Cars, The Silent Crisis Diabetes Among Us,
The Kiss, Ratas, Ratones, Rateros, Get WISE
About Aging, The Titan in the Ring, El Beso
que me Diste

In Development
Rocket Girl, Dark Days, There She Goes,
Morales, My Brother Is a Girl, Laughing
Aztec, Lowrider Bicycles, Cross The Border

Project Types
Features, TV, Talent Management

Tiempo Azul

505 E. 6th St., #3F
New York, NY 10009
Tel 212-673-8065
Fax 212-673-8065
Email.............mnoemi@tiempoazul.com
Email ....tiazul@yahoo.com
Web ....www.tiempoazul.com

Marta Noemi Bautis, President/Producer

Credits
Global Tango, Dreaming the Future, Stories of
Acahualinca, Nicaragua: The Children are
Waiting..., Morir por Amor: Latinas and AIDS,
The Mother, Part 10: Explorations in the
Sacred Theme, Home is Struggle

Project Types
Features

Tornasol Films S.A. (Spain)

Calle Veneras 9-7°
Madrid, Spain 28013
Tel 34 91 542 95 64
Fax 34 91 542 87 10
Web...................www.tornasolfilms.com

Credits
Bear's Kiss, The Navigators, Hermanas, El
Penalti mas Largo del Mundo, Perder es
Cuestión de Método, Inconscientes, Fuera del
Cuerpo, Seres Queridos, Your Next Life, Luna
de Avellaneda, Fond Kiss...Ae, Triple Agent,
O Fascinio, So Far Away, The Galindez File,
La Vida Mancha, Thirteen Chimes, Common
Places, Rosa la China, L'Amore Imperfetto,
The Last Train, Sweet Sixteen, Son of the
Bride, El Lado Oscuro del Corazón 2, Bread
and Roses, Burnt Money, No One Writes to
the Colonel, El Pianista, Martín (Hache)

Project Types
Features

TotalAXIS

9899 Santa Monica Blvd., #340
Beverly Hills, CA 90212
Tel 310-925-4415
Email ....info@totalaxis.com
Web ....www.totalaxis.com

Benjamin Torres, CEO/Producer

Project Types
Entertainment Marketing & Networking

Troublemaker Studios

c/o Rob Newman/ICM
8942 Wilshire Blvd.
Beverly Hills, CA 90211
Tel 310-550-4000
Fax 310-550-4100
Web ....www.loshooligans.com

Robert Rodriguez,
    Director/Producer/Writer
Elizabeth Avellan, Producer

Credits
The Adventures of Shark Boy & Lava Girl in 3-D, Sin City, Spy Kids, Spy Kids 2: Island of Lost Dreams, Spy Kids 3D: Game Over (Dimension Films), From Dusk 'Til Dawn 3 (Buena Vista Distribution), From Dusk 'Til Dawn 2 (Dimension Films), Desperado (Columbia Tri Star), El Mariachi (Columbia Pictures), The Faculty, Bedhead, Roadracers, Four Rooms, Once Upon a Time in Mexico

Project Types
Features

Veintemil Discos

New York, NY
Tel 646-281-8575
Email.................sib1414@hotmail.com
Web ....www.bajomundo.com

Chris Sibilla

Project Types
Production Services

Ventanarosa Productions

9000 Sunset Blvd., Suite 814
Los Angeles, CA. 90069
Tel 323-822-9774

Salma Hayek, Executive Producer

Credits
The Maldonado Miracle, Frida, In the Time of the Butterflies, No One Writes to the Colonel, The Velocity of Gary

Project Types
Features

Agent
Michelle Stern Bohan, William Morris Agency, 310-274-7451

Vision Quest Entertainment

P.O. Box 93515
Hollywood, CA 90093
4107 W. Magnolia Blvd.
Tel 818-842-2757
Fax 818-842-2762
Email ....vqe@att.net
Web ....www.visionquestent.com

Al Gonzalez, Executive Producer

Credits
Viva el Mariachi

In Development
Viva el Mariachi-part 2, Women in Mariachi, Las Divas: an All Female Mariachi Group from L.A., Mothering Children in India, The Mary Ellen Gerber Foundation Story, Downtown Ballerina, The Death Sentence of Jose Maria Martin

Project Types
Features, Documentaries

Volare Films, LLC

14432 S. 40 St.
Phoenix, AZ 85044
Tel 480-229-3143
Fax 623-321-1584
Email ..investorrelation@volarefilms.com
Web ....www.volarefilms.com

Marco Santiago Jr., Producer

Credits
Trafico

In Development
86, Volare, Once Upon a Time in the Desert, Into the Border, Pecan Run

Project Types
Features, Documentaries

production companies

VOY Pictures, LLC

301 N. Canon Dr., Ste. 207
Beverly Hills, CA 90210
Tel 310-550-1019
Fax 310-388-0775
Email ....diezbarroso@voygroup.com
Web ....www.voygroup.com

Emilio Diez Barroso, President
Fernando Espuelas, CEO
Gloria Medel, President of Production
Darlene Caamano, Head of Development
   and Production

Project Types
Features, TV

ZGS Communications, Inc.

2000 N. 14th St., #400
Arlington, VA 22201
Tel 703-528-5656
Fax 703-528-6566
Email ....marketing@zgsonline.com
Web ....www.zgsonline.com

Ron Gordon, President
Eduardo Zavala, Vice President

Credits
Viva Hollywood, True Champions, Latino
Athletes and Their Stories

Project Types
Features, TV

Zokalo Entertainment

5840 S. Van Ness Ave.
Los Angeles, CA 90047
Tel 323-295-0000
Email ....info@zokalo.com
Web ....www.zokalo.com

Jesus Nebot,
   Director/Producer/Writer/Actor

Credits
No Turning Back, Tea with Jesus

In Development
Muneera, Tears in the Dark, The Naked Truth

Project Types
Feature, Documentary, TV

National Association of Latino Independent Producers

film
schools

Note: Where 2004 dates are included in this section, it is for reference only. Please contact individual programs for most current deadlines.

Academy of Art University

Motion Pictures & Television Program:
  BFA
Motion Pictures & Television Program:
  MFA - Narrative or Documentary

Mailing/Physical Address
79 New Montgomery St.
San Francisco, CA 94105

Organization Tel 415-274-2219
Program Tel 1-800-544-ARTS
Email ....admissions@academyart.edu
Web ....www.academyart.edu

Application Available
Online

Application Deadline 2005
Open admissions

Cost of Program
$16,000 - $20,000

American Film Institute

Cinematography: MFA
Directing: MFA
Producing: MFA
Production Design: MFA
Screenwriting: MFA
Editing: MFA

Mailing/Physical Address
2021 N. Western Ave.
Los Angeles, CA 90027

Organization Tel 323-856-7600
Program Tel 323-856-7600
Fax 323-467-4578
Email................shardman@afionline.org
Web ....www.afi.com

Application Available
Online

Application Deadline 2005
December 13, 2004

Cost of Program
$21,000 - $25,000

American University

Visual Media: BA
Film and Video: BA, MA
Film and Electronic Media: MFA
Producing Film and Video (Weekend
  Program): MA

Mailing Address
4400 Massachusetts Ave., NW
Washington, DC 20016

Physical Address
Graduate Admissions
School of Communication
American University
4400 Massachusetts Ave. NW
Washington, DC 20016-8017

Organization Tel 202-885-1000
Program Tel 202-885-2060
Email ......communication@american.edu
Email ....undergradcomm@american.edu
Email ....gradcomm@american.edu
Web ....www.soc.american.edu

Application Available
Online

Application Deadline 2005
Early Decision Freshman Fall Admission:
Nov. 15, 2004
Regular Freshman Fall Admission:
Jan. 15, 2005
Graduate Spring Admission:
Nov. 15, 2004
Graduate Fall Admission June 1, 2005

Cost of Program
$25,000+
Average Non-Resident Tuition

Contact
Kurt Gunderson, Academic Advisor

Arizona State University West

Interdisciplinary Arts and Performance
  with a Concentration on Media Arts: BA
Interdisciplinary Arts and Performance
  with a Concentration on Visual Arts: BA
Interdisciplinary Arts and Performance
  with a Minor in Film and Video: BA
Film and Video: Certificate

Mailing/Physical Address
4701 W. Thunderbird Rd.
Glendale, AZ 85306
Phoenix, AZ 85069-7100

Organization Tel 602-543-6000
Program Tel 602-543-6057
Fax 602-543-6004
Email ....coas@asu.edu
Web ....www.west.asu.edu

Application Available
Online

Application Deadline 2005
Feb. 1, 2005

Cost of Program
$13,000+

Bard College

Film and Electronic Arts: BA
Integrated Arts: BA

Mailing Address
Office of Admission, Bard College
30 Annandale Rd.
Annandale-on-Hudson, NY 12504-5000

Physical Address
School of Communications
Annandale-on-Hudson, NY 12504-5000

Organization Tel 845-758-7472
Fax 845-758-5208
Email ....admission@bard.edu
Web ....www.bard.edu

Application Available
Online

Application Deadline 2005
Jan. 15, 2005

Cost of Program
$29,900+

Biola University

Radio/Television/Film: BA
Motion Picture Production: BA
Motion Picture and Television Directing:
  BA
Screenwriting: BA
Television/Video Production: BA
Audio Production: BA
Media Management: BA

Mailing/Physical Address
13800 Biola Ave.
La Mirada, CA 90639-0001

Organization Tel 562-903-6000
Program Tel.................1-800-OK-BIOLA
(Admissions)
Web................................www.biola.edu

Application Available
Online

Application Deadline 2005
Fall Early Action 1: Dec. 1, 2004
Fall Early Action 2: Jan. 15, 2005
Fall Regular: March 1, 2005

Cost of Program
$25,000+ Average Non-Res Tuition

Boston University

Film Program: BS
Television Program: BS
Film Production: MFA
Screenwriting: MFA
Film Studies: MFA
Television Production: MS
Television Management: MS, MFA

Mailing Address
Department of Film & Television
121 Bay State Rd.
Boston, MA 02215

Physical Address
4400 Massachusetts Ave. NW
Boston, MA 02215

Organization Tel 617-353-2300
Fax 617-353-9695
Email ....admissions@bu.edu
Web ....www.bu.edu

Application Available
Online

Application Deadline 2005
Freshman Fall: Dec. 1, 2004
Graduate Fall: Feb. 1, 2005

Cost of Program
$30,000

Brigham Young University

Visual Arts: BA

Mailing Address
Admissions, A-153 ASB
Provo, UT 84602

Physical Address
Theatre and Media Arts, D-551
Brigham Young University
Provo, UT 84604

Organization Tel 801-422-2507
Program Tel 801-422-2997
Fax 801-422-0005
Email ....admissions@byu.edu
Email ....cfacadvise@byu.edu
Web.................................www.byu.edu

Application Available
Online

Application Deadline 2005
Feb. 15, 2005

Brooks Institute of Photography

Motion Picture/Video: BA
Photographic/Filmmaking Studies:
　Diploma
Visual Journalism: AAD

Mailing/Physical Address
801 Alston Rd.
Santa Barbara, CA 93108

Organization Tel 805-966-3888
Admissions Tel............1-888-304-3456
Email ....admissions@brooks.edu
Web.............................www.brooks.edu

Application Available
Online

Application Deadline 2005
Ongoing

Cost of Program
$16,000 - $20,000

California Institute of the Arts (CalArts)

Film and Video: BFA
Experimental Animation: BFA
Character Animation: BFA
Film Directing: BFA
Integrated Media Program in
　Experimental Animation: BFA
Integrated Media Program in Film and
　Video: BFA

Mailing/Physical Address
School of Film/Video
24700 McBean Parkway
Valencia, CA 91355-2397

Organization Tel 661-255-1050
Admissions Tel............1-800-545-2787
Email ....admiss@calarts.edu
Web ....www.calarts.edu

Application Available
Request Online

Application Deadline 2005
Fall 2005: Jan. 5, 2005

Cost of Program
$25,520

California State University, Fullerton

Radio-TV-Film: BA
Communications with Concentration on
　Entertainment Studies: BA, MA

Mailing/Physical Address
Communications College
800 N. State College Blvd.
Fullerton, CA 92834

Organization Tel 714-278-3517
Email ....rtvf@fullerton.edu
Web ....www.fullerton.edu

film schools

Application Available
Online: www.csumentor.edu

Application Deadline 2005
Oct. 1 to Nov. 30, 2004

Cost of Program
Up to $7,000

California State University, Northridge

Cinema & Television Arts: BA
Mass Communication with an Option in
  Screenwriting: MA

Mailing/Physical Address
Admissions and Records
18111 Nordhoff
Northridge, CA 91330-8207

Organization Tel 818-677-1200
Fax 818-677-3766
Email ......admissions.records@csun.edu
Web................................www.csun.edu
Web ....www.cinemaandtelevision.com

Application Available
Online

Application Deadline Fall 2005
Oct. 1 – Nov. 30, 2004

Cost of Program
$8,500

Chapman University

Film Studies: BA, MA
Screenwriting: BA
Film Production: BFA, MFA
Television: BFA
Broadcast Journalism: BFA
Screenwriting: MFA
Producing for Film and Television: MFA

Mailing/Physical Address
Cecil B. DeMille Hall
333 N. Glassell St.
Orange, CA 92866

Organization Tel 714-997-6815
Fax 714-997-6700
Email ....ftvinfo@chapman.edu
Web...........................www.chapman.edu

Application Available
Online

Application Deadline 2005
Spring: Nov. 1, 2004
Fall: Jan. 31, 2005

Cost of Program
$25,000+

Columbia College, Chicago

Alternative Forms: BA
Film and Video: MFA
Film and Video, Audio: BA
Film and Video, Cinematography: BA
Film and Video, Critical Studies: BA
Film and Video, Directing: BA
Film and Video, Documentary: BA
Film and Video, Editing: BA
Film and Video, Editing: BA
Film and Video, Producing: BA
Film and Video, Screenwriting: BA
Film and Video, Animation: BA

Mailing/Physical Address
600 S. Michigan Ave.
Chicago, IL 60605

Organization Tel 312-663-1600
Email ....admissions@colum.edu
Web ....www.colum.edu

Application Available
Online

Application Deadline 2005
Fall: Jul. 1, 2005
Spring: Dec. 1, 2004
Summer: May 1, 2005

Cost of Program
$16,000 - $18,000

Columbia University

Screenwriting: MFA
Directing: MFA
Producing: MFA
Film Studies: BA, MA

Mailing Address
School of the Arts, Columbia University
305 Dodge Hall
Mail Code 1808
2960 Broadway
New York, NY 10027

Physical Address
School of the Arts, Columbia University
305 Dodge Hall
2960 Broadway
New York, NY 10027

Organization Tel 212-854-2875
Email ......admissions-arts@columbia.edu
Web.........................www.columbia.edu

Application Available
Online

Application Deadline 2005
Film: Dec. 1, 2004
Theater: Jan. 3, 2005
Visual Arts: Feb. 1, 2005
Writing: Jan. 3, 2005

Cost of Program
$25,000+

De Sales University

Television & Film: BA
Theater: BA

Mailing/Physical Address
2755 Station Ave.
Center Valley, PA 18034

Organization Tel 610-282-1100
Email ....Caryn.Lee@desales.edu
Web ....www.desales.edu

Application Available
Online

Application Deadline 2005
Rolling admission system

Cost of Program
$21,000 - $25,000

Contact
Caryn Lee, Admissions Counselor

Emerson College

Visual and Media Arts: BA

Mailing/Physical Address
Visual & Media Arts
120 Boylston St.
Boston, MA 02116-4624

Organization Tel 617-824-8500
Web ....www.emerson.edu

Application Available
Online

Application Deadline 2005
Fall: Jan. 15, 2005

Cost of Program
$23,000+

Florida State University

Film: BFA
Film Production: MFA

Mailing/Physical Address
Florida State University Film School
University Center 3100A
Tallahassee, FL 32306-2350

Organization Tel 850-644-5034
Program Tel 850-644-7728
Fax 850-644-8642
Email ....mbehm@filmschool.fsu.edu
Email ....admissions@admin.fsu.edu
Web ....www.filmschool.fsu.edu

Application Available
Online

Application Deadline 2005
Fall: Dec. 15, 2004

Cost of Program
$12,000 - $16,000

film schools

Hollins University

Film and Photography Major: BA
Short Term Digital Video Production: BA
Screenwriting & Film Studies: MA

Mailing Address
Hollins University
Dean of Admissions
Roanoke, VA 24020

Physical Address
Hollins University
P.O. Box 9707
Roanoke, VA 24020-1707

Organization Tel 1-800-456-9525
Program Tel 540-362-6401
Email ....huadm@hollins.edu
Web ....www.hollins.edu

Application Available
Online

Application Deadline 2005
Undergraduate Fall: Feb. 1, 2005
Graduate Summer: Feb. 15, 2005
Cost of Program
$21,200

Howard University

Film and TV Production: BA, MFA

Mailing/Physical Address
2400 6th St., NW
Washington, DC 20059

Organization Tel 202-806-2763
Email ....admission@howard.edu
Web ....www.howard.edu

Application Available
Online

Application Deadline 2005
Spring: Nov. 1, 2004
Summer: April 1, 2005
Fall: Feb. 15, 2005

Cost of Program
$10,000+

Hunter College - City University of New York

Film: BA
Media: BA
Integrated Media Arts: MFA

Mailing/Physical Address
The Department of Film and Media
Studies at Hunter College
695 Park Ave.
Rm. 433 Hunter North
New York, NY 10021

Organization Tel 212-772-4949
Fax 212-650-3619
Web ....www.cuny.edu

Application Available
Online

Application Deadline 2005
Undergraduate Fall: March 1, 2005
Undergraduate Spring: Oct. 1, 2004
Graduate: Feb. 1, 2005

Cost of Program
$2,800+

L.A. City College

Cinema or Television: AA
Cinema Production: Certificate
Telvision Production: Certificate
Cinema-Video Production: Certificate
Cinematography Skills: Certificate
Cinema Post-Production Skills:
  Certificate
Television Studio Production Skills
  Certificate
Beginning Cinema and Television
  Production Skills: Certificate

Mailing/Physical Address
Cinema - Television Department
Communications Center
855 N. Vermont Ave.
Los Angeles, CA 90029

Organization Tel ..323-953-4000 x2627
Fax 323-953-4013
Email ....obernvg@lacitycollege.edu
Web ....www.lacitycollege.edu

Application Available
Online

Application Deadline
3 months before each semester

Cost of Program
Residents $626
Non-Residents $4,320

Los Angeles Film School

1 Year Filmmaking Program: Certificate

Mailing/Physical Address
6363 Sunset Blvd., #400
Hollywood, CA 90028

Organization Tel 323-860-0789
Program Tel 877-9LA-FILM
Email ....info@lafilm.com
Web..............................www.lafilm.com

Application Available
Online

Application Deadline 2005
Rolling Admissions

Cost of Program
$30,400

Loyola Marymount University Los Angeles

Animation: BA, MFA
Film Production: BA
Narrative or Documentary: MFA
Recording Arts: BA
Screenwriting: BA
Television Production: BA, MFA

Mailing/Physical Address
Office of Admission
Loyola Marymount University
One LMU Dr.
Los Angeles, CA 90045-2659

Organization Tel 310-338-2700
Program Tel 800-568-4636
Fax 310-338-2797
Email ....admissions@lmu.edu
Web ....www.lmu.edu

Application Available
Online

Application Deadline 2005
Fall: Jan. 15, 2005
Spring: Dec. 1, 2004

Cost of Program
$26,000

Miami Dade College

Film Production Technology: A.S.
Radio and Television Broadcast
  Programming: A.S.
Television Production: Certificate

Mailing/Physical Address
School of Entertainment and
Design Technology
Suite 2235
MDC North Campus
11380 NW 27th Ave.
Miami, FL 33167-3418

Organization Tel 305-237-1696
Program Tel 305-237-1373
Fax 305-237-1367
Email ....sedt@mdc.edu
Web ....www.mdc.edu
Director ....Randall De Witt

Application Available
Online

Application Deadline 2005
90 days prior to start of term
International Students: 6 months prior
to start of term

Cost of Program
$7,000+

film schools

New York Film Academy -
New York and Universal Studios

One Year Filmmaking: Certificate
One Year Acting for Film: Certificate
4,6,and 8 week Filmmaking: Certificate
4 week Digital Editing – Final Cut Pro &
  AVID: Certificate
5 Week Digital Filmmaking: Certificate
4 Week Acting for Film: Certificate
Screenwriting: Certificate
3D Animation: Certificate
Advanced Film Directing Workshop:
  Certificate
Evening Sync Sound: Certificate
One Year Screenwriting: Certificate
One Year Producing: Certificate
High School Film Camp – Ages 14-17:
  Certificate
AMC 1 Week Movie Camp: Certificate

Mailing/Physical Address
N.Y.:   100 E. 17th St.
        New York, NY 10003

L.A.:   3801 Barham Blvd.
        Bldg. 9128, Suite 179
        Los Angeles, CA 91608

Organization Tel – N.Y.....212-674-4300
Organization Tel – L.A.....818-733-2600
Fax – N.Y.......................212-477-1414
Fax – L.A.......................818-733-4074
Email ....film@nyfa.com
Web................................www.nyfa.com

Application Available
Online

Application Deadline 2005
Ongoing

Cost of Program
$3,500 - $25,000

New York University
Tisch School of the Arts
Kanbar Institute of Film and TV

Film & Television: BFA
Film & Television: MFA – Narrative or
  Documentary
Cinema Studies: BFA, MA, PhD
Design for Stage and Film: MFA

Mailing Address
Department of Film & TV
70 Washington Sq. S.
New York, NY 10012

Physical Address
721 Broadway, 11th Fl.
New York, NY 10003

Organization Tel 212-229-5150
Program Tel 212-998-1700
Email...........tisch.recruitment@nyu.edu
Web.........................www.nyu.edu/tisch

Application Available
Online

Application Deadline 2005
Dec. 1, 2004

Cost of Program
$31,000

North Carolina School of the Arts

Filmmaking: BFA, Arts Diploma
Design and Production: BFA, MFA,
  Arts Diploma
Film Music Composition: MFA

Mailing/Physical Address
School of Filmmaking
1533 S. Main St.
Winston-Salem, NC 27127-2188

Organization Tel 336-770-3290
Fax 336-770-3370
Email ....admissions@ncarts.edu
Web.............................www.ncarts.edu

Application Available
Online

Application Deadline 2005
Nov. 8, 2004 - Jan. 28, 2005

Cost of Program
$14,000

Northwestern University

Radio/Television/Film: BA, MFA, PhD

Mailing/Physical Address
Department of Radio, Television and
Film
2240 Campus Dr.
Evanston, IL 60208

Organization Tel 847-491-7214
Fax 847-467-1464
Email ....dear-sam@northwestern.edu
Web ....www.communication.
                              northwestern.edu

Application Available
Online

Application Deadline 2005
Early Decision: Nov. 1, 2004
Regular Decision: Jan. 1, 2005

Cost of Program
$25,000+

Ohio University

International Film Scholarship: MA
Film Production and Scholarship: BA,
  MFA

Mailing/Physical Address
School of Film
Lindley Hall 378
Athens, OH 45701

Organization Tel 740-593-1323
Fax 740-593-1328
Email.....................filmdept@ohiou.edu
Web ....www.ohiou.edu

Application Available
Online

Application Deadline 2005
Fall: Feb. 1, 2005
Winter: Dec. 1, 2004
Spring: March 1, 2005
Summer: Feb. 1, 2005

Rochester Institute of Technology

Film & Animation: BFA, MFA

Mailing/Physical Address
School of Photographic Arts & Sciences
One Lomb Memorial Dr.
Rochester, NY 14623

Organization Tel 585-475-2411
Program Tel 585-475-6736
Fax 585-475-7424
Email ....admissions@rit.edu
Web...................................www.rit.edu

Application Available
Online

Application Deadline 2005
Feb. 2, 2005

Cost of Program
$28,600+

Rockport College - International Film Workshops

Photography: MFA, AAD, Certificate
Digital Media: Certificate
Filmmaking: Certificate
Film and Video: AAD
New Media: MFA, AAD
Film: MFA

Mailing Address
P.O. Box 200
2 Central St.
Rockport, ME 04856

Organization Tel 877-577-7700
Fax 207-236-2558
Email ....info@rockportcollege.edu
Web ..www.rockportcollege.edu/pcert.asp

Application Available
Online

Cost of Program
$18,000+

San Jose State University

Radio-Television-Film: BA, minor

Mailing/Physical Address
One Washington Sq.
San Jose, CA 95192-0055

Organization Tel 408-924-3240
Fax 408-924-3229
Email ....contact.sjsu.edu
Web ....www.sjsu.edu

Application Available
Online

Application Deadline 2005
Fall 2005: Feb. 1, 2005
Spring 2006: Nov. 1, 2005

Cost of Program
$14,000+

San Francisco Art Institute

Film: BFA

Mailing/Physical Address
800 Chestnut St.
San Francisco, CA 94133

Organization Tel 415-749-4500
Fax 415-749-4592
Email ....admissions@sfai.edu
Web.................................www.sfai.edu

Application Available
Online

Application Deadline 2005
Fall 2005: Feb. 15, 2005
Spring 2006: Nov. 1, 2005

San Francisco State University

Cinema: BA, MFA
Cinema Studies: MA
Cinema with Emphasis on Animation:
  BA

Mailing/Physical Address
1600 Holloway Ave.
San Francisco, CA 94132

Organization Tel 415-338-1111
Program Tel 415-338-1629
Email ....cinedept@sfsu.edu
Email ....beca@sfsu.edu
Web ....www.sfsu.edu

Application Available
Online

Application Deadline 2005
Fall: Nov. 30, 2004

Cost of Program
$12,750

Savannah College of Art and Design

Film and Television: BFA, MA, MFA
Animation: BFA, MA, MFA
Sound Design: BFA
Visual Effects: BFA, MA, MFA

Mailing Address
Film and Television Department
P.O. Box 3146
Savannah, GA 31402-3146

Physical Address
Hamilton Hall
Indian Ave.
Savannah, GA 31401

Organization Tel 912-525-5100
Fax 912-525-6459
Email ....admission@scad.edu
Web ....www.scad.edu

Application Available
Online

Application Deadline 2005
Rolling admissions

Cost of Program
$20,000

School of the Art Institute of Chicago

Film, Video and New Media: BA, MFA
Visual and Critical Studies: BA, MA

Mailing/Physical Address
37 S. Wabash
Chicago, IL 60603-3103

Organization Tel 312-899-5100
Email ....admissions@artic.edu
Web ....www.artic.edu

Application Available
Online

Application Deadline 2005
Spring 2005: Jan. 15, 2005
Fall 2005: Aug. 15, 2005
Spring 2005: Nov. 15, 2006

Cost of Program
$27,000

School of Visual Arts

Film and Video: BFA
Photography & Related Media: MFA
Film and Video screenwriting,
   production, cinematography, acting,
   directing, digital image, sound design,
   editing and marketing: Certificate

Mailing/Physical Address
209 E. 23rd St.
New York, NY 10010-3994

Organization Tel 202-592-2000
Program Tel 212-592-2100
Fax 212-725-3587
Email...............................admissions@
            adm.schoolofvisualarts.edu
Web ....www.schoolofvisualarts.edu

Application Available
Online

Application Deadline 2005
Spring 2005: Jan. 21, 2005
Fall 2005: Feb. 1, 2005

Cost of Program
$20,000

Stanford University

Documentary Film and Video: MA
Communication: BA, MA, PhD
Media Studies: MA

Mailing/Physical Address
Stanford University
Department of Communication
Stanford, CA 94305-2050

Organization Tel 650-723-1941
Fax 650-725-2472
Email..........krawitz@stanford.edu comm
Email ......inforequest@lists.stanford.edu
Web ....www.stanford.edu

Application Available
Online

Application Deadline 2005
Dec. 15, 2004

Cost of Program
$25,000+

Syracuse University

Filmmaking: BFA
Film Art: MFA

Mailing/Physical Address
Syracuse University
Syracuse, NY 13244

Organization Tel 315-443-1870
Email ....orange@syr.edu
Email Admissions ....admissu@syr.edu
Web ....www.syr.edu

Application Available
Online

Application Deadline 2005
Graduate: Dec. 1, 2004
Undergraduate: Jan. 1, 2005

Cost of Program
$26,730

film schools

Temple University

Film and Media Arts: BFA
Film and Media Arts: MFA - Narrative or
    Documentary
Broadcasting, Telecommunications &
    Mass Media: BFA, MFA
Media Production and Theory: BA

Mailing/Physical Address
Department of Film and Media Arts
09 Annenberg Hall
Temple University 011-00
Philadelphia, PA 19122

Organization Tel 215-204-5273
Program Tel 215-204-7200
Fax 215-204-6641
Email undergrad ....tuadm@
                              mail.temple.edu
Email grad ..graduateschool@temple.edu
Web ....www.temple.edu

Application Available
Online

Application Deadline 2005
Graduate: Dec. 1, 2004
Undergraduate: Spring: Nov. 1, 2004
Fall: April 1, 2005

Cost of Program
$16,000

University of Arizona

Media Arts: BA, BFA, MA

Mailing Address
Media Arts Dept.
P.O. Box 210004
The University of Arizona
Tucson, AZ 85721

Physical Address
Marshall Bldg., Rm. 220
Tucson, AZ 85721

Organization Tel 520-621-7352
Fax 520-621-9662
Email ....marinfo@email.arizona.edu
Web ....www.arizona.edu

Application Available
Online

Application Deadline 2005
Media Arts Fall: Jan. 30, 2005

Cost of Program
$23,000

University of California at Berkeley

Film Studies: BA
Film Studies Track of the Rhetoric
    Department: PhD
Film History and Theory: PhD
Production in Digital Media and New
    Genres: MFA
Documentary Film Production: MA

Mailing Address School of Film
7408 Dwinelle Hall 2670
University of California
Berkeley, CA 94720-2670

Mailing Adress School of Journalism
121 North Gate Hall #5860
University of California at Berkeley
Berkeley, CA 94720-5860

Organization Tel 510-642-6000
Program Tel 510-642-1415
Email ......gradweb@uclink4.berkeley.edu
Web ....www.berkeley.edu

Application Available
Online

Application Deadline 2005
Fall 2005: Dec. 10, 2004

Cost of Program
$24,000+

University of California at Irvine

Department of Film and
  Media Studies: BA

Mailing Address
Office of Admissions and
Relations with Schools
204 Administration
Irvine, CA 92697-1075

Physical Address
Undergraduate Counseling Office
University of California
Irvine, CA 92697-2775

Organization Tel 949-824-6703
Program Tel 949-824-5386
Fax 949-824-2711
Web ....www.uci.edu

Application Available
Online

Application Deadline 2005
Fall: Nov. 1-30, 2004

Cost of Program
$19,720+

University of California at Los Angeles

Film and Television: BA, PhD
Film and Television: MA – Narrative or
  Documentary
Animation: MFA
Production/Directing: MFA
Production/Cinematography: MFA
Screenwriting: MFA
Producers Program: MFA
Moving Image Archive Studies: MA

Mailing Address
School of Theater, Film and Television
405 Hilgard Ave.
Box 951361
Los Angeles, CA 90095-1361

Physical Address
UCLA Undergraduate Admissions, and
Relations with Schools
1147 Murphy Hall
Box 951436
Los Angeles, CA 90095-1436

Organization Tel 310-825-8764
Program Tel 310-825-5761
Fax 310-825-3383
Email..........................info@tft.ucla.edu
Web ....www.ucla.edu

Application Available
Online

Application Deadline 2005
Undergraduate: Nov. 15, 2004
MFA: Nov. 1, 2004
Animation MFA: Feb. 28, 2005
MA/PhD: Dec. 15, 2004

Cost of Program
$22,000 - $24,000

University of California at Los Angeles - Professional Program in Producing and in Screenwriting

School of Theater, Film and Television:
  Certificate

Mailing/Physical Address
102B E. Melnitz
Los Angeles, CA 90095-1622

Organization Tel 310-825-6827
Program Tel 310-825-6124
Fax 310-825-3383
Email ..professionalprogram@tft.ucla.edu
Web ....www.filmprograms.ucla.edu

Application Available
Online

Applications Deadline 2005

Program in Producing
Summer: June 2005 (date TBA)
Fall, Winter & Spring: 30 days prior to
start of quarter
Program in Screenwriting
July 2005 (date TBA)

Cost of Program
$3,950

Contact
Stephanie Moore
Denise Mann

University of California at San Diego

Film, Video, Photography: BFA, MFA

Mailing/Physical Address
Visual Arts – Media
9500 Gilman Dr.
La Jolla, CA 92093-0327

Organization Tel 858-534-4831
Fax 858-534-8651
Email ....admissionsinfo@ucsd.edu
Web ....www.ucsd.edu

Application Available
Online

Application Deadline 2005
Graduate: Dec. 1, 2004
Undergraduate: Nov. 1 - Nov. 30, 2004

University of California at Santa Barbara

Film Studies: BA, MA, PhD

Mailing Address
UCSB
Santa Barbara, CA 93106

Physical Address
Ellison Hall, #1720
Santa Barbara, CA 93106

Organization Tel 805-893-8000
Program Tel 805-893-2347
Fax 805-893-8630
Email ....fsoadmin@filmstudies.ucsb.edu
Web ....www.ucsb.edu

Application Available
Online

Application Deadline 2005
Fall: Nov. 1-30, 2004
Graduate - Fall: Dec. 1, 2004

Cost of Program
$37,700

University of Iowa

Communication Studies: BA
Cinema: BA
Film Studies: MA, PhD
Film and Video Production: MFA

Mailing Address
University of Iowa
Iowa City, IA 52242

Physical Address
105 Becker Communication Studies Bldg.
The University of Iowa
Iowa City, IA 52242-1498

Program Tel 319-335-0575
Fax 319-335-0575
Email ....registar@uiowa.edu
Web ....www.uiowa.edu

Application Available
Online

Application Deadline 2005
Undergraduate Fall: April 1, 2005
Undergraduate Spring: Nov. 15, 2004
Graduate Fall: July 15, 2005
Graduate Spring 2005: Dec. 1, 2004
Graduate Summer: April 15, 2005

Cost of Program
Non Residents: $16,000

University of Miami

Motion Picture Production/
  Producing: MFA
Motion Picture Production/
  Scriptwriting: MA
Film Studies: MA
Communication Studies: PhD
Visual Communication: BA
Film-Video: BA

Mailing Address
University of Miami
Coral Gables
Miami, FL 33124

Physical Address
5100 Brunson Dr.
Frances L. Wolfson Bldg., #3005
Coral Gables, FL 33124

Organization Tel 305-284-2265
Program Tel 800-577-8133
Fax 305-284-3648
Email ....admission@miami.edu
Email......................lherrera@miami.edu
Web.............................www.miami.edu

Application Available
Online

Application Deadline 2005
Undergraduate Early Decision/Action:
Nov. 1, 2004
Undergraduate Regular Decision: Feb. 1,
2005
All Graduate: March 1, 2005

Cost of Program
$27,000+

Contact
George Fernandez
Luis Herrera, Director of Student
Services

University of New Mexico
Media Arts: BA

Mailing/Physical Address
1 University of New Mexico
Albuquerque, NM 87131-0001

Organization Tel 505-277-0111
Program Tel 505-277-6262
Fax 505-277-6314
Email ....apply@unm.edu
Web ....www.unm.edu

Application Available
Online

Application Deadline 2005
Undergraduate Spring: Nov. 15, 2004
Undergraduate Summer: May 1, 2005
Undergraduate Fall: June 15, 2005

Cost of Program
$14,500+

University of New Orleans
Film/Video: BA
Film Production/Directing: MFA
Film Production/Production Design: MFA
Film Production/Creative Writing: MFA

Mailing Address
University of New Orleans
Office of Admissions
103 Administration Bldg.
Lakefront
New Orleans, LA 70148

Physical Address
University of New Orleans
Lakefront
2000 Lakeshore Dr.
New Orleans, LA 70148

Organization Tel 504-280-6595
Program Tel 504-280-6317
Fax 504-280-5522
Email ....admissions@uno.edu
Web...................................www.uno.edu

Application Available
Online

Application Deadline 2005
Undergraduate and Graduate Fall:
July 1, 2005
Undergraduate and Graduate Spring:
Nov. 15, 2004

University of Southern California
Animation and Digital Arts: BA, MFA
Critical Studies: BA, MA, PhD
Film/Televsion Production: BA
Film/Televsion Production: MFA –
    Narrative or Documentary
Interactive Media: MFA
Writing for Screen and Television: BA,
    MFA
Peter Stark Producing Program: MFA
The Business of Entertainment: BS,
    MBA
Summer Production Workshop:
    Certificate

Mailing/Physical Address
School of Cinema-Television
University Park Campus
Los Angeles, CA 90089

Organization Tel 213-740-8358
Program Tel 213-740-2804
Fax 213-740-4013
Email ..cntv-admissions@cinema.usc.edu
Web................................www.usc.edu

Application Available
Online

Application Deadline 2005
Animation and Digital Arts:
Undergraduate: Feb. 15, 2005
MFA: Nov. 15, 2004

Critical Studies, Writing for Screen
and TV:
Undergraduate: Dec. 10, 2004
MA, PhD: Dec. 10, 2004

Film/Televsion Production:
Undergraduate Fall: Dec. 10, 2004
MFA Fall: Nov. 15, 2004
MFA Spring: Sept. 1, 2004

Interactive Media:
MFA Program: Jan. 30, 2005
Peter Stark Program: Dec. 10, 2004
The Business of Entertainment: Must be
in MBA Program
Summer Production Workshop: Rolling
Admissions Jan. 10 – June 23

Cost of Program
$15,000+

University of Texas at Austin

Radio/Television/Film: BA
Screenwriting: MA
Production: MFA - Narrative, Animation
   or Documentary
Ethnic and Minority Issues and the
   Media: MA, PhD
Gender and Sexuality Issues and the
   Media: MA, PhD
International Communication Issues:
   MA, PhD
Media, Culture and Society: MA, PhD
Technology, Culture and Society: MA, PhD

Mailing Address
Office of Admissions
P.O. Box 8058
Austin, TX 78713-8058

Physical Address
Department of Radio-Television-Film
1 University Station A0800
Austin, TX 78712-0108

Organization Tel 512-475-7399
Fax 512-475-7478
Web..............................www.utexas.edu

Application Available
Online

Application Deadline 2005
Graduate: Dec. 1
Undergraduate Summer or Fall 2005:
March 1, 2005
Undergraduate Spring 2005:
Oct. 1, 2004

Cost of Program
$12,000+

Western Carolina University

Film & Video Program: BFA

Mailing/Physical Address:
108 Delk
Cullowhee, NC 28723

Tel 828-227-2324
Fax 828-227-7647
Email ....ssholder@wcu.edu

Application Available
Fall 2005

Application Deadline
TBA

National Association of Latino Independent Producers

diversity
programs

Note: Where 2004 dates are included in this section, it is for reference only. Please contact individual programs for most current deadlines.

ABC Talent Development Programs

The Walt Disney Studios and ABC Entertainment Writing Fellowship Program

500 S. Buena Vista St.
Burbank, CA 91521-4389
Tel 818-560-6894
Email..............abc.fellowships@abc.com
Web ......www.abctalentdevelopment.com

Support Provided
Fellows receive a flat weekly salary of $961.54/wk ($50,000/year) for one year; plus workshops, seminars, and personalized mentorship with creative executives from ABC, Touchstone and the Buena Vista Motion Picture Group.

Deadline
June 2005

Contact
Carmen Smith, VP of Talent
  Development Programs
Frank Gonzalez, Senior Manager, Talent
  Development

ABC Scholarship Grant Program

500 S. Buena Vista St.
Burbank, CA 91521-4389
Tel 818-560-6894
Email..............abc.fellowships@abc.com
Web ......www.abctalentdevelopment.com

Application
Available online

Support Provided
Grants/scholarships support new writing, filmmaking and directing talent. Scholarships and grants help finance creative efforts. For 10 months, grantees are paired with a mentor. Needs to be nominated by a nonprofit organization. Grant of $20,000 to help finance the completion of a screenplay or directing sample.

Deadline
Before March 31, 2005

Contact
Carmen Smith, VP of Talent
  Development Programs
Frank Gonzalez, Senior Manager, Talent
  Development

ABC Television Directing Fellowship Program

500 S. Buena Vista St.
Burbank, CA 91521-4389
Tel 818-560-4000
Email..............abc.fellowships@abc.com
Web ......www.abctalentdevelopment.com

Application
Available online

Description
Three Fellowships will be awarded for a period covering approximately 36 non-consecutive weeks of the television season. Fellows will be employees of ABC, be paid a an hourly wage not to exceed $15.50 for each hour that Fellow is employed.

Support Provided
The program provides personal exposure to television directing, career development, decision-making process and access to professional relationships with executive producers, showrunners, and other executives. The goal of the Directing Initiative is to prepare aspiring directors for later employment opportunities in television.

Deadline
March 1, 2005 - March 31, 2005

Contact
Carmen Smith, VP of Talent
  Development Programs
Frank Gonzalez, Senior Manager, Talent
  Development

diversity programs

ABC Casting Project
500 S. Buena Vista St.
Burbank, CA 91521-4389
Tel 818-560-6894
Email..............abc.fellowships@abc.com
Web ......www.abctalentdevelopment.com

Application
Available online

Description
Opportunities for actors
(SAG/Professional theater company
members) of diverse backgrounds.

Support Provided
Allows actors exposure, direction and
feedback from creative and casting
executives of ABC Entertainment,
Touchstone Television, as well as from
writers and executive producers from
the entertainment industry.

Deadline
Ongoing

Contact
Carmen Smith, VP of Talent
   Development Programs
Randi Chugerman, Manager, Casting &
   Talent Development

ABC Micro-Mini Series Development
500 S. Buena Vista St.
Burbank, CA 91521-4395
Tel 818-460-6055
Email..............abc.fellowships@abc.com
Web ......www.abctalentdevelopment.com

Application
Available online

Description
Series of interstitial short Micro-Mini
program will be three minutes in length.

Support Provided
Three one-minute interstitial acts to
be aired over the course of a single
evening. The Micro-Mini Series may be
repurposed on ABC Family or other
distribution platforms.

Deadline
To be announced

Contact
Carmen Smith, VP of Talent
   Development Programs
Adam Wolman, Executive Consultant,
   Talent Development

ABC Daytime Writing Program
500 S. Buena Vista St.
Burbank, CA 91521-4389
Tel 818-560-6894
Email..............abc.fellowships@abc.com
Web ......www.abctalentdevelopment.com

Application
Available online

Description
Discovers and employs creative talent,
mainly writers of culturally and ethnically
diverse backgrounds interested in
Daytime programming writing.

Support Provided
Workshops, seminars, and personalized
mentorship with creative executives from
ABC, Touchtone and the Buena Vista
Motion Picture Group.

Deadline
Summer 2005

Contact
Carmen Smith, VP of Talent
   Development Programs
Sue Johnson, Director, Talent
   Development, ABC Daytime

ABC Associates Program
500 S. Buena Vista St.
Burbank, CA 91521-4389
Tel 818-560-6894
Email..............abc.fellowships@abc.com
Web ......www.abctalentdevelopment.com

Application
Available online

Description
Management internships in the
television industry.

Support Provided
Provides a broad overview of the entertainment division; also permits time for exploration of specific areas of interest.

Deadline
Summer 2005

Contact
Carmen Smith, VP of Talent
  Development Programs

ABC Production Associates Program
500 S. Buena Vista St.
Burbank, CA 91521-4389
Tel 818-560-6894
Email..............abc.fellowships@abc.com
Web ......www.abctalentdevelopment.com

Application
Available online

Description
12-month paid program for individuals with diverse backgrounds placed in entry-level positions in the production areas of Touchstone Television.

Deadline
March 1, 2005 - April 15, 2005

Contact
Carmen Smith, VP of Talent
  Development Programs
Frank Gonzalez, Senior Manager, Talent
  Development

Academy of Television Arts & Sciences
Education Programs & Services
5220 Lankersheim Blvd.
N. Hollywood, CA 91601-3109
Tel 818-754-2830
Fax 818-761-2827
Web ....www.emmys.com

College Student Internship Program

Description
Offers 35 eight-week paid ($4,000) summer internships in 29 categories of telecommunications work.

Support Provided
In-depth exposure to professional television production, techniques and practices.

Deadline
March 15, 2005

College Television Awards

Description
National competition that provides industry recognition for outstanding student-produced films and videos.

Support Provided
Winners are mentored by television industry professionals. The Academy Foundation awards cash prizes to the winners. Eastman Kodak gives additional product grants and invites the winners to participate in their Emerging Filmmakers Program at the Cannes Film Festival. The Bricker Family award of not less than $4,000 is given to one first or second place winner that best represents a humanitarian concern.

Deadline
March 15, 2005

American Cinema Editors
ACE Internship Program
100 Universal City Plaza,
Ross Hunter Bldg. B, Rm. 202
Universal City, CA 91608
Tel 818-777-2900
Fax 818-733-5023
Email ....amercinema@earthlink.net
Web ......www.ace-filmeditors.org/educate

Application
Available by request

Description
A yearly internship program for college graduates seeking a career in film editing.

Support Provided
Each intern spends one week with three editors: one episodic, one long form television and one feature. There are also field trips to post-production related facilities.

Deadline
November 3, 2004

Contact
Lory Coleman, Head of Internship Program

ACE 2004 Student Editing Competition
100 Universal City Plaza,
Ross Hunter Bldg. B, Rm. 202
Universal City, CA 91608
Tel 818-777-2900
Fax 818-733-5023
Email ....amercinema@earthlink.net
Web ......www.ace-filmeditors.org/educate

Application
Available by request

Description
Participating students edit a set of video dailies. Three finalists will be guests at the annual ACE Eddie Awards in February 2005.

Support Provided
The winner receives a special Student Award and publicity in the Hollywood trade papers.

Deadline
October 3, 2004

Contact
Lory Coleman, Head of Internship Program

American Federation of Television and Radio Artists (AFTRA)
AFTRA Performer Mentor Program
5757 Wilshire Blvd., Suite 900
Los Angeles, CA 90036-3689
Tel 323-634-8181
Tel 323-634-8175
Fax 323-634-8190
Email ....plopez@aftra.com
Web ....www.aftra.org

Application
Available by request

Description
Performer program for students at 2- or 4-year colleges or graduate schools in the fields of television and cinema, or broadcast journalism.

Support Provided
Sponsored tape critiques, shadowing days and special events with feature professional performers and journalists.

Deadline
Rolling

Contact
John Russum, Executive Director

AFTRA Broadcast Mentor Program
5757 Wilshire Blvd., Suite 900
Los Angeles, CA 90036-3689
Tel 323-634-8181
Tel 323-634-8119
Fax 323-634-8190
Email ....ranosa@aftra.com
Web ....www.aftra.org

Application
Available by request

Description
The Broadcast Mentor Program is for students of Broadcast Journalism.

Support Provided
Sponsored tape critiques, shadowing days and special events with professional performers and journalists.

Deadline
Rolling

Contact
Jean Frost, Director of Agency and
　Mentor Programs

Broadcast Training Program/MIBTP
P.O. Box 67132
Century City, CA 90067
Tel 310-551-1035
Fax 310-388-1383
Email ....emailus@theBroadcaster.com
Web ....www.TheBroadcaster.com

Application
Available online

Description
Provides training opportunities to
minority college graduates in
radio/TV news reporting and news
management, and TV/film production.
Training includes the development of
writing, editing, producing and reporting
skills.

Support Provided
For TV/radio reporter trainees, stations
will pay minimum wage to $6.50 an
hour for duration; news management
trainees' salary arrangements vary for
each station.

Deadline
May 2005

Contact
Patrice Williams, CEO

CBS
CBS Diversity Institute
51 W. 52nd St.
New York, NY 10019
Tel 212-975-8941
Fax 212-975-9174
Email........................Diversity@cbs.com
Web.....................www.cbsdiversity.com

Description
Designed to identify and develop
diversity within the acting, writing and
directing community.

Support Provided
The Institute combines three programs:
the CBS Writers Mentoring Program, the
Directing Initiative and the Talent
Showcases.

Contact
Josie Thomas

CBS Writing Mentoring Program
51 W. 52nd St.
New York, NY 10019
Tel 212-975-8941
Fax 212-975-9174
Email........................Diversity@cbs.com
Web.....................www.cbsdiversity.com

Application
Available online

Description
Each participant is teamed with a
mentor, a network executive with whom
they meet on a regular basis to discuss
their work and their career. There will be
a series of small networking gatherings
with various CBS showrunners, in order
to provide a better understanding of
the show-making process and facilitate
relationships.

Support Provided
A structured program of career
development, support and personal
access to executives and decision-making
processes, with the goal of preparing
aspiring writers for later employment
opportunities in television.

diversity programs

Deadline
Please refer to website

Contact
Josie Thomas

CBS Directing Initiative
51 W. 52nd St.
New York, NY 10019
Tel 212-975-8941
Fax 212-975-9174
Email........................diversity@cbs.com
Web......................www.cbsdiversity.com

Application
Available online

Description
The program identifies promising directing candidates and matches them with directors of CBS Television Network drama and comedy series. Aspiring directors of diverse backgrounds with a strong desire to direct on a CBS television series are encouraged to apply. You must be 21 or older to be eligible.

Support Provided
No monetary compensation. A program of personal exposure to the process of television directing, career development and access to executives and decision making process.

Deadline
Rolling admission

Contact
Josie Thomas

CBS Talent Showcases
51 W. 52nd St.
New York, NY 10019
Tel 212-975-8941
Fax 212-975-9174
Email........................Diversity@cbs.com
Web......................www.cbsdiversity.com

Application
No applications

Description
Upcoming showcases will be announced on website. Please submit headshot and resume to the address provided.

DGA—Directors Guild of America
New York DGA Assistant Director Training Program
1697 Broadway
New York, NY 10019
Tel 212-397-0930
Email ....info@dgatrainingprogram.org
Web ....www.DGATrainingProgram.org

Application
Available by request online

Description
Provides opportunities for a limited number of individuals to become assistant directors in film, television and commercials

Support Provided
350 days of on-the-job training, combined with seminars and special assignments. After completion, trainees are eligible to join the DGA as second assistant directors. Trainee weekly salary rates increase over the two year period on a quarterly (six month) basis as follows:
1st quarter: $540/week
2nd quarter: $580/week
3rd quarter: $621/week
4th quarter: $663/week

Deadline
January 14, 2005

Contact
Sandy Forman, Administrator

Los Angeles DGA-Assistant Directors Training Program
14724 Ventura Blvd., Suite 775
Sherman Oaks, CA 91403
Tel 818-386-2545
Email ....mail@trainingplan.org
Web ....www.trainingplan.org

Application
Available online

Description
This non-profit organization trains Second Assistant Directors. Successful completion of this program will allow participants to be placed on the DGA's Southern California Area Qualification List to work as a Second Assistant Director.

Deadline
November 5, 2004

Contact
Janet Dyer, Administrator

FOX Diversity Development
FOX Writers Program
P.O. Box 900
Beverly Hills, CA 90213-0900
Tel 310-369-2976
Tel 310-369-5838
Email ....diversity_program@fox.com
Web ....www.fox.com/diversity

Application
Available online

Description
A Writers' Initiative designed to identify diverse writers for various staff positions on FOX series.

Support Provided
Writers are called in to FOX for initial assessment meetings, and to have their scripts read by FOX Creative Executives. Writers from this pool are interviewed for positions as writers and writers' assistants on FOX Network television series.

Deadline
Between January 1, 2005 and April 15, 2005

Contact
Ron Taylor, Vice President, Diversity Development

FOX Dorsey High School Mentor Program
10201 W. Pico Blvd.
Bldg. 100 / Rm. 4535
Los Angeles, CA 90035
Tel 310-369-2993
Email ....karen.lake@fox.com
Web ....www.fox.com/diversity

Application
Available online

Description
The FOX S.T.A.R. Mentor Program, bridging the school-to-career gap.

Support Provided
One-on-one mentoring sessions between a high school student and a FOX employee; workshops for students on personal development, higher education planning, career choices and life skills.

Contact
Karen Lake
Miriam Brown

FOX Searchlight
FOX Search Lab
10201 W Pico Blvd.
Bldg. 667, Suite 5
Los Angeles, CA 90035
Fax 310-396-1000
Web ....www.foxsearchlight.com

Application
Send required material

Description
This is an incubater for emerging filmmakers. The Lab identifies, supports and showcases the next generation of filmmakers while encouraging new voices and ideas. The Lab is open to international submissions.

Support Provided
The Lab provides a small production budget and equipment to create a short film that serves as an audition piece. The Lab works with selected filmmakers each year to create digital shorts. Each Lab Filmmaker receives a first look deal with FOX Searchlight Pictures.

Deadline
Ongoing

Contact
Kiran Ramchandran

IFP/Los Angeles

Independent Feature Project/Los Angeles Project Involve

8750 Wilshire Blvd., 2nd Fl.
Beverly Hills, CA 90211
Tel 310-432-1280
Tel 310-432-1200
Fax 310-432-1203
Email ....projectinv@ifp.org
Web...................................www.ifp.org

Application
Available online

Description
Mentoring, training and job placement program that provides diverse filmmakers with exposure, experience and connections in the film industry. Two cycles (Fall & Spring) per year for four months each. Twenty participants are selected for each cycle.

Support Provided
Career workshops, individual counseling and access to quality job listings and referrals.

Deadline
April 1, 2005. Applications are accepted once a year for both the Fall and Spring cycles. Next available cycles are Fall 2005 and Spring 2006.

Contact
Ramona Wright, Project: Involve
  Coordinator
Pamela Tom

Inner-City Filmmakers Los Angeles

Inner-City Filmmakers Summer Program

3000 W. Olympic Blvd.
Santa Monica, CA 90404
Tel 310-264-3992
Email............innercityfilm@earthlink.net
Web ....www.InnerCityFilmmakers.com

Application
Available online

Description
Trains inner-city youth in all aspects of filmmaking and helps them to find industry jobs when they graduate from the eight-week summer program.

Support Provided
Hands-on training with the latest in technology—digital cameras, lighting and sound equipment, Final Cut Pro editing and professional Avid editing systems—to further prepare students for the professional world.

Deadline
April 15, 2005

Contact
Fred Heinrich, Founder

Inner-City Filmmakers Job Programs

3000 W. Olympic Blvd.
Santa Monica, CA 90404
Tel 310-264-3992
Email............innercityfilm@earthlink.net
Web ....www.InnerCityFilmmakers.com

Application
Available online

Description
The Inner-City Filmmakers Jobs Program places qualified ICF graduates in paying entry-level jobs at film studios and production companies.

Support Provided
Helps the development of careers in production and postproduction as students build relationships and advance their careers.

Deadline
Ongoing

Contact
Fred Heinrich, Founder

MTV Network
MTV Internship Program
1515 Broadway, 16th Fl.
New York, NY 10036
Tel 212-846-1473
Email.................internships@mtvn.com
Web ....www.MTVNCareers.com

Application
Available online

Description
Allows college students to work in an innovative, progressive, fast-paced and professional environment.
Students must be registered for an internship for academic credit with their college or university, and must provide official documentation upon acceptance of this internship. MTV Networks has internships available in the following departments:
Affiliate Sales & Marketing, National Advertising Sales, Animation, On-Air Graphics (motion graphics), Business Development, Planning & Design, Business and Legal Affairs, Production, Communications, Production Management, Consumer Products, Programming, Creative Services, Promotion, Development, Public Affairs, Editorial Radio Network, Finance, Research, Human Resources, Special Events, Home Video, Talent and Artist Relations, International Travel Management, IS&T, Web Design, Marketing, Wardrobe.
Open to college upperclassmen (juniors/seniors) and eligible sophomores. Must be available at least 2 full days a week for a minimum of 10 weeks (no weekends). The Program runs during the spring, summer and fall semesters.

Support Provided
Students are exposed to all levels of MTV Networks.

Deadline
Application dates for resume submissions are rolling, except Summer - cut off date for resume submission is April 1, 2005. To apply, please send a resume and cover letter indicating the semester you are applying for and the area(s) of interest.

MTV Network Huddle
MTV Network Internship Program
1515 Broadway, 16th Fl.
New York, NY 10036
Tel 212-258-8000
Email ....careers@mtvstaff.com
Web ....www.MTVNCareers.com

Application
Available online

Description
Mentors (at the manager level or above) establish relationships with employees who wish to advance their careers.

Support Provided
Participants meet one-on-one for approximately nine months and often keep up communication beyond that time, occasionally after the mentored participants have left the company.

Deadline
Contact local Human Resources department and complete an application.
April 1, 2005

National Association of Minorities in Communication

L. Patrick Mellon Mentorship Program

600 Anton Blvd., 11th Fl.
Costa Mesa, CA 92626
Tel 714-371-4077
Fax 714-371-2103
Email ....info@namic.com
Web ....www.namic.com

Application
Available online

Description
Makes mentors available for career advancement strategies in the Cable and Telecommunications industry.

Support Provided
Top-level industry professionals mentor for nine months. One-on-one sessions for support, guidance and career advice up to two hours per month.

Deadline
Ongoing

Contact
Marsha Wesley Coleman, L. Patrick Mellon Mentorship Program Manager

NBC

NBC Entertainment Associate Program

Human Resources
3000 W. Alameda Ave.
Burbank, CA 91523
Tel 818-840-4444
Tel 202-885-4445
Email...................epgmassoc@nbc.com
Web ....www.nbcjobs.com

Application
Available online

Description
Hands-on experience in the development and management of entertainment programming. Program Associates analyze/develop scripts and provide creative input to writers and producers on review of scripts, stories, casting and scheduling of programs.

Support Provided
Successful graduates of the program move into Creative Executive positions within the NBC Network or NBC Studios. The program offers competitive compensation including benefits.

Deadline
NBC accepts resumes only when recruiting for open positions. Next open positions anticipated first quarter 2005. Please visit the website at that time.

Contact
Michael Jack, General Manager, Washington, D.C., 202-885-4445

NBC News Associate Program

Human Resources
3000 W. Alameda Ave.
Burbank, CA 91523
Tel 818-840-4444
Tel 202-885-4445
Email ....news.associate@nbc.com
Web ....www.nbcjobs.com

Application
Available online

Description
Fast-track opportunity for people with the goal to learn news gathering and production skills.

Support Provided
News Associates gain real-world experience honing research skills, developing news stories working in a news bureau, participating in field and studio show production, on the nightly news, a morning news program, or on a magazine program. Salary: $33,600/year.

Deadline
February 11, 2005

Contact
Michael Jack, General Manager, Washington, D.C., 202-885-4445

NBC Sales Associate Program
Human Resources
30 Rockefeller Plaza
New York, NY 10112
Tel 818-840-4444
Tel 202-885-4445
Email ....nysales@nbc.com
Web ....www.nbcjobs.com

Application
Available online

Description
Rotations in all aspects of the field of Sales and Marketing. Areas covered during rotations include research, customer service, advertising agencies, business development, technology, Internet and desk experience across NBC, Telemundo and Paxson.

Support Provided
After training, fellows will be eligible for employment at NBC- and Telemundo-owned and operated stations, or national sales offices.

Deadline
Next Sales Associate class to be announced. Please refer to website for information.

Contact
Michael Jack, General Manager, Washington, D.C., 202-885-4445

NBC Internship Program
Human Resources
3000 W. Alameda Ave.
Burbank, CA 91523
Tel 818-840-4444
Tel 202-885-4445
Email ....NYintern@nbc.com
Email ....CAintern@nbc.com
Web ....www.nbcjobs.com

Application
Available online

Description
Students are placed in television broadcast/production areas, business operations and NBC interactive positions related to their major and career goals.

Support Provided
The Internship program offers college students the opportunity to take a first step into the broadcasting industry.

Deadline
Fall: May, June, July, August
Spring: September, November, December
Summer: January, February, March

Contact
Michael Jack, General Manager in Washington, D.C., 202-885-4445

NBC Page Program
Human Resources
3000 W. Alameda Ave.
Burbank, CA 91523
Tel 818-840-4444
Tel 202-885-4445
Email ....NYpage@nbc.com
Email ....CApage@nbc.com
Web ....www.nbcjobs.com

Application
Available online

Description
Applicants will be given the chance to learn about many aspects of network television from the ground up. Primary function is to act as a liaison between NBC and the general public, conduct guided tours and perform various audi-ence services for NBC shows.

Support Provided
Applicants have the opportunity to work in different departments within the company on either short or long term assignments.

Deadline
Ongoing

Emma Bowen Program

Human Resources
3000 W. Alameda Ave.
Burbank, CA 91523
Tel 818-840-4444
Tel 202-885-4445
Email.............Contact the local NBC TV
Station listed online
Web ....www.nbcjobs.com
Web ....www.emmabowenfoundation.com

Application
Available online

Description
Students work for a partner company during summers and school breaks from the end of their junior year in high school until they graduate from college.

Support Provided
Students learn many aspects of corporate operations and develop company-specific skills. Students in the program receive an hourly wage, as well as matching compensation to help pay for college tuition and expenses.

Deadline
Periodically

Minority Writers Program/Network Writing

Human Resources
3000 W. Alameda Ave.
Burbank, CA 91523
Tel 818-840-4444
Tel 202-885-4445
Email ......diversityinitiative@nbcuni.com
Web ....www.nbcjobs.com

Application
Available online

Description
NBC provides funding for a minority staff writer position for all scripted Primetime Series, Daytime and Late Night Programming (including non-NBC Studio produced series).

Support Provided
Funds a staff writer position on all new and returning Primetime Series for up to a total of three seasons for each minority staff writer so hired.

Deadline
Between mid-January and March each year

The NBC Agency Associates Program

Human Resources
3000 W. Alameda Ave.
Burbank, CA 91523
Tel 818-840-4444
Tel 202-885-4445
Email.................agencyassoc@nbc.com
Web ....www.nbcjobs.com

Application
Available online

Description
Hands-on experience while writing and editing on-air promos for NBC's prime time line-up of shows as well as for the various clients of the NBC Agency.

Support Provided
Successful graduates of the program move into Writer/Producer positions within the NBC Agency.

Deadline
NBC accepts resumes only when recruiting for open positions. Open positions anticipated for first quarter, 2005. Please visit the website at that time.

Nickelodeon

Nickelodeon Animation Studio Internship Program

231 W. Olive Ave.
Burbank, CA 91502
Tel 818-736-3673
Fax 818-736-3539
Email.................katie.fiedler@nick.com
Web ....www.nick.com

Application
Please fax cover letter and resume

Description
Internships offered in all areas of animation production.

Support Provided
For school credit only. Non-paid.

Deadline
Ongoing. Programs start September, January and June.

Contact
Katie Fiedler-Garcia, Human Resources
  Assistant

Showtime Networks

Showtime Latino Filmmaker Showcase

10880 Wilshire Blvd., Suite 1600
Los Angeles, CA 90024
Tel 310-234-5300
Fax 310-234-5389
Email............sandra.avila@showtime.net
Web ....www.sho.com

Description
Selects shorts that are 30-minutes or shorter in length produced or directed by a Latino to be showcased on Showtime during Hispanic Heritage month.

Support Provided
There is a license fee for each short selected and the winner gets a $30,000 grant to produce a short film in association with Showtime.

Deadline
May 15, 2006

Contact
Sandra Avila, Program Coordinator

Step Up Women's Network

Step Up Women's Network Professional Mentorship Program

8424-A Santa Monica Blvd., #857
West Hollywood, CA 90069
Tel 323-549-5347
Email..................stepupla@hotmail.com
Web ......www.stepupwomensnetwork.org

Application
Available online

Description
Allows members to earn "points" towards receiving a Professional Mentor in her field in exchange for volunteering with local community partners, participating on Step Up committees, helping recruit new members, etc.

Support Provided
Places women in volunteer opportunities in the entertainment and media industries.

Deadline
Ongoing

Contact
Traci Fleming, Executive Director
Julie Rubin, Program Manager

Streetlights

Production Assistant Program

650 N. Bronson Ave., Suite B108
Hollywood, CA 90004
Tel 323-960-4540
Fax 323-960-4546
Email ....streetlights@streetlights.org
Email ....johnc@streetlights.org
Web ....www.streetlights.org

Description
Designed to help minorities establish careers in the entertainment industry.

Support Provided
240 hours of classroom work and paid on-the-job training that prepares graduates for entry-level jobs as production assistants in film, TV and commercials.

diversity programs

Deadline
Applications accepted year round.

Contact
John Cager, Director of Client Services & Outreach or Dorothy Thompson, Executive Director

Sundance Institute
The Screenwriters Lab
8857 W. Olympic Blvd.
Beverly Hills, CA 90211
Tel 310-360-1981
Email ..featurefilmprogram@sundance.org
Web ....www.sundance.org

Application
Available online

Description
The program offers ten to twelve emerging artists the opportunity to work intensively on their feature film scripts with the support of established screen-writers. January and June sessions at Sundance.

Support Provided
One-on-one problem-solving story sessions with Creative Advisors, who engage in individual dialogues that combine life lessons in craft with practical suggestions to be explored in the next drafts.

Deadline
Applications for consideration for the 2006 Labs starts on February 2005.

Contact
Jason Shinder (CA), Writers Fellowship Program

Filmmakers Lab
8857 W. Olympic Blvd.
Beverly Hills, CA 90211
Tel 310-360-1981
Email ..featurefilmprogram@sundance.org
Web ....www.sundance.org

Application
Available online

Description
Three-week-long hands-on workshop for writers and directors. This lab takes place each June at Sundance.

Support Provided
Participants gain experience rehearsing, shooting and editing scenes from their screenplays on videotape under the mentorship of accomplished directors, editors, cinematographers and actors.

Deadline
Applications for consideration for the 2006 Labs starts February 2005.

Composers Lab
8857 W. Olympic Blvd.
Beverly Hills, CA 90211
Tel 310-360-1981
Email ....peter_golub@sundance.org
Web ....www.sundance.org

Application
Available online

Description
The Sundance Composers Lab, a two-week training program for film com-posers that is run in conjunction with the Sundance Filmmakers Lab.

Deadline
April 1, 2005

Contact
Larin Sullivan (CA), Programming and Composers Lab Coordinator

Native American Initiative
8857 W. Olympic Blvd.
Beverly Hills, CA 90211
Tel 310-360-1981
Email ....native@sundance.org
Web ....www.sundance.org

Application
Available online

Description
Supports Native American writers and directors through the Institute's Feature Film Program, which operates the Institute's Screenwriters and Directors Labs.

Support Provided
Designed to offer emerging screenwriters and directors the opportunity to develop new work.

Deadline
Ongoing

Warner Bros.
Drama Writers Workshop
4000 Warner Blvd.
Bldg. 136, Suite 236
Burbank, CA 91522
Tel 818-954-5700
Web.....................www.warnerbros.com/
writersworkshop

Application
Available online

Description
Exposure to today's top television drama writers, valuable note-giving sessions, as well as supervision by Warner Bros. television executives.

Support Provided
Course runs from January 5 – February 2, 2005 meeting every Wednesday from 12:30 pm to 2:30 pm. Full participation is expected.

Deadline
August 6, 2004

Contact
Debby Pearlman

Comedy Writers Workshop
4000 Warner Blvd.
Bldg. 136, Suite 236
Burbank, CA 91522
Tel 818-954-5700
Web.....................www.warnerbros.com/
writersworkshop

Application
Available online

Description
Exposure to top comedy writers working in television, valuable note-giving sessions and supervision by Warner Bros. Television executives.

Support Provided
Course runs from February 16 - April 20, 2005 meeting every Wednesday from 12:30 pm to 2:30 pm. Full participation is expected.

Deadline
September 3, 2004

Contact
Debby Pearlman

Animation Internship Program
4000 Warner Blvd.
Burbank, CA 91522-0001
Web ....www.wbjobs.com

Description
Internship that develops applicant pool for Animation positions and helps the selected candidates adapt their skills to this unique art form.

Support Provided
The internship provides training to develop a career path for entry-level production personnel, animation writers and artists.

Deadline
Positions become available based on business unit's needs.

Time Warner STARS Program (Summer)
4000 Warner Blvd.
Burbank, CA 91522-0001
Web ....www.wbjobs.com

Application
Submit resume online

Description
Provides college students with a real-life business environment and encourages them to discover their own interests and capacities.

Support Provided
Paid program that exposes college students to career opportunities in the entertainment industry.

Deadline
Positions become available based on business unit's needs in spring for June start date.

Warner Bros. Entertainment
Collegiate Internship Program
4000 Warner Blvd.
Burbank, CA 91522-0001
Web ....www.wbjobs.com

Application
Submit resume online

Description
Provides college students work experience during the academic year for specific disciplines within participating divisions.

Deadline
Positions become available based on business unit's needs.

Corporate Legal Clerkship Program
(Available for credit only)
4000 Warner Blvd.
Burbank, CA 91522-0001
Web ....www.wbjobs.com

Application
Submit resume online

Description
Identifies 1st year Law Students with a strong interest in Entertainment Law and assigns them professional-level projects in various legal divisions.

Deadline
Positions become available based on business unit's needs.

Credit-Only Internship Program
(Available for credit only)
4000 Warner Blvd.
Burbank, CA 91522-0001
Web ....www.wbjobs.com

Application
Submit resume online

Description
Provides college students education-related work experience during the academic year while gaining course credit towards their area of study.

Deadline
Positions become available based on business unit's needs.

Feature Production
Management Trainee Program
4000 Warner Blvd.
Burbank, CA 91522-0001
Web ....www.wbjobs.com

Application
Submit resume online

Description
Provides individuals with the exposure to all facets of the production process.

Support Provided
An understanding of Warner Bros. production methods and an opportunity to develop professional contacts within the production arena.

Deadline
Positions become available based on business unit's needs.

Global Trainee Program
4000 Warner Blvd.
Burbank, CA 91522-0001
Web ....www.wbjobs.com

Application
Submit resume online

Description
Yearlong training both on the job and in a classroom setting within a division in specific disciplines such as Marketing, Sales, Accounting, Production and more.

Deadline
Positions become available based on business unit's needs in spring 2005 for August start date.

Production Assistant Trainee Program
4000 Warner Blvd.
Burbank, CA 91522-0001
Web ....www.wbjobs.com

Application
Submit resume online

Description
Offers the opportunity for individuals with limited exposure to the industry, a chance to explore the Production arena.

Deadline
Positions become available based on business unit's needs.

Writegirl
Tel 323-363-1287
Email ....info@writegirl.org
Web ....www.writegirl.org

Description
Pairs high school girls from high-density communities in central Los Angeles with professional women writers for mentoring and workshops on creative writing. Gives girls techniques, insights and hot topics for great writing in all genres. Monthly group workshops and weekly one-on-one mentoring sessions explore poetry, fiction, creative non-fiction, songwriting, journalism, screenwriting, playwriting, persuasive writing, journal writing, editing and more.

Support Provided
Provides training for all mentors and volunteers and ongoing support to all writing pairs throughout the season.

Contact
Keren Taylor, Executive Director

Youth Mentoring Connection (YMC)
1316 Keniston Ave.
Los Angeles, CA 90019
Tel 323-525-1049
Fax 323-525-1048
Email ....ymc@youthmentoring.org
Web ....www.youthmentoring.org

Application
Available by request

Description
Mentoring program that matches companies such as HBO, Endeavor and Warner Bros. with at-risk youth.

Support Provided
Matches companies with a school or youth center; employees mentor the youth at their corporate offices.

Contact
Tony LoRe, President

National Association of Latino Independent Producers

funding
opportunities

Note: Where 2004 dates are included in this section, it is for reference only. Please contact individual programs for most current deadlines.

Academy of Motion Picture Arts and Sciences Film Scholarship

8949 Wilshire Blvd.
Beverly Hills, CA 90211

Tel 310-247-3000
Email..........................gbeal@oscars.org
Web ....www.oscars.org/foundation/grants

Support Provided
Academy Film Scholars Program supports the creation of innovative and significant works of film scholarship about aesthetic, cultural, educational, historical, theatrical and scientific aspects of motion pictures. Proposed projects may be books, multimedia presentations, curatorial projects, CD-ROMs and internet sites. Projects cannot be film, television or video productions. Two grants of $25,000.

Deadline
August 31, 2005

Program Officer
Greg Beal

Film Festival Grants

Grants have been made to major international film festivals that focus on independent and alternative filmmaking. While the grants have been made for many different purposes, film festivals are encouraged to submit proposals that make festival events more accessible to the general public, especially to segments of the populace who might not normally be able to attend; that give screening access to minority and less visible filmmakers; and that bring the public into contact with films and filmmakers. Individual festival grants have ranged from $5,000 to $30,000, with the amount based upon the size of the festival.

Deadline
On or near July 1, 2005

Program Officer
Greg Beal

Institutional Grants

Grants are given to film-related, nonprofit organizations, schools and colleges. The Academy supports college-based internship programs which enable gifted students to work with prominent filmmakers. Funds are not awarded directly to individuals engaged in the performing arts, to cover the expenses of developing scripts or producing films, nor to fund educational expenses of any nature. The typical funding now ranges from $5,000 to $15,000 per institution.

Deadline
January 26, 2005

The Adolph and Esther Gottlieb Society Foundation

380 W. Broadway
New York, NY 10012

Tel 212-226-0581
Email ....aegf@aol.com
Web ....gottliebfoundation.org

Support Provided
Funding for visual artists who incorporate video and film in their work. Mature film and video artists whose work can be directly interpreted as painting or sculpture may be eligible to apply for the programs; or an artist who works in a combination of performance art, film or video and installation may also qualify. Ten grants of $20,000.

Deadline
December 15, 2005

Program Officer
Sheila Ross

American Antiquarian Society (AAS)

185 Salisbury St.
Worcester, MA 01605-1634

Tel 508-471-2131
Tel 506-471-2139
Fax 508-754-6069
Email ....jmorgan@mva.org
Web ....www.americanantiquarian.org/
                          artistfellowship.htm

Support Provided
Applications for visiting fellowships for historical research by creative and performing artists, writers, filmmakers, journalists and other persons whose goals are to produce imaginative, non-formulaic works dealing with pre-twentieth-century American history. Projects may include documentary films, television programs, screenplays. Grants $1,200.

Deadline
October 15, 2005

Program Officer
James David Moran

Arizona Humanities Council

1242 N. Central Ave.
Phoenix, AZ 85004-1887

Tel..........................602-257-0335 x26
Fax 602-257-0392
Email........amjohnson@azhumanities.org
Web ....www.azhumanities.org

Support Provided
General Grants are available for community-initiated projects that help Arizonans understand and appreciate the humanities. AHC is especially interested in funding projects that bring good humanities scholarship to out-of-school audiences in Arizona. Format may include radio, CD and video productions. Grants up to $3,000. Applicant must have a 501(c)(3) designation or be governmental entity.

Deadlines
February 1, 2005
May 16, 2005
September 12, 2005

Program Officer
Ann-Mary Johnson

Arkansas Humanities Council: Media Projects

10800 Financial Centre Pky., Suite 465
Little Rock, AK 72211

Tel 501-221-0091
Email .... .lavonawilson@sbcglobal.net
Email ....arkhums@sbcglobal.net
Web .... www.arkhums.org

Support Provided
Funds media projects that result in the development of humanities audiovisual resources, including film and video productions, exhibits, audio productions, slide-tape programs, and websites. Preference given to media projects that focus on Arkansas prehistory, history and culture. Major grants of up to $5,000 for film and video preproduction, including development of scripts and production treatments. Funds all format shorts, documentaries, features.

Deadline
February 15 and September 15, 2005. Applications for major grants of up to $25,000 for film and video production are accepted only at the September deadline.

Program Officer
Lavona Wilson

The Arthur Vinning Davis Foundations

225 Water St., Suite 1510
Jacksonville, FL 32202-5185

Tel 904-359-0670
Fax 904-359-0675
Email............arthurvining@bellsouth.net
Web.......................www.jvm.com/davis

Support Provided
Grants primarily provide partial support for major educational series assured of national airing by PBS. Children's series are of particular interest. Consideration also will be given to innovative uses of public television (including online efforts) to enhance educational outreach in schools and communities. Grants $100,000 to $500,000.

Deadline
Rolling

Program Officer
Dr. Jonathan T. Howe

Arts International (Islamic World Arts Initiative)

526 W. 26th St., Suite 512
New York, NY

Tel 212-924-0771
Fax 212-924-0773
Email........ktakeda@artsinternational.org
Web .... www.artsinternational.org

Support Provided
Provides grants in support of projects that foster cultural understanding between the Islamic World and the United States. Professional artists, nonprofit organizations and scholars may apply for support of projects in the areas of contemporary performing, literary, media and visual arts, and arts-related scholarship.

Deadline
December 15, 2005

Program Officer
Kay Takeda

Astrea National Lesbian Action Foundation

116 E. 16 St., 7th Fl.
New York, NY 10003

Tel 212-529-8021
Fax 212-982-3321
Email ....grants@astraea.org
Email ....jkang@astraeafoundation.org
Web..............................www.astraea.org

Support Provided
Support provided for lesbian-led film/video projects that explicitly address lesbian-of-color issues $1,000-$6,000; the average is near $3,000. Funds shorts, features, documentaries.

Deadline
April 1, 2005

Program Officer
Joo-Hyun Kang

California Council for the Humanities: The California Documentary Project

312 Sutter St., Suite 601
San Francisco, CA 94108

Tel.......................415-391-1474 (S.F.)
Tel ....213-623-5993 (L.A.)
Tel ....619-232-4020 (S.D.)
Email ....info@calhum.org
Web ....www.calhum.org

Support Provided
Encourages documentarians to create enduring images and text of contemporary California life, as video documentaries or any digital media. Projects may apply for grants up to $20,000; film, video and radio projects may apply for additional funds of up to a total of $80,000. To be eligible for the additional funds, projects must be suitable for statewide/national broadcast. Consult website for futher guidelines.

funding opportunities

Deadline
October 1, 2006

Program Officer
Los Angeles: Felicia Kelley
San Francisco: Susana Loza
San Diego: Amy Rouillard

Center for Alternative Media and Culture

P.O. Box 0832, Radio City Station
New York, NY 10101

Tel 212-977-2096

Support Provided
Supports independent media projects in post-production that address the economy, class issues, poverty, women, war and peace, race and labor. Grants range $100-$10,000.

Center for Independent Documentary

680 S. Main St.
Sharon, MA 02067

Tel 781-784-3627
Fax 781-784-8254
Email...............info@documentaries.org
Web ....www.documentaries.org

Support Provided
Seeks proposals from independent producers for the production of documentaries on contemporary issues. Applicants receive a variety of services and resources.

Deadline
Rolling

Program Officer
Susan Walsh

Colorado Endowment for the Humanities

1490 Lafayette St., Suite 101
Denver, CO 80218

Tel 303-894-7951
Fax 303-864-9361
Email................................info@ceh.org
Web ....www.ceh.org

Support Provided
Awards pre-production development of script and narrative treatments for all media formats, including films and video tapes. Must be centered on one or more disciplines of the humanities. Applicants may request up to $10,000. A $10,000 proposal must have at least $3,000 in matching funds.

Deadline
September 1, 2004

Program Officer
Mark Skinner

Connecticut Humanities Council Cultural Heritage Development Fund

955 S. Main St.
Middletown, CT 06457

Tel 800-628-8272
Tel 860-685-2260
Fax 860-704-0429
Email...................... chc@ctheritage.org
Web ....www.ctculture.org

Connecticut Non-Profit Grants

Support Provided
Awards grants to Connecticut-based nonprofit organizations, including educational television stations, for public projects in the humanities.

Deadline
November 1, 2005

Program Officer
Bruce Fraser

Exhibition Grants

Support Provided
Grants support research and scripting of temporary, traveling and permanent exhibitions (both traditional and online); creation of living history programs of significant aspects of Connecticut history and heritage (includes catalogues, interpretive brochures, walking tours and guidebooks, audiovisual presentations, interactive computer/videodisc displays and online exhibitions and tours). Grants $15,500.

Deadline
For proposals seeking more than $5,000: 2/1/05, 5/1/05, 8/1/05, 11/1/05 or the first working day thereafter.
For proposals under $5,000: The first day of every month or the first working day thereafter.
For proposals seeking $2,500 or less: Rolling deadline.

Program Officer
Bruce Fraser

Implementation Grants

Support Provided
Actual production of heritage programs once planning is complete. Applications should reflect thoughtful humanities content, well-developed project scripts, clear work-plans and detailed production budgets and comprehensive plans for project marketing. Grants up to $75,000.

Deadline
For proposals seeking more than $5,000: 2/1/05, 5/1/05, 8/1/05, 11/1/05 or the first working day thereafter.
For proposals under $5,000: The first day of every month or the first working day thereafter.
For proposals seeking $2,500 or less: Rolling deadline.

Program Officer
Bruce Fraser

Corporation for Public Broadcasting Diverse Voices

401 9th St. NW
Washington, DC 20004-2129

Tel 202-879-9600
Fax 202-879-9700
Email ....programming@cpb.org
Web ....www.cpb.org

Support Provided
This program development and mentoring project is a strategic and focused expansion of previous P.O.V. efforts to showcase emerging media makers of diverse backgrounds for public broadcasting's national audience. In collaboration with stations and the Minority Consortia, P.O.V. will seek out and mentor minority producers to bring multicultural programming to the series. A CPB Diversity Fund Project. Grants around $500,000.

Deadline
Please check the website for information on 2005 funding.

Program Officer
Cheryl Head

Corporation for Public Broadcasting: New Voices, New Media Fund

401 9th St. NW
Washington, DC 20004-2129

Tel 202-879-9600
Fax 202-879-9700
Email ....programming@cpb.org
Web ....www.cpb.org

Support Provided
Funding for innovative, educational and informational public television programming. Documentary programs and series, children's programming, news programming.

Deadline
September 15, 2005

Program Officer
Cheryl Head

Creative Capital Foundation

65 Bleecker St., 7th Fl.
New York, NY 10013

Tel 212-598-9900
Fax 212-598-4934
Email ....info@creativity-capital.org
Web.................www.creative-capital.org

Support Provided
Revolving fund supporting artists
pursuing innovative, experimental
approaches. All forms of film and video,
including experimental documentary,
animation, experimental media,
non-traditional narrative in all formats
and interdisciplinary projects. Most
initial grants (about 15 in each
discipline) will be in the $5,000 range,
with a few (about five) in the
$15-20,000 range for projects further
along in their development.

Deadline
March 14, 2005

Program Officer
Dona Pena

Delaware Division of the Arts Individual Artists Fellowships

820 N. French St.
Wilmington, DE 19801

Tel 302-577-8278
Fax 302-739-5304
Email ......kristin.pleasanton@state.de.us
Web ....www.artsdel.org

Support Provided
Provides individul Artist Fellowships
to Delaware creative artists working
in the visual, performing, media,
interdisciplinary, folk and literary arts.
Also available are opportunity grants
for unique, short-term professional
development and/or presentation
opportunities. Please refer to website
for further guidelines.

Deadline
August 1, 2004

Program Officer
Kristin Pleasanton

Delaware Humanities Forum

100 W. 10th St., Suite 1009
Wilmington, DE 19801

Tel 302-657-0650
Tel 1-800-752-2060
Fax 302-657-0655
Email ....delawarehumanities@dhf.org
Web ....www.dhf.org
Web ....www.delawarehumanities.org

Support Provided
Supports humanities programs for
the public sponsored by nonprofit
organizations and schools in Delaware.
Supports: Grants, Speakers Bureau,
Visiting Scholars to the schools and
Dover Lecture Series. Average grant is
$5,500 up to $10,000. Teachers and
scholars in the humanities must be
involved in planning, presenting and
evaluating the project.

Deadline
First Draft Due by January 1, April 1, July 1, October 3, 2005

Final Draft due by February 1, May 2, August 1, November 1, 2005

Decision due by March 30, June 30, September 30, December 30, 2005

Executive Director
Marilyn Whittington

Program Officer
Jeanne Sadot

Digital Media Educational Center

Email ....kate@filmcamp.com

Support Provided
Supports independent feature directors looking for means to complete their films, while offering Avid-authorized training to career editors.

The Durfee Foundation Artists: Resource for Completion

1453 3rd St., Suite 312
Santa Monica, CA 90401

Tel 310-899-5120
Fax 310-899-5121
Email ....admin@durfee.org
Web ....www.durfee.org

Support Provided
The ARC (Artists' Resource for Completion) grants provide rapid, short-term assistance to individual artists in Los Angeles County who wish to complete work for a specific, imminent opportunity that may significantly benefit their career. Artists in any discipline are eligible to apply. The applicant must already have secured an invitation from an established organization to present the proposed work. Grants up to $2,500.

Deadline
February 1, 2005; May 3, 2005; August 2, 2005; November 1, 2005

Program Officer
Caroline D. Avery

Echo Lake Fund

213 Rose Ave., 2nd Fl.
Venice, CA 90291

Tel 310-399-9164
Fax 310-399-9278
Email ..contact@echolakeproductions.com

Support Provided
Film fund for independent narrative features, not documentaries. For both producing and financing projects, the script and the director are crucial. Grants range $500,000 - $1,000,000.

Deadline
Rolling

Program Officer
Mark Dempsey

Experimental Television Center

109 Lower Fairfield Rd.
Newark Valley, NY 13811

Tel 607-687-4341
Email ....etc@experimentaltvcenter.org
Web ....www.experimentaltvcenter.org

Support Provided
Provides support to electronic media and film artists and organizations in New York State to encourage creative work (not students); to facilitate the exhibition of moving-image and sound art to audiences in all regions of the State; and to strengthen organizations with active media programs

Finishing Funds

Support Provided

Provides individual artists with grants up to $2,000 to help with the completion of diverse and innovative moving-image and sonic art projects, and works for the Web and new technologies. Eligible forms include media as single or multiple channel presentations, computer-based moving-imagery and sound works, installations and performances, interactive works and works for new technologies, CD-ROM, multimedia and the Web. Also supports new media, and interactive performance. Work must be surprising, creative and approach the various media as art forms; all genres are eligible, including experimental, narrative and documentary art works.

Deadline

March 15, 2005. Projects must be completed by the following Fall.

Presentation Funds

Support Provided

Provides grants to not-for-profit organizations throughout New York State. Support is available for personal presentations by independent electronic media and film artists. The program seeks to encourage events which increase understanding of and appreciation for independent media work in all areas of the State. Events must be open to the public; courses, classes and workshops with limited enrollments are not eligible. The intention of this program is to provide partial assistance; organizations must also provide additional support for the event. The maximum amount an organization may receive annually is about $1,000; if the organization receives support from the New York State Council on the Arts, the maximum award is about $700.

Deadline

Rolling

Media Arts Technical Assistance Fund

Support Provided

Designed to help non-profit media arts programs in New York State stabilize, strengthen or restructure their media arts organizational capacity, services and activities. Provides up to $2,000 per project. Can assist with the hiring of consultants or other professionals to help with organizational, managerial and programming issues that influence the media arts activities of your organization. Can also help with attendance at conferences, festivals and meetings, with field-wide networking opportunities, or with other activities which contribute to organizational and staff development or the building of critical skills. Organizations must be receiving support from NYSCA's Electronic Media and Film Program.

Deadline

Applications are accepted quarterly, with a postmark deadline of January 1, April 1, July 1 and October 1, 2005. Forms are available on the web.

Program Officer

Sherry Miller Hocking

Film Arts Foundation

145 9th St., Suite 101
San Francisco, CA 94103

Tel 415-552-8760 x315
Fax 415-552-0882
Email ....info@filmarts.org/
Email ....merrie@filmarts.org
Web ....www.filmarts.org

Support Provided
Funds different projects, from documentaries, experimental, features, educational videos. Grants from $1,000 to $4,000 for residents of the Bay Area. STAND (Support, Training and Access for New Directors) is a mentorship program for folks that have never made a film/tape before. Additional information on the website.

Deadline
July 30, 2005

Program Officer
Gail Silva

Fleischhacker Foundation

P.O. Box 29918
San Francisco, CA 94129-0918

Tel 415-561-5350
Fax 415-561-5350
Email ....info@fleishhackerfoundation.org
Web ......www.fleishhackerfoundation.org

Support Provided
Offers grants for Arts & Culture and Collegiate (K-12) Education. Grants between $1,000 and $10,000 for dance, film/video and media, music, theatre and visual arts. For organizations in the greater San Francisco Bay area.

Deadline
January 15, 2005 for May decision. July 15, 2005 for Fall decision. Note: these are postmark deadlines; please mail applications via regular mail.

Program Officer
Christine Ebel

Flintridge Foundation

1040 Lincoln Ave., Suite 100
Pasadena, CA 91103-3263

Tel 626-449-0839
Tel 800-303-2139
Fax 626-585-0011
Email ....awards@flintridgefoundation.org
Web ....www.flintridgefoundation.org

Biennial Awards for Visual Artists

Support Provided
The Foundation distributes ten biennial grants of $25,000 each to mature artists (five artists from California and five from Oregon/Washington), whose work demonstrates high artistic merit and a distinctive voice for 20 or more years. In addition, artists may not be nationally renowned, and they must have lived at least nine months per year in the tri-state region for the last three years. The primary goal of the Awards program has been to recognize and support artists and the process of art-making both directly and indirectly by providing artists with more time and resources to work. Artists working in visual disciplines—fine arts, crafts, and performance and media work based in the visual arts tradition—are eligible. (Dance, theatre, independent film and video are not eligible.)

Deadline
Early 2005

Program Officer
Pamela Gregg, Director of Programs
Angie Kim, Program Officer

Ford Foundation

320 E. 43rd St.
New York, NY 10017

Tel 212-573-5000
Fax 212-351-3677
Email................secretary@fordfound.org
Email ......office-secretary@fordfound.org
Web ....www.fordfound.org/grant/
guidelines.html

Media, Arts and Culture

Support Provided
In Media our work strengthens free
and responsible media that address
important civic and social issues, and
promotes policies and regulations that
ensure media and information systems
serve the public's diverse constituencies
and interests. In addition, we support
high-quality productions that enrich
public dialogue on such core issues
as building democratic values and
pluralism.
In Arts and Culture our goal is to
increase opportunities for cultural and
artistic expression for people of all
backgrounds; to foster documentation,
dissemination and transmission of both
new and traditional creative art forms;
to broaden audience involvement and
access, and to improve the livelihoods
of artists and their opportunity to
contribute to civic life.
Supports public broadcasting and the
independent production of film, video
and radio programming; and supports
efforts to engage diverse groups in work
related to the media and to analyze the
media's effect on society. Supports
high-quality productions that enrich
public dialogue on such core issues
as building democratic values and
pluralism. Grants vary from case to case.
All formats are accepted.

Deadline
Rolling

Program Officer
Pamela Meyer, Orlando Bagwell

The Foundation Center

79 5th Ave.
New York, NY 10003

Tel 212-620-4230
Fax 212-691-1828
Web ....www.fdncenter.org/onlib

Support Provided
Online resource for researching funders,
with tips on proposal writing.

The Fund for Jewish Documentary Filmmaking

330 7th Ave., 21st Fl.
New York, NY 10001

Tel.......................212-629-0500 x215
Fax 212-629-0508
Email ....grants@jewishculture.org
Email ..nschwartzman@jewishculture.org
Web ....www.jewishculture.org

Support Provided
The Fund is designed to support the
creation of original documentary films
and videos that promote thoughtful
consideration of Jewish history, culture,
identity, and contemporary issues among
diverse public audiences. No grant will
exceed $50,000 or 50% of the total
project budget, whichever is less. Most
grant awards are expected to fall in the
$20,000-30,000 range.

Deadline
March 10, 2005

The Ronnie Heyman Prize for an
Emerging Visual Artist

Support Provided
To recognize and support an emerging
visual artist who is creating a body of
work that reflects the Jewish experience.
Fund will provide a grant/prize for
$2,500.

Deadline
November 4, 2005

Program Officer
Nancy Schwartzman

Funding Exchange/Paul Robeson Fund for Independent Media

666 Broadway, Rm. 500
New York, NY 10012

Tel 212-529-5300
Tel........................212-529-5356 x307
Fax 212-982-9272
Email ....duong@fex.org
Email ....grants@fex.org
Web..................................www.fex.org

Support Provided
Grants provided for film, video and
radio projects of all genres that address
critical social and political issues; that
will reach a broad audience; that
include a progressive political analysis
combining intellectual clarity with
creative use of the medium. Prioritizes
projects that give voice to marginalized
communities and to those traditionally
excluded from mainstream media. Funds
all formats including documentaries,
shorts, and features. Video and Film
projects in preproduction or distribution
may apply. Radio projects in any stage
may apply. Guidelines can be down-
loaded at www.fex.org. Grants range
$5,000-$20,000.

Deadline
May 15, 2005

Program Officer
Trinh Duong

HBO America Undercover

1100 6th Ave.
New York, NY 10036

Tel 212-512-1670
Fax 212-512-7452
Email ....gregrhem@hbo.com
Email ....lana.iny@hbo.com
Web ....www.hbo.com

Support Provided
Provides production funds for American
Indie documentaries.

Program Officer
Greg Rhem

Hollywood Film Foundation

433 Camden Dr., Suite 600
Beverly Hills, CA 90210

Tel 310-288-3040
Email ..hollyinfo@hollywoodnetwork.com
Web ....www.hollywoodfilmfestival.com

Support Provided
Awards grants in the following
categories: Experimental, Digital
Moviemaking, Post-Production and
Partial Budget. Grants for up to
50 percent of budget.

Deadline
March 31, 2005

funding opportunities

IFP/Chicago Production Fund
1104 S. Wabash, Suite 403
Chicago, IL 60605

Tel 312-235-0161
Tel 312-235-0161
Fax 312-235-0162
Email......productionfund@ifpchicago.org
Email............................chicago@ifp.org
Web..................................www.ifp.org
Web ....www.chi.ifp.org

Support Provided
In-kind donation of production
equipment and services, up to $90,000
for the next short film. Applicants must
be IFP/Chicago members and the film
must be shot in the Midwest region.

Deadline
June 10, 2004

Program Officer
Rebekah Cowling

IFP MSP/McKnight Artists Program
401 N. 3rd St., Suite 450
Minneapolis, MN 55401

Tel..........................612-338-0871 x11
Fax 612-338-4747
Email..........nhinrichsbideau@ifpmsp.org
Email.....................wkruse@ifp.msp.org
Email ....word@ifp.msp.org
Web..............................www.ifpmsp.org

McKnight Artists Fellowship for Filmmakers
Support Provided
McKnight Artists Fellowship for filmmakers. Awards two $25,000 grants for
documentaries, narrative, animation and
multimedia. Open to Minnesota residents.
Applicants must have a demonstrable
and ongoing career in filmmaking with a
minimum of 2 films completed.

Deadline
March 4, 2005

Program Officer
Nicole Hinrichs-Bideau

McKnight Artists Fellowship for Screenwriters
Support Provided
Grants two $25,000 fellowships for
excellence in screenwriting as
demonstrated by at least 2 completed
and registered screenplays. Minnesota
residents. (Need to live at least one
continuous year in the state.)

Deadline
February 2005

Program Officer
Nicole Hinrichs-Bideau

Illinois Humanities Council Media Grants
203 N. Wabash Ave., Suite 2020
Chicago, IL 60601-2417

Tel 312-422-5580
Fax 312-422-5588
Email ....ihc@prairie.org
Email ....lfm@prairiedog.org
Web ....www.prairie.org

Support Provided
Funding for development, research of
scripts (up to $4,000) or production
and post production (up to $10,000).
Projects must relate to the humanities.
Production company must be based in
Illinois, or the theme be related to
Illinois. Funds documentaries and
narratives in film and video.

Deadline
Mini Grant: January 15, April 15,
July 15 & October 15, 2005

Major Grant: Draft: January 10,
June 1, 2005

Application: February 15, July 15, 2005
Recommends submitting 3 weeks in
advance

Program Officer
Luis Ramiro

Independent Television Service (ITVS)

501 York St.
San Francisco, CA 94110

Tel.........................415-356-8383 x232
Email..............marlene_velasco@itvs.org
Web ....www.itvs.org

Open Call

Support Provided
Provides production license agreements for public television programs.
Production funds for documentaries and narratives. Funds provided will cover the production or post-production budget, or portion; must be last funds in.

Deadline
Spring round, February 11, 2005
Fall round, August 5, 2005

Program Officer
Marlene Velasco-Begue

LInCS

Support Provided
Co-production funds for independent producers who partner with a local PBS station. Provides production license agreements for public television documentaries and narratives. Funds provided will cover the production budget and a cap at $1,000.

Deadline
May 26, 2005

Program Officer
Marlene Velasco-Begue

International Film Financing Conference (IFFCON)

360 Ritch St.
San Francisco, CA 94107

Tel 415-281-9777
Fax 415-495-2381
Email ....info@iffcon.com
Web..............................www.iffcon.com

Support Provided
To open doors between independent producers and the international industry, persuading both to participate in a forum in which they get to know each other, develop relationships, and forge financial partnerships that are not dependent upon nonprofit subsidy. Annualy, only 60 independent filmmakers are accepted into the full three-day event based in San Francisco, with a fairly even ratio of "buyers" and "sellers."

Jerome Foundation

125 Park Sq. Ct.
400 Sibley St.
St. Paul, MN 55101-1928

Tel 651-224-9431
Toll Free 1-800-995-3766
Fax 651-224-3439
Email.............mediaarts@jeromefdn.org
Email ....info@jeromefdn.org
Web ....www.jeromefdn.org

Support Provided
Grant program for individual media artists living and working in the five boroughs of New York City and the State of Minnesota. Funds documentaries, feature, shorts for all media (anything but commercials, promotional, industrial and education). Grants for budgets $200,000 or under, not including in-kind donation for New York and $175,000 budgets for Minnesota.

Deadline
NY: Ongoing; MN: May 2004

Program Officer
Robert Byrd

John D. and Catherine T. MacArthur Foundation

140 S. Dearborn St., Suite 1100
Chicago, IL 60603

Tel 312-726-8000
Email ....media@macfound.org
Web ....www.macfound.org

Support Provided
Funding for independent documentary films and programming that address subject matter close to MacArthur's grantmaking strategies; but also, occasionally, projects on other subjects of overall relevance to the Foundation's mission. Typically range from $50,000 to $300,000.

Deadline
Rolling

Program Officer
Kathy Im

Kansas Arts Commission

700 SW Jackson St., Suite 1004
Topeka, KS 66603-3761

Tel 785-296-3335
Fax 785-296-4989
Email ....KAC@arts.state.ks.us
Email ....bob@arts.state.ks.us
Web ....www.arts.state.ks.us

Support Provided
Limited number of Kansas Artist Fellowships in various disciplines. Awards $5,000. Disciplines include film and video.

Deadline
September, 2004

Program Officer
Lindsay Howgill

Latino Public Broadcasting

6777 Hollywood Blvd., Suite 500
Los Angeles, CA 90028

Tel 323-466-7110
Web ....www.lpbp.org
Email ....info@lpbp.org

Support Provided
Supports the development, production, acquisition and distribution of non-commercial educational and cultural television programming that is representative of Latino people, or addresses issues of particular interest to Latino Americans. Funds range from $5,000 to $100,000 for programs of most genres, including drama, comedy, animation, documentary or mixed genre. Considers projects at any production stage.

Deadline
June 6, 2005

Program Officer
Luca Bentivoglio, Executive Director
Luis Ortiz, Program Manager

Louisiana Division of the Arts: Artists Fellowship

P.O. Box 44247
Baton Rouge, LA 70804-4247

Tel 225-342-8180
Fax 225-342-8173
Email ....arts@crt.state.la.us
Web ....www.crt.state.la.us/arts

Support Provided
Fellowship award for $5,000 depending on the artist's work. Artists must submit sample of their work. Project Assistance program grants $1,000-$20,000 to artists in different discipline including documentary films. There are also $500 mini grants available.

Deadline
Fellowship – September 1, 2005
Project Assistance – March 1, 2005

Mini grants – August 1, 2005 and December 1, 2005

Program Officer
Anne Russo

Maine Humanities Council

674 Brighton Ave.
Portland, ME 04102

Tel 207-773-5051
Fax 207-773-2416
Email ......ejorgens@mainehumanities.org
Web ....www.mainehumanities.com

Support Provided
The Humanities Council occasionally supports scripting or post-production of films, but media is not a primary area of focus. Films must have humanities content, strong scholarly involvement, viable business plan, and be related to Maine. Documentaries and narratives film and video. Grant normally not more than $3,000. Requires draft proposal before deadline.

Deadline
April 10, 2005 and October 10, 2005

Program Officer
Victoria Bonebakker and Erik Jorgensen

Maryland Humanities Council

Executive Plaza One, Suite 503
11350 McCormick Rd.
Hunt Valley, MD 21031-1002

Tel 410-771-0650
Fax 410-771-0655
Email ....shardy@mdhc.org
Web...............................www.mdhc.org

Support Provided
Projects must be a public program, the disciplines of the humanities must be central to the project, humanities scholars must be involved in the project and funding must support projects that would not normally occur without council support. Maryland topics priorities. All formats.

Opportunity Grants
$1,200 or less.

Deadline
Rolling

Major Grants
$1,201 - $10,000

Deadline
Proposals are submitted twice a year: once for projects beginning after January 1, 2005: draft proposal due September 1, 2004 and final grant proposal due October 15, 2004. For projects beginning after July 1, 2005: draft proposal due March 1, 2005 and final grant proposal due April 15, 2005.

Program Officer
Steven Hardy

Massachusetts Foundation for the Humanities

66 Bridge St.
Northampton, MA 01060

Tel 413-584-8440
Fax 413-585-8454
Email......................KOConnell@mfh.org
Email...........................hwood@mfh.org
Email ....arogers@mfh.org
Web ....www.mfh.org

Support Provided
Films and videos that explore humanities themes with special interest to people of Massachusetts. Pre-Production grants up to $10,000 (please refer to website for the most current information regarding grant sizes). Post-Production up to $5,000.

Deadline
May 2005 - November 2005

Program Officer
Kristin O'Connell

funding opportunities

Minnesota State Arts Board Artist Fellowship

400 Sibley St., Suite 200
Saint Paul, MN 55101-1928

Tel 651-215-1600
Email .... msab@arts.state.mn.us
Web ....www.arts.state.mn.us

Support Provided
Rewards outstanding individual artists who are Minnesota residents. Grant amounts range from $2,000 to $6,000.

Deadline
May 16, 2005

Program Officer
Amy Frimpong

Moxie Films

107 Suffolk St., Studio 517
New York, NY 10002
Tel 212-982-5008
Fax 212-353-3707
Email.................. info@moxie-films.com
Web ....www.moxie-films.com

Support Provided
Provides the means for complete production, postproduction, and theatrical distribution to the selected documentary proposal. Enlisting the support of AVID Technology, Panasonic Broadcast & Television Systems Company and The Screening Room, the award has increased to over $150,000 in products and services including: Panasonic HD 24P Camera package access, production budgeting/scheduling software, post-production services, theatre screening access, expendables and more.

Deadline
October 30, 2004

Founder/Director
Drew R. Figueroa

National Asian American TV Communications Association (NAATA)

145 9th St., Suite 350
San Francisco, CA 94103

Tel.........................415-863-0814 x122
Fax 415-863-7428
Email ....mediafund@naatanet.org
Web ....www.naatanet.org

Open Call For Production Fund

Support Provided
For Asian Pacific American programming for public TV. All formats are considered: features, shorts, documentaries for public television programming. Funds range from $20,000-$50,000.

Deadline
June 25, 2004

Program Officer
Pia Shaa

National Black Programming Consortium

145 E. 125th St., Suite 3R
New York, NY 10035

Tel ....212-828-7588 x 3
Email ....info@nbpc.tv/grants
Web ....www.nbpc.tv/grants

Support Provided
Funds both independent and station based producers creating quality film and video projects about the African American and African Diaspora. Grant awards range between $1,000 and $80,000.

Deadline
May 31, 2005

Program Officer
Leslie Fields-Cruz

National Endowment for the Arts

1100 Pennsylvania Ave. NW
Washington, DC 20506
Tel 202-682-5400
Web ....webmgr@arts.endow.org

Support Provided
Supports projects for radio and television arts programs that are intended for national braodcast. Grants range from $20,000 to $200,000.

Deadline
September 9, 2005

Program Officer
Laura Welsh

The National Endowment for the Humanities: Planning, Scripting and Production Grant

1100 Pennsylvania Ave. NW
Washington, DC 20506

Tel 202-606-8269
Email ....publicpgms@neh.gov
Web ....www.neh.gov

Support Provided
NEH supports projects that use the medium of television to address significant figures, events or developments in the humanities and that draw their content from humanities scholarship. Projects may be in the form of either documentary programs or historical dramatizations and must be intended for national distribution during prime time on either broadcast or cable networks. Grants up to $30,000 for planning, $60,000 to $70,000 for scripting and $40,000 to $800,000 for production.

Deadline
November 3, 2004 for projects beginning in July 2005

Program Officer
David Weinstein

Lead Program Analyst
Margaret Scrymser

The National Science Foundation

4201 Wilson Blvd.
Arlington, VA 22230

Tel 703-292-5090/5111
Email ....info@nsf.gov
Web ....www.nsf.gov

Support Provided
Supports media projects designed to deepen the appreciation of science and technology and the understanding of the impact science and technology have on today's society.

Deadline
December 2004

Nevada Humanities Committee

P.O. Box 8029
Reno, NV 89154-5080

Tel 775-784-6587
Email ....winzeler@unr.nevada.edu
Web............ .www.nevadahumanities.org

Support Provided
Media grants used to support the production of films, videos, radio programs or educational Web-based projects. Grants up to $10,000.

Deadline
March 10, 2005

Executive Director
Judith Winzeler

New Hampshire Humanities Council

19 Pillsbury St., P.O. Box 2228
Concord, NH 03302-2228

Tel 603-224-4071
Fax 603-224-4072
Web ....www.nhhc.org

Support Provided
Awards grants to public programs in the humanities, such as film viewing and discussion series, and script development for documentary films. Grants are up to $1,500 to support small projects and over $15,000 to support major projects.

Deadline
February 1, 2005 for project grant drafts
January 3, 2005 for mini-grants

Program Officer
Toby Ball

New York Foundation for the Arts

155 Ave. of the Americas, 14th Fl.
New York, NY 10013-1507

Tel 212-366-6900
Tel........................212-366-6900 x217
Email........................ nyfaafp@nyfa.org/
Email ....smiller@nyfa.org
Web................................www.nyfa.org

Support Provided
Artists' Fellowships are $7,000 cash awards made to individual originating artists living and working in the state of New York for use in career development. Grants are awarded in 16 artistic disciplines, with applications accepted in eight categories each year. For additional information, visit www.nyfa.org/afp.

Deadline
July 1, 2005

Program Officers
Margie Lempert
Shawn Miller

New York State Council on the Arts

NYSCA Electronic Media and
Film Program
175 Varick St., 3rd Fl.
New York, NY 10014-4604

Tel 212-627-4455
Tel 212-741-3003
Web...............................www.nysca.org

The New York State Council on the Arts (NYSCA) is a state funding agency that provides support for activities of non-profit arts and cultural organizations in New York State and helps to bring artistic programs of high quality to the citizens of the state.

Distribution

Support Provided
Funding is available to organizations that distribute film, new media, sound art or video work. Organizations may request support for core distribution activities, expanding a collection into new formats, marketing, closed captioning and subtitling, or packaging of titles into collections. The program encourages projects that address changing trends for radio distribution and experiments in distributing Web-based art or using the Internet for delivery or marketing of film and electronic media.

Deadline
March 1, 2005

Program Officer
Karen Helmerson

Exhibitions

Support Provided
Exhibition support is available for the public presentation of film, video, sound art, new electronic media, and installation work offered on-site (in cinemas, community centers, galleries, libraries, or museums) or via broadcast, cable, radio, satellite, or Internet dissemination. Funding is available for projects on a variety of scales and design, including festivals, series, installations, and touring programs, as well as for year-round programming. The presentation of work by independent artists is strongly encouraged.

Deadline
March 1, 2005

Program Officer
Karen Helmerson

General Support Program

Support Provided
General Program Support (GPS) offers unrestricted support for ongoing media arts programming. GPS is designed to support qualifying organizations that have a consistent track record of artistic achievement, public service, and managerial competence in their media art programming. GPS support reflects NYSCA's recognition of the artistic and programmatic capabilities of qualified arts and cultural organizations.

Deadline
March 1, 2005

Program Officer
Karen Helmerson

NEXTPIX

295 Greenwich St., Suite 348
New York, NY 10007

Tel 212-465-3125
Fax 212-658-9627
Email ....info@nextpix.com
Web .... www.nextpix.com

Support Provided
Seeks to foster the best and brightest new talent in digital video, film and animation, and to help promote that talent by providing supplemental post-production funds through its "firstPix" grant program. Gives grants for both documentary and narrative features. Budget cannot exceed $250,000. The DV/film should have a positive humanitarian message.

Deadline
September 15, 2004

Program Officer
Diana Takata

funding opportunities

NYSCA Electronic Media and Film Grants

1104 S. Wabash, Suite 403
Chicago, IL 60605

Tel 312-235-0161
Fax 312-235-0162
Email ....nysca-grant@ifp.org
Web .... http://www.ifp.org/nysca

Support Provided
Funding is available from New York State Council on the Arts, coordinated through IFP/New York, to support the distribution of recently completed work by independent media artists residing in New York State. Grants are given for audio/radio, film and video productions, computer-based work, and installations incorporating these media. Artists may request funding up to a maximum amount of $5,000, though grants awarded are generally lower. The work proposed for support must have been completed between August 2003 and December 2004.

Deadline
January 3, 2005

Program Officer
Elizabeth Donius

Ohio Humanities Council

471 E. Broad St., Suite 1620
Columbus, OH 43215-3857

Tel 614-461-7802
Fax 614-461-4651
Email ....ohc@ohiohumanities.org
Web .... www.ohiohumanities.org

Support Provided
Supports media projects when they convey the humanities effectively to large, diverse audiences. Any nonprofit organization operating in Ohio may apply. The disciplines of the humanities must be central to the project, humanities scholars must be involved in the project. Up to $20,000.

Deadline
July 15, 2004 and December 15, 2004

Program Officer
Jack Shortlidge

Oklahoma Humanities Council

428 W. California, Suite 270
Oklahoma City, OK 73102

Tel 405-235-0280
Email........ohc@okhumanitiescouncil.org
Web ....www.okhumanitiescouncil.org

Support Provided
Awards Mini Grants are up to $1,000; Major Grants maximun award is $5,000; and Challenge Grants are up to $15,000 to support Oklahoma projects; including film and video production, designed to increase public understanding and appreciation of the humanities.

Deadlines
Mini: First working day of each month. Major and Challenge: February 25, 2005 for draft application and April 1, 2005

Program Officer
David Pettyjohn

Open Door Completion Fund

145 9th St., Suite 350
San Francisco, CA 94103

Tel 415-863-0814
Fax 415-863-7428
Email ....mediafund@naatanet.org
Web ....www.naatanet.org

Support Provided
Finishing funds for all formats: features, shorts, documentaries for public television programming. Funds range from $20,000-$50,000 for post production.

Deadline
Rolling

Program Officer
Pia Shaa

The Open Society Institute – Oppenheimer Camera New Filmmaker Equipment Grant Program

666 S. Plummer St.
Seattle, WA 98134

Tel 206-467-8666
Fax 206-467-9156
Email ....filmgrant@
oppenheimercamera.com
Web ....www.oppenheimercamera.com

Support Provided
Gives new filmmakers access to a professional 16 mm camera system for their first serious new production in the dramatic, narrative, documentary or experimental form. Program does not support commercials, industrials, PSAs, music video or pornography.

Deadline
Rolling

Program Officer
Marty Oppenheimer

Pacific Pioneer Film Fund

P.O. Box 20504
Stanford, CA 94309

Tel 650-996-3122
Email......................armin@stanford.edu
Web .... www.pacificpioneerfund.com

Support Provided
To support emerging documentary filmmakers. The term "emerging" is intended to denote a person committed to the craft of making documentaries, who has demonstrated that commitment by several years of practical film or video experience. Grants limited to filmmakers or videographers who live and work in California, Oregon and Washington. Grant Range $1,000 – $10,000. All subjects.

Deadline
Applications are accepted on an ongoing basis. Application deadlines in January 1, 2005 and May 1, 2005. Rejected applicants must wait one year to reapply.

Executive Director
Armin Rosencranz

Panavision New Filmmakers Program

6219 DeSoto Ave.
Woodland Hills, CA 91367-2602

Tel 818-316-1000
Tel 818-316-1111
Web ....www.panavision.com

Support Provided
Panavision's New Filmmakers Program donates 16mm camera packages to short, nonprofit film projects of any genre, including graduate student thesis films. Highly competitive—only two packages available. Filmmakers must secure equipment and liability insurance.

Deadline
Submit proposals five to six months before you intend to shoot.

Program Officer
Ric Halpern

Pen Writers Fund and Fund For Writers and Editors With AIDS

568 Broadway
New York, NY 10012

Tel........................212-334-1660 x101
Tel........................212-334-1660 x116
Email ....motika@pen.org
Web ....www.pen.org

Support Provided
The PEN Fund for Writers and Editors with HIV/AIDS, administered under the PEN Writers Fund, gives grants of up to $1,000 to professional writers and editors who face serious financial difficulties because of HIV or AIDS-related illness.

Deadline
The Writers Fund Committee meets approximately every two months to review applications.

Program Officer
Stephen Motika

Pennsylvania Council on the Arts Fellowships

216 Finance Bldg.
Harrisburg, PA 17120

Tel 717-787-6883
Email....................keswartz@state.pa.us
Web ....www.artsnet.org/pca/

Support Provided
The PCA supports outstanding Pennsylvania artists by awarding Fellowships on an annual basis. The range of awards is $5,000 to $10,000. Disciplines funded are Documentary and Experimental.

Deadline
August 1, 2005

Program Officer
Carolyn Savage

Pew Fellowships in the Art

230 S. Broad St., Suite 1003
Philadelphia, PA 19102

Tel 215-875-2285
Fax 215-875-2276
Email ....pwarts@mindspring.com
Web ....http://www.pewarts.org

Support Provided
This program awards grants of $50,000 to artists working in a wide variety of performing, visual, and literary disciplines. Up to twelve fellowships are awarded annually to artists living and working in the five-county Philadelphia area.

Deadline
December 3, 2004

Program Officer
Christine R. Miller

Playboy Foundation Media Grants

680 N. Lake Shore Dr.
Chicago, IL 60611

Tel 312-373-2435
Web...... www.playboy.com/pd-foundation

Support Provided
Funding to documentary film and video projects. Grants range from $1,000 to $5,000.

Deadline
Please write for application

P.O.V./American Documentary, Inc.
32 Broadway, 14th Fl.
New York, NY 10004

Tel 212-989-8121
Fax 212-989-8230
Web ....www.pbs.org/pov

Support Provided
Through a summer series and year-round specials, P.O.V. brings 12-16 new films each year to public television viewers, presenting non-fiction work by diverse voices. P.O.V. must provide broadcast premiere of the program. Considers primarily completed work for standard acquisitions. Occasionally provides funds for completion costs such as: sound editing, mixing, negative cutting, on-line editing, etc. Completion funding will be applied towards the acquisition fee for broadcast rights. P.O.V. is continuing its Film Fund that provides limited co-production financing for select projects.

Deadline
June 2005

Executive Director
Cara Mertes

The Puffin Foundation
20 E. Oakdene Ave.
Teaneck, NJ 07666-4111

Tel 201-836-8923
Fax 201-836-1734
Email ....puffingrant@mindspring.com
Web ...... http://www.puffinfoundation.org

Support Provided
The Puffin Foundation continues to make grants that encourage emerging artists in art, music, theater, and literature whose works, due to their genre and/or social philosophy might have difficulty being aired. The Foundation does not fund large film/documentary proposals. Amount: $1,000-$2,500.

Deadline
December 23, 2004

Program Officer
Gladys Miller-Rosenstein

Rhode Island Council for the Humanities
385 Westminster St., Suite 2
Providence, RI 02903

Tel 401-273-2250
Fax 401-454-4872
Email...............grants@rihumanities.org
Web.....................www.rihumanities.org

Support Provided
Support the production of films, videotapes, audiotapes, CD-ROMS, Internet Projects, and live programming that are strong in humanities content.

Deadlines
To be eligible to submit a proposal, work samples must be submitted at least two weeks in advance of the proposal deadline for technical evaluation.
Spring Grant Cycle: May 1, 2005
Fall Grant Cycle: Nov 1, 2005

Program Officer
Sue Ellen Kroll

Roy W. Dean Film and Video Grants
1455 Mandalay Beach Rd.
Oxnard, CA 93035-2845
Tel 866-689-5150
Email ....caroleedean@worldnet.att.net
Web ..www.fromtheheartproductions.com

Editing Grant

Support Provided
Takes filmmakers to New Zealand and offers off-line editing for the editing grants. Available for shorts and low budget features as well as documentary.

Deadline
July 2005

Program Officer
Carole E. Dean

L.A. Film Grant

Support Provided
Grant for Los Angeles shorts and low budget independents as well as documentary filmmakers. Grants for student filmmakers, independent producers and independent production companies producing documentaries or other socially aware film projects for television, film or video. Goods and services around $50,000.

Deadline
May 30, 2005

Program Officer
Carole E. Dean

L.A. Video Grant

Support Provided
Grant for Los Angeles shorts and low budget independents as well as documentary filmmakers. Grants for student filmmakers, independent producers and independent production companies producing documentaries or other socially aware video projects for television, film or video. Goods and services around $50,000.

Deadline
June 30, 2005

Program Officer
Carole E. Dean

NY Film Grant

Support Provided
Grant for New York shorts and low budget independents as well as documentary filmmakers. Grants for student filmmakers, independent producers and independent production companies producing documentaries or other socially aware projects for television, film or video. Goods and services around $50,000.

Deadline
April 2005

Program Officer
Carole E. Dean

Writing Grant

Support Provided
Takes filmmakers to New Zealand to write in a beautiful setting and offers off-line editing for the editing grants. Available for shorts and low budget features as well as documentary.

Deadline
August 30, 2005

Program Officer
Carole E. Dean

The Seventh Generation Fund

P.O. Box 4569
Arcata, CA 95518

Tel 707-825-7640
Fax 707-825-7639
Email ....lc7gen@pacbell.net
Web http://www.7genfund.org

Support Provided
The Seventh Generation Fund provides technical assistance in the form of workshops, conferences, training, and grant funding for projects. Amount: Small Grants ranging from $600 to $10,000 per year in assistance to seed emerging organizations.

Deadlines
Reviewed quarterly: March 1, June 1, September 1, December 1, 2005

Program Officer
Leo Canez

The Soros Justice Fellowships of the U.S. Justice Fund – The Soros Justice Media Fellowship

400 W. 59th St., 3rd Fl.
New York, NY 10019

Tel 212-548-0170
Email...................... kblack@sorosny.org
Email ....ncordova@sorosny.org
Web ....www.soros.org/crime

Support Provided
Seeks dynamic journalists working in media, photography, radio and documentary film and video to improve the quality of media coverage of incarceration and criminal justice issues. Must be a 501(c)(3) tax-exempt organization, or have a tax-exempt fiscal agent.

Deadline
March 25, 2005

Program Officer
Kate Black
Nidia E. Cordova-Vazquez
  (program assistant)

South Carolina Arts Commission Quarterly Grants

1800 Gervais St.
Columbia, SC 29201

Tel 803-734-8681
Fax 803-734-8526
Web........................www.state.sc.us/arts

Support Provided
Provides grants for projects for organizations, cultural visions for rural communities and quarterly projects for artists. Nonprofit organizations must be incorporated and registered in the state of South Carolina. Individuals must maintain a permanent residence in South Carolina prior to the application date and throughout the grant period.

Deadline
October 1, 2005

Program Officer
Susan Leonard

The Standby Program

1135 W. 26th St., 12th Fl.
New York, NY 10001

Tel 212-2037858
Fax 212-206-7884
Email..........................info@standby.org
Web ....www.standby.org

Support Provided
Provide post-production services to artists and nonprofits, provide technical consultation, and do publications to serve the media arts field.

Sundance Documentary Fund

8857 W. Olympic Blvd.
Beverly Hills, CA 90211

Tel 310-360-1981
Email .... sdf@sundance.org
Web ....www.institute.sundance.org

Support Provided
Grant-giving program available to filmmakers around the world to support full length documentaries in development and production about contemporary human rights, freedom of expression, social justice and civil liberties issues. Does not accept historical projects, biographies or series. Documentary film or video projects that range in length from full broadcast hour to long format feature. Development funds up to $15,000. Production funds up to $75,000.

Deadline
Rolling

Program Officer
Diane Weyermann, Anna Proulx

funding opportunities

Texas Filmmakers' Production Fund

1901 E. 51st St.
Austin, TX 78723

Tel 512-322-0145
Email ....tfpf@austinfilm.org
Web .... www.austinfilm.org

Support Provided
Annual grant awarded to emerging film and video artists in the state of Texas. Funds all genres (narrative, documentary, experimental, animation) and hybrids thereof. Cannot consider multimedia projects at this time. Projects must be independent productions. No consideration will be given to industrials, promotional pieces, or "works-for-hire." $1,000 to $15,000 in a cash award, up to $6,000 in Kodak film stock, and up to $1,000 in videotape stock.

Deadline
June 1, 2005

Program Officer
Elisabeth Sikes

U.S. Mexico Fund for Culture

Web ....http://www.fidemexusa.org.mx/
english/home.html

Support Provided
The Fund grants economic support to projects of excellence that reflect the artistic and cultural diversity of Mexico and the United States, and that enrich cultural exchange and promote lasting ties among artists, scholars, independent groups and cultural institutions in both countries. Amounts range from $2,000 - $30,000 depending on the type of project.

Deadline
December 12

Utah Humanities Council: Research Fellowship Grants

202 W. 300 North
Salt Lake City, UT 84103

Tel 801-359-9670
Email ....johnson@utahhumanities.org
Web ....www.utahhumanities.org

Annual Fellowships

Support Provided
Two annual fellowships are offered to humanities scholars:
• The Albert J. Colton Fellowship supports a research project on a topic of national or international significance.
• The Delmont R. Oswald Fellowship supports a research project in Utah studies. Research fellowships, which provide a $3,000 stipend, are evaluated and approved by UHC's Board of Directors.

Deadline
September 15, 2005 for 1st draft

Program Officer
Brandon Johnson

Quick Grants

Support Provided
Supports direct program costs of smaller projects, with a simplified and expedited process. Eligible requests include:
• small projects using proven formats and scholars
• film, video, exhibit or book programs with discussion led by a humanities scholar
• planning or consultant grants, hiring a consultant to plan and help prepare a competitive grant application.
Provides up to $500. Reviewed year-round and approved by the Executive Director. The maximum provided will increase to $1,500.

Deadline
Application must be received 4-6 weeks prior to need.

Program Officer
Marisa Black

Visual Studies Workshop
Media Center

31 Prince St.
Rochester, NY 14607

Tel 585-442-8676
Email ....info@vsw.org
Web ....www.vsw.org

Support Provided
The Media Center supports film and video-making through its low-cost equipment rental to independent producers and members of the community, its training workshops, and its screening and exhibition programs. Awards artists, independent producers and nonprofits working on non-commercial projects reduced rates for production and post production equipment.

Deadline
Rolling

The Wallace Alexander Gerbode
Foundation

111 Pine St., Suite 1515
San Francisco, CA 94111

Tel 415-391-0911
Fax 415-391-4587
Email...........................info@gerbode.org
Web ....www.fdncenter.org/
grantmaker/gerbode/

Support Provided
Grants for media projects proposed by 501(3) organizations. Focused in San Francisco Bay Area and Hawaii.

Deadline
Ongoing

Program Officer
Stacie Ma'a

Women in Film Foundation
Film Finishing Fund

8857 W. Olympic Blvd., Suite 201
Beverly Hills, CA 90211

Tel 310-657-5144
Email ....jane@wif.org
Web....................................www.wif.org

Support Provided
Offers grants to assist filmmakers who have completed principal photography and whose projects will be in post-production by a given date. Please note that student projects are not eligible. You do not have to be a Women In Film member to apply for the FFF. Grants up to $5,000.

Deadline
March 4, 2005

Program Officer
Jane La Bonte

funding opportunities

National Association of Latino Independent Producers

distributors

Alfa-Film Enterprises, Inc.
264 S. La Cienega Blvd., Suite 1138
Beverly Hills, CA 90211
Tel 323-882-6193
Fax 323-882-6103
Email ....sidarvof@earthlink.net

Olga Fradis, VP, Distribution &
 Acquisitions

Amazefilms
8491 Sunset Blvd., Suite 90069
Hollywood, CA 90069
Tel 323-761-7000
Email ....info@amazefilms.com
Web.....................www.amazefilms.com

Ruden Dua, President

American Public Television
55 Summer St.
Boston, MA 02110
Tel 617-338-4455
Fax 617-338-5369
Email......................info@aptonline.org
Web ....www.aptonline.org

Cynthia Fenneman, President

Andrea International
3201 Bayview Dr.
Manhattan Beach, CA 93001
Tel 310-720-4567
Fax 310-546-9551
Email ....drost7@aol.com
Web ....www.andre-int.com

Shirin Drost, President/CEO

ArcLight Films
1201/39 McLaren St.
North Sydney 2060, Australia
Tel 61-2-9955-8825
Fax 61-2-9955-8828
Email ....info@arclightfilms.com
Web ....www.arclightfilms.com

Victor Symris, Chairman
Gary Hamilton, Managing Director

Arenas Entertainment
100 N. Crescent Dr., Garden Level
Beverly Hills, CA 90210
Tel 310-385-4401
Fax 310-385-4458
Email ....info@arenasgroup.com
Web ....www.arenasgroup.com

Diana Lesmez, VP, Development,
 Production & Acquisitions

Ariztical Entertainment Group
405 E. Wetmore Rd., Suites 117-516
Tucson, AZ 85705
Tel 520-622-2400
Fax 520-622-2992
Email ....mjshoel@ariztical.com
Web ....www.ariztical.com

Michael J. Shoel, President

Artistic License Films
250 W. 57th, Suite 2602
New York, NY 10107
Tel 212-265-0119
Fax 212-262-9299
Email...........................info@artlic.com
Web ....www.artlic.com

Sande Zeig, President
Vicky Waldron Wight

distributors

Artist View Entertainment

12500 Riverside Dr., Suite 201
North Hollywood, CA 91607
Tel 818-752-2480
Fax 818-752-9339
Email ....celina@artistviewent.com
Web ....www.artistviewent.com

Scott J. Jones, President

BCI Eclipse. LLC

810 Lawrence, Suite 100
Newbury Park, CA 91320
Tel 805-375-9998
Fax 805-375-9908
Web......................www.bcieclipse.com

Jeff Hayne, Product Development
  Manager

Bristol Media International

200 W. 57th St., #506
New York, NY 10019
Tel 212-245-6000
Fax 212-245-5464
Email.................info@bristolmedia.com
Web ....www.bristolmedia.com

Amy Mitchell, Director, Sales and
  Acquisitions

Buena Vista International

500 S. Buena Vista St.
Burbank, CA 91521
Tel 818-560-1000
Web ....www.disney.com

Patrick Fitzgerald, Sr. VP, Sales &
  Distribution

BuyIndies.com

P.O. Box 20082
New York, NY 10014
Tel 887-889-7477
Email......................info@buyindies.com
Web ....www.buyindies.com

Michele Meek, President and Co-Funder
Geoffry Meek, Chief Technology Officer
  and Co-Funder

Captive Entertainment

6535 Wilshire Blvd., Suite 130
Los Angeles, CA 90048
Tel 323-658-7760
Fax 323-658-7885
Email ....captive@captive-
                            entertainment.com

Paul Poste, VP, Sales & Acquisitions

Celluloid Dreams

2 rue Turgot
Paris France 75009
Tel 33-1-49-70-03-70
Email ....charlotte@celluloid-dreams.com

Charlotte Mickie, Managing Director

Channel 4 Television

124 Horseferry Rd.
London, UK SWIP 2TX
Tel 44-207-395-4444
Email ....info@channel4.co.uk
Web www.channel4.com

Tim Highsted, Sr., Editor, Acquired
  Feature Films

Cicada Pictures, Inc.

65 Roebling St., #204
Brooklyn, NY 11211
Tel 718-384-5166
Fax 718-486-5124
Email ....jdissard@bway.net

Jean-Michel Dissard, Producer

The Cinema Guild
130 Madison Ave., 2nd Fl.
New York, NY 10016
Tel 212-685-6242
Fax 212-685-4717
Email.................info@cinemaguild.com

Handeh Kemmer, Director of
  Acquisitions

Cinnamon Productions, Inc.
19 Wild Rose Rd.
Westport, CT 06880
Tel 203-221-0613
Fax 203-227-0840
Email ....cinnaprods@aol.com
Web ....www.nativevideos.com

John C. May, VP, Acquisitions

Columbia TriStar Home Entertainment
10202 W. Washington Blvd.
Culver City, CA 90232
Tel 310-244-4000
Fax 310-244-2626
Web ....www.sonypictures.com

Elizabeth Stewart, VP, International
  Distribution

CS Associates
200 Dexter Ave.
Watertown, MA 02472
Tel 617-923-0077
Fax 617-923-0025
Email ....programs@csassociates.com

Charles Schuerhoff, President

Curb Entertainment International Corporation
3907 W. Alameda Ave., 2nd Fl.
Burbank, CA 91505
Tel 818-843-8580
Fax 818-566-1719
Email.................curbfilm@earthlink.net
Web...........www.curbentertainment.com

Glen Reynolds, Director/Head,
  Acquisitions and Business Affairs

Desert Island Fims, Inc.
11 Coggeshall Circle
Middletown, RI 02842
Tel 401-846-3453
Fax 401-846-0919
Email ....info@desertislandfilms.com
Web..............www.desertislandfilms.com

Marc Berlin, President

Dimension Films (c/o Miramax Films)
375 Greenwich St.
New York, NY 10013
Tel 212-941-3800
Tel 323-822-4100
Fax 212-941-3949
Web ....www.dimensionfilms.com

Gere Hausfater, Executive VP, Co-Head
Andrew Rona, Co-Head, Productions

Ebs/L.A.
3000 W. Olympic Blvd.
Santa Monica, CA 90404
Tel 310-449-4065
Fax 310-449-4061
Email ....acquistions@ebsla.com
Web ....www.ebsla.com

Richard Cooper, Head, Acquisitions

distributors

Echelon Entertainment

400 S. Victory Blvd., Suite 203
Burbank, CA 91502
Tel 818-558-1820
Fax 818-558-1877
Email....................info@echelonent.com
Web ....www.echelonent.com

Gloria Marrison, President/Director,
　Acquisitions

Echo Bridge Entertainment

75 2nd Ave., Suite 500
Needham, MA 02494
Tel 781-444-6767
Fax 781-444-6472
Email ....info@ebellc.com
Web.............................www.ebellc.com

Michael Rosenblatt, Managing Partner,
　Acquisitions

Emerging Pictures

245 W. 55th St., 4th Fl.
New York, NY 10119
Tel 212-245-6767
Fax 212-202-4984
Email ....ira@emergingpictures.com

Ira Deutchman, President and CEO
Scott Karpf, Director of Development

Entertainment 7

15030 Ventura Blvd., Suite 762
Sherman Oaks, CA 91403
Tel 818-709-9595
Fax 818-709-9597
Email..............................bill@ent7.com
Web...............................www.ent7.com

Bill Wildes, Sales Executives

Excalibur Media Group, LLC

3130 Bonita Rd., Suite 206
Chula Vista, CA 91910
Tel 619-662-1655
Fax 619-662-3789
Email.............rgarcia@excaliburmg.com
Web ....www.excaliburmg.com

Sergio Garcia, President
Armando Espinoza, President

Fabrication Films

6725 W. Sunset Blvd., #250
Los Angeles, CA 90028
Tel 323-655-4663
Fax 323-467-8225
Email ....glerenynolds@hotmail.com
Web...............www.fabricationfilms.com

Glen Reynolds, President, Motion
　Pictures

Fantastic Films International

3854 Clayton Ave.
Los Angeles, CA 90027
Tel 323-661-7088
Fax 323-661-7188
Email ....roxane@ffimail.com
Web ..www.fantasticfilmsinternational.com

Roxane Barbat, President

Film Artists Distribution (F.A.D)

P.O. Box 323
Canoga Park, CA 91305
Tel 818-344-0569
Fax 818-344-0569
Email ....pilliczar@netzero.net

Saundra Winchester, Head, Acquisitions

The Film Source Company

P.O. Box 131690
Staten Island, NY 10313
Tel 212-644-2090
Fax 718-370-3972
Email ....info@filmsourceco.com
Web ....www.filmsourceco.com

Alex Massis, President

Filmax Internatinal

Miguel Hernandez, 81-87
Distrito Economico L' Hopitalet
L' Hopitalet de Llobregat
Barcelona Spain 08908
Tel 34-9-33-36-85-55
Fax 34-9-32-63-08-24
Email ....m.yebra@filmax.com
Web ....www.filmaxinternational.com

Antonia Nava, SVP of Sales and
　Co-Production

Filmmakers Alliance Productions

5419 Hollywood Blvd., #420
Los Angeles, CA 90027
Tel 213-228-1152
Fax 213-228-1156
Email ....info@filmmakersalliance.com

Liam Filnn, Head of Production

Filmmakers Library

124 E. 40th St.
New York, NY 10016
Tel 212-808-4980
Fax 212-808-4983
Email ....info@filmakers.com

Su Oscar, Co-President

Films Around the World

417 E. 57th St., Suite 31B
New York, NY 10022
Tel 212-599-9500
Fax 212-599-6040
Email.....................alexjr@pipeline.com
Web ....www.filmsaroundtheworld.com

Alex W. Kogan Jr., President

Films Transit International, Inc.

252 Gouin Blvd. E., #100
Montreal, QC H3L IA8 Canada
Tel 514-844-3358
Fax 514-844-7298
Email ......janrofekamp@filmstransit.com

Diana Holtzberg, U.S., Sales and
　Acquisitions

Fine Line Features

116 N. Robertson Blvd.
Los Angeles, CA 90048
Tel 310-854-5811
Fax 310-659-1453
Web ....www.flf.com

Guy Stodel, Sr. VP, Acquisitions & Co-
　Productions

First Look Pictures

8000 Sunset Blvd., E. Penthouse
Los Angeles, CA 90046
Tel 323-337-1000
Fax 323-337-1037
Email ....info@firstlookmedia.com
Web ....www.firstlookmedia.com

Peter Lawson, Manager, Acquisition

distributors

First Run Features

153 Waverly Pl.
New York, NY 10014
Tel 212-243-0600
Fax 212-989-7649
Email ....info@firstrunfeatures.com
Web ....www.firstrunfeatures.com

Seymour Wishman, President
Gary Crowdus

Focus Features

100 Universal City Plaza, Bldg. 9128-2
Universal City, CA 91608
Tel 818-777-7373
Web ....www.focusfeatures.com

Jason Resnick, VP, Acquisitions

Fox Latin American Channel

1440 S. Sepulveda Blvd., 3rd Fl.
Los Angles, CA 90025
Tel 310-444-8595
Fax 310-969-0849
Web ....www.canalfox.com

Mauricio Rios, Associate Director,
   Programming

Fox Searchlight Pictures

10201 W. Pico Blvd., Bldg. 38
Los Angeles, CA 90035
Tel 310-369-1000
Fax 310-369-2359
Web ....www.foxsearchlight.com

Peter Rice, President
Claudia Lewis, VP

Freestyle Releasing, LLC

506 Santa Monica Blvd., Suite 210
Santa Monica, CA 90401
Tel 310-395-3500

Mark Borde
Mike Doban
Susan Jackson

Galavision

605 3rd Ave., 12th Fl.
New York, NY 10158
Tel 212-455-5300
Fax 212-953-0198
Web ....www.galavision.com

Pablo Quintero, Operations Director

Global Cinema Group

1007 Broxton Ave., Suite 210
Los Angeles, CA 90024
Tel 310-443-7788
Fax 310-443-7739
Email ....ishectman@
                globalcinemagroup.com

Peter Elson, President

Go Fish Pictures

1000 Flower St.
Glendale, CA 91201
Tel 818-695-7742
Fax 818-695-7741
Email ....jfilippini@gopictures.com

Joan Filippini, Head,
   Distribution/Acquisitions

Gold Circle Releasing

9420 Wilshire Blvd., Suite 250
Beverly Hills, CA 90212
Tel 310-278-4800
Fax 310-278-0885
Web ....www.goldcirclefilms.com

David Garber, Distribution &
   Acquisitions

Ground Zero

6701 Center Dr. W., Suite 655
Los Angeles, CA 90045
Tel 310-410-3030
Fax 310-410-3003

Anthony Perez, CEO
Nestor Miranda, Executive Producer

H3O Filmed Entertainment, Inc.
1415 W. Georgia St., Suite 1804
Vancouver, BC 3C8 Canada
Tel 604-662-3345
Fax 604-662-7720
Email ....production@h3ofilm.com
Web www.h3ofilm.com

John Curtis, President

Harmony Gold
7655 Sunset Blvd.
Los Angeles, CA 90046
Tel 323-851-4900
Fax 323-851-5599
Email ....sales@harmonygold.com
Web....................www.harmonygold.com

Melissa Wohl, VP, Sales & Acquisitions

HBO/Cinemax Documentary Films
1100 Ave. of the Americas
New York, NY 10036
Tel 212-512-1000
Web ....www.hbo.com

Gregory Rhem, Manager

HBO Latin America Group
4000 Ponce de Leon Blvd., Suite 800
Coral Gables, Fl 33134
1100 Ave. of the Americas
New York, NY 10036
Tel ....305-648-8100 (FL)
Fax ....305-648-8170 (FL)
Tel ....212-512-1012 (NY)
Fax.........................212-512-7458 (NY)
Web ....www.hbo-la.tv

Roberto Rios, VP, Programming &
  Acquisitions

Here! Films
10990 Wilshire Blvd., Penthouse
Los Angeles, CA 90024
Tel 310-806-4288
Fax 310-806-4268
Email ....herefilms@
                regententertainment.com
Web............................www.heretv.coom

Mark Reinhart, Executive VP,
  Distribution & Acquisitions
Judy Scott, VP, Acquisitions

Hollywood Classics
2450 Mission St., Suite 5
San Marino, CA 91108-1696
Tel 626-403-8480
Fax 626-403-8473
Email........jflynn@hollywoodclassics.com
Web ....www.hollywoddclassics.com

Melanie Tebb, Sales

Home Vision Entertainment
4423 N. Ravenswood Ave.
Chicago, IL 60640
Tel 773-878-2600
Fax 773-878-2895
Email ....license@homevision.com
Web ....www.homevision.com

Sonia Rosario, VP, Production

Horizon Entertainment
1040 Hamilton St., Suite 207
Vancouver, BC V6B 2R9 Canada
Tel 604-632-1707
Fax 604-632-1607
Email ....caroline@filmhorizon.com
Web ....www.filmhorizon.com

Michele Taverna, Sales & Acquisitions

Ideas for Films
7 Ave. Emile Deschanel
Paris, France 75007
Tel 33-1-45-51-42-54
Fax 33-1-45-51-27-84
Email ....patrickjucaud@ideas4films.com
Web www.ideas4films.com

Patrick Jucaud, Marketing Manager

IDP Distribution (Independent Distribution Partnership)
1133 Broadway, Suite 926
New York, NY 10010
Tel 212-367-9435
Fax 212-367-0853

Michael Silberman, President/CEO

IFC Films
11 Penn Plaza, 15th Fl.
New York, NY 10001
Tel 646-273-7200
Fax 646-273-7250
Web ....www.ifcfilms.com

Jonathan Sehring, President
Sarah Lash, Director of Acquisitions

IFM World Releasing, Inc.
1328 E. Palmer Ave.
Glendale, CA 91205
Tel 818-243-4976
Fax 818-550-9728
Email ....ifmfilm@aol.com
Web...........................www.ifmfilm.com

Antony I. Ginnane, President

Innovation Film Group
506 Santa Monica Blvd., #210
Santa Monica, CA 90401
Tel 310-314-6444
Fax 310-314-0455
Web.........www.innovationfilmgroup.com

Mark Borde, President

Interactive Film Sales International, Inc.
4240 Promenade Way, Suite 334
Marina del Rey, CA 90292
Tel 310-823-7778
Fax 310-868-2723
Email ....daniel.sales@att.net
Web ....www.interactivefilmsales.com

Mariam Arthur, VP, Acquisitions

Intermat, Inc.
44 E. 32nd St., Penthouse
New York, NY 10016
Tel 212-251-8676
Fax 212-214-0779
Email ....info@intermat.tv
Web..............................www.intermat.tv

Mathew Tombers, Managing Director

Laguna Films
6930 Hayvenhurst Ave
Van Nuys, CA 91406
Tel 1-800-852-9840
Email ....support@lagunafilms.com
Web ....www.lagunafilms.com

Lakeshore International
5555 Melrose Ave.
Gloria Swanson Bldg., 4th Fl.
Hollywood, CA 90038
Tel 323-956-4222
Fax 323-862-1456
Email ....info@lkshore
Web ....www.lakeshoreentertainment.com

Bic Tran, VP, Acquisitions &
   Co-Productions

Laemmle/Zeller Films
522 N. Larchmont Blvd.
Los Angeles, CA 90004
Tel 323-860-0270
Fax 323-860-0279
Email ....stevenzeller@gsemg.com

Steven Zeller, President
Greg Laemmle, President

Lantern Lane Entertainment, LTD
P.O. Box 8187
Calabasas, CA 91372-8187
Tel 818-222-2309
Fax 818-224-4028
Email..............dgarber@lanternlane.com
Web ....www.lanternlane.com

Rob Lynch, VP Sales & Acquisitions

Leisure Time Features
40 Worth St., Suite 1214
New York, NY 10013
Tel 212-267-4501
Fax 212-267-4501
Email ....bpleisure@aol.com
Web ....www.leisurefeat.com

Bruce Pavlow, President

Leo Films
6249 Langdon Ave.
Van Nuys, CA 91411
Tel 818-782-6541
Fax 818-782-3320
Email ....lustgar@pachbell.net
Web ....www.leofilms.com

Steve Lustgarten, President

Lifetime Entertainment Services
309 W. 49th St.
New York, NY 10019
Tel 212-424-7379
Email ....npacifico@lifetimetv.com
Web ....www.lifetimetv.com

Val Boreland, VP of Scheduling and
   Acquisitions

Lightning Entertainment
301 Arizona Ave., Suite 400
Santa Monica, CA 90401
Tel 310-255-7999
Fax 310-255-7998
Email ....jdickstein@lightning-ent.com
Web ....www.lightning-ent.com

Joe Dickstein, VP, Acquisitions

Lions Gate Films
2700 Colorado Ave.
Santa Monica, CA 90404
Tel 310-449-9200
Fax 310-255-3870
Web.........................lionsgatefilms.com

Tom Ortenberg, President,
   Realising/Acquisitions
Jason Constantine, VP Acquisitions

Little Magic Productions, Inc.
14 E. 4th St., Suite 502
New York, NY 10012
Tel 212-533-8300
Fax 212-533-9305
Email ....littlemagicny@aol.com

Kiki Miyake, President

distributors

Little Studio Films, Inc.

9899 Santa Monica Blvd., Suite 139
Beverly Hills, CA 90212
Tel 310-552-4842
Email..international@littlestudiofilms.com
Web................www.littlestudiofilms.com

Alexia Melocchi, President

Lot 47 Films

13 Laight St., 6th Fl.
New York, NY 10011
Tel 212-925-7800
Fax 212-965-5655
Email............................info@lot47.com
Web www.lot47.com

Gregory B. Williams, CEO

MAC Releasing

1640 S. Sepulveda Blvd., Suite 218
Los Angeles, CA 90025
Tel 310-477-8426
Fax 310-996-1892
Web ....www.macreleasing.com

Carl Hampe, Head of Acquisitions

Madstone Films

85 5th Ave., 12th Fl.
New York, NY 10003
Tel 212-989-4500
Fax 212-989-7744
Web ....www.madstonefilms.com

Tom Gruenberg, Co CEO

Magnolia Pictures

115 W. 27th St., 8th Fl.
New York, NY 10001
Tel 212-924-6701
Fax 212-924-6742
Email.................info@magpictures.com
Web ....www.magpictures.com

Eamonn Bowles, President
Tom Quinn, Director, Acquisitions

Manga Entertainment, Inc.

215 W. Superior St., 6th Fl.
Chicago, Il 60610
Tel 312-751-0020
Fax 312-751-2483
Email......................manga@manga.com
Web ....www.manga.com

Kaoru Mfaume, Acquisitions

Manhattan Pictures International

369 Lexington Ave., 10th Fl.
New York, NY 10017
Tel 212-453-5055
Fax 212-453-5080
Email ....info@manhattanpics.com
Web ....www.manhattanpics.com

Gayle Cohen, VP, Acquisitions

Maverick Entertainment

1191 E. Newport Center Dr., Suite 210
Ft. Lauderdale, FL 33442
Tel 954-422-8811
Fax 954-429-0565
Email ....ap@maverickentertainment.com
Web ....www.maverickentertainment.com

Doug Schwab, President
Alberto Perez de la Mesa, Director of
  Latin Product

Maxmedia, LLC

1620 Broadway
Santa Monica, CA 90404
Tel 310-828-6313
Fax 310-829-0599
Email ....info@maxmedia.org
Web ....www.maxmedia.org

Matt Pascale, Acquisitions &
  Development
Jeffrey Winter, Acquisitions &
  Development

Metrodome Distribution
33 Charlotte St., 5th Fl.
London, UK WIT IRR
Tel 44 20 715 344 29
Email........akeyte@metrodomegroup.com

Kate Falconer, Acquisitions Manager

MGM Home Entertainment
2500 Broadway St.
Santa Monica, CA 90404
Tel 310-449-3000
Web ....www.mgm.com

Malik Ducard, VP, Worldwide Business
   Development & Acquisitions

Miramax International
99 Hudson St., 5th Fl.
New York, NY 10013
Tel 212-219-4100
Fax 212-219-4562
Web.........................www.miramax.com

Matt Brodlie, Sr. VP of Acquisitions
Adrianne Bucco

Monarch Films, Inc.
368 Danforth Ave.
Jersey City, NJ 07305
Tel 201-451-3770
Fax 201-451-3877
Email ....art@mfilms.com

Arthur Skopinsky, President

MTV Networks Latin America
1111 Lincoln Rd.
Miami Beach, FL 33139
Tel 305-535-3700
Web ....www.mtvla.com

Antoinette Zel, President

New Video/Docurama
126 5th Ave.
New York, NY 10025
Tel 212-206-8600
Fax 212-206-9001
Email ....info@docurama.com

Mark Kahden, VP, Acquisitions

New Yorker Films
85 5th Ave., 11th Fl.
New York, NY 10003
Tel 212-645-4600
Fax 212-645-3030
Email..............info@newyorkerfilms.com
Web ....www.newyorkerfilms.com

Daniel Talbot, President

Newmarket Film Group
597 5th Ave., 7th Fl.
New York, NY 10017
Tel 212-303-1700
Fax 212-421-1163
Email ....info@newmarketfilms.com
Web ....www.newmarketfilms.com

Bob Berney, President

Omni Content Distribution, Inc.
P.O. Box 64397
Los Angeles, CA 90064
Tel 310-478-4700
Fax 310-478-7147
Email ....info@omnicd.com
Web ....www.onmicd.com

Tristan Cavato, VP of Acquisitions &
   New Media

distributors

Palm Pictures
601 W. 26th St., 11th Fl.
New York, NY 10001
Tel 212-320-3678
Fax 240-266-6247
Email ....david.koh@palmpictures.com
Web ....www.palmpictures.com

David Koh, Head, Acquisitions

Paramount Classics
5555 Melrose Ave., Chevalier, Suite 215
Hollywood, CA 90038-3197
Tel 323-956-2000
Fax 323-862-1212
Web...........www.paramountclassics.com

David Dinerstein, Co-President
Ruth Vitale, Co-President
Joe Matukewicz, Manager, Acquisitions

Passion River Films
Greenestreet Film Center
9 Desbrosses St., 2nd Fl.
New York, NY 10013
Tel 212-966-5877
Fax 212-966-5914
Email ....info@passionriver.com

Allen Chou, President of Acquisitions

Patriot Pictures
9065 Nemo St.
West Hollywood, CA 90069
Tel 310-274-0745
Fax 320-274-0925
Email ....sduff@patriotadvisors.com

Michael Mendelsohn, President

PBS
1320 Braddock Pl.
Alexandria, VA 22314-1698
Tel 703-739-5000
Fax 703-739-0775
Web ....www.pbs.org

Gustavo Sagastume, VP, Programming
Cheryl Jones, Senior Director, Program
   Development and Independent Film

Performance Syndication, Inc.
1929 N. Serrano Ave.
Hollywood, CA 90027
Tel 323-465-6515
Fax 323-469-1876
Email ....performance_synd@hotmail.com

Kris Gangadean, President

Picture This! Entertainment
7471 Melrose Ave., Suite 7
Los Angeles, CA 90046
Tel 323-852-1398
Fax 323-658-7265
Email......................gaypicture@aol.com
Web ....www.picturethisent.com

Doug Witkins, President

Plexifilm
580 Broadway, Suite 1004
New York, NY 10012
Tel 212-965-9220
Fax 212-965-9262
Email ....info@plexifilm.com
Web.........................www.plexifilm.com

Gary Hustwit, President

+Entertainment
468 N. Camden Dr., Suite 250
Beverly Hills, CA 90210
Tel 310-860-5604
Fax 310-860-5194
Email........................mail@plusent.com
Web ....www.plusent.com

Porchlight Entertainment
11777 Mississippi Ave.
Los Angeles, CA 90025
Tel 310-477-8400
Fax 310-477-5555
Email ....info@porchlight.com
Web........................www.porchlight.com

Zac Reeder, Head, Acquisitions

Premiere Films, Inc.
614 Hipodromo St.
San Juan, PR 00909
Tel 787-724-0762
Fax 787-723-4562
Email ......dnieves@premierefilmsinc.com
Email ..rrodriguez@premierefilmsinc.com
Web ....www.premierefilmsinc.com

Danny Nieves, Vice President and
  General Manager
Richard Rodriguez, Print Comptroller

Pretty Pictures
42 rue Edouard Vaillant
Montreuil, France 93100
Tel 33-1-48-51-16-11
Fax 33-1-48-51-16-10
Email ....info@prettypictures.fr

Adrian Dannatt, VP of Acquisitions
  Advisor

Redbus Film Distribution
Ariel House, 74A Charlotte St.
London, UK WIT 4QJ
Tel 44-207-299-8800
Fax 44-207-299-8801
Email.........................info@redbus.com
Web ....www.redbus.com

Simon Franks, Chief Executive

Regent Entertainment, Inc.
10990 Wilshire Blvd., 18th Fl.
Los Angeles, CA 90024
Tel 310-806-4288
Fax 310-806-4268
Email ..ggeorge@regententertainment.com
Web ....www.regententertainment.com

Paul Colichman, President
John Lambert, President, Acquisitions

Rialto Pictures
594 Broadway, Suite 1004
New York, NY 10012
Tel 212-717-6773
Fax 212-288-8543
Web ....www.rialtopictures.com

Bruce Goldstein, Co-President

Rigel Entertainment
4201 Wilshire Blvd., Suite 555
Los Angeles, CA 90010
Tel 323-954-8555
Fax 323-954-8592
Email ....admin@rigel.tv
Web ....www.rigel.tv

John Laing, President

Roadside Attractions
421 S. Beverly Dr., 8th Fl.
Beverly Hills, CA 90212
Tel 310-789-4710
Fax 310-789-4711
Email ....info@roadsideattractions.com
Web ....www.roadsideattractions.com

Howard Cohen
Eric d'Arbeloff

distributors

Sabeva Film Distribution

13603 Marina Pointe Dr., #A611
Marina del Rey, CA 90292
Tel 310-821-3290
Fax 310-821-3872
Email............................damianchapa@
                    sabevadistribution.com
Web ....www.sabevadistribution.com

Damian Chapa, CEO

Samuel Goldwyn Films

9570 W. Pico Blvd., 4th Fl.
Los Angeles, CA 90035
Tel 310-860-3100
Fax 310-860-3195

Peter Goldwyn, Manager of Acquisitions

Screen Gems

10202 W. Washington Blcd.
Culver City, CA 90232
Tel 310-244-4000

Benedict Carver, Sr. VP, Acquisitions
Gilbert Dumontet, Sr. VP, Acquisitions

Seventh Art Releasing

7551 Sunset Blvd., Suite 104
Los Angeles, CA 90046
Tel 323-845-1455
Fax 323-845-4717
Email ....seventhart@7thart.com
Web www.7thart.com

Udy Epstein, Founder
Stephen Kral, Executive VP, Acquisitions

Shadowdance Pictures

264 S. La Cienega Blvd., Suite 1166
Los Angeles, CA 90211
Tel 323-936-1916
Fax 323-936-8728
Email.....info@shadowdancepictures.com
Web ......www.shadowdancepictures.com

Miranda Kwok, President

Shoreline Entertainment, Inc.

1875 Century Park E., Suite 600
Los Angeles, CA 90067
Tel 310-551-2060
Fax 310-201-0729
Email .mail@shorelineentertainment.com
Web ....www.shorelineentertainment.com

Morris Ruskin, President

Showcase Entertainment

21880 Oxnard St., Suite 150
Woodland Hills, CA 91367
Tel 818-715-7005
Fax 818-715-7009
Web ....www.showcaseentertainment.com

Cara Shapiro, Director, Acquisitions

Showtime Networks, Inc.

1633 Broadway
New York, NY 10019
Tel 212-708-1600
Web ....www.sho.com

Matthew Duda, Executive VP, Program
    Acquisitions & Planning
Richard Espinosa, Manager of
    Acquisitions

Showtime's Latino Filmmaker Showcase Program

10880 Wilshire Blvd., Suite 1600
Los Angeles, CA 90024
Tel 310-234-5200
Web ....www.sho.com

Gary Garsenkel, VP of Acquistion

Singa Home Entertainment
400 S. Victoria Blvd., Suite 203
Burbank, CA 91502
Tel 818-558-1820
Fax 818-558-1877
Email ....info@echelonent.com
Web ....www.echelonent.com

Gloria Morrison, President, Development
& Acquisitions

Skouras Films
1556 17th St., 2nd Fl.
Santa Monica, CA 90404
Tel 310-586-1888
Fax 310-586-3803
Email..........dstephan@skourasfilsm.com
Web ....www.skourasfilms.com

David Stephan, Director, Acquisitions

Solid Entertainment
610 Santa Monica Blvd., Suite 204
Santa Monica, CA 90401
Tel 310-319-3440
Fax 310-319-3442
Email ....solident.com
Web ....www.solidentertainment.com

Michael Propper, VP, Acquisitions
Richard Propper, Director, International
Licensing

Solo Entertainment Group
9350 Wilshire Blvd., Suite 212
Beverly Hills, CA 90212
Tel 310-205-6280
Fax 310-205-6281

Karin Cohen, VP, Acquisitions & Co-
Productions

Sony Pictures Classics
550 Madison Ave., 8th Fl.
New York, NY 10022
Tel 212-833-8833
Web ....www.sonypictures.com

Michael Barker, Co-President
Dylan Leiner, Sr. VP, Acquisitions and
Production

Spike TV
1515 Broadway, 42nd Fl.
New York, NY 10036
Tel 212-846-6833
Fax 212-846-1752
Email ....ivana.schechtegarcia@
spiketv.com

Keith Brown, VP, News and Docs
Ivana Schechter-Garcia, Director, News
and Docs

Starpoint Entertainment/ Evolution Pictures
645 Wilcox Ave., Suite 3B
Los Angeles, CA 90004
Tel 323-620-4477
Fax 323-466-0964
Email ....david@starpointent.com

David Kim, President

The Steel Company
9220 Sunset Blvd., Suite 212
Los Angeles, CA 90069
Tel 310-274-7221
Fax 310-274-7507
Email ....gsteelco@aol.com

Gordon Steel, President
Tyler Erskine, Acquisitions Coordinator

Strand Releasing

1460 4th St., Suite 302
Santa Monica, CA 90401
Tel 310-395-5002
Fax 310-395-2502
Email ....strand@strandreleasing.com
Web ....www.strandreleasing.com

Marcus Hu, Partner

Stratosphere Entertainment

767 5th Ave., Suite 4700
New York, NY 10153
Tel 212-605-1010
Fax 212-813-0300
Email.........................stratent@aol.com

Angela Schapiro, VP, Business Affairs

Subcine

611 Broadway, Suite 836
New York, NY 10012
Tel 212-253-6273
Web ....www.subcine.com

Alex Rivera, President

Sundance Channel

1633 Broadway, 8th Fl.
New York, NY 10019
Tel 212-654-1500
Fax 212-654-4738
Email ..feedback@sundancechannel.com
Web ....www.sundancechannel.com

Larry Greenberg, Director of Acquisitions

Sundance Home Entertainment

1633 Broadway, 8th Fl.
New York, NY 10019
Tel 212-654-1500
Fax 212-654-4738
Email ..feedback@sundancechannel.com
Web ....www.sundancechannel.com

Mike Haney, Vice President

Telemundo Network

2290 W. 8th Ave.
Hialeah, FL 33010
Tel 305-884-8200
Direct...........................305-889-7308
Web ....www.telemundo.com

Kathleen Vedoya, VP, Reality
    Programming & Acquisitions

Tepuy International

2745 Ponce de Leon Blvd.
Coral Gables, FL 33134
Tel 305-774-0033
Fax 305-477-7372
Email ....marcos@tepuy.com
Web ....www.tepuy.com

THINK Film

155 Ave. of the Americas, 7th Fl.
New York, NY 10013
Tel 646-293-9400
Fax 646-293-9407
Web ....www.thinkfilmcompany.com

Randy Manis, Sr. VP, Acquisitions &
    Business Affairs
Daniel Katz, Director of Acquisitions

Thirteen/WNET NY

450 W. 33rd St.
New York, NY 10001
Tel 212-560-1313

Margaret Smilow, Director of Culture and
    Arts Documentaries

TLA Releasing, TLA Video

234 Market St., 5th Fl.
Philadelphia, PA 19106
Tel 215-733-0608
Fax 215-733-0637
Email ....contact@tlarealeasing.com
Web ....www.tlavideo.com

Richard Wolff, Director of Acquisitions

Transcontinental Films & TV

650 N. Bronson Ave., Suites 108-207
Los Angeles, CA 90004
Tel 323-464-2279
Fax 323-464-3212

Robert Kilgore, VP, Acquisitions

Trident Releasing

8401 Melrose Pl., 2nd Fl.
Los Angeles, CA 90069
Tel 323-655-8818
Fax 323-655-0515
Email ....tridentrel@aol.com

Jean Ovrum, Co-Founder/Partner
Victoria Plummer, Co-Founder/Partner

Trio Network/NBC Universal

30 Rockefeller Plaza
New York, NY 10112
Tel 212-413-5000

Megan Kew, Coordinator, Acquisitions

Troma, Inc.

733 9th Ave.
New York, NY 10019
Tel 212-757-4555
Fax 212-399-9885
Email ....info@troma.com
Web..............................www.troma.com

Jonathan Lees, Director, Events &
    Publicity, Acquisitions

Turner Entertainment Networks

1050 Techwood Dr.
Atlanta, GA 30318-5604
Tel 404-827-1500
Fax 404-885-4947
Web..............................www.turner.com

Jonathan Katz, Exec. VP, Program
    Planning & Acquisitions

TVA Films

376 Victoria Ave.
Montreal, QC H32 1C3 Canada
Tel 514-284-2525
Fax 514-985-4461

Pierre Lampron, President

Twentieth Century Fox Home Entertainment

2121 Ave. of the Stars, 25th Fl.
Los Angeles, CA 90067
Tel 310-369-5369

Mike Dunn, President

United Artists

10250 Constellation Blvd.
Los Angeles, CA 90067
1350 6th Ave., 24th Fl.
New York, NY 10019
Tel ....310-449-4000 (L.A.)
Tel ....212-708-0306 (N.Y.)
Fax ....310-586-8358 (L.A.)
Fax ....212-708-0465 (N.Y.)
Email ....jturner@unitedartists.com
Web ....www.unitedartists.com

Jack Turner, VP, Acquisitions and
    Productions

Universal International Television

100 Universal City Plaza
Universal City, CA 91608
Tel 818-777-1000
Web ....www.universalstudios.com

Natalie Osborne, VP, Sales &
    Acquisitions

Universal Television Distribution

100 Universal City Plaza
Universal City, CA 91608
Tel 818-777-1000
Web ....www.universalstudios.com

Urban Entertainment

9200 Sunset Blvd., Suite 321
Los Angeles, CA 90069
Tel 310-724-5630
Fax 310-724-5635
Web ....www.urbanentertainment.com

Michael Jenkinson, CEO/Founder

Urban Home ENT

140 Walker St., Loft A
Atlanta, GA 30013
Tel 678-508-6445
Email ....bluscreenmedia@aol.com
Web ....www.urbanhomeent.com

Barret Dungy, CEO

USA Networks Latin America

1440 S. Sepulveda Blvd., 3rd Fl.
Los Angeles, CA 90025
Tel 310-444-8592
Web ....www.usalatinamerica.com

Steve Patscheck, VP, Programming

Vanguard International Cinema

1901 Newport Blvd., Suite 225
Costa Mesa, CA 92627
Tel 949-258-2000
Fax 949-258-2010
Email..........fthor@vanguard-cinema.com
Web ....www.vanguardcinema.com

Freyr Thor, President

Venevision International

550 Biltmore Way, Suite 1180
Coral Gables, FL 33134
Tel 305-442-3411
Fax 305-448-4762
Email ....wphelan@cisneros.com
Web ....www.venevisioninternational.com

Julio Noriega, Division Manager

Ventura Distribution, Inc

2590 Conejo Spectrum St.
Thousand Oak, CA 91320
Tel 805-498-7800
Fax 805-498-7842
Email..............................international@
venturadistribution.com
Web ....www.venturadistribution.com

Daniel Malaguiua, VP, Studio Latino
Mauricio Buendia, Spanish Market
Arturo Chavez, Product Manager

Venture Entertainment Group, Inc.

P.O. Box 55113
Sherman Oaks, CA 91413
Tel 818-981-7813
Fax 818-981-3466
Email....................venture818@aol.com
Web www.venture818.com

Leigh Leshner, President

Video Sound

21 Meridian Rd., Suite 103
Edison, NJ 08820
Tel 732-548-4555
Fax 732-548-9532
Email ....info@video-sound.com
Web ....www.video-sound.com

Lal Dadlaney, President, Acquisitions

VIEW Video

34 E. 23rd St.
New York, NY 10010
Tel 212-674-5550
Fax 212-979-0266
Email ....bob@view.com
Web ....www.view.com

Warner Independent Pictures

4000 Warner Blvd.
Burbank, CA 91522
Tel 818-977-5491
Web ....www.wbitv.com

Paul Federbush, Sr. VP, Acquisitions and
Productions

Warwick Pictures

One Warwick Plaza
7822 Candlegreen Lane
Houston, TX 77071
Tel 281-754-4009
Email ....bert.weil@warwickpictures

Bert Weil, Executive VP

Wellspring Media

419 Park Ave. S., 20th Fl.
New York, NY 10016
Tel 212-686-6777
Fax 212-685-2625
Email ....movies@wellspring.com
Web.......................www.wellspring.com

Marie Theresa Guirgis, Head of
Acquisitions
Rob Williams, Manager of Acquisitions
Vanessa Arteaga, Director of Production
Development for Documentaries

Women Make Movies

462 Broadway, Suite 500WS
New York, NY 10013
Tel 212-925-0606
Fax 212-925-2052
Email............................info@wmm.com
Web ....www.wmm.com

Debra Zimmerman, Executive Director

World Film Magic Dist. Corp.

1149 N. Gower, #210
Hollywood, CA 90038
Tel 323-785-2118
Email ....worldfilmmagic@hotmail.com
Web ....www.worldfilmmagic.com

Roman Alvarado, President
Jose Gonzalez, CEO
Francisco Olea, CFO
Louis Hernandez, Public Relations

World Media Sales, USA

605 W. Huntington Dr., Suite 518
Monrovia, CA 91016
Tel 626-798-0850
Fax 928-441-5857
Email........................sthawkins@jps.net

Steve Hawkins, GM & Acquisitions

Xenon Pictures

1440 9th St.
Santa Monica, CA 90401
Tel 310-451-5510
Fax 310-395-4058
Email ....info@xenonpictures.com
Web ....www.xenonpictures.com

York Entertainment

4565 Sherman Oaks Ave.
Sherman Oaks, CA 91403
Tel 818-788-4050
Fax 818-788-4011
Email ....treston@yorkentertainment.com
Web ....www.yorkentertainment.com

Vicky Judah, VP, Acquisitions

distributors

Zeitgeist Films, LTD
247 Centre St., 2nd Fl.
New York, NY 10013
Tel 212-274-1989
Fax 212-274-1644
Email...............mail@zeitgeistfilms.com
Web ....www.zeitgeistfilms.com

Emily Russo, Co-President
Nancy Gerstman, Co-President

ZIA Film Distribution, LLC
369 Montezuma Ave., Suite 320
Santa Fe, NM 87501
Tel 505-438-9299
Fax 505-438-6137
Email.......................sales@ziafilm.com

Bobbi Valentine, President

National Association of Latino Independent Producers

**hispanic
american
films**

Note: This section includes American narrative features, 1970-2005, made by Latinos, and/or reflecting Latino themes, stories and key cast.

30 Days Until I'm Famous (2004)
Director ....Gabriela Tagliavini
Producer ....Kevin Bannerman
Screenwriter ....Laura Angelica Simon
DP ....Bernd Heinl
Cast............................Alanna Ubach, Udo Kier
Production Co. ....Maverick Entertainment,
                          Screenvest G. Productions
Distributor ....VH1 Television

187 Shadow Lane (2003)
Director ....Frank Nunez
Producer ....John Fuentes, Frank Nunez
Screenwriter ....John Fuentes
DP ....Shawn Livermon
Cast............................Danny Romo, Robert Zepeda,
                          Tonantzin Carmelo
Production Co. ....Little Boyz Dreams,
                          Skitree Pictures

El Alambrista (The Illegal) (1977)
Director ....Robert M. Young
Producer ....Michael Hausman, Irwin W. Young
Screenwriter ....Robert M. Young
DP ....Robert M. Young
Cast............................Domingo Ambriz, Trinidad Silva,
                          Linda Gillen
Production Co. ....Filmhaus
Distributor ....PBS, First Run Features, Visions

Almost a Woman (2001)
Director ....Betty Kaplan
Producer ....Ronald Colby, Anne Hopkins
Screenwriter ....Esmeralda Santiago
DP ....Carlos González
Cast............................Wanda de Jesús, Miriam Colon,
                          Cliff De Young
Production Co. ....Alt Films
Distributor ....PBS

American Me (1992)
Director ....Edward James Olmos
Producer ....Edward James Olmos, Sean Daniel,
                          Robert Young
Screenwriter ....Floyd Mutrux, Desmond Nakano
DP ....Reynaldo Villalobos
Cast............................Sal López, Vira Montes,
                          Roberto Martín Marquez
Production Co. ....Universal Pictures
Distributor ....Universal Pictures

Amigos (1985)
Director ....Ivan Acosta
Producer ....Camilo Vila
DP ....Henry Vargas
Cast............................Blanca de Abril, Luisa Gil,
                          Ruben Rabasa
Production Co. ....Manicote Productions
Distributor ....Hargrove Entertainment, Inc.

... and the Earth Did Not Swallow Him (1994)
Director ....Severo Perez
Producer ....Paul Espinosa
Screenwriter ....Tomas Rivera, Severo Perez
DP ....Virgil L. Harper
Cast............................Jose Alcala, Art Bonilla,
                          Evelyn Guerrero
Production Co. ....American Playhouse, Kino
                          International Corp., Tierra
                          Productions, SP Film, KPBS
Distributor ....Kino International Corp., PBS

The Arturo Sandoval Story (2000)
Director ....Joseph Sargent
Producer ....Celia de Costas,
                          Andy Garcia (Exec.)
Screenwriter ....Timothy J. Sexton
DP ....Donald M. Morgan
Cast............................Andy Garcia, Mia Maestro,
                          Gloria Estefan
Production Co. ....Cine Son Entertainment,
                          HBO Films
Distributor ....HBO, High Fliers Video Distribution

The Ballad of Gregorio Cortez (1982)
Director ....Robert M. Young
Producer ....Moctesuma Esparza,
                          Michael Hausman
Screenwriter ....Victor Villaseñor,
                          Robert M. Esparza
DP ....Raynaldo Villalobos
Cast............................Edward James Olmos,
                          James Gammon, Tom Bower
Production Co. ....Embassy Pictures Corporation,
                          National Endowment for the
                          Humanities
Distributor ....Embassy Pictures

La Bamba (1987)

Director ....Luis Valdez
Producer ....Bill Borden, Taylor Hackford
Screenwriter ....Luis Valdez
DP ....Adam Greenberg
Cast............................Lou Diamond Phillips,
                             Esai Morales, Rosana De Soto
Production Co. ....Columbia Pictures Corporation,
                             New Visions Pictures
Distributor ....Columbia Pictures

Bandido (2003)

Director ....Roger Christian
Producer ....Roger Christian, Carlos Gallardo
Screenwriter ....Scott Duncan, Carlos Gallardo,
                             Ned Kerwin
DP ....Mike Southon
Cast............................Carlos Gallardo, Edy Arellano,
                             Kim Coates, Manuel Vela
Production Co. ....Televisa, Videocine
Distributor ....Arcangelo Entertainment Inc.,
                             Fries Film Group

Before Night Falls (2000)

Director ....Julian Schnabel
Producer ....Jon Kilik
Screenwriter ....Julian Schnabel (screenplay),
                             Reynaldo Arenas (memoir),
                             Cunningham O'Keefe (screenplay),
                             Lázaro Gómez
DP ....Guillermo Rosas,
                             Xavier Perez Grobet
Cast............................Javier Bardem, Olivier Martinez,
                             Andrea Di Stefano, Johnny Depp
Production Co. ....El Mar Pictures
Distributor ....Fine Line Features

The Big Squeeze (1996)

Director ....Marcus de Leon
Producer ....Zane W. Levitt, Liz McDermott,
                             Mark Yellen
Screenwriter ....Marcus de Leon
DP ....Jacques Haitkin
Cast............................Danny Nucci, Peter Dobson,
                             Bert Santos
Production Co. ....Zeta Entertainment Ltd.
Distributor ....First Look Pictures Releasing

The Blue Diner (2001)

Director ....Jan Egleson
Producer ....Natatcha Estebanez
Screenwriter ....Natatcha Estebanez, Jan Egleson
DP ....Teresa Medina
Cast............................Miriam Colón, Jose Yenque,
                             Fernando Ruiz
Production Co. ....CPB, Goldheart Pictures, PBS,
                             The Blue Diner Film Project,
                             WGBH Boston
Distributor ....First Look Home Entertainment

Born In East L.A (1987)

Director ....Cheech Marin
Producer ....Peter MacGregor-Scott
Screenwriter ....Cheech Marin
DP ....Alex Phillips Jr.
Cast............................Paul Rodriguez, Cheech Marin,
                             David Perez
Production Co. ....Clear Type
Distributor ....Universal Pictures

Breaking Pan with Sol (1993)

Director ....Nancy de los Santos
Producer ....Francine Jacome
Screenwriter ....Nancy de los Santos
Cast............................Bertila Damas
Production Co. ....Hispanic Film Project,
                             MCA/Universal Television
Distributor ....MCA/Universal Television

Casa de los Babys (2003)

Director ....John Sayles
Producer ....Hunt Lowry, Alejandro Springall,
                             Lemore Syvan
Screenwriter ....John Sayles
DP ....Mauricio Rubinstein
Cast............................Angelina Pelaez, Lizzie Martinez,
                             Vanessa Martinez, Amanda
                             Alvarez, Said Martinez
Production Co. ....Blue Magic Pictures,
                             Springall Pictures
Distributor ....IFC Films

The Cisco Kid (1994)

Director ....Luis Valdez
Producer ....Gary M. Goodman,
                             Robert Katz, Barry Rosen,
                             Moctesuma Esparza (Exec.)
Screenwriter ....Luis Valdez, Michael Kane,
                             O. Henry
DP ....Guillermo Navarro
Cast............................Jimmy Smits, Cheech Marin,
                             Sadie Frost
Production Co. ....Esparza/Katz Productions,
                             Goodman/Rosen Productions,
                             Turner Pictures

Clarity of Smoke (Experimental 1999)

Director ....Frances Negrón-Muntaner
Producer ....Frances Negrón-Muntaner
Screenwriter ....Frances Negrón-Muntaner
DP ....Tom Brunstetter
Production Co. ....Art Center/South Florida
Distributor ....Art Center/South Florida,
                          Artful Truth

Clean (2004)

Director ....Nyle Cavazos García
Producer ....Nyle Cavazos García, Jane Gaffney
Screenwriter ....Nyle Cavazos García, Jane Gaffney
DP ....Jon Salzman
Cast...........................Paolo Cascardo, Patrick Fabian,
                          Tamara Mello

Come and Take It Day (2001)

Director ....Jim Mendiola
Producer ....Jim Mendiola, Rose Hanson,
                          Howard Carey
Screenwriter ....Jim Mendiola
DP ....Shane F. Kelly
Cast...........................Jesse Borrego, Rick Delgado,
                          Jesse De Luna
Distributor ....ITVS

Culture Clash in AmeriCCa (2004)

Director ....Emilio Estevez
Producer ....Diana Lesmez, Daniel Martinez
Screenwriter ....Richard Montoya, Ric Salinas,
                          Herbert Siguenza
DP ....Stephen C. Confer
Cast...........................Richard Montoya, Ric Salinas,
                          Herbert Siguenza
Production Co. ....Arenas Entertainment,
                          The Media Shop
Distributor ....Arenas Entertainment

A Day Without a Mexican (2004)

Director ....Sergio Arau
Producer ....Isaac Artenstein
Screenwriter ....Sergio Arau, Yareli Arizmendi,
                          Sergio Guerrero
DP ....Alan Caudillo
Cast...........................Caroline Aaron, Tony Abatemarco,
                          Melinda Allen
Production Co. ....Eye on the Ball Films,
                          Jose and Friends, Inc.,
                          Plural Entertainment España S.L
Distributor ....Televisa Cine

Desperado (1995)

Director ....Robert Rodriguez
Producer ....Bill Borden, Robert Rodriguez
Screenwriter ....Robert Rodriguez
DP ....Guillermo Navarro
Cast...........................Antonio Banderas, Salma Hayek,
                          Quentin Tarantino
Production Co. ....Columbia Pictures Corporation,
                          Los Hooligans Productions
Distributor ....Columbia Pictures

The Disappearance of Garcia Lorca (1997)

Director ....Marcos Zurinaga
Producer ....Marcos Zurinaga, Moctesuma
                          Esparza, Robert Katz
Screenwriter ....Marcos Zurinaga (screenplay),
                          Ian Gibson (novel),
                          Juan Antonio Ramos (screenplay),
                          Neil Cohen (screenplay)
DP ....Juan Ruiz-Anchia
Cast...........................Esai Morales, Andy Garcia,
                          Edward James Olmos,
                          Miguel Ferrer, Tony Plana
Production Co. ....Antena 3 Television,
                          Enrique Cerezo Producciones
                          Cinematográficas S.A.,
                          Esparza/Katz Productions,
                          Le Studio Canal+, Miramar Films
Distributor ....Triumph Films,
                          Columbia TriStar (DVD)

Doña Bárbara (1998)

Director ....Betty Kaplan
Producer ....David Frost, Peter Rawley,
                          María de la Paz Mariño
Screenwriter ....Rómulo Gallegos, Betty Kaplan
DP ....Hector Collodoro, Carlos González
Cast...........................Víctor Cárdenas,
                          Audry Gutierrez Alea,
                          Jorge Perugorría, Esther Goris
Production Co. ....Luz Arbero LLC
Distributor ....MCA/Universal Pictures

Empire (2002)

Director ....Franc Reyes
Producer ....Daniel Bigel, Michael Mailer
Screenwriter ....Franc Reyes
DP ....Kramer Morgenthau
Cast...........................John Leguizamo, Peter Sarsgaard,
                          Sonia Braga
Production Co. ....Arenas Entertainment,
                          Bigel/Mailer Films,
                          Universal Pictures
Distributor ....Universal Pictures

Foto Novelas: In the Mirror (TV Short 1997)
Director ....Carlos Avila
Producer ....Kurt Kaya
Cast...........................Elizabeth Cueva
Production Co. ....ITVS

Foto Novelas: Mangas (TV Short 1997)
Director ....A.P Gonzalez
Producer ....Kurt Kaya, Carlos Avila
Cast...........................Ulises Cuadra
Production Co. ....ITVS

Foto Novelas: Seeing Through Walls (TV Short 1997)
Director ....Carlos Avila
Producer ....Kurt Kaya
Cast...........................Casey Biggs, Roxann Dawson
Production Co. ....ITVS

Foto Novelas: The Fix (TV Short 1997)
Director ....Carlos Avila
Producer ....Kurt Kaya
Cast...........................Veryle Rupp
Production Co. ....ITVS

Foto Novelas II: Broken Sky (TV Series 2003)
Director ....Carlos Avila
Producer ....Debra J. Olchick
Screenwriter ....Bennett Cohen, Edit Villareal
DP ....Carlos Gonzalez
Cast...........................Robert Beltran, Victor Campos, Richard Coca, Diana Uribe
Production Co. ....Echo Park Films

Foto Novelas II: Junkyard Saints (TV Movie 2002)
Director ....Carlos Avila
Producer ....Debra J. Olchick
DP ....James L. Carter
Cast...........................León Singer, Jeremey Ray Valdez, Lorina Zapata

Fragile (2005)
Director ....Jaume Balagueró
Producer ....Carlos Fernández, Julio Fernández, Antonia Nava
Screenwriter ....Jaume Balagueró, Jordi Galcerán
Cast...........................Calista Flockhart, Yasmin Murphy, Elena Anaya
Production Co. ....Castelao Productions S.A
Distributor ....Filmax

Frida (2002)
Director ....Julie Taymor
Producer ....Lindsay Flickinger, Sarah Green, Nancy Hardin, Salma Hayek, Jay Polstein, Roberto Sneider, Lizz Speed
Screenwriter ....Hayden Herrera, Clancy Sigal, Diane Lake, Gregory Nava & Anna Thomas
DP ....Rodrigo Prieto
Cast...........................Salma Hayek, Mía Maestro, Amelia Zapata, Alfred Molina, Diego Luna
Production Co. ....Handprint Entertainment, Lions Gate Films Inc., Miramax Films, Trimark Pictures, Ventanarosa Productions
Distributor ....Miramax Films

Gaby: A True Story (1987)
Director ....Luis Mandoki
Producer ....Pinchas Perry
Screenwriter ....Luis Mandoki, Martín Salinas
DP ....Lajos Koltai
Cast...........................Liv Ullman, Norma Aleandro, Robert Loggia
Production Co. ....G. Brimmer Productions, TriStar Pictures
Distributor ....TriStar Pictures

The Gatekeeper (2002)
Director ....John Carlos Frey
Producer ....John Carlos Frey, Jack Lorenz
Screenwriter ....John Carlos Frey
DP ....Kris Denton
Cast...........................John Carlos Frey, Joel Pascual, Joel Brooks
Production Co. ....Gatekeeper Productions
Distributor ....Abranomara Inc.

Gotta Kick It Up! (2002)
Director ....Ramón Menendez
Producer ....Meghan Cole, Christopher Morgan
Screenwriter ....Meghan Cole, Nancy de los Santos
DP ....Clark Mathis
Cast...........................Camille Guaty, America Ferrera, Joanna Flores
Production Co. ....The Disney Channel
Distributor ....The Disney Channel

Hangin' With the Homeboys (1991)

Director ....Joseph B. Vasquez
Producer ....Richard Brick
Screenwriter ....Joseph B. Vasquez
DP ....Anghel Decca
Cast...........................Doug E. Doug, Mario Joyner,
                                    John Leguizamo
Production Co. ....Juno Pix, New Line Cinema
Distributor ....New Line Cinema,
                                    New Line Home Video

Harlem Blues (2003)

Director ....Andy Diaz
Producer ....Andy Diaz
Screenwriter ....Andy Diaz
DP ....Salvador Bolivar
Cast...........................Steven Beckford, Yvonne Delano,
                                    Andy Diaz
Distributor ....Spartan Entertainment

Heartbreaker (1983)

Director ....Frank Zuniga
Producer ....Chris Anders, Chris De Nebe
Screenwriter ....Vincent Gutierrez
DP ....Michael Lonzo
Cast...........................Fernando Allende, Miguel Ferrer,
                                    Robert Dryer
Production Co. ....Emerson
Distributor ....Monarex

Highway Patrolman (1991)

Director ....Alex Cox
Producer ....Lorenzo O'Brien
Screenwriter ....Lorenzo O'Brien
DP ....Miguel Garzón
Cast...........................Roberto Sosa, Bruno Bichir
Production Co. ....Cable Hogue Co. Ltd., Marubeni
                                    Corporation, Together Brothers
                                    Productions, Ultra
Distributor ....First Look Pictures Releasing

Hour of the Assassin (1987)

Director ....Luis Llosa
Producer ....Luis Llosa
Screenwriter ....Matt Leipzig
DP ....Cusi Barrio
Cast...........................Erick Estrada, Robert Vaughn,
                                    Alfredo Alvarez Calderón
Distributor ....Concorde Pictures, Video Arte

The House of Ramon Iglesia (1986)

Director ....Luis Soto
Producer ....Laura Mola, Luis Soto
Screenwriter ....Jose Rivera
DP ....Stephen Bower
Cast...........................Jaime Sánchez, Nick Corri,
                                    Roberto Badillo
Production Co. ....LSF Productions Inc.
Distributor ....America Playhouse, PBS

How Did It Feel? (2004)

Director ....Daniel Feraldo
Producer ....Marvin V. Acuna, Lucinda Clare,
                                    Daniel Feraldo, Jacob Mosler
Screenwriter ....Daniel Feraldo
Cast...........................Judith Benezra, Tom Bresnahan,
                                    Lucinda Clare
Production Co. ....Acuna Entertainment

How the Garcia Girls Spent Their Summer (2005)

Director ....Georgina García Riedel
Producer ....Olga Arana, Jose C. Mangual,
                                    Georgina García Riedel
Screenwriter ....Georgina García Riedel
DP ....Tobias Datum
Cast...........................America Ferrera, Elizabeth Peña,
                                    Steven Bauer, Rick Najera
Production Co. ....Loosely Based Pictures

Hunting of Man (2003)

Director ....Joe Menendez
Producer ....Roni Eguia
Screenwriter ....Joe Menendez
DP ....Brian Baugh
Cast...........................Douglas Spain, Rube Garfias,
                                    Jon Molerio

Imagining Argentina (2003)

Director ....Christopher Hampton
Producer ....Santiago Pozo, Diane Sillan,
                                    Jose Maria Cunillas, Lourdes Díaz,
                                    Michael Peyser
Screenwriter ....Christopher Hampton
DP ....Guillermo Navarro
Cast...........................Antonio Banderas,
                                    Emma Thompson, Horacio Flash
Production Co. ....Arenas Entertainment,
                                    Myriad Pictures, Inc.,
                                    Green Moon Productions,
                                    Multivideo, Imagining Argentina
                                    Productions
Distributor ....Arenas Entertainment

The Impostor (2002)
Director ....Joe Menendez
Producer ....Barbara Carratala Bonds
Screenwriter ....Joe Menendez
DP ....Nino Neuboeck, David Singh
Cast...........................Robert Arevalo, Angie Lucia,
Morris Perez
Production Co. ....Narrow Bridge Films
Distributor ....Spectrum Films

In The Time of the Butterflies (2001)
Director ....Mariano Barroso
Producer ....Helen Barlett, Tony Bill,
Mike Medavoy, Craig Roessler
Screenwriter ....Judy Klass, David Klass
DP ....Xavier Perez Grobet
Cast...........................Salma Hayek,
Edward James Olmos, Mía Maestro
Production Co. ....Metro-Goldwyn-Mayer,
Ventanarosa Productions
Distributor ....MGM Home Entertainment,
Showtime Networks, Inc.

Killing Pablo (2005)
Director ....Joe Carnahan
Producer ....Mark Gordon, Bob Yari,
Jason Zelin, Gregory Nava (Exec.)
Screenwriter ....Joe Carnahan
Cast...........................Javier Bardem, Paul Vasquez
Production Co. ....Paramount Pictures, DreamWorks
SKG, El Norte Productions,
Green Moon Productions,
Stratus Film Co.
Distributor ....DreamWorks Distribution LLC,
Paramount Pictures

Kiss Me a Killer (1991)
Director ....Marcus de Leon
Producer ....Catherine Cyran, Craig J. Nevius
Screenwriter ....Marcus de Leon,
Christopher Wooden

Latin Boys Go to Hell (1997)
Director ....Ela Troyano
Producer ....Jurden Bruning
Screenwriter ....Ela Troyano, Andre Salas
DP ....James Carman
Cast...........................Irwin Ossa, John Bryant Davila,
Alexis Artiles
Distributor ....Strand Releasing

The Latin Divas of Comedy (2005)
Director ....Jorge Gaxiola
Producer ....Rick Telles, Yvette Yates,
Scott Montoya (Exec.)
Cast...........................Sara Contreras, Ludo Vike,
Monique Marvez,
Alex Reymundo
Production Co. ....Payaso Entertainment
Distributor ....Paramount Pictures

The Lost City (2004)
Director ....Andy Garcia
Producer ....Andy Garcia (Exec.)
Screenwriter ....G. Cabrera Infante, Andy Garcia
DP ....Emmanuel Kadosh
Cast...........................Andy Garcia, Dustin Hoffman,
Bill Murray
Production Co. ....Lions Gate Films, CineSon
Entertainment, Platinum Equity,
Crescent Drive Pictures
Distributor ....Lions Gate Films Inc.

Luminarias (2000)
Director ....Jose Luis Valenzuela
Producer ....Sal López
Screenwriter ....Evelina Fernández
DP ....Eric Allaman
Cast...........................Evelina Fernández, Scott Bakula
Production Co. ....Sleeping Giant Productions,
July Street Entertainment
Distributor ....Artist View Entertainment,
New Latin Pictures

Malachance (2004)
Director ....Gerardo Naranjo
Producer ....Karina Pyudik, David Selig,
Linda Sena
Screenwriter ....Gerardo Naranjo
DP ....Max Goldman
Cast...........................James Ransone, Stewart Skelton,
Brandon Quinn
Production Co. ....Perro Negro Productions,
Parthenon Films, Inc.

Manito (2002)
Director ....Eric Eason
Producer ....Allen Bain, Steve Carrillo,
Jesse Scolaro, Lou Torres
Screenwriter ....Eric Eason
DP ....Didier Gertsch
Cast...........................Franky G, Leo Minaya,
Manuel Jesus Cabral
Production Co. ....Smashing Entertainment,
The 7th Floor
Distributor ....Film Movement

El Mariachi (1992)

Director ....Robert Rodriguez
Producer ....Robert Rodriguez,
                          Carlos Gallardo
Screenwriter ....Robert Rodriguez
DP ....Robert Rodriguez
Cast...........................Carlos Gallardo,
                          Consuelo Gómez,
                          Jaime de Hoyos
Production Co. ....Columbia Pictures Corporation,
                          Los Hooligans Productions
Distributor ....Columbia Pictures

El Matador (2003)

Director ....Joey Medina
Producer ....Jason Rorhbacker
Screenwriter ....Joey Medina
DP ....Tom Hobb
Cast...........................Andrew M. Aybar, Sheila Korsi,
                          Robert Wolfskill
Distributor ....Maverick Entertainment

The Milagro Beanfield War (1998)

Director ....Robert Redford
Producer ....Moctesuma Esparza,
                          Robert Redford
Screenwriter ....John Nichols, David Ward
DP ....Robbie Greenberg
Cast...........................Ruben Blades, Sonia Braga,
                          Julie Carmen
Production Co. ....Esparza Films, Universal Pictures
Distributor ....Universal Pictures

A Million to Juan (1994)

Director ....Paul Rodriguez
Producer ....Steven Paul, Mark Amin,
                          Gary Binkow
Screenwriter ....Robert Grasmere, Francisca Matos,
                          Mark Twain
DP ....Bruce Douglas Johnson
Cast...........................Paul Rodriguez, Tony Plana,
                          Bert Rosario
Production Co. ....Crystal Sky Communications,
                          Prism Entertainment Corporation,
                          Trimark Pictures
Distributor ....Samuel Goldwyn Company

Money for Nothing (1993)

Director ....Ramón Menendez
Producer ....Tom Musca
Screenwriter ....Ramón Menendez, Tom Musca,
                          Carol Sobieski
DP ....Tom Sigel
Cast...........................John Cusack, Debi Mazar,
                          Benicio del Toro
Production Co. ....Hollywood Pictures
Distributor ....Saul Zaentz Film Center

My Family (Mi Familia) (1995)

Director ....Gregory Nava
Producer ....Anna Thomas
Screenwriter ....Gregory Nava, Anna Thomas
DP ....Edward Lachman, Jason Poteet
Cast...........................Jimmy Smits, Edward James
                          Olmos, Esai Morales
Production Co. ....American Playhouse,
                          American Zoetrope,
                          Majestic Films International,
                          Newcomb Productions
Distributor ....New Line Cinema

Never Trust a Serial Killer (2002)

Director ....Juan Garza
Producer ....Juan Garza, Lorenzo O'Brien,
                          Daniel Villareal
Screenwriter ....Juan Garza, Daniel Villareal
DP ....Christopher Bernal
Cast...........................Cris Franco, Del Zamora,
                          Valente Rodriguez

El Norte (1983)

Director ....Gregory Nava
Producer ....Anna Thomas, Trevor Black,
                          Bertha Navarro
Screenwriter ....Gregory Nava, Anna Thomas
DP ....James Glennon
Cast...........................Zaide Silvia Gutierrez,
                          David Villalpando,
                          Ernesto Gómez Cruz,
                          Lupe Ontiveros
Production Co. ....American Playhouse,
                          Channel Four Films, Independent
                          Productions, Island Alive
Distributor ....Artisan Entertainment

hispanic american films

No Turning Back (2001)
Director ....Jesus Nebot, Julia Montejo
Producer ....Jesus Nebot
Screenwriter ....Jesus Nebot, Julia Montejo
DP ....Ian Fox
Cast............................Cindy Benson, Joe Estevez,
                                    Joey Lanai
Production Co. ....CARTEL, Zocalo Entertainment
Distributor ....Zenpix

The Novice (1995)
Director ....Judy Hecht Dumontet
Producer ....Gilbert Dumontet,
                                    Judy Hecht Dumontet
DP ....Mark Parry
Cast............................Sophie Chahinian, Luis Avalos,
                                    Jesús Mendoza
Distributor ....PBS

Of Love and Shadows (1994)
Director ....Betty Kaplan
Producer ....Betty Kaplan, Paul Mayersohn,
                                    Richard B. Goodwin
Screenwriter ....Donald Freed
DP ....Felix Monti
Cast............................Antonio Banderas,
                                    Jennifer Connelly
Production Co. ....Miramax Films, Aleph Productions
                                    S.A, Pandora Cinema
Distributor ....Miramax Films

Once Upon a Time in Mexico (2003)
Director ....Robert Rodriguez
Producer ....Robert Rodriguez,
                                    Elizabeth Avellán, Carlos Gallardo
Screenwriter ....Robert Rodriguez
DP ....Robert Rodriguez
Cast............................Antonio Banderas, Salma Hayek,
                                    Johnny Depp, Mickey Rourke,
                                    Eva Mendes
Production Co. ....Columbia Pictures Corporation,
                                    Dimension Films,
                                    Troublemaker Studios
Distributor ....Sony Pictures Entertainment,
                                    Dimension Films

Once Upon a Wedding (2004)
Director ....Matia Karrell
Producer ....Robert Benjamin, Scott Rosenfelt
Screenwriter ....Reuben Gonzalez
DP ....Steven Finestone
Cast............................Charlotte Ayanna, Esai Morales,
                                    Cristián de la Fuente, Kuno Becker,
                                    Valeria Andrews
Production Co. ....Cinematropical Pictures LLC,
                                    La Boca Productions LLC,
                                    Trailopolis Entertainment Group LLC
Distributor ....Outrider Pictures

Only Once in a Lifetime (1979)
Director ....Alejandro Grattan
Producer ....Moctesuma Esparza,
                                    Alejandro Grattan
DP ....Turner Brown
Cast............................Claudio Brook, Estrellita López,
                                    Miguel Robelo
Production Co. ....Moctesuma Esparza, Sierra Madre
Distributor ....Movietime

The Original Latin Kings of Comedy (2002)
Director ....Jeb Brien
Producer ....Jeb Brien, Scott L. Montoya,
                                    Paul Rodriguez
DP ....Strand Croker
Cast............................Nayib Estefan, George Lopez,
                                    Joey Medina, Paul Rodriguez,
                                    Alex Reymundo
Production Co. ....Checkmate Entertainment,
                                    Paramount Pictures,
                                    Payaso Entertainment
Distributor ....Paramount Pictures

Pain Flower (1996)
Director ....Fred Garcia
Producer ....Fernando Cano
Screenwriter ....Fred Garcia
Cast............................Jesse Borrego, Gabriel R. Martinez
Production Co. ....Yerba Buena Productions Inc.

La Pastolera (1991)
Director ....Luis Valdez
Producer ....Richard D. Soto,
                                    Phillip Esparza (Exec.)
Screenwriter ....Luis Valdez
DP ....Chuy Elizondo
Cast............................Linda Ronstandt, Paul Rodriguez,
                                    Robert Beltran
Production Co. ....El Teatro Campesino,
                                    Richard Soto Productions
Distributor ....PBS

Picking Up the Pieces (2000)
Director ....Alfonso Arau
Producer ....Paul L. Sandberg,
                         Alfonso Arau (Exec.)
Screenwriter ....Bill Wilson
DP ....Vittorio Storaro
Cast...........................Woody Allen, Sharon Stone,
                         Alfonso Arau
Production Co. ....Comala Films Productions,
                         Kushner-Locke Company,
                         Ostensible Productions
Distributor ....Cinemax

Piñero (2001)
Director ....León Ichaso
Producer ....John Penotti, Fisher Stevens,
                         Tim Williams
Screenwriter ....León Ichaso
DP ....Claudio Chea
Cast...........................Benjamin Bratt,
                         Giancarlo Esposito,
                         Talisa Soto, Rita Moreno,
                         Nelson Vasquez
Production Co. ....GreeneStreet Films Inc.,
                         Lower East Side Films
Distributor ....Miramax Films

Price of Glory (2000)
Director ....Carlos Avila
Producer ....Moctezuma Esparza,
                         Arthur Friedman, Robert Katz
Screenwriter ....Phil Berger
DP ....Affonso Beato
Cast...........................Jimmy Smits, Jon Seda,
                         Clifton Collins Jr., Ron Pearlman
Production Co. ....New Line Cineman,
                         Arthur Friedman Productions,
                         Esparza/Katz Productions
Distributor ....New Line Cinema

The Princess and the Barrio Boy (2000)
Director ....Tony Plana
Producer ....Steven Paul
Screenwriter ....Julie Chambers
DP ....Mario Garcia Joya
Cast...........................Mirasol Nichols, Nicolas Gonzalez,
                         Edward James Olmos
Production Co. ....Showtime Networks Inc.
Distributor ....Crystal Sky,
                         Showtime Networks Inc.

Puerto Rican Mambo: Not a Musical (1993)
Director ....Ben Model
Producer ....Ben Model
Screenwriter ....Luis Caballero, Ben Model
DP ....Rosemary Tomosky-Franco
Cast...........................Luis Caballero, John Leguizamo,
                         Jeff Eyres
Production Co. ....Piñata Films, Inc.
Distributor ....Cabriolet Films

Raising Victor Vargas (2002)
Director ....Peter Sollet
Producer ....Peter Sollet, Scott Macaulay,
                         Robin O'Hara, Alain de la Mata
Screenwriter ....Peter Sollet (screenplay),
                         Eva Vives (story)
DP ....Tim Orr
Cast...........................Judy Marte, Melonie Díaz, Victor
                         Rasuk, Altagracia Guzman,
                         Silvestre Rasuk, John Ramos
Production Co. ....Forensic Films, Le Studio Canal+,
                         Studio Canal
Distributor ....Samuel Goldwyn Films, Fireworks
                         Pictures

Real Women Have Curves (2002)
Director ....Patricia Cardoso
Producer ....George LaVoo, Effie Brown
Screenwriter ....Josefina López, George LaVoo
DP ....Jom Denault
Cast...........................America Ferrera, Lupe Ontiveros,
                         Ingrid Oliu, George Lopez
Production Co. ....HBO Independent Productions,
                         LaVoo Productions,
                         Newmarket Film Group
Distributor ....HBO Independent Productions

Robbing Peter (2004)
Director ....Mario F. de la Vega
Producer ....T. Todd Flinchum, Lisa Y. Garibay,
                         Mario F. de la Vega
Screenwriter ....Mario F. de la Vega
DP ....Jaime Reynoso, Blake Scripps
Cast...........................Louie Olivos Jr., Victor Martínez
Production Co. ....Prickly Pear Productions

hispanic american films

123

Roosters (1993)

Director ....Robert M. Young
Producer ....Susan Block-Reiner,
                                     Norma I. Cohen, Kevin Reidy
Screenwriter ....Milcha Sanchez Scott
DP ....Reynaldo Villalobos
Cast...........................Edward James Olmos,
                                     Sarah Lassez, KCET Los Angeles
Production Co. ....American Playhouse, Olmos
                                     Productions
Distributor ....IRS Media

Rum & Coke (1999)

Director ....Maria Escobedo
Producer ....Charles Gherardi
Screenwriter ....Maria Escobedo, Charles Gherardi
DP ....Dick Fisher
Cast...........................Diana Marquis,
                                     Juan Carlos Hernández,
                                     Christopher Marazzo
Production Co. ....Rainforest Films,
                                     Rum and Coke Inc.
Distributor ....Koan Inc.

Runnin' at Midnite (2001)

Director ....Pablo Toledo
Producer ....Lawrence Toledo, Jennifer
                                     Santiago, Pablo Toledo
Screenwriter ....Pablo Toledo
DP ....Robert Ballo
Cast...........................Paul Appleby, Daniel Chacón,
                                     Melody Chubb
Production Co. ....Hope Street Productions
Distributor ....El Matador Entertainment

Rhythm of the Saints (2003)

Director ....Sarah Rogacki
Producer ....Cyn Cañel Rossi, Yvette Tomlinson
Screenwriter ....Cyn Cañel Rossi
DP ....Matthew Clark
Cast...........................Sarita Choudhury, Danielle Alonso,
                                     Gano Grills
Production Co. ....Cynalex Productions LLC

Seguín (1980)

Director ....Jesús Salvador Treviño
Producer ....Severo Perez
Screenwriter ....Jesús Salvador Treviño
DP ....Judy Irola
Cast...........................Rose Portillo, Edward James
                                     Olmos, Pepe Serna
Production Co. ....KCET Los Angeles

Selena (1997)

Director ....Gregory Nava
Producer ....Moctesuma Esparza,
                                     Robert Katz
Screenwriter ....Gregory Nava
DP ....Edward Lachman
Cast...........................Jennifer Lopez, Jackie Guerra,
                                     Constance Marie,
                                     Alexandra Meneses, Jon Seda,
                                     Edward James Olmos,
                                     Jacob Vargas, Lupe Ontiveros
Production Co. ....Esparza/Katz Productions,
                                     Q Productions Inc.
Distributor ....Warner Bros.,
                                     Warner Home Video (DVD)

Short Eyes (1977)

Director ....Robert M. Young
Producer ....Lewis Harris, Robert M. Young
Screenwriter ....Miguel Piñero
DP ....Peter Sova
Cast...........................Bruce Davison, Jose Perez,
                                     Nathan George
Distributor ....Film League

Speeder Kills (2003)

Director ....Jim Mendiola
Producer ....Faith Radle
Screenwriter ....Jim Mendiola
DP ....Jim Mendiola
Cast...........................Xelina Flores, Amalia Ortiz
Production Co. ....BadAss Pictures

Spy Kids (2001)

Director ....Robert Rodriguez
Producer ....Robert Rodriguez,
                                     Elizabeth Avellan,
                                     Guillermo Navarro
Screenwriter ....Robert Rodriguez
DP ....Guillermo Navarro
Cast...........................Antonio Banderas, Carla Gugino,
                                     Alexa Vega
Production Co. ....Dimension Films,
                                     Troublemaker Studios
Distributor ....Dimension Films

Spy Kids 2: Island of Lost Dreams (2002)
Director ....Robert Rodriguez
Producer ....Elizabeth Avellan,
                         Robert Rodriguez
Screenwriter ....Robert Rodriguez
DP ....Robert Rodriguez
Cast...........................Antonio Banderas, Carla Gugino,
                         Alexa Vega
Production Co. ....Dimension Films,
                         Troublemaker Studios
Distributor ....Dimension Films,
                         Miramax Films

Spy Kids 3-D: Game Over (2003)
Director ....Robert Rodriguez
Producer ....Elizabeth Avellan,
                         Robert Rodriguez
Screenwriter ....Robert Rodriguez
DP ....Robert Rodriguez
Cast...........................Antonio Banderas, Carla Gugino,
                         Alexa Vega
Production Co. ....Dimension Films,
                         Troublemaker Studios,
                         Los Hooligans Productions
Distributor ....Dimension Films,
                         Miramax Films

Staccato Purr of the Exhaust (1996)
Director ....Luis M. Meza
Producer ....Luis M. Meza, Mark Miremont
Screenwriter ....Luis M. Meza
Cast...........................Michelle Beauchamp,
                         Dennis Brooks, Ron Garcia
Production Co. ....Skunkboy Ink

Stand & Deliver (1988)
Director ....Ramon Menendez
Producer ....Iya Labunka, Lindsay Law,
                         Tom Musca
Screenwriter ....Ramon Menendez, Tom Musca
DP ....Tom Richmond
Cast...........................Edward James Olmos,
                         Esther Harris, Mark Phelan
Production Co. ....American Playhouse, Warner Bros.
Distributor ....Warner Bros.

Star Maps (1997)
Director ....Miguel Arteta
Producer ....Matthew Greenfield
Screenwriter ....Miguel Arteta, Matthew Greenfield
DP ....Chuy Chavez
Cast...........................Douglas Spain, Efrain Figueroa,
                         Martha Velez
Production Co. ....Flan de Coco Films, King Films
Distributor ....Fox Searchlight Pictures

El Súper (1979)
Director ....León Ichaso,
                         Orlando Jimenez Leal
Producer ....Manuel Arce, León Ichaso
Screenwriter ....Manuel Arce, León Ichaso
Cast...........................Reynaldo Medina, Elizabeth Peña,
                         Hilda Lee
Production Co. ....Max Mambru Films
Distributor ....New Yorker Films

A Time of Destiny (1988)
Director ....Gregory Nava
Producer ....Anna Thomas
Screenwriter ....Gregory Nava, Anna Thomas
DP ....James Glennon
Cast...........................William Hurt, Timothy Hutton,
                         Melissa Leo
Production Co. ....Alive Films, Columbia Pictures
                         Corporation, Nelson Entertainment
Distributor ....Columbia Pictures

Tortilla Heaven (2005)
Director ....Judy Hecht Dumontet
Producer ....Gilbert Dumontet, Jose M.
                         Iturralde, Courtney Mizel
Screenwriter ....Judy Hecht Dumontet,
                         Julius Robinson
DP ....Chuy Chavez
Cast...........................Jose Zuñiga, Miguel Sandoval,
                         George Lopez, Lupe Ontiveros,
                         Irene Bedard

Tortilla Soup (2001)
Director ....María Ripoll
Producer ....John Bard Manulis
Screenwriter ....Hui-Ling Wang, Ang Lee,
                         James Schamus,
                         Ramón Menendez,
                         Tom Musca, Vera Blasi
DP ....Savier Perez-Grobet
Cast...........................Hector Elizondo, Elizabeth Peña,
                         Jacqueline Obradors,
                         Tamara Mello, Raquel Welch
Production Co. ....Samuel Goldwyn Films,
                         Starz! Encore Entertainment
Distributor ....Samuel Goldwyn Films

Twelve and Holding (2005)
Director ....Michael Cuesta
Producer ....Brian Bell, Michael Cuesta,
                         Jenny Schweitzer, Leslie Urdang
Screenwriter ....Anthony Cipriano
DP ....Romeo Tirone
Cast...........................Bruce Altman, Jayne Atkinson,
                         Jesse Camacho
Production Co. ....Canary Films, Serenade Films

hispanic american films

Undefeated (2003)

Director ....John Leguizamo
Producer ....Robin O'Hara, Scott Macaulay,
                           Enrique Chediak
Screenwriter ....John Leguizamo, Frank Pugliese
DP ....Enrique Chediak
Cast............................John Leguizamo, Clifton Collins Jr.,
                           Adrian Martinez
Production Co. ....Forensic Films,
                           Hart-Sharp Entertainment,
                           Lower East Side Films
Distributor ....HBO Films

Vote for Me (2002)

Director ....Nelson Denis
Screenwriter ....Nelson Denis
DP ....Salvador Bolivar
Cast............................Malik Yoba, Angel Salazar,
                           Gloria Irizarry

A Walk in the Clouds (1995)

Director ....Alfonso Arau
Producer ....David Zucker, Jerry Zucker,
                           Emmanuel Lubezki
Screenwriter ....Cesare Zavattini,
                           Vittorio de Benedetti,
                           Robert Mark Kamen
DP ....Leo Brouwer
Cast............................Keanu Reeves, Aitana
                           Sanchez Gijon, Anthony Quinn,
                           Angelica Aragon
Production Co. ....20th Century Fox
Distributor ....20th Century Fox

Washington Heights (2002)

Director ....Alfredo De Villa
Producer ....Alfredo De Villa, Manny Perez,
                           Luis Dantas, Tom Donahue
Screenwriter ....Alfredo De Villa, Nat Moss,
                           Junot Díaz, Manny Perez
DP ....Claudio Chea
Cast............................Tomas Milian, Manny Perez,
                           Danny Hoch, Jude Ciccolella
Production Co. ....AsDuesDon, Ex-Bo Productions,
                           Stolen Car Productions
Distributor ....Mac Releasing LLC

Woman on Top (2000)

Director ....Fina Torres
Producer ....Alan Poul
Screenwriter ....Vera Blasi
DP ....Thierry Arbogast
Cast............................Penelope Cruz, Muirlo Benício,
                           Harold Perrineau Jr.

Zoot Suit (1982)

Director ....Luis Valdez
Producer ....Peter Burnell
Screenwriter ....Luis Valdez
DP ....David Myers
Cast............................Daniel Valdez, Edward James
                           Olmos, Charles Aidman
Production Co. ....Universal Pictures
Distributor ....Universal Pictures

hispanic american films

Note: This section includes American Documentary Features, 1970-2005, made by Latinos and/or reflecting Latino themes and stories.

The 20th Century: American Tapestry (Documentary 1999)
Director ....Gregory Nava
Producer ....Barbara Martinez Jitner,
    Gregory Nava
DP ....Stephen Consentino,
    Kirk Gardner, Frances Kenny,
    Barbara Martinez Jitner
Production Co. ....Showtime Networks, Inc.,
    El Norte Productions,
    Buena Vista Television,
    5759 Productions
Distributor ....Showtime Networks, Inc.

90 Miles (Documentary 2001)
Director ....Juan Carlos Zaldívar
Producer ....Nicole Betancourt,
    Juan Carlos Zaldívar
Screenwriter ....Juan Carlos Zaldívar
DP ....Nicole Betancourt,
    Juan Carlos Maciquez
Production Co. ....90 Miles LLC

1492 Revisited (Documentary 1992)
Director ....Paul Espinosa
Producer ....Paul Espinosa
Distributor ....PBS

Abriendo Camino (Documentary 2005)
Director ....Lillian Jimenez
Producer ....Bienvenida Matías, Lillian Jimenez
DP ....Elia Lyssey
Production Co. ....Latino Educational Media Center

Accordion Dreams (Documentary 2001)
Director ....Hector Galán
Producer ....Hector Galán
Screenwriter ....Hector Galán
DP ....Kieter Kaupp
Production Co. ....Galán Productions
Distributor ....Galán Productions

The Acculturation of Indigenous Art (Documentary 2003-2005)
Director ....Russell Alexander Orozco
Producer ....Russell Alexander Orozco
Screenwriter ....Russell Alexander Orozco

AIDS In the Barrio: Eso No Me Pasa a Mi (Documentary 1989)
Director ....Peter Biella,
    Frances Negrón-Muntaner
Producer ....Alba Martínez,
    Frances Negrón-Muntaner
Screenwriter ....Peter Biella,
    Frances Negrón-Muntaner
DP ....Peter Biella
Production Co. ....AIDS Film Initiative
Distributor ....Cinema Guild

Al Otro Lado (Documentary 2004)
Director ....Natalia Almada
Producer ....Natalia Almada

The American Dream (Documentary 2003)
Director ....Sonia Fritz
Producer ....Frances Lausell
Screenwriter ....Sonia Fritz
DP ....Sonia Fritz
Production Co. ....Isla Films
Distributor ....Cinema Guild

Americanos: Latino Life in the United States (Documentary 2000)
Director ....Susan Todd, Andrew Young
Producer ....Nick Athas, Edward James Olmos
DP ....Andrew Young
Cast..........................Jennifer Broncamontes,
    Carlos Santana, Tito Puentes
Production Co. ....BAK Productions,
    Olmos Productions,
    Reflections Joint Venture

America Tropical (Documentary 1971)
Director ....Barry Nye
Producer ....Jesús Salvador Treviño
Screenwriter ....Jesús Salvador Treviño
DP ....Barry Nye
Cast..........................Victor Millan
Production Co. ....KCET
Distributor ....The Cinema Guild

Ballad of and Unsung Hero (Documentary 1983)
Director ....Isaac Artenstein
Producer ....Paul Espinosa
Screenwriter ....Paul Espinosa
Distributor ....PBS

Beyond the Dream (Documentary 2005)
Director ....Paul Espinosa, Lyn Goldfarb,
                          Jed Riffe, Emiko Omori
Producer ....Paul Espinosa, Lyn Goldfarb,
                          Jed Riffe, Emiko Omori,
                          Alison Sotomayor (Asso.)
Production Co. ....Beyond the Dream LLC
Distributor ....PBS

Beyond Borders: John Sayles in Mexico (Documentary 2003)
Director ....Bruno de Almeida
Producer ....Bruno de Almeida,
                          Rene Simon Cruz Jr.
DP ....Rene Simon Cruz Jr.,
                          Bruno de Almeida
Cast...........................John Sayles, Marcia Gay Harden,
                          Rita Moreno
Production Co. ....Arco Films, Esperanza Films,
                          Independent Film Channel
Distributor ....Independent Film Channel

Beyond the Sea (Documentary 2003)
Director ....Lisandro Perez-Rey
Screenwriter ....Lisandro Perez-Rey
DP ....Lisandro Perez-Rey
Distributor ....WPBT

Bill Viola, A Twenty-Year Retrospective (Documentary 1998)
Producer ....Pedro Celedon

Biography of David Ben-Gurion (Documentary 2004)
Director ....Joshua Alper
Producer ....Olga Arana (Assoc.),
                          Donald Lucitana
Screenwriter ....Joshua Alper
Production Co. ....Greystone Film Television
Distributor ....Biography Channel

Biography of Mario Vargas Llosa (Documentary 2004)
Director ....Mauricio Bonnett
Producer ....Olga Arana, Marcela Cuneo,
                          Jose Manuel Lorenzo
Screenwriter ....Mauricio Bonnett, Marcela Cuneo
DP ....Paulo Jacinto dos Reis
Production Co. ....Amazonas Films LLC
Distributor ....Canal + España

Birthwrite (Documentary 1989)
Director ....Luis R. Torres
Producer ....Jesús Salvador Treviño,
                          Charles R. Allen
Screenwriter ....Jesús Salvador Treviño
DP ....Scot Olson
Cast...........................Cheech Marin
Production Co. ....KCET
Distributor ....The Cinema Guild

Biscayne National Park: Legacy of Environmental Pioneers (Documentary 1997)
Producer ....Polita Glynn
Distributor ....WRNL Public Television Channel 17

Bitter Harvest (Documentary 1997)
Director ....Ray Telles
Producer ....Ray Telles
Screenwriter ....Ray Telles
DP ....John Claibourne, Jim Raeside
Production Co. ....KQED TV
Distributor ....KQED TV

Book Wars (Documentary 2000)
Director ....Jason Rosette
Producer ....John Montoya, Jason Rosette
Screenwriter ....Jason Rosette
DP ....Jason Rosette
Cast...........................Peter Whitney, Rick Sherman,
                          Marvin
Production Co. ....Carmerado, NYC
Distributor ....Avatar Films, Carmerado,
                          Transit Media Communications

The Border (Documentary 2000)
Producer ....Paul Espinosa, Hector Gonzalez,
                          Matthew Sneddon
Screenwriter ....Paul Espinosa
Production Co. ....Espinosa Productions,
                          KPBS Television
Distributor ....PBS

Border Visions/Visiones Fronterizos (Documentary 2003)
Director ....Evangeline Griego
Producer ....Evangeline Griego
Production Co. ....About Time Productions

Bragging Rights: Stickball (Documentary 2001)
Director ....Sonia N. Gonzalez
Producer ....Sonia N. Gonzalez
DP ....Elia Lyssi, Dylan Verrechia
Cast...........................Charlie Ballard, Carlos Diaz,
Joviana Mercado
Production Co. ....Chica Luna Productions

Brave New Valley (Documentary 2005)
Director ....Jennifer Maytorena Taylor
Producer ....Jennifer Maytorena Taylor
Screenwriter ....Jennifer Maytorena Taylor
Production Co. ....Specific Pictures, KQED-TV,
San Francisco (Co Production)

Break Through: The Changing Face of Science in America (Documentary Series 1996)
Director ....Trudi Brown, Natatcha Estebanez,
Thomas Ott, Yolanda Parks,
Eric Stange, Elizabeth Taylor-Mead,
Joseph Tovares
Producer ....Henry Hampton (Exec.)
Cast...........................Andre Braugher, George Castro,
France Cordova
Production Co. ....Blackside Inc.

Brincando El Charco (Documentary 1994)
Director ....Frances Negrón-Muntaner
Producer ....Frances Negrón-Muntaner
Screenwriter ....Frances Negrón-Muntaner
Cast...........................Frances Negrón-Muntaner
Production Co. ....HipSpic
Distributor ....Women Make Movies

The Bronze Screen: 100 Years of the Latino Image in American Cinema (Documentary 2002)
Director ....Nancy de los Santos, Alberto
Domínguez, Susan Racho
Producer ....Nancy de los Santos, Alberto
Domínguez, Susan Racho
Screenwriter ....Nancy de los Santos, Susan Racho
Cast...........................Benicio del Toro, Anthony Quinn,
Dolores del Rio
Distributor ....HBO

Cachao...Como Su Ritmo No Hay Dos (Documentary 2003)
Director ....Andy Garcia
Producer ....Andy Garcia
Cast...........................Alfredo Armenteros, Andy Garcia
Production Co. ....CineSon Entertainment

Carnalitos (Documentary 1973)
Director ....Richard Davies
Producer ....Bobby Páramo

Carnival in Rio 2003 (Documentary 2003)
Director ....Terry Gastrow, Deborah Calla
Producer ....Deborah Calla
Production Co ....Globo International
Distributor ....Travel Channel

Carnival in Rio 2004 (Documentary 2004)
Director ....Deborah Calla
Producer ....Deborah Calla
Screenwriter ....Adam Stephan
Production Co ....Globo International
Distributor ....Discovery Channel

Carnivals of the Caribbean (Documentary 2004)
Director ....Sonia Fritz
Producer ....Frances Lausell
Screenwriter ....Sonia Fritz
DP ....Jaime Costas
Production Co. ....Isla Films

Celia Cruz and Friends (PBS Concert 1999)
Producer ....Frank Borres
Production Co ....American View Productions
Distributor ....PBS

The Challenge (Documentary 2005)
Director ....Frank Borres
Producer ....Frank Borres
Screenwriter ....Frank Borres, Anthony García
Production Co. ....American View Productions
Distributor ....Connecticut Public Broadcasting

Chicana (Documentary 1979)
Director ....Sylvia Morales
Distributor ....Women Make Movies

Chicano Artists (Documentary 2001)
Director ....Deborah Calla
Producer ....Deborah Calla
Distributor ....HBO Latino

hispanic american films

Chicano! History of the Mexican American Civil Rights Movement (Documentary Series 1996)

Producer ....Jose Luis Ruiz (Exec.),
                          Hector Galán, Robert Cozens,
                          Sylvia Morales, Mylene Moreno,
                          Susan Rancho
Screenwriter ....Sylvia Morales
DP ....Dieter Kaupp, Tom Taylor
Production Co. ....Galán Productions
Distributor ....PBS

Chicano Park (Documentary 1988)

Director ....Marilyn Mulford, Mario Barrera

Chicanos Story (Documentary 1982)

Director ....Luis Valdez

Children of the Street (Documentary 2002)

Director ....Eva S. Aridijis
Producer ....Eva S. Aridijis
DP ....Juan Pablo Chapela Barnetche,
                          Carlos Cárdenas,
                          Bernadette Pampuch

Cholo Joto (Documentary 1993)

Director ....Augie Robles

Cinco Vidas (Documentary 1972)

Director ....Jose Luis Ruiz

College Track (Documentary 2004)

Director ....Maria Agui Carter
Producer ....Maria Agui Carter
Screenwriter ....Maria Agui Carter
Distributor ....PBS

Color of Money (Documentary 2004)

Director ....Frank Borres
Producer ....Robert Alvarado
Screenwriter ....Frank Borres, Robert Alvarado
Production Co. ....American View Productions
Distributor ....Connecticut Public Broadcasting

Connecticut Tobacco Valley (Documentary 2001)

Director ....Frank Borres
Producer ....Frank Borres
Screenwriter ....Frank Borres
Production Co. ....American View Productions
Distributor ....Connecticut Public Broadcasting

Control Room (Documentary 2004)

Director ....Jehane Noujaim
Producer ....Rosadel Varela
Screenwriter ....Julia Bacha, Jehane Noujaim
DP ....Jehane Noujaim
Cast............................Tom Mintier, Samier Khader
Distributor ....Magnolia Pictures

El Corazón De Loisaida (The Heart of Loisaida) (Documentary 1979)

Director ....Bienvenida Matías, Marcy Reaven
Producer ....Bienvenida Matías, Marcy Reaven
DP ....Tom Sigel,
                          Juan Antonio Ruiz Anchia
Distributor ....Company Cinema Guild

Corpus: A Home Movie for Selena (Documentary 1999)

Director ....Lourdes Portillo
Producer ....Lourdes Portillo
Screenwriter ....Lourdes Portillo

The Cost of Cotton (Documentary 1978)

Director ....Luis Argueta
Distributor ....PBS

Countdown to Armageddon (Documentary 2004)

Director ....David Devries
Producer ....Olga Arana, Glenn Kirschbhaum
Screenwriter ....David Devries
Production Co. ....Greystone Film Television
Distributor ....History Channel

The Couple in the Cage (Documentary 1997)

Director ....Paula Heredia

Cristal (Documentary 1974)

Director ....Severo Perez
Producer ....Severo Perez

Cuba: A Personal Journey (Documentary 1983)

Director ....Hector Galán
Producer ....Hector Galán
Screenwriter ....Hector Galán
DP ....Fred Tutman
Production Co. ....Galán Productions
Distributor ....PBS

Cuba Mia (Documentary 2001)

Director ....Rhonda M. Mitrani
Producer ....Rhonda M. Mitrani
Production Co. ....Elizabeth Dascal

The Dark Magic Show (Documentary 2003-2004)
Producer ....Gustavo Stebner

The Devil's Music (Documentary 2000)
Director ....Maria Agui Carter
Producer ....Maria Agui Carter
Screenwriter ....Maria Agui Carter
Distributor ....PBS

El Diablo Nunca Duerme (Documentary 1994)
Director ....Lourdes Portillo
Producer ....Lourdes Portillo
Screenwriter ....Lourdes Portillo
DP ....Kyle Kibbe
Production Co. ....ITVS, Xochiti Films

A Donde Va Vicente? (Where Is Vicente Going?) (Documentary 2003)
Director ....Michelle Salcedo

Don Ricardo Alegria (Documentary 2000)
Director ....Miguel Zallas Garcia
Producer ....Rafael Rivera-Viruet
Screenwriter ....Rafael Rivera-Viruet (Co)
Production Co ....Tropical Vision Entertainment
Distributor ....Tropical Vision Entertainment

The Doorman (Documentary 1999)
Director ....Alfredo de Villa
Producer ....Caroline Bourmachard
DP ....Frank Reyes
Production Co. ....Whole 9 Productions
Distributor ....HBO

Los Duros (Documentary 2005)
Director ....Leon Gast, Chad Carlberg
Producer ....Pablo Bressan, Fred Roos,
                           John Tempereau
Production Co. ....Going Going Productions
Distributor ....Going Going Productions

La Fabri-k (The Cuban Hip Hop Factory) (Documentary 2004)
Director ....Lisandro Perez-Rey
Producer ....Lisandro Perez-Rey
Screenwriter ....Lisandro Perez-Rey
Production Co. ....Gato Films

Una Familia Mexicana (Documentary 1980)
Director ....Jose Araujo
Producer ....Jose Araujo
Screenwriter ....Jose Araujo

Farmingville (Documentary 2004)
Director ....Carlos Sandoval,
                           Catherine Tambini
Producer ....Carlos Sandoval,
                           Catherine Tambini
Screenwriter ....Carlos Sandoval
DP ....Karola Ritter, Catherine Tambini
Production Co. ....Camino Bluff Productions, Inc.
Distributor ....Docurama, ITVS, POV/American
                           Documentary

Favorite Poem Project (Documentary 1997)
Director ....Juanita Anderson (Exec.)

Fear and Learning at Hoover Elementary (Documentary 1997)
Director ....Laura Angelica Simon
Producer ....Laura Angelica Simon
DP ....Suki Medencevic
Distributor ....PBS, P.O.V., Fear & Learning

Fighting the Tide (Documentary 1999)
Director ....Manny Santos
Distributor ....PBS

The Fight in the Fields (Documentary 1996)
Director ....Ray Telles, Rick Tejada-Flores
Producer ....Ray Telles, Rick Tejada-Flores
Screenwriter ....Ray Telles, Rick Tejada-Flores
DP ....Vicente Franco
Production Co. ....ITVS, Paradigm Productions
Distributor ....Cinema Guild

The First Photograph - Nicephobe Niepce (Documentary 2004)
Director ....Pedro Celedon
Producer ....Pía Dominguez
DP ....Andrés Garretón

For The Record: Guam in WWII (Documentary 2005)
Director ....Frances Negrón-Muntaner
Producer ....Frances Negrón-Muntaner,
                           Cris Borja, Bienvenida Matías
Screenwriter ....Frances Negrón-Muntaner,
                           Cris Borja
DP ....Edwin Pagan, David Gonzalez
Production Co. ....Polymorphous Pictures
Distributor ....ITVS

French Furniture - Marquetry in the 18th Century Europe (Documentary 2004)
Director ....Pedro Celedon
Producer ....Pía Dominguez
DP ....DeWayne Rude

Forgotten Americans (Documentary 2000)
Director ....Hector Galán
Producer ....Hector Galán
Screenwriter ....Hector Galán
Production Co. ....Galán Productions
Distributor ....PBS

Garment Workers (Documentary 1975)
Director ....Susan Racho
Production Co. ....Susan Racho

Getting To Heaven (Documentary 1996)
Director ....Alfredo Bejar

Go Back To Mexico! (Documentary 1994)
Director ....Hector Galán
Producer ....Hector Galán
Screenwriter ....Hector Galán
DP ....Dieter Kaupp
Production Co. ....Galán Productions
Distributor ....PBS

The Good War and Those Who Refused To Fight It (Documentary 2000)
Director ....Judith Ehrlich, Rick Tejada-Flores
Producer ....Judith Ehrlich, Rick Tejada-Flores
Screenwriter ....Judith Ehrlich, Rick Tejada-Flores
Cast...........................Edward Asner
Production Co. ....ITVS, Paradigm Productions
Distributor ....CPB, MacArthur Foundation, ITVS

The Head of Joaquin Murrieta (Documentary 2005)
Director ....John Valadez
Producer ....John Valadez
Distributor ....PBS

Hispanic Americans (Documentary 1998)
Producer ....Francisco Ramirez,
                                   Radames Soto (Exec.),
                                   Richard Perin (Exec.)
Screenwriter ....Jim Medrinos
Production Co. ....Blue Pearl Entertainment, Films for the Humanities & Sciences

The History of Puerto Rican Politics (Documentary 2005)
Director ....Rafael Rivera-Viruet
Producer ....Rafael Rivera-Viruet
Screenwriter ....Rafael Rivera-Viruet
Production Co ....Terramax Entertainment
Distributor ....Terramax Entertainment

History Told On Walls (Documentary 1991)
Director ....Pedro Celedon
Producer ....Pía Dominguez
Screenwriter ....Pedro Celedon
DP ....DeWayne Rude
Distributor ....Barefoot Productions

Home Front (Documentary 2001)
Director ....Jennifer Maytorena Taylor
Producer ....Jennifer Maytorena Taylor
Screenwriter ....Jennifer Maytorena Taylor
DP ....Sophie Constantinou
Production Co. ....Specific Pictures
Distributor ....KQED-TV

Home Is the Struggle (Documentary 1991)
Director ....Marta Bautis
Distributor ....Women Make Movies

Homeless Diaries (Documentary 1996)
Director ....Frances Negrón-Muntaner
Producer ....Frances Negrón-Muntaner
Screenwriter ....Frances Negrón-Muntaner
DP ....Dan Moyer
Distributor ....Polymorphous Pictures, Inc.

The Hunt for Pancho Villa (Documentary 1993)
Director ....Hector Galán
Producer ....Paul Espinosa, Hector Galán
Screenwriter ....Paul Espinosa, Hector Galán
Narrator.....................Linda Hunt
DP ....Lee Daniel
Production Co. ....Galán Productions
Distributor ....PBS

I Am Joaquin (Documentary 1969)
Director ....Luis Valdez
Screenwriter ....Corky Gonzales

The Idea We Live In (La Idea Que Habitamos) (Experimental 1991)
Director ....Pilar Rodriguez-Aranda
Producer ....Pilar Rodriguez-Aranda
Production Co. ....Anarcafilms
Distributor ....Anarcafilms

I Love My Freedom, I Love My Texas (Documentary 2002)

Director ....Hector Galán
Producer ....Hector Galán
Screenwriter ....Hector Galán
DP ....Dieter Kaupp, Gustavo Aguilar
Production Co. ....Galán Productions
Distributor ....Galán Productions

Impresario (Documentary 2002)

Director ....Eren McGinnis, Ari Palos
Production Co. ....Dos Vatos Productions
Distributor ....PBS

Inner Heart (Documentary 2003)

Director ....Jackie Gonzalez-Carlos

Innermotion: The Dance of Incest (Documentary 2003)

Director ....Sylvie Rokab
Producer ....Sylvie Rokab
Co-producer...............Cristiana Carron
DP. ....Sylvie Rokab
Production Co. ....In the Daylight Productions, Inc

In Search of Aztlan (Documentary 2002)

Producer ....Alfonso Espinosa

In Search of My Cultural Heroes (Documentary 2003)

Producer ....Yvette Vega

In The Shadow of Love (Documentary 1988)

Director ....Paul Espinosa
Producer ....Paul Espinosa
Screenwriter ....Paul Espinosa
Distributor ....PBS

In The Wake of the Flood (Documentary)

Director ....J. Carlos Peinado
Producer ....J. Carlos Peinado, Daphne Ross

Jasper Johns: Ideas in Paint (Documentary 1989)

Director ....Rick Tejada-Flores
Producer ....Rick Tejada-Flores
Cast...........................Jasper Johns

My Journey Home (Documentary 2004)

Director ....Renee Tajima-Pena,
                            Lourdes Portillo
Producer ....Renee Tajima-Pena (Exec.),
                            Jeff Bieber (Exec.),
                            Evangeline Griego (Line)
DP ....Vicente Franco, Jonathan Schell
Production Co. ....WETA-TV
Distributor ....PBS

Julia, Todo De Mi (Julia: All in Me) (Documentary 2002)

Director ....Ivonne Belen
Producer ....Ileana Ciena
Cast...........................Angelica Aragón, Nydia Caro,
                            Ileana Ciena
DP ....Jochi Melero
Production Co. ....Paradiso Films

Kentucky Theater (Documentary 2003)

Director ....Ari Palos
Producer ....Eren McGinnis
Production Co ....Dos Vatos Productions

KordaVision, Una Revelación Cubana (A Cuban Revelation) (Documentary 2004)

Director ....Hector Cruz Sandoval

Lalo Guerrero: The Original Chicano (Documentary 2005)

Director ....Nancy de Los Santos, Dan Guerrero
Producer ....Nancy de Los Santos, Dan Guerrero
Screenwriter ....Nancy de Los Santos, Dan Guerrero
Production Co ....Original Chicano Productions
Distributor ....Latino Public Broadcasting

La Lupe: A Mirror of the Time (Documentary 2005)

Director ....Ela Troyano
Producer ....Ela Troyano
Production Co. ....ITVS, PBS, LPB

The Last Conquistador (Documentary 2005)

Director ....Cristina Ibarra, John Valadez
Producer ....Cristina Ibarra, John Valadez
Production Co. ....Kitchen Sink
Distributor ....PBS, LPB

Live Nude Girls Unite! (Documentary 2000)
Director ....Vicky Funari, Julia Query
Producer ....John Montoya
Screenwriter ....Vicky Funari, Julia Query
DP ....Vicky Funari, Sarah Kennedy,
                            John Montoya, Julia Query
Cast...........................Stephanie Batey, Julia Query, Dr.
                            Joyce Wallace
Production Co. ....Constant Communication,
                            Farm Fresh Films, Lazy Eight,
                            Namesis Vigilante Productions,
                            Query Productions, Pix + Stone
Distributor ....First Run Features

Living in Democracy Hawaiian Style (Documentary 2005)
Director ....Jennifer Maytorena Taylor
Producer ....Mari Tuti Baker
Screenwriter ....Mari Tuti Baker

The Lemon Grove Incident (Documentary 1986)
Director ....Frank Christopher
Producer ....Paul Espinosa
Screenwriter ....Paul Espinosa
DP ....Russell Carpenter
Distributor ....PBS

The Lovely Faces of Tite Curet (Documentary 2003)
Producer ....Frances Lausell
Director ....Sonia Fritz
Screenwriter ....Sonia Fritz, Chuco Quintero
Cast...........................Tite Curet, Cheo Feliciano,
                            Ruben Blades
Production Co. ....Isla Films

Una Lucha Por Mi Pueblo (Documentary 1990)
Director ....Federico Antonio Reade

Made In L.A (Documentary 2005)
Director ....Almudena Carracedo
Producer ....Almudena Carracedo,
                            Robert Bahar
DP ....Almudena Carracedo

Las Madres: The Mothers of Plaza de Mayo (Documentary 1986)
Director ....Lourdes Portillo,
                            Susana Blaustein Muñoz
Producer ....Lourdes Portillo (Co.),
                            Susana Blaustein Muñoz
Screenwriter ....Lourdes Portillo
Distributor ....First Run Features

Maid in America (Documentary 2004)
Director ....Anayansi Prado
Producer ....Anayansi Prado, Kevin Leadingham
DP ....Kevin Leadingham
Production Co. ....Impacto Films
Distributor ....Women Make Movies

Maof: A Foundation's Vision & Mission (Documentary 2003)
Director ....Alison Sotomayor
Producer ....Alison Sotomayor

Maria Del Mar Bonet (Documentary 2003)
Director ....Margarita Ramon

Matters of Race: The Divide (Documentary 2003)
Director ....John Valadez
Producer ....John Valadez
Production Co. ....Roja Productions
Distributor ....PBS

Mbamba (Documentary 1989)
Director ....Olivia Chumacero

The Meaning of the Interval (Documentary 1987)
Director ....Edín Velez

Meta Mayan II (Documentary 1981)
Director ....Edín Velez

Mi Hijo Mi Hija Amor (Documentary)
Director ....Jose Luis Partida

Los Mineros (Documentary 1990)
Director ....Hector Galán, Paul Espinosa
Screenwriter ....Paul Espinosa
Production Co. ....American Experience
Distributor ....PBS

Minority Perspective (Audience Talk 1996)
Director ....Frank Borres
Producer ....Frank Borres
Screenwriter ....Frank Borres
Production Co. ....American View Productions
Distributor ....Connecticut Public Broadcasting

Mi Otro Yo (Documentary 1988)
Director ....Phillip Brookman, Amy Brookman

Mirrors of the Heart (Documentary 1993)
Director ....Lourdes Portillo
Producer ....Lourdes Portillo
Screenwriter ....Lourdes Portillo
Production Co. ....WGBH
Distributor ....PBS

Mission San Jose (Documentary 1996)
Director ....Roger Castillo
Producer ....Roger Castillo
Screenwriter ....Roger Castillo
Distributor ....Maverick International

The Mother: Mitos Maternos (Documentary 1994)
Director ....Marta Bautis
Distributor ....Women Make Movies

De Mujer a Mujer (Documentary 1993)
Director ....Beverley Sanchez-Padilla
Production Co. ....Indigena Productions

Nasci Mulher Negra (Documentary 1999)
Director ....Maria Luisa Mendoca
Producer ....Kit Miller,
　　　　　　　　　　　　　Rick Tejada-Flores (Exec.)
Cast...........................Benedita da Silva, Zeze Mota,
　　　　　　　　　　　　　Bárbara Santos

Neighbors: The US and Mexico (Documentary 1985)
Director ....Jesús Salvador Treviño,
　　　　　　　　　　　　　Jose Luis Ruiz
Producer ....Jesús Salvador Treviño,
　　　　　　　　　　　　　Jose Luis Ruiz
Screenwriter ....Jesús Salvador Treviño
DP ....Jose Luis Ruiz
Cast...........................Luis R. Torres
Production Co. ....Interamerican Satellite
Distributor ....The Cinema Guild

The New Americans (Documentary Series 2004)
Director ....Susana Aikin, Carlos Aparicio,
　　　　　　　　　　　　　Steve James, Indu Krishnan,
　　　　　　　　　　　　　Gordon Quinn, Rene Tajima-Pena
Exec. Producer ....Steve James, Gordon Quinn,
Series Producer ....Gita Saedi
Segment Producers ....Evangeline Griego, Fennel Doremus
DP ....Carlos Aparicio, Roddy Blelloch,
　　　　　　　　　　　　　Vicente Franco, Peter Gilbert,
　　　　　　　　　　　　　Steve James, Danna Kupper,
　　　　　　　　　　　　　Gordon Quinn, Scott Sinkler,
　　　　　　　　　　　　　Viren Thambidorai
Production Co. ....Kartmenquin Films
Distributor ....PBS

The New Tijuana (Documentary 1990)
Producer ....Paul Espinosa
Screenwriter ....Paul Espinosa
Production Co. ....San Diego State University, PBS

Nicaragua: The Children Are Waiting (Documentary 2002)
Director ....Marta Noemi Bautís
Producer ....Marta Noemi Bautís
Screenwriter ....Marta Noemi Bautís
DP ....Marta Noemi Bautís

No Porque Lo Diga Fidel Castro (Documentary 1988)
Director ....Graciela Sanchez
Distributor ....Frameline

Nuyorican Dream (Documentary 1999)
Director ....Laurie Coyller
Producer ....Katy Chevigny, Laurie Coyller,
　　　　　　　　　　　　　Julia Pimsleur
DP ....Aurora Aguero
Production Co. ....Big Mouth Productions

La Ofrenda: The Days of the Dead (Documentary 1988)
Director ....Lourdes Portillo
Producer ....Lourdes Portillo (Co.)
Screenwriter ....Lourdes Portillo

La Onda Chicana (Documentary 1976)
Director ....Efraín Gutierrez

Paño Arte: Images from Inside (Documentary 1997)
Director ....Evangeline Griego
Producer ....Evangeline Griego
DP ....Robert Diaz Leroy
Production Co ....About Time Productions
Distributor ....About Time Distribution

Papapapa (Documentary 1997)
Director ....Alex Rivera
Producer ....Alex Rivera

The Paris Review: Early Chapters (Documentary 2001)
Director ....Paula Heredia

Passages (Documentary 2000)
Director ....Gabriela Bohm
Producer ....Gabriela Bohm
Production Co. ....Bohm Productions

Paulina (Documentary 1998)
Director ....Vicky Funari
Producer ....Vicky Funari,
                         Jennifer Maytorena Taylor
Screenwriter ....Vicky Funari,
                         Jennifer Maytorena Taylor,
                         Paulina Cruz Suarez
DP ....Marie Cristine Camus
Distributor ....First Run Pictures,
                         Icarus International Sales,
                         Salsa Distribution

Perfiles En El Tiempo (Documentary 1996)
Director ....Emilia Anguita Huerta
Producer ....Emilia Anguita Huerta

Playgrounds of Our Past (Documentary 1997)
Director ....Frank Borres
Producer ....Frank Borres
Screenwriter ....Frank Borres
Production Co. ....American View Productions
Distributor ....Connecticut Public Broadcasting

Power Mapping (Documentary 1998)
Director ....Margarita Ramon

Promises (Documentary 2001)
Director ....Carlos Bolado, B.Z Goldberg,
                         Justine Shapiro
Producer ....B.Z Goldberg, Justine Shapiro
DP ....Alan Buchbinder, Yoram Millo
Production Co. ....Promises Film Project
Distributor ....Cinemien, Solaris Distribution

Puerto Rican I.D (Documentary 1996)
Director ....Frances Negrón-Muntaner
Producer ....Frances Negrón-Muntaner
Screenwriter ....Frances Negrón-Muntaner
DP ....Dan Moyer
Production Co. ....ITVS
Distributor ....ITVS

Puerto Rican Passages (Documentary 1993)
Director ....Frank Borres
Producer ....Frank Borres
Screenwriter ....Frank Borres
Production Co. ....American View Productions
Distributor ....American Programming Service

Qoyllur Ritty: Mistery and Legend (Documentary 1999)
Director ....Olga Arana
Producer ....Olga Arana
Production Co. ....ABR Productions
Distributor ....Antena 3 Peru

R3 (Documentary 2003)
Director ....Betty Thomas
Producer ....Jonathan Prince
Screenwriter ....Peter Murrieta
Cast..........................Joseph Lawrence, Broke Totman
Production Co. ....Revolution Studios
Distributor ....Columbia Pictures

Race Is the Place (Documentary 2005)
Director ....Ray Telles, Rick Tejada-Flores
Producer ....Ray Telles, Rick Tejada Flores
Screenwriter ....Ray Telles, Rick Tejada Flores
DP ....Bobby Shepard, Vicente Franco,
                         Emiko Omori
Cast..........................Lalo Guerrero, Culture Clash,
                         Amiri Baraka, Mayda del Valle,
                         Haunani Kay Trask, WIllie Perdomo
Production Co. ....Paradigm Productions,
                         KERA Dallas

Rag Top Ralph (Documentary 1984)
Director ....Juan Garza

Raza Si, Guerra No (Documentary 2003)
Producer ....Sonny Richard E. Espinoza

La Raza Unida (Documentary 1972)
Director ....Jesús Salvador Treviño
Producer ....Jesús Salvador Treviño
Screenwriter ....Jesús Salvador Treviño
DP ....Richard B. Davies
Production Co. ....KCET
Distributor ....The Cinema Guild

Reaching Out to Lesbian, Gay, Bisexual Youth (Documentary 1996)
Director ....Sylvie Rokab
Producer ....Sylvie Rokab
Distributor ....Cinema Guild

Rediscovering a Lost World (Documentary 1996)
Director ....Manny Santos
Producer ....Manny Santos
Distributor ....PBS

Regarding Vieques (Documentary 2005)
Director ....Frances Negrón-Muntaner
Producer ....Frances Negrón-Muntaner
Screenwriter ....Frances Negrón-Muntaner
DP ....David Gonzalez,
                                  Frances Negrón-Muntaner
Production Co. ....Polymorphous Pictures, Inc.

Remember the Alamo (Documentary 2004)
Director ....Joseph Tovares
Producer ....Joseph Tovares
Screenwriter ....Joseph Tovares
Production Co. ....WGBH
Distributor ....PBS

Requiem 29 (Documentary 1971)
Director ....David Garcia
Production Co. ....Moctezuma Esparza Film

Ringl and Pit (Documentary 1995)
Director ....Juan Mandelbaum
Cast...........................Ellen Auerbach, Grete Stem
Distributor ....First Run Features, Icarus Films

Rivera in America (Documentary)
Director ....Rick Tejada-Flores

Rumble Over West Side Story (Documentary 2001)
Director ....Maria Agui Carter
Producer ....Maria Agui Carter
Screenwriter ....Maria Agui Carter
Distributor ....PBS

Salve A Ubanda (Hail Ubanda) (Documentary 1987)
Director ....Jose Araujo
Producer ....Jose Araujo
Screenwriter ....Jose Araujo

San Juan - Ciudad De Todos (Documentary 2000)
Director ....Miguel Zallas Garcia
Producer ....Rafael Rivera-Viruet
Screenwriter ....Ramon Almodovar,
                                  Rafael Rivera-Viruet
Production Co. ....Tropical Vision
                                  Entertainment Group
Distributor ....Tropical Vision
                                  Entertainment Group

Santeros (Documentary 1986)
Director ....Ray Telles
Producer ....Ray Telles
Screenwriter ....Ray Telles
DP ....Mark Adler
Production Co. ....Teresita Productions
Distributor ....Tapestry International

School Goods Enough for All (Documentary 1998)
Director ....Frank Borres
Producer ....Frank Borres
Screenwriter ....Frank Borres
Production Co. ....American View Productions
Distributor ....Connecticut Public Broadcasting

The Secret Curl (Documentary 1993)
Screenwriter ....Ana Marie de la Peña Portela

Señorita Extraviada (Missing Young Woman) (Documentary 2001)
Director ....Lourdes Portillo
Producer ....Gemma Cubero del Barrio
DP ....Kyle Kibbe
Production Co. ....Xochitl Films
Distributor ....Balcony Releasing,
                                  Women Make Movies

hispanic american films

September 11 - segment "Mexico"- (2002)
Director ....Alejandro González Iñarritú
Producer ....Alejandro González Iñarritú
Screenwriter ....Alejandro González Iñarritú
Production Co. ....CIH Shorts, Zeta Film
Distributor ....Bac Films, BIM

The Sequoia Presidential Yacht (Documentary 2002)
Director ....Ilse Fernandez

La Sierra (Documentary 2004)
Director ....Scott Dalton, Margarita Martinez
Producer ....Margarita Martinez, Scott Dalton

Silent Crisis: Diabetes Among Us (Documentary 2002)
Director ....A. P. Gonzalez, Erma Elzy-Jones
Producer ....Deirdre Dix Hunt
Cast...........................Debbie Allen, Del Atkins
DP ....Jack Rayzor
Production Co. ....Discovery Health, Edge of Dream Productions, USA Pictures

Si Se Puede (Documentary 1973)
Director ....Rick Tejada-Flores

Soldados: Chicanos in Vietnam (Documentary 2002)
Director ....Charley Trujillo, Sonya Rhee
Producer ....Sonya Rhee
DP ....Laure Sullivan
Distributor ....PBS

Sometimes My Feet Go Numb (Documentary 1994)
Director ....Lourdes Portillo
Producer ....Lourdes Portillo

Somos (Documentary 2002-2004)
Director ....María Bures
Producer ....María Bures
Distributor ....PBS

Songs of the Homeland (Documentary 1995)
Producer ....Hector Galán
Cast...........................Freddy Fender
Distributor ....Galán Inc.

Split Decision (Documentary 2001)
Director ....Marcy Garriot
Producer ....Roman Morales
Cast...........................Chuy Chávez
Production Co. ....La Sonrisa Productions, Inc.
Distributor ....First Run Features

Tango: Duel or Dance (Documentary 2000)
Director ....Maria Agui Carter
Producer ....Maria Agui Carter
Screenwriter ....Maria Agui Carter
Distributor ....PBS

That Old Gang of Mine (Documentary 1996)
Director ....Carlos de Jesus
Producer ....Carlos de Jesus

They Speak of Hope: The Church in El Salvador (Documentary 1986)
Director ....Ferm Hagadom
Producer ....Ferm Hagadom
Production Co. ....Esperanza Films Inc., Lutheran World Ministries
Distributor ....Lutheran World Ministries

Through The Eyes of Larry Harlow - El Judio Maravilloso (Documentary 1998)
Director ....Orlando Guzman
Producer ....Rafael Rivera-Viruet
Screenwriter ....Rafael Rivera-Viruet
Cast...........................Larry Harlow
Production Co. ....Tropical Visions Entertainment Group
Distributor ....Tropical Visions Entertainment Group

Tibes Ceremonial Park (Documentary 2004)
Producer ....Frances Lausell
Director ....Sonia Fritz
Producer ....Frances Lausell
Screenwriter ....Sonia Fritz, Stella Soto
DP ....Jaime Costas
Production Co. ....Isla Films

True Hearted Vixens (Documentary 2001)
Director ....Mylene Moreno
Producer ....Mylene Moreno
Screenwriter ....Mylene Moreno
DP ....Jennifer Lane
Production Co. ....ITVS, Souvenir Pictures Inc.

El Turista Soy: Luis Agujeta Y
Su Cante Gitano (Documentary 2003)
Producer ....Trina Bardusco
Distributor ....HBO Latino

Twenty Years...y que? (Documentary 1990)
Director ....Nancy de los Santos,
    Alberto Dominguez
Producer ....Nancy de los Santos,
    Alberto Dominguez
Screenwriter ....Nancy de los Santos
Production Co ....Chicano Moratorium USA
Distributor ....Chicano Moratorium USA

Uneasy Neighbors (Documentary 1989)
Director ....Paul Espinosa
Screenwriter ....Paul Espinosa
Production Co. ....Paul Espinosa
Distributor ....PBS

The Unexpected Turn of Jim Sagel
(Documentary 2003)
Director ....Pilar Rodriguez-Aranda
Producer ....Pilar Rodriguez-Aranda
Production Co. ....Anarcafilms
Distributor ....Anarcafilms

Unprecedented: The 2000 Presidential Election
(Documentary 2002)
Director ....Richard Ray Perez, Joan Sekler
Producer ....Richard Ray Perez
Screenwriter ....William Haugse,
    Richard Ray Perez, Joan Sekler
DP ....Rebecca Flores, Brian Long,
    Richard Ray Perez
Cast...........................Peter Coyote, Ed Baker, Jeb Bush
Production Co. ....Alternavision Films, Los Angeles
    Independent Media Center

Unwanted (Documentary 1975)
Director ....Jose Luis Ruiz

The U.S.-Mexican War 1846-1848
(Documentary Series 1998)
Director ....Ginny Martin
Producer ....Paul Espinosa, Andrea Boardman,
    Sylvia Komatsu, Robert Tranchin
Screenwriter ....Robert Trachin
DP ....Ginny Martin, Allen Moore,
    Bill Zarchy
Cast...........................Antonia Castañeda,
    Israel Cavazos Garzas
Production Co. ....KERA Dallas
Distributor ....PBS

Vaquero: The Forgotten Cowboy (Documentary
1988)
Director ....Hector Galán
Producer ....Hector Galán
Screenwriter ....Hector Galán
Production Co. ....Galán Productions
Distributor ....PBS

Vayan Con Diós (Documentary)
Director ....Sylvia Morales
Producer ....Sylvia Morales
Screenwriter ....Sylvia Morales
Production Co. ....KCET
Distributor ....KCET

Visiones: Latino and Art Culture (Documentary
Series 2004)
Director ....Hector Galán
Producer ....Ray Santistéban (Senior),
    Hector Galán (Exec.),
    Paul Espinosa, John Valdez,
    Natatsha Estébanez, Alex Rivera,
    Rick Leal, David Martinez,
    Gustavo Vazques, Yvette Pita
DP ....Tom Taylor, Gustavo Aguilar
Production Co. ....Galán Productions,
    National Association of
    Latino Arts and Culture
Distributor ....PBS, Galán Inc.

Viva 16! (Documentary 1994)
Director ....Valentin Aguirre, Augie Robles

Voices from Texas (Documentary 2003)
Director ....Ray Santisteban
Producer ....Ray Santisteban, Ray Flores (Co.)
Distributor ....ITVS

Watercolors - Cezanne's Still Life
(Documentary 2004)
Director ....Pedro Celedon
Producer ....Pía Dominguez
DP ....DuWayne Rude

Weather Underground (Documentary 2003)
Director ....Sam Green, Bill Siegel
Producer ....Carrie Lozano, Sam Green, Bill
    Siegel, Marc Smolowitz
DP ....Andy Black, Federico Salsano
Production Co. ....Free History Project
Distributor ....Shadow Distribution

139

When You Think of Mexico: Commercial Images of Mexico (Documentary 1986)
Director ....Yolanda Lopez

Wilkins - Pionero Del Rock En Español (Documentary 2003)
Director ....Rafael Rivera-Viruet
Producer ....Rafael Rivera-Viruet
Production Co ....Terramax Entertainment
Distributor ....Terramax Entertainment

Yo Soy (I Am) (Documentary 1985)
Director ....Jesús Salvador Treviño,
                             Jose Luis Ruiz
Producer ....Jesús Salvador Treviño,
                             Jose Luis Ruiz
Screenwriter ....Jesús Salvador Treviño
DP ....Jose Luis Ruiz
Cast...........................Daniel Valdez
Production Co. ....Interamerican Satellite
Distributor ....The Cinema Guild

Yo Soy Chicano (Documentary 1972)
Director ....Barry Nyle
Producer ....Jesús Salvador Treviño
Screenwriter ....Jesús Salvador Treviño
DP ....Barry Nyle
Cast...........................Victor Millan
Production Co. ....KCET
Distributor ....The Cinema Guild

You're On the Air (Documentary 1995)
Director ....Frank Borres
Production Co ....American View Productions
Distributor ....Connecticut Public Broadcasting

The Zoot Suit Riots (Documentary 2002)
Director ....Joseph Tovares
DP ....Michael Chin
Cast...........................Hector Elizondo
Distributor ....PBS

*Note: The following section includes U.S. narrative films with **Latinos in key creative positions.***

21 Grams (2003)
Director ....Alejandro González Iñarritú
Producer ....Alejandro González Iñarritú,
     Robert Salerno
Screenwriter ....Guillermo Arriaga
DP ....Rodrigo Pietro
Cast...........................Sean Penn, Naomi Watts,
     Danny Huston
Production Co. ....This Is That Productions,
     Y Productions
Distributor ....Focus Features

The Ambulance (1990)
Director ....Larry Cohen
Producer ....Moctesuma Esparza, Robert Katz
Screenwriter ....Larry Cohen

Anaconda (1997)
Director ....Luis Llosa
Producer ....Verna Harrah, Carole Little,
     Leonard Rabinowitz
Screenwriter ....Hans Bauer, Jim Cash,
     Jack Epps Jr.

Angel Eyes (2001)
Director ....Luis Mandoki
Producer ....Bruce Berman, Mark Canton,
     Elie Samaha
Screenwriter ....Gerald Di Pego

The Assasination of Richard Nixon (2004)
Director ....Nils Mueller
Producer ....Alfonso Cuarón, Jorge Vergara
Screenwriter ....Niels Mueller, Kevin Kennedy

The Avenging Angel (1995)
Director ....Craig. R Baxley
Producer ....Jay Benson, Tom Berenger,
     Patrick Curtis,
     Moctesuma Esparza,
     Robert Katz, Heather Lowe,
     Dennis Nemec
Screenwriter ....Dennis Nemec

Axel and Antoinette: The Secret Love Story (2005)
Producer ....Julio Bove, Luis Mandoki
Screenwriter ....Evelyn Farr
Production Co. ....Bosco Entertainment,
     Mandolin Entertainment

The Big Bounce (2004)
Director ....George Armitage
Producer ....George Armitage, Steve Bing,
     Jorge Saralegui
Screenwriter ....Sebastian Gutierrez

Bird (1988)
Director ....Clint Eastwood
Producer ....Clint Eastwood,
     David Valdes (Exec.)
Screenwriter ....Joel Oliansky

Blade II (2002)
Director ....Guillermo del Toro
Producer ....Peter Frankfurt, Patrick J. Palmer,
     Wesley Snipes
Screenwriter ....David S. Goyer

Born Yesterday (1993)
Director ....Luis Mandoki
Producer ....D. Constantine Conte
Screenwriter ....Douglas McGrath

Break of Dawn (1988)
Director ....Isaac Artenstein
Producer ....Jude Pauline Eberhard
Screenwriter ....Isaac Artenstein

Butter (1998)
Director ....Peter Gathings Bunche
Producer ....Moctesuma Esparza (Exec.),
     Julian Fowles
Screenwriter ....Peter Gathings Bunche

The Cell (2000)
Director ....Tarsem Singh.
Producer ....Julio Caro
Screenwriter ....Mark Protosevich
Cast...........................Jennifer Lopez

Chuck & Buck (2000)
Director ....Miguel Arteta
Producer ....Matthew Greenfield
Screenwriter ....Mike White

Club Dread (2004)
Director ....Jay Chandrasekhar
Producer ....Richard Perello, Lance Hool (Exec.)
Screenwriter ....Broken Lizard

Crazy in Alabama (1999)
Director ....**Antonio Banderas**
Producer ....Linda Goldstein Knowlton, Debra
                             Hill, Diane Sillas Issacs, Meir Teper
Screenwriter ....Mark Childress

Crime Zone (1988)
Director ....**Luis Llosa**
Producer ....**Luis Llosa**
Screenwriter ....Daryl Haney

Crocodile Dundee in Los Angeles (2001)
Director ....Simon Wincer
Producer ....Paul Hogan, **Lance Hool**
Screenwriter ....Paul Hogan

Crossover Dreams (1985)
Director ....**Leon Ichaso**
Producer ....**Manuel Arce**
Screenwriter ....**Manuel Arce, Leon Ichaso**

Daybreak (1993)
Director ....Stephen Tolkin
Producer ....John Bard Manulis,
                             Kathryn F. Galán (Exec.)
Screenwriter ....Stephen Tolkin

The Dead Pool (1988)
Director ....Buddy Van Horn
Producer ....**David Valdes**
Screenwriter ....Steve Sharon

Death and the Compass (1992)
Director ....Alex Cox
Producer ....Karl Braun, **Lorenzo O' Brien**
Screenwriter ....**Jorge Luis Borges**, Alex Cox

Eight Hundred Leagues Down The Amazon (1993)
Director ....**Luis Llosa**
Producer ....**Luis Llosa**
Screenwriter ....Jackson Barr, Laura Schiff

Elvis Is Alive! I Swear I Saw Him Eating Ding Dongs Outside The Piggly Wiggly's (1988)
Director ....**Robert Diaz Leroy**
Producer ....**Al Gomez**
Screenwriter ....**Robert Diaz Leroy**
Cast...........................Gina Bernstein, Vicki Lawrence,
                             Rip Taylor

Faces of Fear (2001)
Director ....**Rick Telles**
Producer ....**Cris Abrego, Roberto Cardenas**
Screenwriter ....James Eagan, Martin Kunert,
                             Eric Manes

The Faculty (1998)
Director ....**Robert Rodriguez**
Producer ....**Elizabeth Avellan**,
                             Robert Rodriguez
Screenwriter ....Kevin Williamson

Flipper (1996)
Director ....Alan Shapiro
Producer ....Robert Florio, Perry Katz,
                             James J. McNamara,
                             Lance Hool (Exec.)
Screenwriter ....Alan Shapiro

Follow Me Home (1995)
Director ....**Peter Bratt**
Producer ....**Benjamin Bratt, Peter Bratt**,
                             Alan Renshaw, **Irene Romero**
Screenwriter ....**Peter Bratt**

Four Rooms (1995)
Director ....Allison Anders, Alexandre Rockwell,
                             Robert Rodriguez,
                             Quentin Tarantino
Producer ....Lawrence Bender
Screenwriter ....Allison Anders, Alexandre Rockwell,
                             Robert Rodriguez
                             Quentin Tarantino

French Kiss (1995)
Director ....Lawrence Kasdan
Producer ....**Kathryn F. Galán**, Meg Ryan,
                             Eric Fellner, Tim Bevan
Screenwriter ....Adam Brooks

From Dusk Till Dawn (1996)
Director ....**Robert Rodriguez**
Producer ....Gianni Nunnari, Meir Teper
Screenwriter ....Quentin Tarantino

From Dusk Till Dawn 2: Texas Blood Money (1999)
Director ....Scott Spiegel
Producer ....Gianni Nunnari, Meir Teper,
                             Robert Rodriguez (Exec.)
Screenwriter ....Scott Spiegel, Duane Whitaker

From Dusk Till Dawn 3: The Hangman's Daughter (2000)
Director ....P. J. Pesce
Producer ....Michael S. Murphey, Meir Teper,
        Gianni Nunnari,
        Robert Rodriguez (Exec.)
Screenwriter ....**Alvaro Rodriguez**

Full Fathom Five (1990)
Director ....Carl Franklin
Producer ....**Luis Llosa**, Roger Corman
Screenwriter ....Bart Davis

Gangs (1988)
Director ....**Jesús Salvador Treviño**
Producer ....Frank Doelger, Howard Meltzer
Distributor ....CBS Television

Gettysburg (1993)
Director ....Ronald F. Maxwell
Producer ....**Moctesuma Esparza,** Robert Katz
Screenwriter ....Ronald F. Maxwell

Go Fish (1994)
Director ....**Rose Troche**
Producer ....**Rose Troche,** Guinevere Turner
Screenwriter ....**Rose Troche,** Guinevere Turner
DP ....Ann T. Rossetti
Cast..........................Jamita Ajalon, Tracy Kimme,
        Joana Brown
Production Co. ....Can I Watch, Islet, KPVI, Samuel
        Goldwyn Company
Distributor ....Hallmark Home Entertainment,
        Samuel Goldwyn Company

Gods and Generals (2003)
Director ....Ronald F. Maxwell
Producer ....**Moctesuma Esparza** (Exec.),
        Ronald F. Maxwell
Screenwriter ....Ronald F. Maxwell

The Good Girl (2002)
Director ....**Miguel Arteta**
Producer ....Matthew Greenfield
Screenwriter ....Mike White

Great Expectations (1998)
Director ....**Alfonso Cuarón**
Producer ....Art Linson
Screenwriter ....Mitch Glazer

The Green Mile (1999)
Director ....Frank Darabont
Producer ....Frank Darabont, **David Valdes**
Screenwriter ....Frank Darabont

Harry Potter and the Prisoner of Azkaban (2004)
Director ....**Alfonso Cuarón**
Producer ....Chris Columbus, David Heyman,
        Mark Radcliffe
Screenwriter ....Steve Kloves

Heart and Souls (1993)
Director ....Ron Underwood
Producer ....Sean Daniel, Nancy Roberts,
        Cari-Esta Albert
Screenwriter ....Brent Maddock, S.S Wilson,
        Gregory Hansen, Erick Hansen

Hellboy (2004)
Director ....**Guillermo del Toro**
Producer ....Lawrence Gordon, Lloyd Levin,
        Mike Richardson
Screenwriter ....**Guillermo del Toro**

Hellboy 2 (2006)
Director ....**Guillermo del Toro**
Producer ....Lawrence Gordon, Lloyd Levin,
        Mike Richardson
Screenwriter ....Mike Mignola, **Guillermo del Toro**

Heroes Stand Alone (1989)
Director ....Mark Griffiths
Producer ....**Luis Llosa**
Screenwriter ....Thomas McKelvey Cleaver

In the Line of Fire (1993)
Director ....Wolfgang Petersen
Producer ....Jeff Apple, **David Valdes** (Exec.)
Screenwriter ....Jeff Maguire

Introducing Dorothy Dandridge (1999)
Director ....Martha Coolidge
Producer ....Larry Y. Albucher,
        Moctesuma Esparza (Exec.)
Screenwriter ....Shonda Rhimes, Scott Abbott

Jack and Marilyn (2002)
Director ....**Edward James Olmos**
Producer ....Daniel De Liege, Cheryl DuBois,
        Edward James Olmos, Steve Perry
Screenwriter ....Paul Portuguese

Just the Ticket (1999)
Director ....Richard Wenk
Producer ....**Andy Garcia**, Gary Lucchesi
Screenwriter ....Richard Wenk

King of the Jungle (2001)
Director ....Seth Zvi Rosenfeld
Producer ....Scott Macaulay, Robin O'Hara,
                            Bob Potter, **John Leguizamo** (Exec.)
Screenwriter ....Seth Zvi Rosenfeld

Let the Devil Wear Black (1999)
Director ....Stacy Title
Producer ....Matt Salinger,
                            Sergio Aguero (Exec.)
Screenwriter ....Jonathan Penner, Stacy Title

L.I.E (2001)
Director ....**Michael Cuesta**
Producer ....Rene Bastian, **Michael Cuesta,**
                            Linda Moran
Screenwriter ....Stephen M. Ryder, Michael Cuesta,
                            Gerald Cuesta

Like Father Like Son (1987)
Director ....Rod Daniel
Producer ....**David Valdes**, Brian Grazer
Screenwriter ....Steven Bloom, Lorne Cameron,
                            David Hoselton

A Little Princess (1995)
Director ....**Alfonso Cuarón**
Producer ....Mark Johnson
Screenwriter ....Richard LaGravanese,
                            Elizabeth Chandler

Lives in Hazard (1994)
Director ....Susan Todd, Andrew Young
Producer ....**Edward James Olmos**

The Magic Pearl (1997)
Director ....Bob Curtis
Producer ....Carol Corwin, Bob Curtis,
                            Phil Roman (Exec.)
Screenwriter ....Joseph Kleinman,
                            Juliane Klemm

The Maldonado Miracle (2003)
Director ....**Salma Hayek**
Producer ....Paul W. Cooper
Screenwriter ....Susan Aronson, Don Schain,
                            Eve Silverman
Distributor ....Showtime Networks Inc.

The Man From Elysian Fields (2001)
Director ....George Hickenlooper
Producer ....**Andy Garcia**, David Kronemeyer,
                            Andrew Pfeffer, Donald Zuckerman
Screenwriter ....Phillip Jayson Lasker

Man On Fire (2004)
Director ....Tony Scott
Producer ....Lucas Foster, Tony Scott,
                            Lance Hool (Exec.)
Screenwriter ....Brian Helgeland

Il Mare (2006)
Director ....**Alejandro Agresti**
Producer ....Doug Davison, Roy Lee
Screenwriter ....David Auburn
Cast...........................Sandra Bullock, Keanu Reeves
Production Co. ....Vertigo Entertainment
Distributor ....Warner Bros.

McHale's Navy (1997)
Director ....Bryan Spicer
Producer ....Bill Sheinberg, Jon Sheinberg,
                            Sid Sheinberg, **Lance Hool** (Exec.)
Screenwriter ....Peter Crabbe

Message in a Bottle (1999)
Director ....**Luis Mandoki**
Producer ....Kevin Costner, Denise Di Novi,
                            Jim Wilson
Screenwriter ....Gerald Di Pego

Mimic (1997)
Director ....**Guillermo del Toro**
Producer ....Ole Bornedal, B. J. Rack,
                            Bob Weinstein
Screenwriter ....**Guillermo del Toro,**
                            Matthew Robbins

Missing In Action (1984)
Director ....Joseph Zito
Producer ....Yoram Globus, Menahem Golan,
                            Lance Hool
Screenwriter ....**Lance Hool**, James Bruner

Modigliani (2004)
Director ....Mick Davis
Producer ....**Philippe Martinez,**
                            Stephanie Martinez,
                            Marcos Zurinaga (Exec.),
                            Andy Garcia (Exec.)
Screenwriter ....Mick Davis

Monster-in-Law (2005)
Director ....Robert Luketic
Producer ....Chris Bender, Richard Brener,
                              Julio Caro, Magnus Kim,
                              J.C Spink, Paula Weinstein
Screenwriter ....Anya Kochoff,
                              Richard LaGravanese
Cast...........................**Jennifer Lopez,** Jane Fonda,
                              Michael Vartan

New Crime City (1994)
Director ....Jonathan Winfrey
Producer ....Roger Corman, **Luis Llosa**
Screenwriter ....Rob Kerchner, Charles Philip Moore

One Man's Hero (1999)
Director ....**Lance Hool**
Producer ....**Conrad Hool, Lance Hool,**
                              William J. MacDonald
Screenwriter ....Milton S. Gelman

One More Day For Hiroshima (2004)
Director ....**Luis Mandoki**
Producer ....Jan Fantl, Adrian Rudomin,
                              Sam Sleiman
Screenwriter ....Sam Sleiman, Evan Spiliotopoulos

Open Range (2003)
Director ....Kevin Costner
Producer ....**David Valdes,** Kevin Costner,
                              Jake Eberts
Screenwriter ....Lauran Paine, Craig Storper

Options (1988)
Director ....**Camilo Vila**
Producer ....Edgar Bold, Lance Hool
Screenwriter ....John J. Strauss, Edward Decter

The Others (2001)
Director ....**Alejandro Amenábar**
Producer ....**Fernando Bovaria,**
                              Jose Luis Cuerda, Sunmin Park
Screenwriter ....**Alejandro Amenábar**

Perfect Lover (2001)
Director ....**Gabriela Tagliavini**
Producer ....Lauren Moews
Screenwriter ....Gabriela Tagliavini

A Perfect World (1993)
Director ....Clint Eastwood
Producer ....Clint Eastwood, **David Valdes,**
                              Mark Johnson
Screenwriter ....John Lee Hancock

Pink Cadillac (1989)
Director ....Buddy Van Horn
Producer ....**David Valdes**
Screenwriter ....John Eskow

Pure Luck (1991)
Director ....Nadia Tass
Producer ....Sean Daniel, **Lance Hool**
Screenwriter ....Francis Veber

Queen of the Damned (2002)
Director ....Michael Rymer
Producer ....**Jorge Saralegui**
Screenwriter ....Michael Petroni, Scott Abbott

Radioactive Dreams (1985)
Director ....Albert Pyun
Producer ....**Moctesuma Esparza,**
                              H. Frank Dominguez (Exec.)
Screenwriter ....Albert Pyun

Red Planet (2000)
Director ....Antony Hoffman
Producer ....Bruce Berman, Mark Canton,
                              Jorge Saralegui
Screenwriter ....Chuck Pfarrer

The Rookie (1990)
Director ....Clint Eastwood
Producer ....**David Valdes,** Steven Siebert,
                              Howars G. Kasanjian
Screenwriter ....Boaz Yakin, Scot Spiegel

Rough Riders (1997)
Director ....John Milius
Producer ....Allan A. Apone, Tom Berenger,
                              Moctesuma Esparza (Exec.)
Screenwriter ....John Milius, Hugh Wilson

hispanic american films

Selma, Lord, Selma (1999)
Director ....Charles Burnett
Producer ....Christopher Seitz,
Moctesuma Esparza (Exec.),
Robert Katz (Exec.)
Screenwriter ....Rachel West Nelson,
Sheyann Webb

Showtime (2002)
Director ....Tom Dey
Producer ....**Jorge Saralegui**, Jane Rosenthal
Screenwriter ....**Jorge Saralegui** (story),
Keith Sharon, Alfred Gough,
Miles Millar

Sniper (1993)
Director ....**Luis Llosa**
Producer ....Robert L. Rosen
Screenwriter ....Michael Frost Beckner,
Crash Leylan

Spanglish (2004)
Director ....James L. Brooks
Screenplay..................James L. Brooks
Producer ....Julie Ansell, Richard Sakai,
Christy Haubegger (Exec.),
Joan Bradshaw (Exec.)

The Specialist (1994)
Director ....**Luis Llosa**
Producer ....Jerry Weintraub
Screenwriter ....Alexandra Seros

Squanto: A Warrior's Tale (1994)
Director ....Xavier Koller
Producer ....**Kathryn F. Galán**
Screenwriter ....Darlene Craviotto
Distributor ....Buena Vista Pictures

The Stars Fell on Henrietta (1995)
Director ....James Keach
Producer ....**David Valdes**, Clint Eastwood
Screenwriter ....Philip Railsback

Sugar Hill (1994)
Director ....**Leon Ichaso**
Producer ....Marc Abraham, Greg Brown,
Rudy Langlais,
Steven R. McGlothen
Screenwriter ....Barry Michael Cooper

Swing Vote (1999)
Director ....David Anspaugh
Producer ....Richard Brams, Jonathan Littman,
Andy Garcia (Co. Exec.)
Screenwriter ....Ron Bass, Jane Rusconi

The Telephone (1988)
Director ....Rip Torn
Producer ....**Moctesuma Esparza**, Robert Katz
Screenwriter ....Harry Nilsson, Terry Southern

Three Blind Mice (2003)
Director ....Mathias Ledoux
Producer ....**Carolyn Caldera**,
Jean-Luc De Fanti,
Guillaume Godard,
Maryvonne Le Meur,
Mathias Ledoux
Screenwriter ....Mikael Ollivier

The Ties That Bind (2001)
Director ....Tom McLoughlin
Producer ....Tom Berry, Matthew Hastings,
Kelley Feldsott Reynolds,
Andy Garcia (Exec.)
Screenwriter ....**Miguel Tejada-Flores**,
Scott Williams

The Time Machine (2002)
Director ....Simon Weels
Producer ....**David Valdes**, Walter F. Parkes
Screenwriter ....John Logan

To Die Standing (1990)
Director ....Louis Morneau
Producer ....**Luis Llosa**, Roger Corman
Screenwriter ....Roy Grayson Bell, Daryl Haney

Tom and Jerry: The Movie (1992)
Director ....**Phil Roman**
Producer ....**Phil Roman**
Screenwriter ....Dennis Marks

Touched (2005)
Director ....Timothy Scott Bogart
Producer ....**Marvin V. Acuna**, Grazka Taylor
Screenwriter ....Timothy Scott Bogart

Trapped (2002)
Director ....**Luis Mandoki**
Producer ....**Luis Mandoki**, Mimi Polk Gitlin
Screenwriter ....Greg Lles

The Truth About Cats & Dogs (1996)
Director ....Michael Lehmann
Producer ....**Cari-Esta Albert**
Screenwriter ....Audrey Wells

Turbulence (1997)
Director ....Robert Butler
Producer ....**David Valdes,** Martin Ransohoff
Screenwriter ....Jonathan Brett

Two Days (2003)
Director ....Sean McGinly
Producer ....Mohit Ramchandai,
                            Marvin V. Acuna (Exec.)
Screenwriter ....Sean McGinly

Ultra Warrior (1990)
Director ....Augusto Tamayo San Román,
                            Kevin Tent
Producer ....**Luis Llosa**, Mike Elliott
Screenwriter ....Len Jenkin, Dan Kleinman

Unforgiven (1992)
Director ....Clint Eastwood
Producer ....Clint Eastwood,
                            David Valdes (Exec.)
Screenwriter ....David Webb Peoples

Unlawful Passage (1994)
Director ....**Camilo Vila**
Producer ....Tom Broadbridge, Josi W. Konski,
Screenwriter ....Peter L. Dixon

Vanilla Sky (2001)
Director ....Cameron Crowe
Producer ....Cameron Crowe, Tom Cruise,
                            Paula Wagner
Screenwriter ....**Alejandro Amenábar**, Mateo Gil

The Warden (2001)
Director ....Stephen Gyllenhaal
Producer ....**Natalie Chaidez**
Screenwriter ....**Natalie Chaidez**, David Roessell

Watchers III (1994)
Director ....Jeremy Stanford
Producer ....**Luis Llosa**
Screenwriter ....Dean R. Koontz, Michael Palmer

When a Man Loves a Woman (1994)
Director ....**Luis Mandoki**
Producer ....Jon Avnet, Jordan Kerner
Screenwriter ....Ronald Bass, Al Franken

White Hunter Black Heart (1990)
Director ....Clint Eastwood
Producer ....Clint Eastwood,
                            David Valdes (Exec.)
Screenwriter ....Peter Viertel, James Bridges,
                            Burt Kennedy

White Palace (1990)
Director ....**Luis Mandoki**
Producer ....Griffin Dunne, Amy Robinson,
                            Mark Rosemberg
Screenwriter ....Ted Tally, Alvin Sargent

Why Do Fools Fall In Love (1998)
Director ....**Gregory Nava**
Producer ....Paul Hall, Stephen Nemeth
Screenwriter ....Tina Andrews

hispanic american films

National Association of Latino Independent Producers

filmmakers

Note: Names marked with an asterisk (*) indicate a NALIP member. Names marked with two asterisks (**) indicate a NALIP Board of Trustees member. To update and/or submit new information, please email directly to LMRG@nalip.info.

Luis Cady Abarca*
New York, NY 10012
Tel 212-529-3977
Email............................Cadab@aol.com

Carlos Abascal*
HBO Latin America
Sunrise, FL 33323
Tel 954-217-5300
Fax 954-217-5380
Email ....cabascal@hbo-la.com

Bonnie Abaunza
Director of Artist Relations
Amnesty International
Culver City, CA 90232
Tel 310-815-0450
Tel 310-815-0457
Email ....babaunza@yahoo.com
Web ....www.amnesty.org

Media Advocate

Beatriz Acevedo
President
Hip TV
Santa Monica, CA 90401
Tel 310-998-8580
Email ....beatrizacevedo@worldnet.att.net

Damian Acevedo*
Hollywood, CA 90046
Tel 818-481-2979
Email ....reeldamian@mac.com
Web ....www.damiandp.com

Agent: Leslie Alyson, Montana Artists Agency, 323-845-4144, lalyson@montanartists.com

Director of Photography, DIZZEE RASCAL: STAND UP TALL, 2004, Smuggler, Music Video

Director of Photography, FLORSHEIM: COLOR BLIND, 2004, V12, Commercial
Director of Photography, KFC: DOWN HOME, 2004, Smuggler, Commercial
Director of Photography, LA CLIPPERS: ELTON BRAND, 2004, 3rd Eye Filmworks, Commercial

Martin Acevedo*
San Antonio, TX 78230
Email ..macevedo@txlawyerscommittee.org

Stephen Acevedo*
Tallahassee, FL 32304
Email ....Sacevedo@aol.com

Belinda Acosta*
Journalist
Austin Chronicle
Austin, TX 78751
Tel 512-653-3918
Fax 512-458-6910
Email............tveye@austinchronicle.com

John Acosta*
Aventura, FL 33180
Email ....john_direct@hotmail.com

Marvin Acuña*
Manager
Acuña Entertainment
Santa Monica, CA 90404
Tel 310-828-0209
Fax 310-828-0210
Email ....marvin@acunaentertainment.com
Web ....www.acunaentertainment.com

Agent: Skyrzyniarz & Associates, 310-786-876

Producer, HOW DID IT FEEL, 2004, Feature
Producer, TWO DAYS, 2003, Feature

Ricardo Acuña*
Los Angeles, CA 90041
Tel 323-478-1928
Email ......writericardoacuna@yahoo.com

Alejandro Agresti
Agresti Films S.R.L.
Buenos Aires,   Argentina
Tel 5411-4384-5883
Fax 310-247-1111

Agent: Stuart Manashill, UTA,
310-273-6700

Director, IL MARE, 2006, Vertigo
Entertainment, Feature
Director, Producer, Writer, A LESS BAD
WORLD, 2004, Buena Vista International,
Feature
Director of Photography, THE MASTER AND
HIS PUPIL, 2003, Cinemien, Feature
Director, VALENTIN, 2002, Miramax Films,
Feature

Sergio Aguero*
Andale Pictures
Los Angeles, CA 90024
Tel 310-820-2111
Fax 310-207-6308
Email ....saguero@3monkeysla.com

Executive Producer, Y TU MAMÁ TAMBIÉN,
2001, IFC Films, Feature
Executive Producer, LET THE DEVIL WEAR
BLACK, 1999, A-Pix Entertainment,
Feature

Maria Agui-Carter*
Iguana Films
Cambridge, MA 02138
Tel 617-429-1258
Cell 617-429-1258
Email ....iguanafilms@earthlink.net
Web ....www.iguanafilms.com

Producer, REBEL, 2005, Iguana Films,
Documentary
Director, Producer, Writer, COLLEGE TRACK,
2004, PBS/Roundtable Media,
Documentary
Director, Producer, Writer, REALIDADES,
2002, Prentice Hall/Mondi Films,
Documentary

Director, Producer, Writer, EN CONTACTO,
2001, Heinle & Heinle/Video Production
Group, Documentary
Director, Producer, Writer, INTERACCIONES,
2001, Heinle & Heinle/Video Production
Group, Documentary
Director, Producer, Writer, RUMBLE OVER
WEST SIDE STORY, 2001, PBS,
Documentary

Carlos Aguilar*
Ethnic Pictures
Arleta, CA 91331
Email..........angelsoverhavana@msn.com

Claire Aguilar*
Director of Programming
ITVS
San Francisco, CA 94110
Tel 415-356-8383
Fax 415-356-8491
Email ....claire_aguilar@itvs.org

Gustavo Aguilar*
Galan Inc.
Austin, TX 78741
Tel 512-327-1333
Email ....chanfle8@hotmail.com

Corey Aguirre*
Abrazo Productions
Yorba Linda, CA 92887
Tel 714-777-6810
Email ....mareflections@aol.com

Jorge Aguirre*
Maldito Perrito Productions Co.
New York, NY 10002
Tel 212-477-3143
Cell 917-687-2674
Fax 206-350-6573
Email ....mailjorge@earthlink.net

Producer, Writer, CIRCUMCISED CINEMA,
2004-2005, Si TV/Maya Pictures, TV
Series
Producer, THE PERFECT DRESS, 2004,
TLC/Lion Television, TV Series

Director, Producer, HISTORY DETECTIVES, 2003-2004, PBS/Lion Television, TV Series
Director, Producer, Writer, IS MY NEIGHBOR LATINO?, 2002, Latino Public Broadcasting, Interstitial
Producer, A MORE PERFECT UNION, 2001, WNET/MPT, Short
Writer, IF YOU WERE THERE, 2001, Noggin Television, TV Series, Animated
Director, THE ABSENTEE FATHER, 2001, Sundance Channel, Short

Margarita D. Aguirre*

Abrazo Productions
Yorba Linda, CA 92887
Tel 714-777-6810
Email ....mareflections@aol.com

Luis Aira*

Ofrenda Inc.
Los Angeles, CA 90068
Tel 323-851-6145
Fax 323-851-9078
Email ....donna@ofrenda.com
Web ....www.ofrenda.com

Manager: Donna Casey-Aira, 323-851-6145, donna@ofrenda.com

Attorney: Harris Tulchin & Associates, 310-914-7979, entesquire@aol.com

Director, Writer, GIRL IN 3D, 2004, Ofrenda Inc., Feature
Director, IKEA, 2004, Ofrenda Inc., TV Commercial
Director, JOHN KERRY, 2004, Ofrenda Inc., TV Commercial
Director, SEARS, 2004, Ofrenda Inc., TV Commercial
Director, WELLS FARGO, 2004, Ofrenda Inc., TV Commercial
Director, CARL'S JR., 2003, Ofrenda Inc., TV Commercial

Victor Albarran

Marina Del Rey, CA 90272
Tel 310-993-6843

Line Producer, DREAMING OF JULIA, 2003, Arza-Gerard, Feature
Line Producer, MERRY CHRISTMAS, 2002, Lolafilms S.A., Feature
Line Producer, NATALE SUL NILO, 2002, Lolafilms S.A., Feature

Carlos Albert*

Fuerza Films
North Hollywood, CA 91606
Tel 818-764-6534
Cell 818-324-2282
Fax 818-764-6534
Email ....largelatinlead@netscape.net
Web ....www.nowcasting.com/carlosalbert

Agent: Miguel Mueller, Schiowitz, Clay, Ankrum & Ross, 323-463-8355

Actor, ARRESTED DEVELOPMENT, 2004, FOX, TV Series
Actor, BOLD AND THE BEAUTIFUL, 2003-2004, Bell-Phillips TV Productions, TV Series
Actor, THE HANDLER, 2003, Viacom, TV Series
Producer, I NEVER WANT TO WORK FOR JOHN WOO, 2002, Fuerza Films, Short
Director, Producer, THE FULL MIGUEL, 2002, Fuerza Films, Short

Magdalena Albizu*

Brooklyn, NY 11205
Tel 718-622-0083
Cell 646-996-0457
Email ....nubianlatina@msn.com

Production Assistant, EL VACILOR, 2004, Babylegs Entertainment, Feature
Production Assistant, PARTY, 2004, Feature
Editor, ORAL HISTORY PROJECT, 2003-2004, DrDream.com, Documentary
Associate Producer, EXPEXTING BROKEN SHOW, 2001, Posedon Productions, Feature

Felix Alcala
Bastrop, TX 78602

Agent: Susan Sussman, Diverse Talent Group, 310-300-5430

Director, HAWAII, 2004, NBC, TV Series
Director, FLASHPOINT, 2002, Touchstone Television, TV Series
Director, FOR THE PEOPLE, 2002, Lifetime Television, TV Series
Director, HACK, 2002, CBS, TV Series
Director, TAKEN, 2002, Dreamworks, TV Series
Director, THE SHIELD, 2002, Fox Network, TV Series
Director, CSI, 2000, CBS Television, TV Series

Martin Alcala
Simi Valley, CA 93063
Tel 310-369-5868
Email.......handsofwisdom@earthlink.net

Production Accountant, JUSTIN TO KELLY, 2003, J2K Prods., Inc., Feature
Production Accountant, COAL MINER'S STORY, 2002, Touchstone, TV Movie
Supervising Producer, DAWG, 2001, Gold Circle Films, Feature
Production Accountant, INSOMINA, 2001, Warner Bros., Feature

Russell Alexander-Orozco*
About Time Productions
Los Angeles, CA 90026
Tel 323-666-0690
Email ....AboutTimeProd@aol.com
Web ....www.Alexander-Orozco.com

Director, Producer, Writer, THE WALL IN LINCOLN HEIGHTS, 2004-2005, Public Broadcasting, Documentary
Writer, THE "O" TAPES, 2004, RoseWorks, Documentary
Director, Producer, Writer, THE ACCULTURATION INDIGENOUS ART, 2003-2005, Documentary
Writer, Producer, KEEPERS OF THE ARTS, 2002-2005, Cable, TV Documentary
Writer, RESOLUTION, 2002-2004, Feature
Producer, THE WAVE, 2002, Eye Awake Studio, Short

Fabio Alexandre da Silva*
Rio de Janeiro, Rio 22790735 Brazil
Cell..........................55-21-9384-2216
Email ....fabio.alexandre@tvglobo.com.br

Production Manager, TO THE LEFT OF THE FATHER, 1997, Videofilms Production Company, Feature
Production Coordinator, THE CANGACEIRO REVENGE, 1991, TV Globo, TV Episode
Production Coordinator, THE MASTER OF THE WORLD, 1991, TV Globo, TV Soap Opera
Production Coordinator, THE CARRIER, 1990, TV Globo, TV Series

Frank Algarin*
New York, NY 10025
Tel 212-222-9206
Fax 212-222-5429
Email ....batibiri@earthlink.net

Natalia Almada*
Altamura Films
Brooklyn, NY 11211
Tel 718-782-4501
Cell 347-228-8368
Fax 718-782-4501
Email..........nataliaalmada@hotmail.com
Web ....www.altamurafilms.com

Director, Editor, Producer, AL OTRO LADO, 2004, Altamura Films, Documentary
Associate Producer, Editor, REVOLUCIÓN, 2004, El Sueño, Documentary
Director, Director of Photoraphy, Editor Producer, LOST HIGHWAY/TIFT MERRITT EPK, 2003, EPK
Director, Director of Photography, Editor, Producer, ALL WATER HAS A PERFECT MEMORY, 2002, Women Make Movies, Short

Iris Almaraz*
Bella Donna Films
Los Angeles, CA 90063
Cell 213-447-1002
Email ....iris@bdfilms.biz
Web ....www.bdfilms.biz

2nd Assistant Director, ERICA 1988, 2004,
   Short
Director of Photography, Producer, Editor,
   IT'S A PLEASURE, 2004, Short
Editor, JUAN THE BRAVE, 2004, Short
Director, Editor, LA PUTA, 2004, Short
Editor, REFLEXION, 2004, Short
Director, Director of Photography, Editor,
   Producer, UNTITLED, 2004, Short

Raquel Almazan*
La Lucha Arts Company
Sunnyside, NY 11104
Tel 305-527-3395
Fax 718-392-9814
Email ....raquelalmazan@hotmail.com
Web ....www.raquelalmazan.com

Actor, Director, Producer, Writer, DEATH OF
   THE DOLL, 2004, La Lucha Arts Group,
   Short
Actor, ESCAPING JUAREZ, 2004, El Museo
   del Barrio, Stage Play
Acting Instructor, Director, WOMENS PRISON
   PROJECT, 2004, Art Spring Organization,
   Performance
Actor, RED BIRD, 2003, Andromedia
   Productions, Short
Actor, Director, Producer, Writer, SHE
   WOLVES: A HYBRID JOURNEY OF
   WOMEN THROUGH TIME, 2002 - 2005,
   La Lucha Arts Group, Experiemental
Actor, Dramaturgy, ANOMIE, 2001, Artemis
   Arts Organization, Peformance

Maxim Almenas*
Maxim Media Productions
Fort Lee, NJ 07024
Tel 917-714-6708
Cell 917-714-6708
Fax 201-585-1904
Email ....maximediainc@yahoo.com

Director, Producer, Reporter, THE ROOF,
   2004, mun2/Telemundo/NBC, TV Series
Director, Producer, INSIDE-OUT, 2002,
   Maxim Media Productions, Music Video
Writer, Producer, NEWS AT 10, 2002,
   Tribune/WB11, On Air Promotions
Production Assistant, NIGHTLY NEWS, 2001,
   NBC Entertainment, On-Air Promotions
Associate Producer, QUE PASA TV (NYC),
   1997, Que Pasa Productions, TV Series

Diane Almodovar*
Assistant Vice President Latin Music
BMI
Miami, FL 33126
Tel 305-266-3636
Fax 305-266-2442
Email ....dalmodovar@bmi.com
Web ....www.bmi.com

German Alonso*
South El Monte, CA 91733
Tel 626-524-4445
Email...............jalonso11@earthlink.net

Director, Writer, MEXMAN, 2004, Short

Pedro Alonso*
Downey, CA 90241
Tel 562-861-6927
Email...............cybex095@hotmail.com

Carlos Alvarado
Agent
Alvarado Rey Agency
Los Angeles, CA 90048
Tel 323-655-7978
Fax 323-655-2777

Elvia Alvarado*
South Pasadena, CA 91030
Tel 626-441-9016
Email ....ealvar8324@aol.com

Roman Alvarado
President
World Film Magic Distribution Corp.
Hollywood, CA 90038
Tel 323-785-2118
Web ....www.worldfilmmagic.com

*Agent: World Film Magic Distribution
Corp.*

Patricia Alvarado-Nuñez*

La Plaza - WGBH
Boston, MA 02134
Tel 617-300-2289
Email ....patricia_alvarado@wgbh.org
Web ....www.wgbh.org/laplaza

Co-Producer, FIDEL, 2004, WGBH-American
   Experience, Documentary
Producer, PAQUITO D'RIVERA IN STUDIO,
   2004, WGBH-La Plaza, Music Special
Producer, EL TIANTE, 2003, WGBH-La
   Plaza, Documentary
Producer, LAST CHANCE DNA, 2002,
   WGBH-La Plaza, Documentary
Producer, CYRO BATISTA & BEAT THE DON-
   KEY, 2001, WGBH-La Plaza, Music
   Special
Producer, GETTING TO FENWAY, 2001,
   WGBH-La Plaza, Documentary

Louis Alvarez

Center for New American Media
New York, NY 10018
Tel 212-630-9971
Cell ....louis@cnam.com
Web ....www.cnam.com

Director, Producer, Writer, SMALL BALL: A
   LITTLE LEAGUE STORY, 2004,
   Documentary
Co-Executive Producer, Director, SEX:
   FEMALE, 2003, CNAM, Documentary
Co-Executive Producer, Director, PEOPLE
   LIKE US: SOCIAL CLASS IN AMERICA,
   2001, CNAM, TV Documentary
Director, Producer, MOMS, 1999,
   Documentary
Director, VOTE FOR ME: POLITICS IN AMER-
   ICA, 1996, PBS, TV Special

Gina Amador*

Silent Bay Entertainment
Palos Verdes Peninsula, CA 90274
Tel 818-668-2030
Email ....gamador@silentbay.com

Claudia Amaya

Co-Executive Director
The Latin American Cinema Festival of
New York
Bronx, NY 10468
Tel 917-353-2290
Fax 718-228-3540
Email ....claudia@lacinemafe.org
Web ....www.cinemafe.org

Producer, AMY IN THE CAFÉ, 2000, City
   College of New York-City Visions, Short
Producer, BECOMING AMERICAN, 2000,
   City College of New York, Short
Director, Producer, Writer, SILENT DAWN,
   2000, City College of New York,
   Documentary

Alejandro Amenabar

Web ....www.amenabar.com

Composer, Director, Editor, Executive
   Producer, Writer, THE SEA INSIDE, 2004,
   Fine Line Features, Feature
Composer, Director, Orchestrator, Writer, THE
   OTHERS, 2001, Dimension Films, Feature
Writer, VANILLA SKY, 2001, Paramount
   Pictures, Feature
Composer, BUTTERFLY TONGUES, 1999,
   Miramax Films, Feature
Composer, Director, Writer, OPEN YOUR
   EYES, 1997, Artisan Entertainment,
   Feature
Associate Producer, Composer, Director,
   Writer, TESIS, 1996, Tanelorn Films Inc.,
   Feature

Daniel Anaya*

Los Angeles, CA 90042
Tel 323-550-8610
Email ....eyeandi@pacbell.net

Mario Anaya*

Mar Productions
Los Angeles, CA 90010
Tel 213-388-8695
Fax 213-388-4453
Email ....oceanmar@aol.com

Rafael Andreu*
Director of Animation Films
Ramm Animation
Miami Beach, FL 33140
Tel 305-532-1575
Tel 305-742-8420
Email ....randreu@rammprod.com
Web ....www.rammprod.com

Co-Director, Producer, EL DIABLO LLEGO A
   LA HABANA, 2004, 24/30 Companies
   LLC, Short
Director, 100 MILLAS/ HORA, 2003, Sony
   Discos, Music Video
Director, Editor, Producer, SEGUNDO AIRE,
   2003, Various, TV Series, Animated
Director, BONGO, 2002, Sony Tropical, Music
   Video
Director, DEL TREQUE AL CHEQUE, 1999,
   TV Azteca, TV Series, Animated
Co-Producer, MAFALDA, 1996, Various, TV
   Series, Animated

Cruz Angeles*
Brooklyn, NY 11234
Tel 718-252-1272
Email...............cruzangeles@yahoo.com

Director, Editor, Producer, Writer, ABUELA'S
   REVOLT, 2001, Short
Unit Production Manager, ALL ABOUT
   GEORGE, 2000, Short

Emilia Anguita Huerta*
Andromeda Productions, Inc.
Coral Gables, Fl 33146
Tel 305-662-6298
Cell 305-984-4494
Fax 305-447-8579
Email........emilia@andromedavisual.com
Web ....www.andromedavisual.com
Director, Producer, RED BIRD, 2004,
   Andromeda Productions, Short
Director, Producer, SOMBRAS Y BARRO,
   1995, Andromeda Productions, Short
Director, Producer, SÍNTOMA: MADRE -
   NIÑA, 1994, Andromeda/USB, Venezuela,
   Documentary
Director, CARIBE, 1992, Radio Caracas
   Television, TV

Jaime Angulo
Festival Director
Miami Latin Film Festival
Miami, FL 33176
Tel 305-279-1809
Email ....jangulo@hispanicfilm.com
Web ....www.hispanicfilm.com

Kary Antholis*
VP of Development and Production
HBO Films
Santa Monica, CA 90404
Tel 310-382-3255
Web ....www.hbo.com/films

Executive Producer, THE CAPE, 1996, MTM
   Enterprises Inc., TV Series
Director, ONE SURVIVOR REMEMBERS,
   1995, HBO, Documentary
Producer, THE SHADOW OF HATE, 1995,
   Guggenheim Productions, Documentary

Jorge Luis Aquino Calo*
Aquino Calo Picture Inc.
San Juan, PR 00936
Tel 787-466-2948
Email ....jorgeluis@caribe.net

Charles Aragon*
Valley Center, CA 92082
Tel 760-749-2017
Email ....chasaragon@worldnet.att.net

Frank Aragon*
1211 Entertainment
Covina, CA 91722
Tel 323-707-2964
Email.............frankthedirector@aol.com

Actor, Director, Producer, Writer, LAND OF
   1000 DANCES, 2000, Our Ocean Films,
   Feature
Director, Editor, Producer, Writer, MY
   FATHER'S LOVE, 1999, Feature

Oriana Aragon*
Escondido, CA 92025
Tel 760-747-9111
Email ....orianarc@aol.com

Bernat Aragones
Fuerza Films
Hollywood, CA 90028
Tel 323-957-2687
Fax 818-764-6534
Email ....largelatinlead@netscape.net
Web www.my8by10.com

Producer, I NEVER WANT TO WORK FOR
    JOHN WOO, 2002, Documentary
Producer, THE FULL MIGUEL?, 2001,
    Documentary

Alfonso Arambula*
Bay Harbor, FL 33154
Tel 305-761-9862
Email.............ponchingas@hotmail.com

Olga Arana*
Santa Monica, CA 90403
Tel 310-393-8636
Fax 310-899-1598
Email ....oarana@aol.com

Producer, HOW THE GARCIA GIRLS SPENT
    THEIR SUMMER, 2005, Loosely Based
    Pictures, LLC, Feature
Producer, BIOGRAPHY:MARIO VARGAS
    LLOSA, 2003, Sogecable-Canal Plus
    Spain/A&E Mundo, Documentary
Researcher, MOSTLY TRUE STORIES, 2003,
    AFI & Showtime, TV Series
Producer, WHAT REALLY HAPPENED DUR-
    ING THE CUBAN MISSILE CRISIS, 2002,
    AFI & Showtime, Short
Director, Producer, SAVING THE WHITE
    WINGED GUAN, 2000, Antena 3,
    Documentary

Jesse Aranda*
Los Angeles, CA 90028
Tel 310-480-6028
Email ....jar_anda@yahoo.com

Alfonso Arau
Mexico, DF Mexico
Tel 52-55-10-89-06-26
*Agent: Nick Reed, ICM, 310-550-4000,
nreed@icmtalent.com*

Manager: Peter Safran, 310-305-5181

Producer, LOS HIJOS DEL TOPO, 2004,
    Titan Producciones, Feature
Director, Producer, ZAPATA, 2004, Latin Arts
    LLC, Feature
Director, A PAINTED HOUSE, 2003, CBS, TV
    Movie
Director, THE MAGNIFICENT AMBERSONS,
    2002, A&E, TV Movie
Producer, PICKING UP THE PIECES, 2000,
    Cinemax, Feature
Director, A WALK IN THE CLOUDS, 1995,
    20th Century Fox, Feature
Director, LIKE WATER FOR CHOCOLATE,
    1992, Miramax, Feature
Director, TACOS DE ORO, 1985, Hermes
    Films International, Feature

Sergio Arau
Eye On The Ball Films
Los Angeles, CA 90046
Tel 323-935-0634
Fax 323-935-4188
Email ....keepyoureye@aol.com

Director, Writer, A DAY WITHOUT A MEXI-
    CAN, 2004, Alta Vista, Feature
Director, A DAY WITHOUT A MEXICAN,
    1998, Short
Director, EL MURO, 1998, Short

José Araujo*
Tupa Films
Brooklyn, NY 11215
Tel 718-768-0358
Fax 718-832-5766
Email ....araujo@tupafilms.com
Web ....www.tupafilms.com

Director, Producer, Writer, O SERTAO DAS
    MEMÓRIAS/LANDSCAPES OF MEMORY,
    1996, Tupa Films, Feature
Director, Producer, Writer, SALVE A UMBAN-
    DA/HAIL UMBANDA, 1987, Tupa Films,
    Documentary
Director, Producer, Writer, UNA FAMILIA
    MEXICANA 14 AÑOS DESPUES, 1980,
    Tupa Films, Documentary

Leslie Arcia*
Blue Desert Entertainment
Miami, FL 33183
Tel 305-586-8777
Email..................26leslie@bellsouth.net

Production Manager, RED BIRD, 2004, Short
Producer, EL CRIMEN PERFECTO, 2002, Short
Producer, THE SOLDIERS, 2002, Short

Lucero Arellano
Program Manager
California Arts Council
Sacramento, CA 95814
Tel 916-322-6338
Fax 916-322-6575
Email..........larellano@caartscouncil.com
Web ....www.cac.ca.gov

Media Advocate

Roberto Arevalo*
Founder, Director
The Mirror Project
Atlanta, GA 30303
Tel 404-651-0574
Tel 404-651-0574
Cell 404-509-4204
Fax 404-651-0574
Email..............roberto@mirrorproject.org
Web ....www.mirrorproject.org
Producer, UNDERSTANDING VIOLENCE,
    2003, The Mirror Project, Short
Educator, WE GROW UP SO FAST, 2003, The
    Mirror Project, Short
Producer, PORVENIR, 2000, The Mirror
    Project, Short
Producer, WITHOUT MAKE-UP, 1999, The
    Mirror Project, Short

Edward Luis Arguelles*
Trecena Entertainment
Los Angeles, CA 90027
Tel 323-257-1540
Email......................trecena@excite.com

Director, Producer, NOTHING STOPS A BUL-
    LET LIKE A JOB, 2004, Homeboy
    Industries/Trecena Films, PSA
Researcher, FEAR, 2001, MTV Networks, TV
    Series
Director, Producer, XICANO RHAPSODY,
    1998, Trecena Entertainment, Short

Maite Arguelles
Mexico, 04220 Mexico
Web ....www.hartosindios.com

Unit Production Manager, CASA DE LOS
    BABYS, 2003, IFC Films, Feature
Producer, HERE WAS THE ANTHEM, 2002,
    Documentary Short
Art Department Coordinator, THE TIGER OF
    SANTA JULIA, 2002, Videocine, Feature
Production Coordinator, IN THE TIME OF
    BUTTERFLYS, 2001, MGM, Showtime, TV
    Movie
Producer, SANTITOS, 1999, New Yorker
    Films, Feature

Luis Argueta
New York, NY 10027
Tel 212-866-5332
Tel 212-654-4779
Fax 212-316-3926

Director, Executive Producer, Writer,
    COLLECT CALL, 2002, Maya Media Corp.,
    Feature
Director, Writer, EL SILENCIO DE NETO,
    1994, Buenos Dias, Feature
Director, THE COST OF COTTON, 1978,
    PBS, Documentary

Victoria Arias-Fraasa
Film Production Services.com
Los Angeles, CA
Tel 323-937-0633
Cell 323-849-5753
Email..............Victoria@Fraasafilms.com
Web ....www.FilmProductionServices.com

Production Facilities & Services

filmmakers

Eva S. Aridjis
Brooklyn, NY 11215
Tel 718-623-2405
Email ....earidjis@nyc.rr.com

Director, CHILDREN OF THE STREET, 2003,
    Documentary
Director, Editor, Writer, BILLY TWIST, 1998,
    Documentary
Director, TAXIDERMY, 1998, Short

Fidel Arizmendi*
Marina del Rey, CA 90292
Tel 213-248-0581
Email.............................rdna@anet.net

Yareli Arizmendi
Eye On The Ball Films
Los Angeles, CA 90046
Tel 323-935-0634
Fax 323-935-4188
Email ....keepyoureye@aol.com

*Agent: Cunningham-Escott-Selvin-Doherty
Talent Agency, 212-477-6622,
lavoices@cedtalent.com*

*Attorney: Rudy Valner, Esq.,
rvalner@aol.com*

Actor, Writer, A DAY WITHOUT A MEXICAN,
    2004, Televisa Cine, Feature

Eddie T. Arnold**
Vice President Government Affairs
Nielsen Media Research
Washington, DC 20006
Tel.....................202-637-2063 x6124
Email ....eddie.arnold@nielsonmedia.com
Web ......www.nielsenmediaresearch.com

Media Advocate

Marisa Aronoff*
Fox Broadcasting Company
Los Angeles, CA 90036
Tel 310-369-0034
Fax 310-369-4690
Email ....marisaaronoff@yahoo.com

Ishmael Arredondo Henriquez
Codices Entertainment
Hollywood, CA 90078
Tel 323-462-5448
Fax 323-462-5448
Email ....ishmaelo@pacbell.net

Producer, THE SPIRIT OF MY MOTHER,
    2001, Codices Entertainment, Feature
Producer, SIN PAPELES, 1997, Codices
    Entertainment, Short

Guillermo Arriaga
Beverly Hills, CA 90212

*Agent: Shana Eddy, UTA,
310-273-6700*

Associate Producer, Writer, 21 GRAMS,
    2003, Focus Features, Feature
Writer, THE HIRE: POWDER KEG, 2001,
    Films, Short
Associate Producer, AMORES PERROS,
    2000, Lion's Gate Films, Feature

Vanessa Arteaga
Sr. Programming Production Executive
Wellspring Media
New York, NY 10016
Tel 212-686-6777
Email ....varteaga@wellspring.com
Web........................www.wellspring.com

Isaac Artenstein
Cinewest
Hollywood, CA 90028
Tel 323-295-0773
Email ....cinewest@aol.com

Producer, A DAY WITHOUT A MEXICAN,
    2004, Eye on the Ball Films, Feature
Co-Producer, EL GRITO, 2000, Beret Films,
    Feature
Producer, LOVE ALWAYS, 1997, Legacy
    Releasing Corporation, Feature

Miguel Arteta
Flan de Coco Films
Los Angeles, CA 90040
Tel 323-666-8485

Agent: David Lubliner, WMA,
310-859-4000

Director, CRACKING UP, 2004, Fox, TV
   Series
Director, THE GOOD GIRL, 2002, Fox
   Searchlight, Feature
Director, SIX FEET UNDER, 2001, HBO, TV
   Series
Director, CHUCK & BUCK, 2000, Artisan
   Entertainment, Feature
Writer, LIVIN' THING, 1998, Filmmakers
   Forum, Feature
Director, Writer, STAR MAPS, 1997, 20th
   Century Fox, Feature

Janis Astor del Valle*
Gigi Productions
Bronx, NY 10474
Tel 917-529-5290
Tel 646-245-9725
Cell 646-245-9725
Fax 212-219-2058
Email ....gigijanis@aol.com

Director, Writer, A SOUTH BRONX TALE,
   2004, Okay Kurty Productions, Short
Director, Producer, GIRLS TALKIN' TRASH,
   2004, Gigi Productions, Documentary
Performer, Writer, TRANS PLANTATIONS,
   2004, Cynalex Productions, One-Woman
   Play
Peformer, Writer, JANUARY, 2002, Dixon
   Place, Stage Play

Monica Aswani*
New York, NY 10017
Email ....monica@blueelephant.tv

Marilyn R. Atlas*
Manager, Producer
Marilyn Atlas Management
Los Angeles, CA 90048
Tel 310-278-5047
Fax 310-278-5289
Email ....matlas704@yahoo.com

Producer, ADD ME TO THE PARTY, 2005,
   Feature
Producer, SUBURBAN TURBAN, 2005,
   Feature
Producer, REAL WOMEN HAVE CURVES,
   2002, HBO Films, Feature
Producer, A CERTAIN DESIRE, 1986,
   Feature

Bernadette Aulestia
Marketing Executive
HBO Pictures
New York, NY
Tel 212-512-1000
Email ....bernadette.aulestia@hbo.com

Elizabeth Avellan
Los Hooligans Productions
Austin, TX 78701
Web ....www.loshooligans.com

Agent: Robert Newman, ICM,
310-550-4000 ,
rnewman@icmtalent.com

Producer, SIN CITY, 2005, Feature
Producer, THE ADVENTURES OF SHARK
   BOY & LAVA GIRL IN 3-D, 2005,
   Dimension Films, Feature
Producer, SECUESTRO EXPRESS, 2004,
   Feature
Producer, ONCE UPON A TIME IN MEXICO,
   2003, Sony Pictures Entertainment,
   Feature
Producer, SPY KIDS 3D: GAME OVER, 2003,
   Miramax Films, Feature
Producer, SPY KIDS 2: ISLAND OF THE
   LOST DREAMS 2002, 2002, Dimension
   Films, Feature
Producer, SPY KIDS, 2001, Dimension Films,
   Feature
Producer, FROM DUSK TILL DAWN, 1996,
   Miramax Films, Feature
Producer, DESPERADO, 1995, Columbia
   TriStar, Feature
Producer, EL MARIACHI, 1992, Columbia
   Pictures, Feature

Davah Avena
Los Angeles, CA 90027
Tel 323-662-5281
Email ....guavis@hotmail.com
Web ....www.inhotpursuit.com

Director, IN HOT PURSUIT, 2003, Short

Carlos Avila
Echo Park Films
Glendale, CA 91202
Tel 818-773-7846
Fax 818-242-7234
Email ....echoparkfilms@aol.com

Agent: Rhonda Gomez, Broder, Webb,
Chervin, Silbermann Agency,
310-281-3400

Director, Executive Producer, Writer, FOTO
NOVELAS 2: JUNKYARD SAINTS, 2003,
PBS, TV Series
Director, PRICE OF GLORY, 2000, New Line
Cinema, Feature
Director, Executive Producer, Writer, FOTO
NOVELAS: IN THE MIRROR, 1997, PBS,
TV Series
Executive Producer, Writer, LA CARPA, 1993,
American Playhouse, TV Series

Isaac Avila
Aztlan Entertainment M.P
Los Angeles, CA 90015
Tel 213-738-7917
Fax 213-738-7918
Email ......info@aztlanentertainment.com
Web ....www.aztlanentertainment.com

Production Facilities & Services, THE
LOWRIDER SHOW, Charter
Communications, TV Special

Magi Avila*
Los Angeles, CA 90078
Tel 323-833-8761
Email ....magiavila@aol.com
Web ....www.magiavila.com

Attorney: Steve Blalock, 310-497-4168,
swblolock@yahoo.com

Host, KAR PLUS AND MILLER TOYOTA,
2004, The LuCa Group, Infomercial

Host, QUALITY TOYOTA & THEODORA R
FORD, 2004, The LuCa Group,
Informercial
Actress, FANTASIA, 2003, Universal
Pictures, TV Movie
Actress, THE PET, 2003, Try Costal, Feature
Actress, NUEVO CALIFORNIA, 2002, San
Diego Repertory Theatre, Stage Play

Mario Avila
Midcoast Pictures
Collinsville, OK 74021
Tel 918-527-8796
Email ......mario@midcoast-pictures.com
Web ....www.midcoast-pictures.com

Producer, CHOICES, 2003, Midcoast
Pictures, Short
Writer, OKLAHOMA TRAGEDY, 2003,
Midcoast Pictures, Feature
Producer, DOWN THE ROAD, 2002, Road
Pictures, Feature
Writer, LA CABANA (THE CABIN), 2002,
Midcoast Pictures, Feature

Sandra Avila
Program Coordinator
Showtime Networks, Inc.
Los Angeles, CA 90024
Tel 310-234-5300
Fax 310-234-5389
Email...........sandra.avila@showtime.net
Web ....www.sho.com

Coordinator, LATINO FILMMAKER SHOW-
CASE, 2004, Showtime, TV Series

Nicolas Aznarez*
Mojo A Band Apart
Los Angeles, CA 90046
Tel 323-951-4477
Fax 323-951-4401
Email ......nicolas.mojo@abandapart.com

Andre Baca*
Millbrae, CA 94030
Tel 415-613-3726
Email ....grin56@hotmail.com

Shawna Baca*
4 Elements Entertainment
Los Angeles, CA 90034
Tel 310-980-8906
Email ....shawnabaca@hotmail.com
Web.....................www.ShawnaBaca.com

*Manager: Shapiro West & Associates,
310-278-8896*

Director, Writer, 3:52, 2005, Short
Associate Producer, DOLOROSAS, 2004,
   Cisneros Films, Short
Associate Producer, MAN, WHERE'S MY
   SHOE, 2004, SaReNDiBity Films, Short
Director, Executive Producer, Writer, ROSE'S
   GARDEN, 2003, Irene Belle Films, Short
Actress, Executive Producer, Writer, IMPER-
   SONAL IMPRESSION, 2002, Irene Belle
   Fiilms, Short

Evelyn Badia*
Evebad Productions, Inc.
Brooklyn, NY 11215
Tel 917-539-1677
Tel 718-768-7483
Email ....evebad@aol.com

Director, Producer, HEAD START, 2004,
   Evebad Productions, Industrial
Producer, LANCERS, CITIBANK, 2004,
   Rodrigues, Mejer Adv., TV Commercial
Producer, OLD NAVY, HOME DEPOT, 2004,
   The Vidal Partnership, TV Commercial
Director, Producer, SPRING CREEK TOWERS,
   2004, Evebad Productions, Industrial
Director, Producer, Writer, UNDER THE
   SKIN, 2004, Evebad Productions, Short
Director, GONNA GET CONTEST, 2003,
   Evebad Productions, TV Commercial

Michael Baez*
Baez Entertainment, Inc.
Van Nuys, CA 91411
Tel 818-901-9081
Tel 212-769-6989
Cell 646-623-4972
Email ....Baezent@yahoo.com
Web ....www.BaezEnt.com

Director, Producer, Writer, DEVIL'S KISS,
   2002, Baez Entertainment, Short

Director, Producer, Writer, NUDE IN NY,
   2000-2004, Baez Entertainment, Stage
   Play/TV
Director, LIGHTS, CAMERA, ACTION, 1997,
   Baez Entertainment, Stage Play/TV
Director, Producer, Writer, SPANISH
   HARLEM, 1997, Boricua Film Works,
   Feature
Director, Producer, Writer, CONSEQUENCES,
   1996, Latino Jams Filmworks, Short

Dan Baker*
Orilla, Ontario L3V6H1 Canada
Tel 705-327-9059
Email ....danb@jackfields.com

Mario Balibrera*
Culver City, CA 90230
Tel 310-390-7817

Charisma Baltodano*
Orinda, CA 94563
Email ....Charizb@aol.com

Art Department

Antonio Banderas
Beverly Hills, CA 90212

*Agent: Emanuel Nunez, CAA,
310-288-4545*

Actor, LEGEND OF ZORRO, 2005, Sony
   Entertainment, Feature
Actor, SHREK 2, 2004, Universal, Feature
Actor, AND STARRING PANCHO VILLA AS
   HIMSELF, 2003, HBO Films, TV Movie
Actor, IMAGINING ARGENTINA, 2003,
   Arenas, Feature
Actor, ONCE UPON A TIME IN MEXICO,
   2003, Sony Pictures Entertainment,
   Feature
Actor, SPY KIDS 3-D: GAME OVER, 2003,
   Dimension Films, Feature
Actor, SPY KIDS 2: ISLAND OF LOST
   DREAMS, 2002, Dimension Films, Feature
Actor, SPY KIDS, 2001, Dimension Films,
   Feature
Director, CRAZY IN ALABAMA, 1998, Hatbox
   Productions/TriStar, Feature
Actor, THE MASK OF ZORRO, 1998,
   Columbia Tristar, Feature

Marcos Baraibar*
Baraibar Productions
Austin, TX 78746
Tel 512-736-2753
Email ....baraibar@mail.utexas.edu

Norbeto Barba
Los Angeles, CA 90067
Tel 310-578-9530

Agent: Susan Sussman, Diverse Talent Group, 310-201-6565

Director, AMERICAN DREAMS, 2003, NBC, TV Series
Director, LEVEL 9, 2000, Paramount TV, TV Series
Director, RESURRECTION BLVD., 2000, Showtime, TV Series
Director, TERROR IN THE MALL, 1998, Warner Bros. Television, TV Movie

Trina Bardusco*
Latino Media Works
New York, NY 10009
Tel 347-837-1542
Email ....trina@latinomediaworks.com
Web ....www.latinomediaworks.com

Casting Director, EL VACILON, 2004, Babylegs Entertainment
Casting Director, ERROL MORIS COMMERCIALS: CITIBANK, TYLENOL, AT&T, 2004, TV Commercials
Casting Director, HABLA, 2004, HBO Latino, TV Series
Casting Director, LECHON, 2004, HBO, Short
Director, Producer, EL TURISTA SOY: LUIS AGUJETA Y SU CANTE GITANO, 2003, HBO Latino, Documentary

Eduardo Barraza*
Chula Vista, CA 91913
Tel 619-733-3329
Email ....eduardobarraza@gmail.com

Ruben Barrera*
Vamos Productions
Kingsville, TX 78363
Tel 361-595-5205
Tel 361-228-4200
Email ....the_thinking_man@hotmail.com

Pablo Barrios*
Smithtown, NY 11787
Email ....pbarrios2783@netscape.net

Frank Barron*
Producer, Media Relations
Cosmo TV Network
Irvine, CA 92614
Tel 949-222-4411
Fax 949-222-4407
Email ....fb@cosmotvnetwork.com

Joe Basquez*
Composer/Sound Designer
MelSar Productions
Austin, TX 78720
Tel 512-219-0174
Cell 512-470-3455
Email ....j_basquez@yahoo.com

Composer, J.F. QUE?, 2004, Austin LP, short film
Sound Designer, LA PASTORELA, 2004, Austin Latino Theater Alliance, stage play
Web Designer, LA PASTORELA, 2004, Austin Latino Theater Alliance, stage play
Sound Designer, ULTIMA ASCENSION, 1999, Origina Systems, video game

Marta Bautis
Tiempo Azul Productions
New York, NY 10009
Tel 212-673-8065
Fax 212-673-8065
Email ....mbautis@nyc.rr.com

Director, Producer, NICARAGUA: THE CHILDREN ARE WAITING, 2002, Tiempo Azul Productions, Documentary
Director, Producer, THE MOTHER: MITOS MATERNOS, 1994, Women Make Movies, Documentary

Director, Producer, HOME IS THE STRUG-
GLE, 1991, Women Make Movies,
Documentary

Carmen Bautista*
New York, NY 10026
Email ....cb1218@yahoo.com

José Bayona*
Unicorn Films
Corona, NY 11368
Tel 347-351-0207
Cell 347-351-0207
Fax 718-606-1447
Email ....josebayona@yahoo.com
Web ....www.josebayona.com

Director, Writer, FAR AWAY NEIGHBORS,
2005, Feature
Script Supervisor, VIOLET OF A THOUSAND
COLORS, 2005, Feature
Director, REQUIEM FOR A LIFE, 2004, Stage
Play/ Feature
Director, BUS STOP, 2003, NYU, Short
Producer, THE BUGCHASER, 2003, Mouse
Head Productions, Short

Veronica Bellver*
Mexico City, DF 04210 Mexico
Tel 54-11-47-42-44-76
Email ....verobellver@hotmail.com

Mary Beltran*
Assistant Professor, Dept. of
Communication
University of Wisconsin
Madison, WI 53706
Tel 608-262-8788
Email ....mcbeltran@wisc.edu

Salvador Benavides*
Indio Z Films
Los Angeles, CA 90029
Tel 323-665-6102
Email ....salvadorbenavides@juno.com
*Agent: John Hugh, Ann Waugh Agency,
818-980-0141, hamhu@pacbell.net*

Actor, Director, Writer, CABEZA DE COL-
IFLOR, 2004, Short
Actor, DARKNESS MINUS TWELVE, 2004,
Antonio Negret Films, Short
Actor, DEATH OF SALVADOR DALI, 2004,
Dali Freud Films, Short
Assistant Director, GOLDEN EAGLE AWARDS,
2004, Nosotros, Nosotros Awards
Ceremony/Gala
Set Designer, RICARDO MONTALBAN THE-
ATRE, 2004, Nosotros Opening Night Gala

Jellybean Benitez
Jellybean Productions
New York, NY 10003
Tel 212-777-5678
Fax 212-777-7788
Web ....www.Jellybean-recordings.com

Associate Producer, DUMMY, 2002, Artisan
Entertainment, Feature
Associate Producer, ANGEL EYES, 2001,
Warner Bros., Feature
Executive Producer, FOR LOVE OR COUN-
TRY: THE ARTURO SANDOVAL STORY,
2000, HBO, TV Movie
Co-Producer, TAINA, 2000, Nickelodeon, TV
Series
Executive Producer, NUYORICAN DREAM,
1999, Big Mouth Productions,
Documentary

Luca Bentivoglio
Executive Director
Latino Public Broadcasting
Los Angeles, CA 90028
Tel 323-466-7110
Fax 323-466-7521
Email ....lucabenti@lpbp.org
Web ....www.lpbp.org

Daniel Bernardi*
Associate Professor, Hispanic Research
Center
University of Arizona
Tempe, AZ 85287
Tel 480-727-8588
Cell 520-971-8075
Email ....daniel.bernardi@asu.edu

filmmakers

María Berns*

Broken Doll Films
El Paso, TX 79912
Tel 915-833-0421
Email ....mariaberns@yahoo.com

Director, Writer, OF DEER AND BUTTER-
FLIES, 2005, Feature
Producer, WOMEN ON THE EDGE, 2005, TV
Play
Writer, PROCERES DEL FREE SHOP, 2004,
Stage Play
Director, Writer, BLACK ICE, 2002, Short
Director, Writer, JAMAICA IN WINTER, 2001,
Short
Director, Writer, SPLENDORS BEFORE
DEATH, 2000, Short
Director, Writer, A RUSSIAN DIARY, 1999,
Short
Director, Writer, LA NOVIA, 1998, Short
Director, Writer, HISTORIA MINIMA DE UNA
SEDUCCION, 1993, Short

Jennifer Berry*

Boulder, CO 80306
Tel 303-786-7600
Tel 818-247-5091
Email ....Magilian@aol.com

Rudy Beserra**

Sr. Vice President of Latin Affairs
Coca Cola Company
Atlanta, GA 30301
Email ....rbeserra@na.ko.com
Web........................www.cocacola.com

Nelson Betancourt*

Executive Director
Orlando Latin American Film Festival
Orlando, FL 32812
Tel 407-273-4079
Email ....leafstormpictures@earthlink.net

Producer, AMCHITKA, 2004, Documentary

Maria Bird-Pico*

San Juan, PR 00926
Email.................mbird@sanjuanstar.net

Daniel Birman

Mexico City, DF 11560 Mexico
Tel 52-55-10-55-23-33
Cell.......................52-55-51-02-92-22
Fax 52-55-52-80-89-52
Email..daniel.birman@alamedafilms.com
Web ....www.alamedafilms.com

Producer, EL CRIMEN DEL PADRE AMARO,
2002, Samuel Goldwyn Films, Feature

Vera Blasi

Beverly Hills, CA 90212

Agent: Blair Belcher, UTA,
310-273-6700

Writer, TORTILLA SOUP, 2001, Samuel
Goldwyn Films, Feature
Writer, WOMAN ON TOP, 2000, Fox
Searchlight Pictures, Feature

Gabriela Bohm

Los Angeles, CA 90064
Tel 310-842-8088
Fax 310-815-8177
Email ....gabriela@bohmproductions.com
Web ....www.bohmproductions.com

Director, Producer, ANIORANZAS, 2004,
Bohm Productions, Documentary
Director, Producer, PASSAGES, 2000, Bohm
Productions, Documentary

Carlos Bolado

Sincronia/BBM Productions
Berkeley, CA 94709
Tel 505-525-8998
Email ....bolex@pobox.com

Director, PROMESAS, 2001, PBS/POV/IVTS,
Documentary
Editor, POR LA LIBRE, 2000, Fox Home
Entertainment, Feature
Director, Writer, BAJO CALIFORNIA, THE
LIMIT OF TIME, 1998, Columbia Pictures
Mexico, Feature
Editor, COMO AGUA PARA CHOCOLATE,
1992, Miramax, Feature

Angelo Bolanos*
Born Powerful Films
Patterson, NJ 07522
Tel 973-904-006
Tel 951-346-7572
Email ....bpa7@yahoo.com

Jorge Bonamino*
Right Cut Media Inc.
Coconut Grove, FL 33133
Tel 305-788-2326
Fax 786-552-897
Email ....pipob@sion.com

Blanca Bonilla*
Fe Productions
Jamaica Plain, MA 02130
Tel 617-524-8154
Email ....bblinkie@aol.com

Maria Piedad Bonilla*
Piñata Productions
Beverly Hills, CA 90210
Tel 310-358-1943
Cell 310-490-8151
Fax 310-358-0812
Email ....pinatamgmt@aol.com

DVD Project Manager, GWAR, 2002, Venus
  New Media, DVD
Casting Director, INGLES SIN BARRERAS,
  2002, Lexicon, Educational Course
Dialect Coach, Extras Casting Director, BLOW,
  2001, New Line Cinema, Feature
Producer, SANTA FE, 1991, The Palace in
  Los Angeles, Live Concert Event
Producer, Writer, CONTACTO AND LA BUENA
  VIDA, 1990, Telemundo Network, TV
  Segment

Josefina Bonilla-Ruiz*
West Roxbury, MA 02132
Tel 617-821-1615
Email..............................jfina@rcn.com
Web ....www.feproduction.com

Margarita Borda*
Sunshots Productions
Miami, FL 33155
Tel 305-667-4887
Cell 305-898-6607
Email ....marborda_2000@yahoo.com
Web ....www.sunshotsproductions.com

Director, Producer, FINDING THE PAST,
  2004, Sunshots Productions, Documentary
Director, Producer, THE POWER OF GIVING,
  2004, WPBT Channel 2 PBS, TV Segment
Director, Producer, TLINKIT CARVING, 2003,
  Sunshots Productions, Documentary

Eddie Borges*
Los Angeles, CA 90027
Email ....eddieborges@hotmail.com

Jesse Borrego*
Venice, CA 90291
Tel 323-464-0870

*Manager: Liberman-Zerman Management,
323-464-0870*

Actor, 24, 2004, Fox Television, TV Series
Actor, THE MALDONADO MIRACLE, 2003,
  Showtime, Feature
Actor, HELL SWARM, 2000, Wilshire Court
  Productions, TV Movie
Actor, BOUND BY HONOR, 1993, Hollywood
  Pictures, Feature
Actor, MI VIDA LOCA, 1993, Sony Pictures
  Classics, Feature

Frank Borres
American View Productions
Bridgeport, CT 06604
Tel 203-366-5033
Fax 203-366-5044
Email......................americanv@snet.net
Web ..www.americanviewproductions.com

Director, Producer, YOU'RE ON THE AIR,
  2002, PBS, Documentary
Director, Producer, CELIA CRUZ AND
  FRIENDS, 2000, PBS, TV Special
Director, Producer, PUERTO RICAN PAS-
  SAGES, 1993, PBS, Documentary

filmmakers

Victor Bowleg*
Tucson, AZ 85702
Tel 520-740-5779
Email ....vbowleg@hotmail.com

Maria Bozzi
Programs Director
IFP-LA
Beverly Hills, CA 90211
Tel 310-432-1200
Email ....mbozzi@ifp.org

Cynthia Braden*
Hawthorne, CA 90250
Email.........cynthiabraden@hotmail.com

James Brennan*
Culver City, CA 90232
Tel 310-259-0646
Email ....jbrennan@mandalan.com

Pablo Bressan*
Miami Beach, FL 33139
Tel 305-458-0197
Fax 305-532-8621
Email pablo@goinggoingproductions.com

Producer, LOS DUROS, 2005, Going-Going
  Productions, Documentary

Evelyn Brito*
Boston, MA 02119
Tel 617-670-9094
Email ....britoevelyn@hotmail.com

Abraham Alfonso Brown*
Santa Monica, CA 90404
Tel 310-829-3948
Email ....sarcasm4all@aol.com

Bette Brown*
Comadre Productions
West Columbia, TX 77486
Tel 281-988-8888
Tel 281-989-0897

Georgia Brown-Quiñones*
Sologaistoa Peace Making Through Film
Dallas, TX 75204
Tel 214-855-1297
Tel 214-368-9881
Fax 214-855-1297
Email ....quinones20007@cs.com

Attorney: Lizabeth Hasse, Esq.,
415-433-4380,
lhasse@creativelawgroup.com

Adrian Brunello*
Musa Music Producciones
Irvine, CA 92614
Email ....agentbrunello@hotmail.com

Cynthia Buchanan*
Comadre Productions
Carrizo Springs, TX 78834
Tel 830-876-3034
Cell 281-989-0897
Fax 830-876-3034
Email ....producer@azteceagles.net
Web ....www.azteceagles.net

Maria Bures*
Buresa Media
Miami, FL 33145
Tel 305-856-2929
Cell 305-632-1503
Fax 305-858-0357
Email ....buresa@aol.com

Director, Producer, CONVERSANDO CON
  LETICIA, 2004, VS Brooks, TV Series
Director, Producer, I DO, 2004, Buresa
  Media, PSA
Director, Producer, RETO A LA MODA, 2004,
  SBS, TV Pilot
Director, Producer, LILLY AND I..., 2003,
  Buresa Media, Documentary
Director, Producer, SOMOS, 2002-2004,
  Buresa Media/LPB, Documentary

Raza Burgee*
Razablade Productions
Van Nuys, CA 91407
Tel 310-842-5583
Email ....Razabld@juno.com

Ernie Bustamante*
20th Century Fox Television
Los Angeles, CA 90035
Email ....ermie.bustamante@tvbyfox.com

Assistant to Executive Producer, BOSTON
    LEGAL, 2004, David E. Kelley
    Productions, TV Series

Darlene Caamano-Loquet
Vice President, Production
Voy Pictures
Beverly Hills, CA 90210
Tel 310-550-1019
Fax 310-388-0775
Email.................contact@voygroup.com
Web ....www.voy.tv

Alberto Caballero*
Knightmare Pictures
Los Angeles, CA 90069
Tel 310-854-6518
Email ....acabal@adelphia.net

Technical Director, ACTION, 2004, Chicago
    Museum of Science and Industry ,
    Industrial
Technical Director, DELILAH'S NIGHT CLUB,
    2003-2004, Electrosonic Themed
    Systems, Industrial
Director, Producer, Writer, MI ABUELA,
    1999, KnightMare Pictures, Feature
Producer, THE LIGHT HOUSE, 1996, Water
    Mark Productions, Feature

Kirk Cabezas*
Editor-In-Chief
Estrenos Magazine
Encino, CA 91311
Tel 818-998-3707
Tel 866-378-7366
Fax 818-998-3736
Email ....kirkcabe@aol.com
Web ....www.estrenosdevideo.net

Media Advocate

Mayra Cabrera*
Highland, NY 12528
Email ....cricketg@att.net

Juan Caceres*
New York, NY 10031
Tel 212-491-3892
Fax 212-926-7030
Email ....SupaJuan@aol.com
Web ....www.nuevayorkfilms.com

Director, Producer, Writer, ROCK STEADY,
    JUICY, 2004, Short

Al Cadena*
Yale University
New Haven, CT 06511
Email ....bigfilfy@yahoo.com

Nora Cadena*
Austin, TX 78757
Tel 512-380-0229
Email ....noracadena@earthlink.net

Paul F. Cajero
Los Angeles, CA
Tel 323-667-3454

Co-Producer, CLUBHOUSE, 2004, CBS, TV
    Series
Unit Production Manager, DR. VEGAS, 2004,
    CBS , TV Series
Production Manager, KAREN SISCO, 2003,
    Universal Network Television, TV Series
Producer, KINGPIN, 2003, NBC, TV Series
Production Manager, UNDECLARED, 2001,
    Fox, TV Series

Elizabeth Caldas*

Office of the Mayor, NYC
New York, NY 10128
Tel 212-788-7816
Fax 212-788-3229
Email ....ecaldas@cityhall.nyc.gov

Carolyn Caldera*

Caldera/De Fanti Entertainment
Los Angeles, CA 90027
Tel 323-906-9500
Email.................ccaldera@earthlink.net

Producer, THREE BLIND MICE, 2002,
    Viacom, Feature
Associate Producer, SELENA, 1997, Warner
    Bros, Feature
Associate Producer, THE DISAPPEARANCE
    OF GARCIA LORCA, 1997, Columbia
    TriStar, Feature
Production Supervisor, THE CISCO KID,
    1994, Turner, TV Movie
Executive Assistant, GETTYSBURG, 1993,
    New Line Cinema, Feature

Julio Calderon

Los Angeles, CA

*Agent: Michael Margules, Paradigm
Agency, 310-967-0200*

Writer, THE ORTEGAS, 2003, Fox
    Broadcasting, TV Series
Writer, BROTHERS GARCIA, 2001,
    Nickelodeon Networks, TV Series

Elizabeth Calienes*

Los Angeles, CA 90064
Email...............calienes@sakonline.com
Web ....www.sakonline.com

Production Designer, CAYO, 2005, Feature
Production Designer, BLACKBERRIES, 2004,
    Feature
Production Designer, HOW THE GARCIA
    GIRLS SPENT THEIR SUMMER, 2004,
    Loosely Based Pictures, LLC., Feature
Production Designer, SHUI HEN, 2003, AFI
    & Sugar Cane Productions, Short
Production Designer, SINGULARITY, 2003,
    Fox Searchlab, Short

Deborah Calla*

Calla Productions
Santa Monica, CA 90405
Tel 310-392-3775
Fax 310-399-5594
Email ....debcalla@callaproductions.com
Web ....www.callaproductions.com

Attorney: Darrell Miller, 310-826-0300

Director, Producer, CARNIVAL IN RIO -
    2004, 2004, Travel Channel, Documentary
Executive Producer, JERGENS, 2004,
    National re-launch campaign (3 spots),
    Commercial
Executive Producer, VALTREX, 2004,
    National Commercial, Commercial
Producer, CARNIVAL IN RIO - 2003, 2003,
    Travel Channel, Documentary
Producer, LOST ZWEIG, 2002, Grupo Novo,
    Feature

Cecilia Camacho*

Bell Gardens, CA 90201
Tel 562-928-7942

Celia Camacho*

Celia Camacho Studios
Downey, CA 90241
Tel 562-869-6000

Michael Camacho

Agent
Creative Artists Agency (CAA)
Beverly Hills, CA 90212
Tel 310-288-4545
Fax 310-288-4800
Email ....mcamacho@caa.com
Web ....www.caa.com

Ray Camacho*

Thump Records
Huntington Beach, CA 92648
Tel 310-308-8031
Email ....rcolympian@aol.com

Juan Jose Campanella

Argentina

Manager: John Ufland, 310-550-9600

Director, CLICK, 2005, Columbia Pictures, Feature
Co-Writer, Director, LUNA DE AVELLANEDA, 2004, Feature
Director, DRAGNET, 2002, ABC, TV Series
Director, Writer, EL HIJO DE LA NOVIA, 2001, Columbia TriStar, Feature
Director, LAW & ORDER CRIMINAL INTENT, 2001, NBC, TV Series
Director, LAW & ORDER SVU, 2000, NBC, TV Series

Félix Leo Campos*

AfterDark CATV PRoductions, Inc
Bronx, NY 10459
Tel 718-842-4460
Fax 718-842-4480
Email ......AfterdarkCATVPro@yahoo.com

Producer, ALTO EXTERMINATING SERVICE, 2004, Cablevision, Commercial
Producer, NY LATINAS AGAINST DV, 2004, Documentary
Associate Producer, AMERICAN JUSTICE, 2003, A&E, TV Series
Director, NUYORICAN POET CAFÉ, 2003, Live Event

Walter Carasco

CEO &Founder
Imagen Entertainment
Burbank, CA 91505
Tel 818-845-1424
Fax 818-845-1113
Email............info@imagentertainment.tv
Web ....www.imagentertainment.tv

Johnny Carbajal*

Crossover Films
Los Angeles, CA 90032
Tel 323-227-5581
Email ....johnnycarbajal@hotmail.com

Laura Cardona

New York, NY 10003
Tel 646-924-9267
Email ....tislaura@yahoo.com

Editor, Assistant, JOE REDNER CAMPAIGN COMMERCIALS, 2003, TV Promo
Editor, Assistant, WALT DISNEY WORLD HIGHLIGHT VIDEO, 2003, Action Sports International, TV Promo
Editor, Assistant, FIGHTING FOR LIFE IN THE DEATH BELT, 2002-2003, TV

Ricardo Cardona-Marty*

Ciudad Universidad, Trujillo Alto 00976 PR
Tel 787-531-6958
Email ....rycar_m@yahoo.com

Patricia Cardoso

Santa Monica, CA 90406
Tel 310-850-2107
Fax 310-450-4677
Email ....lechuga@earthlink.net

Agent: Barbara Mandell, ICM, 310-550-4000

Manager: Rosalie Swedlin, 323-964-9220

Director, NAPPILY EVER AFTER, 2005, Universal Pictures, Feature
Director, THE JANE PLAN, 2005, Feature
Director, REAL WOMEN HAVE CURVES, 2002, HBO, Feature
Director, Writer, EL REINO DE LOS CIELOS: THE WATER CARRIER, 1996, UCLA, Short
Director, Writer, AIR GLOBE, 1990, UCLA, Short

Juan M. Carillo

Interim Director
California Arts Council
Sacramento, CA 95814
Tel 800-201-6201
Email ....jcarrillo@caartscouncil.com
Web ....www.cac.ca.gov

Julissa Carmona*

Carmona Inc.
Yonkers, NY 10705
Tel 914-423-1001
Email.............julissa@carmona-inc.com
Web ....www.carmona-inc.com

Director, BREAKING UP IS HARD TO DO,
  2004, Emogene Shadwick Productions,
  Short
Director, Writer, BURNING RED, 2004,
  Carmona Inc., Short
Director, Writer, WHATEVER IT TAKES, 2003,
  Carmona Inc., Short
Associate Producer, BACK TEAR, 2002,
  Underdog Entertainment, Commercial
Script Supervisor, SYMANTIX, 2002,
  Blackout Entertainment, Music Video

Gladys Caro*

Los Angeles, CA 90036
Email ....ycarocaro@sbcglobal.net
Web...........................www.colicidi.com

Michael Caro*

Regional Manager, San Diego
Latin Style Magazine
San Diego, CA 91932
Tel 619-934-8768
Email ....latinstyle3@cox.net
Web ....www.latinstylemag.com

Yvonne Caro Caro*

Los Angeles, CA 90036
Cell 323-445-4541
Email ....ycarocaro@sbcglobal.net

Agent: Joel Kleinman, BKI,
323-874-9800, bki@anet.net

Manager: (Voice Management) ICM,
310-550-4380

Attorney: Matthew Swanlund,
310-315-8282

Actress, DIRTY DANCING II, 2004, Miramax,
  Feature
Actress, Producer, TINA MODOTTI, A DREAM
  OF REVOLUTION, 2004, Highways, Play
Actress, PSICOSIS, 2003, Telemundo, TV
  Series

Almudena Carracedo*

Los Angeles, CA 90028
Tel 323-850-0622
Cell 323-633-1529
Email ....acarracedo2@yahoo.com
Web ....www.madeinla.com

Director, Director of Phography, Producer,
  MADE IN LA, 2004, Feature
Director, Director of Photraphy, Editor,
  Producer, WELCOME, A DOCUMENTARY
  JOURNEY OF IMPRESSIONS, 2003,
  Documentary

Octavio Carranza

Carranza Brothers
Los Angeles, CA 90294
Tel 323-650-6649
Cell 310-699-5273
Email ....Octavio@LAart.com

Producer, Writer, ARTURO - EL SONADOR,
  2002, Film Festival Circuit, Short

Salvador Carrasco*

Salvastian Pictures
Santa Monica, CA 90403
Tel 310-576-6785
Email ....SalvastianPics@aol.com
Web ....www.theotherconquest.com

Director, THE BROTHERS GARCIA, 2000,
  Nickelodeon, TV Series
Director. Editor, Writer, LA OTRA CON-
  QUISTA, 1998, Carrasco & Domingo Films,
  Feature

Carlos Carreras

Agent
United Talent Agency (UTA)
Beverly Hills, CA 90212
Tel 310-273-6700
Email ....carrerasc@unitedtalent.com

Juliette Carrillo*
Venice, CA 90291
Tel 310-664-0778
Email ....cilantro@earthlink.net

Director, AS VISHNU DREAMS, 2004,
  Cornerstone/East West, Stage Play
Director, ANNA IN THE TROPICS, 2003,
  South Coast Repertory, Stage Play
Director, Writer, SPIRAL, 2002, AFI, Short
Director, Producer, HISPANIC PLAYWRIGHTS
  PROJECT, 1997-2004, South Coast
  Repertory, Stage Play Festival

Elvira Carrizal*
New York, NY 10027
Tel 917-558-5864
Email ....elviracl@yahoo.com

Director, ANNA IN THE TROPICS, 2005,
  Stage Play
Director, Writer, ESCAPING JUAREZ, 2004,
  Stage Play
Director, Writer, IGNACIO'S KEYS, 2004,
  Short
Director, Writer, Director of Photography,
  EDWIN'S PORTRAIT, 2003, Short
Producer, Writer, Director of Photography,
  SAMUEL'S RISE, 2003, Short
Director of Photography, SAVING FACE,
  2003, Short

José Casado*
New Haven, CT 06511
Tel 646-729-4518
Email ....casaluz1@yahoo.com

Editor, LUCHA LIBRE: LIFE BEHIND THE
  MASK, 2004, KPI Films, Documentary
Director, INDECISION, 2002, Casaluz
  Filmworks, Short
Editor, NUMEROUS TV PROGRAMS: HISTO-
  RY CHANNEL, BRAVO, 1999-2005,
  Documentary

Michael B. Case*
Philadelphia, PA 19144
Tel 215-844-7593
Email ....ArtistCasey@aol.com

Rudy Casillas
Program Manager
PBS KUAT-TV
Tucson, AZ 85721
Tel 520-621-5379
Email ....rcasillas@kuat.arizona.edu
Web..................................www.kuat.org

Carlos Castañeda*
San Antonio, TX 78216
Tel 210-344-6378
Fax 210-344-6378
Email ....ccastanedatx@sbcglobal.net
Web.......www.geocities.com/castanedatx

Producer, NEW MORNING, 2003-3004, The
  Hallmark Channel, Documentary
Director, PSA "LIFETIME DECISIONS",
  2003, OLLU - College for Texans,
  Commercials

Laura Castañeda*
Reporter, Producer
Pass Press International
San Diego, CA 92103
Tel 619-585-3359
Tel 619-855-4140
Email ....presspasslc@aol.com

Host, Producer, STORIES DEL AL FRON-
  TERA2, 2004, KPBS-TV, TV Series
Producer, CUNA: MEDICINE MAN, 2003,
  UCSD-TV, TV Series
Producer, LA CUCARACHA, 2003, Cox
  Communications, TV Series
Producer, MUJERES SANAS PARA FAMILIAS
  SALUDABLES, 2003, UCSD-TV, TV Series
Producer, AMERICA'S MOST WANTED,
  2001, Fox TV, TV Series

Leticia Castañeda*
Oxnard, CA 93030
Email ....filmxical@msn.com

Marisa Castaneda
University of Mexico
Albuquerque, NM 87198
Tel 505-268-0987
Fax 505-268-0988
Email ....mcastan@unm.edu
Web ....www.marisacastaneda.com

Producer, FAMILY SAUSAGE, 2003, Short
Director, Editor, Producer, FOUND BOY,
   2003, Short
Producer, ICARUS HAS FALLEN, 2002, Short

Liliana Castellanos*
New York, NY 10002
Tel 212-505-0344
Email ....liliprisas@yahoo.com

Alex Castillo*
Castle Sun Pictues
Los Angeles, CA 90046
Tel 310-770-4710
Email ....alex.castillo@comcast.net
Web ....www.castlesun.com

Begoña Castillo*
Los Angeles, CA 90007
Tel 213-925-1852
Fax 213-745-6652
Email ....maerbale@yahoo.com

Emma Castillo*
Junior Producer
Conill
Torrance, CA 90505
Tel 310-214-6420
Email ....emma.castillo@conill-la.com

Raul Castillo*
Brooklyn, NY 11205
Tel 917-804-7434
Email ....odioelinternet@hotmail.com

Roger Castillo*
Fawn Mountain Films
Boerne, TX 78015
Tel 210-698-1191
Cell 210-260-6931
Email ..castillo@fawnmountainfilms.com
Web ....www.fawnmountainfilms.com

Editor, Producer, A SLIGHT DISCOMFORT,
   2001, Potential Productions, Documentary
Director of Photography, Editor, Producer,
   Writer, MISSION SAN JOSE, 1996,
   Maverick International, Documentary
Editor, ON FIRE WITH FAITH, 1990,
   Hispanic Telecommunications,
   Documentary

Karina Castorena*
Los Angeles, CA 90029
Tel 323-630-9909
Email ....karinastarr@yahoo.com

Fernando Alberto Castroman
Playa del Rey, CA 90293
Tel 310-822-2281
Cell 310-874-4062
Email ....nando@earthlink.net

1st Assistant Director, ER, 2003, NBC, TV
   Series
1st Assistant Director, RESURRECTION
   BLVD., 2000, Showtime, TV Series
1st Assistant Director, AVALON: BEYOND
   THE ABYSS, 1999, UPN, TV Movie

Allen Cazares*
Chula Vista, CA 91913
Email...................Allencazares@cox.net

Manuel Ceballos*
Tucson, AZ 85712
Emailmceballos_desaracho@hotmail.com

Pedro Celedon*
Barefoot Productions
Hollywood, CA 90028
Tel 323-461-9773
Fax 323-913-1331
Email ....pceledon@e-nfomercial.com

Producer, A CONTINENT ENFLAMED, 2004,
   NEH, Documentary
Producer, FULL BLOOM, 2002, Michelle
   Mattei Productions, Documentary
Producer, A TALE OF THREE LIVES, 1999,
   KCET-TV, TV
Producer, BILL VIOLA, A TWENTY-YEAR
   RETROSPECTIVE, 1998, KCET-TV,
   Documentary
Producer, THE CROSSING OF THE
   ATLANTIC, 1992, TVN Chile, TV

Brandi Centeno*
North Hollywod, CA 91601
Email..........................Guzelik@aol.com

Ivan Cevallos
Ethos Group, Inc.
South Pasadena, CA 91030
Tel 626-388-2100
Email ....icevallos@ethosagency.com

Director, PIÑATA STAND, 2003, Commercial
Producer, 14 WAYS TO WEAR LIPSTICK,
   1999, Feature

Mike & Gibby Cevallos
Cevallos Brothers Productions
Valley Village, CA 91601
Tel 818-822-9261
Email ....mick58@earthlink.net
Web ....www.cevallosbros.com

Writers, THE MISADVENTURES OF MAYA
   AND MIGUEL, 2004-2005, PBS, TV
   Series
Co-Creators, Directors, Writers, THE BROTH-
   ERS GARCIA, 2000, Nickelodeon, TV
   Series
Directors, Writers, BARBACOA THE MOVIE,
   1998, Feature

Flor de Maria Chahua*
Experiencia Latina
Berkeley, CA 94712
Tel 310-770-0522
Email ....experiencialatina@yahoo.com

Nancy Chaidez
Agent
Nancy Chaidez Agency & Associates
Los Angeles, CA 90048
Tel 323-655-6455
Fax 323-655-1255
Email ....talria@aol.com

Natalie Chaidez
Beverly Hills, CA 90212
Email ....chaidezinc@aol.com

*Agent: Peter Benedek, UTA,
310-273-6700*

Co-Producer, Writer, NEW YORK UNDERCOV-
   ER, 2005, Fox, TV Series
Co-Executive Producer, Writer, SKIN, 2003,
   Fox Film Corporation, TV Series
Producer, Writer, THE WARDEN, 2001,
   Turner Network Television, TV Movie
Producer, Writer, JUDGING AMY, 1999, CBS
   Television, TV Series
Producer, TRINITY, 1998, NBC, TV Series

Brenda Chavez*
New York, NY 10028
Tel 212-801-6834
Email.......................chavezb@gtlaw.com

Carol Chavez*
Dallas, TX 75235
Tel 214-678-9438
Email..........girlwhodreams@netzero.com

Chuy Chavez
Beverly Hills, CA 90210

*Agent: Melanie Ramsayer, The Gersh
Agency, 310-274-6611*

Director of Photography, ARE YOU THE
   FAVORITE PERSON OF ANYBODY, 2005,
   Short

Director of Photography, TORTILLA HEAVEN, 2005, Feature
Director of Photography, PUERTO VALLARTA SQUEEZE, 2003, Showcase Entertainment, Feature
Director of Photography, ZURDO, 2003, Fantasmas Films, Feature
Director of Photography, CHUCK AND BUCK, 2002, Artisan Entertainment, Feature

David Chavez*

Executive Producer
Latin Pointe, Inc.
Olathe, KS 66062
Tel 913-397-8850
Fax 913-397-0890
Email ....dchavez@latinpointe.com
Web ....www.latinpointe.com

Producer, PAUL RODRIGUEZ ALL STAR COMEDY TRIBUTE, 2004, DVD
Producer, ALMA AWARDS, 2002, 2005, Live Show

Joaquin Chavez*

Omnicron
San Ysidro, CA 92173
Tel 526-803-8526
Email ....lobotmex@mailcity.com

Writer, GETTING TO KNOW THE THIRD NATION, 2004, Documentary

Maria Chavez*

South Miami, FL 33134
Tel 305-442-0048
Tel 305-665-0179
Cell 305-588-0087
Fax 305-661-2676
Email ....mariakc@aol.com

Production Manager, MANCHURIAN CANDI-DATE, FLORIDA, 2004, Sony Pictures, Feature
Production Manager, ADAPTATION, 2002, Feature
Location Manager, BAD BOYS 2, 2002, Columbia Pictures, Feature
Production Manager, SWEET HOME ALABA-MA, 2002, Feature

Maria Elena Chavez*

Los Angeles, CA 90006
Tel 323-449-8613
Email ....latinavision@earthlink.net

Director, Writer, DOLORES HUERTA TRIB-UTE, 2004, Dolores Huerta Foundation, Documentary
Coordinator, IFP/LA LOS ANGELES FILM FESTIVAL, 2004, IFP/LA, Film Festival
Production Assistant, IMAGEN AWARDS, 2004, The Imagen Foundation, Awards Show
2nd Assistant Director, PURA LENGUA, 2004, Maritza Alvarez, Short
Director, Writer, STRUGGLING FOR LEGAL-IZATION, 2004, United Farm Workers, AFL-CIO, Documentary
Director, Writer, JERRY VERACRUSE TRIB-UTE, 2003, Pacific Federal, Documentary

Sarah Chavez*

LatinPointe, Inc.
Olathe, KS 66062
Tel 913-397-8850

Yvonne Chavez*

Investment Officer
Low Income Investment Fund
Huntington Park, CA 90255
Tel.......................213-627-9611 x110
Fax 213-627-2528
Email ....ychavez@liifund.org

Federico Chavez Blanco

Sueña Bien Inc./Hot Charros
San Antonio, TX 78201
Tel 210-734-2092
Cell 210-415-8260
Email ....frede@suenabien.com
Web ....www.suenabien.com

Composer, Music Arrangement, LA DUDA, 2003, Azteca TV, TV Soap Opera
Composer, EL PAIS DE LAS MUJERES, 2002, Azteca TV, TV Soap Opera
Composer, CUANDO SEAS MIA, 2001, Azteca TV, TV Soap Opera
Composer, MAREA BRAVA, 1999, Azteca TV, TV Soap Opera

Claudio Chea
Santa Monica, CA 90403

Agent: Montana Artists Agency ,
323-845-4144

Director of Photography, WASHINGTON
  HEIGHTS, 2002, Mac Releasing LLC,
  Feature
Directorof Photography, AZÚCAR AMARGA ,
  2001, First Look Pictures, Feature
Director of Photography, PIÑERO , 2001,
  New Films International, Feature
Director of Photography, CROSSOVER
  DREAMS, 1985, Miramax Films, Feature

Calixto Chinchilla*
Festival Director
New York International Latino Film
Festival
New York, NY 10023
Tel 212-265-8452
Fax 212-307-7445
Email ....calixto@nylatinofilm.com
Web ....www.nylatinofilm.com

Ileana Ciena
Guaynabo, PR 00969
Tel 787-287-9281
Email ....montaje@prtc.net

Producer, JULIA, TODO EN MI, 2002,
  Documentary

George Cisneros*
New Media Artist
Vu-Ture Arts
San Antonio, TX 78207
Tel 210-527-0377
Email ....cisneros@dcci.com

Susan Claassen*
Tucson, AZ 85719
Tel 520-884-0672
Email ....belsuz@aol.com

A. Sayeeda Clarke*
New York, NY 10036
Email..........as_clarke_2000@yahoo.com

Barbara Guadalupe Bustillos Cogswell*
President, Photographer
Bustillos & Company
Media Productions, LLC
Tempe, AZ 85282
Tel 480-768-1561
Cell 480-296-6152
Fax 480-768-1561
Email ....barbara@docu-mama.com
Web ....www.docu-mama.com

Manager: Dale Cogswell,
480-768-1561, www.docu-mama.com

Photographer, AZ NITE LIFE, 2005, TV
  Magazine Series
Photographer, Producer, MARIACHI MEM-
  OIRS, 2005, Documentary
Photographer, Writer, PATRIOTIC FREEDOM:
  BIKERS, 2005, Documentary
Photographer, ANHEUSER-BUSCH PROJECT,
  2004, In House Project, Commercial
Photographer, Writer, LOS LOBOS RETRO-
  SPECT, 2004, Documentary
Photographer, THE ART OF HULA, 2004,
  Documentary

Howard Cohen*
Roadside Attractions
Beverly Hills, CA 90212
Tel 310-789-4710
Fax 310-789-4711
Email ..howard@roadsideattractions.com
Web ....www.roadsideattractions.com

Evelyn Collazo*
Administrative Assistant to Chief
Administrator
Henry Street Settlement
New York, NY 10002
Tel 212-598-0400
Fax 212-874-7587
Email ....emcfoto@aol.com

Jose Colomer

Colomer Productions
Los Angeles, CA
Tel 310-713-4059
Email ....colomerproductions@yahoo.com

Director, EL NUEVO SHOW DE PAUL
  RODRIGUEZ, 2002, Univision, TV Special
Director, LIFE,CAMERA, ACTION, 2002, Fox
  Family Channel, Documentary
Director, LIVE FROM THE ACADEMY
  AWARDS, 2002, Tribune Entertainment,
  TV Special
Director, AL DÍA CON MARÍA CONCHITA,
  1998, Telemundo, TV Show
Director, REAL T.V., 1997, 20th Century Fox,
  TV Series

Ezequiel Colon-Rivera*

Jersey City, NJ 07302
Email ....ecolonrivera@hotmail.com

Dolores Colunga-Stawitz

VP, Secretary
Story Makers, Inc.
Houston, TX 77291
Tel 281-591-7479
Email ....stmkr@aol.com
Web ....www.storymakersinc.com

Agent: Denise Coburn, Actors, ETC,
713-785-4995

Diana Contreras

Diosa Productions
Northridge, CA 91326
Tel 818-360-0813
Email ....diana.shakti@verizon.net

Director, POR UN AMOR, 1999, Diosa
  Productions, Short
Director, LUMINARY, 1998, Diosa
  Productions, Short
Director, PORTRAIT OF LIGHT, 1996, Diosa
  Productions, Short

Ernie Contreras*

Los Angeles, CA 90068
Tel 323-876-3424
Cell 323-447-4069
Fax 323-876-3424
Email ....cemtr@sbcglobal.net

Agent: Mark Ross, Paradigm,
310-277-4400

Writer, FAIRY TALE: A TRUE STORY, 1997,
  Paramount, Feature
Writer, THE PAGEMASTER, 1994, Twentieth
  Century Fox, Feature
Writer, THE SMURFS, 1990,
  Hanna-Barbera/Turner, TV Series, Animated
Writer, TELEVISION ANIMATION,
  1988-1993, Hanna-Barbera, TV Animation

Rosemary Contreras*

Los Angeles, CA 90048
Cell 818-648-4206
Email ....rosemarycontreras@hotmail.com

Writer, GO, DIEGO, GO!, 2005, Nick Jr., TV
  Series, Animated
Director, Writer, LATINA TRAILBLAZER
  ELLEN OCHOA, 2001, Latino Public
  Broadcasting, Interstitial

Samuel Cordoba*

Graphic Artist, Production Designer
Los Angeles, CA 90027
Tel 323-667-2072
Cell 213-840-6847
Fax 323-667-2072
Email ....samuel@lookpictures.net
Web ....www.lookpictures.net

Production Designer, OIL AND WATER, 2002,
  Short
Production Designer, THE TREE, 2002, Short
Production Designer, STRIKE, 2001, Short
Graphic Designer

Lori Cordova*

Catering By Lori Cordova Inc.
Santa Barbara, CA 93101
Tel 805-733-3141
Fax 805-733-3142
Email ....loricordova@verizon.net
Web ......www.cateringbyLoriCordova.com

Caterer, EL NIÑO, 2004, Mojo Productions, Feature
Caterer, Craft, JACK SATIN, 2004, Feature
Caterer, Craft, HOW THE GARCIA GIRLS SPENT THEIR SUMMER, 2003, Loosely Based Pictures LLC., Feature
Caterer, Craft, ANIMA, 2002, AFI, Short

Sergio Coronado*
North Hills, CA 91343
Tel 818-415-3056
Email ....sergiocoronado@msn.com

Field Producer, CRAFTING COAST TO COAST (SEASON 1 & 2), 2004, 2005, Weller/Grossman Productions HGTV, TV Series
Production Manager, HARSH REALITY (PILOT), 2004, 20th Television Syndication, Talk Show
Associate Producer, IT'S A MIRACLE, 2003, 2004, Weller/Grossman Productions PAX-TV, TV Series
Production Manager, BEHIND CLOSED DOORS (PILOT), 2003, Sony Pictures TV, Talk Show
Production Manager, BOY MEETS BOY, 2003, Evolution Film, Tape BRAVO, TV Series

Carlos Corral*
MindWarp Entertainment
Austin, TX 78741
Tel 512-922-4379
Email ....ccorral@mindwarpet.com
Web ....www.mindwarpet.com

Manuel Correa
Strictly Kings Productions
New York, NY 10023
Cell 646-209-0177
Email ....contact@
strictlykingsproductions.com

Producer, Writer, PEOPLES, 2003, Strictly Kings Productions, Feature
Production Manager, LOVE SONG - HARVEY MILK, 2001, Hypnotic, Short
Director, Writer, WUNDER, 2001, Jetlag Productions, Short

Alex D. Cortez*
Santa Ana, CA 92701
Tel 714-791-1238
Email ....alexdcortez@yahoo.com
Web ....www.cortezvision.com

Producer, BETRAYAL AND VIOLATIONS, 2005, Documentary
Producer, DIMITRI GONZALEZ EL VEN-GADOR, 2005, Feature
Producer, HIP HOP HOODIOS:"KIKE ON THE MIC", 2005, Music Video

David Cortez*
MEXUS
Santa Fe, NM 87501
Tel 505-988-9233
Cell 202-425-5435
Email ....cortezdl@mac.com

Attorney: David Dirks, daviddirks18@hotmail.com

Director of Photography, BEHIND THE WHITE COAT, 2005, PAC 8 Los Alamos NM, Educational Program
Producer, CHICANO BUILT, 2005, Poetry Music Entertainment
Director of Photography, Editor, CULTURAL COMPETENCY, 2004, Anarcafilms Santa Fe Public Schools, Educational
Director of Photoraphy, Editor, HISTORY ART AND CULTURE OF MEXICO, 2004, Anarcafilms Gregorio Luke, Educational Lecture

Oscar Cortez*
Goleta, CA 93117
Tel 650-784-1598
Email ....oscaracortez@hotmail.com

Maria Elena Cortinas*
Cinemaria Productions
Los Angeles, CA 90062
Tel 323-298-7315
Email ....cinemaria2002@yahoo.com

Director, Producer, QUE TAL, THE DOCU-MENTARY, 2005, Documentary
Still Photographer, NATE AND THE COLONEL, 2004, Feature
Associate Producer, UNSUNG COWBOY, 1998, Short

Co-Director, Producer, GO WEST, 1996, Short
Director, NUMBERS COUNT, 1995, National
MS Society, PSA
Director, ENUF SAID, 1994, National MS
Society, Music Video

Valintino Costa*

Publicity and Event Coordinator
EV Public Relations
Tucson, AZ 85704
Tel 520-292-2035
Cell 520-235-1862
Email ....tinoc72@yahoo.com

2nd 2nd Assistant Director, HOW THE GAR-
CIA GIRLS SPENT THEIR SUMMER,
2005, Loosely Based Pictures, LLC.,
Feature
2nd Assistant Director, THE CONNECTICUT
KID, 2003, TCK Productions, Feature

Oscar Luis Costo

MARdeORO Films Inc.
San Marino, CA 91108
Tel 626-799-1388
Fax 626-799-2388
Email ....mardeoro@earthlink.net

*Agent: Jack Leighton, Innovative Artists,
310-656-0400*

Producer, THE LAST RIDE, 2004, USA
Network, TV Movie
Director, ENCRYPT , 2003, USA Films, TV
Movie
Producer, STEALING CHRISTMAS, 2003,
USA Films, TV Movie
Producer, SAINT/SINNER, 2002, USA Films,
TV Movie
Producer, HITCHED, 2001, USA Films, TV
Movie

Manny Coto

Beverly Hills, CA 90212

*Agent: Greg Hodes, Endeavor Talent
Agency, 310-248-2000*

Executive Producer, Writer, ODYSSEY 5,
2002, Columbia TriStar, TV Series
Executive Producer, Writer, STAR TREK:
ENTERPRISE, 2001, Paramount Pictures,
TV Series

Director, ZENON: THE SEQUEL, 2001, The
Disney Channel, TV Movie
Director, THE OTHER ME, 2000, The Disney
Channel, TV Movie

Richard Crudo

Los Angeles, CA 90049
Tel 310-288-1125
Email ....rpcarn@aol.com

*Agent: Montana Artists Agency,
323-845-4144*

Director of Photography, NAILED RIGHT IN,
2005, Lions Gate Films, Feature
Director of Photography, BRING IT ON
AGAIN, 2004, Universal Pictures, Feature
Director of Photography, OUT OF REACH,
2004, Roundabout Entertainment Inc.,
Feature
Director of Photography, GRIND, 2003,
Warner Bros., Feature
Director of Photography, DOWN TO EARTH,
2001, Paramount Pictures, Feature

Kaye Cruz*

24 Hour Entertainment Inc.
San Antonio, TX 78240
Tel 210-573-6990
Cell 210-573-6990
Fax 210-691-0803
Email ....onair@juno.com

Producer, THE BACKROAD, 2004, New Tribe
Films, Short
Executive Producer, VENTANA RADIO IM,
2004, 24 Hour Entertainment Inc.,
Broadband Broadcast Project Design
Executive Producer, VENTANA-TV, 2003, 24
Hour Entertainment Inc., Broadband
Broadcast Project Design

Rene Simon Cruz*

Esperanza Films, Inc.
Santa Monica, CA 90404
Tel 310-899-9336
Fax 310-899-9007
Email ....renecruz@esperanza.com
Web.......................www.esperanza.com

*Attorney: Michael Morales, Esq.,
310-278-0066*

Producer, THE CULT OF QUENTIN TRRANTI-NO, 2005, IFC Originals, Documentary
Director, Writer, THE SALTED EARTH, 2005, Esperanza Films Inc./Steel Petal Films, Feature
Producer, MARY J. BLIGE "LIVE", 2004, Sanctuary Records, HD Concert DVD
Producer, CROSS THE LINE, 2003, Horizon Films, Feature
Producer, DRIVE TIME, 2003, Independent Film Channel, TV Series Pilot
Producer, INDEPENDENT FOCUS, 2002-2003, Independent Film Channel, Talk Show

Jason Cuadrado*
Cinemonster Films
New York, NY 10031
Email ....cinemonster@hotmail.com

Alfonso Cuaron
Burning Bright Features
New York, CA 10013
Tel 212-219-7610
Fax 212-601-5916

Agent: Steve Rabineau, WMA, 310-859-4000

Producer, ASSASSINATION OF RICHARD NIXON, 2004, Monsoon Pictures, Feature
Producer, CRONICAS, 2004, Producciones Anhelo, Feature
Director, HARRY POTTER AND THE PRISONER OF AZKABAN, 2004, Warner Bros., Feature
Director, THE CHILDREN OF MEN, 2003, Beacon Communications, Feature
Director, Producer, Y TU MAMA TAMBIEN, 2001, IFC, Feature
Director, GREAT EXPECTATIONS, 1998, 20th Century Fox, Feature
Director, LITTLE PRINCESS, 1995, Warner Bros., Feature
Director, FALLEN ANGELS, 1993, Showtime, TV Series

Carmen Cuba
Beverly Hills, CA 90212
Tel 213-503-4405
Email ....cubaahse@aol.com

Agent: Sean Elliott, Endeavor Talent Agency, 310-248-2000

Casting Director, DEEP WATER, 2005, Halcyon Entertainment, Feature
Casting Director, ONE POINT O, 2004, Armada Films, Feature
Casting Director, THE BUTTERFLY EFFECT, 2004, New Line Cinema, Feature
Casting Director, SWITCHED, 2003, ABC Family, TV Series
Casting Director, BLACK WIDOW MAMA, 2002, Important Pictures, Feature

Michael Cuesta
New York, NY 10001
Tel 516-909-4787
Email ....howie516@aol.com

Agent: ICM, 310-550-4000

Director, Producer, 12 AND HOLDING, 2005, Feature
Director, Producer, Writer, L.I.E., 2001, Lot 47 Films, Feature
Director, SIX FEET UNDER, 2001, HBO, TV Series

Mary Cuevas*
Long Beach, CA 90802
Email ....marycuevas@earthlink.net

Tania Cuevas-Martinez*
Oakland, CA 94611
Tel 646-236-1935
Email...............efilms2012@yahoo.com

Patricia Cunliffe*
Joie de Vivre Productions
Altadena, CA 91003-6635
Tel 626-797-9926
Fax 626-296-0342
Email......................cunliffe@juno.com
Web ......www.joiedevivreproductions.com

Director, Producer, A LANGUAGE OF PAS-
SION, 2004, Joie de Vivre Productions,
Documentary
Director, Producer, CHILI & TORTILLAS,
2002, Joie de Vivre Productions, Short
Director, Producer, RHIANNON'S BRIDGE,
2000, Joie de Vivre Productions,
Experimental
Host, Producer, SEASONED MEN AND
THEIR PASSIONS, 1999, Joie de Vivre
Productions, TV Show
Costume Designer, GIRL OF THE YEAR,
1998, M. Roman Productions, Stage Play
Graphic Designer

Monique Gabriela Curnen*
New York, NY 10027
Cell 917-533-7190
Email ....mcurnen@hotmail.com

Actress, ANGEL, 2004, Feature
Actress, MARIA FULL OF GRACE, 2004,
HBO Films/Fine Line, Feature
Actress, THE JURY, 2004, Fox TV, TV Series
Actress, HOLLYWOOD CALLING, 2001,
Feature

Tania Cypriano*
Vival Pictures
New York, NY 10014
Tel 212-691-5303

Producer, DAME LA MANO, 2001, PVH Films
the Netherlands, Feature
Producer, DESTINO EXPORTADOR, 2001, TV
Cultura-Brazil, TV Series
Producer, BILL MOYER: EARTH ON EDGE,
2000, PBS, TV Series
Producer, CASA GRANDE E SENZALA, 2000,
GNT-Brazil, TV Series
Producer, NO MIRROR, 1991, Vival Pictures,
Feature
Producer, VIVA EU!, 1989, VideoVideo-Brazil,
Third World Newsreel-USA, Feature

Vanessa Dalama*
Miami, FL 33183
Tel 786-346-5723
Tel 305-380-1712
Email....................crazygrl419@aol.com

Marcia L. Daley
Attorney
Sanchez & Amador, LLP
Los Angeles, CA 90017
Tel 213-291-3101
Fax 213-955-7201
Email ....daley@sanchez-amador.com

Ignacio Darnaude
Executive Vice President, International
Creative Advertising
Columbia TriStar
Culver City, CA 90232
Tel 310-244-4000
Fax 310-244-0898

Elizabeth Datrindade*
New York, NY 10016
Email ....edatrin@iwon.com

Angel David*
New York, NY 10024
Tel 212-769-1137
Email..................nyangeldavid@aol.com

Director, Writer, THE LONG GOODNIGHT,
2004, Short
Director, CUCHIFRITO, 2003, INTAR
Theatre, Stage Play
Director, EL SALVADOR, 2002, Legend
Theatre Co., Stage Play
Writer, BY REASON OF..., 1994, INTAR
Theatre, Stage Play

Gilbert Davila
VP, Multicultural Marketing
Walt Disney Company
Burbank, CA 91521
Tel 818-560-6905
Email ....gilbert.davila@disney.com

Carlos de Jesus

Professor, Dept. of Film and Television
Tisch School of the Arts, NYU
New York, NY 10003
Tel 212-691-4930
Tel 212-998-1729
Fax 212-995-4062
Email ....carlos.dejesus@nyu.edu

Director, Producer, THAT OLD GANG OF
    MINE, 1996, Filmmakers Library,
    Documentary
Director, Producer, WATCH YOUR MOUTH,
    1977, PBS, TV Series
Director, Producer, IMAGENES, 1973-1976,
    PBS-New Jersey, Weekly Variety Program

Victor de Jesus*

Burbank, CA 91522
Tel 818-954-2007
Email ....vdejesus@aol.com

Agent: Tanya Lopez, ICM,
310-550-4000, lopezti@icmtalent.com

Manager: Caldera/De Fanti,
323-906-9500, ccaldera@sbcglobal.net

Writer, THIRD WATCH, 2003, WBTV/JWP, TV
    Series
Production Manager, PRISON SONG, 2001,
    New Line Cinema, Feature
Production Manager, GHOST DOG, 1999,
    Feature
Production Manager, THE 24 HOUR WOMAN,
    1999, Shooting Gallery, Feature
Production Manager, SUBWAY STORIES,
    1997, HBO Films, TV Movie
Associate Producer, I LIKE IT LIKE THAT,
    1994, Sony Pictures, Feature

Maggie de la Cuesta*

Polymorphous Pictures
New York, NY 10027
Tel 212-222-4134
Cell 305-519-3372
Email ....tibutort12@aol.com

Christian de la Fe*

Coral Gables, FL 33143
Email ....erniedelafe@yahoo.com

Neil de la Peña*

Hollywood, CA 90028
Email ....ndlp@mindspring.com

Nonny de la Peña

Los Angeles, CA 90001
Email ....nonnydlp@verizon.net

Director, Producer, THE WHISTLE BLOWER,
    2004, Court TV, TV Special
Director, Producer, Writer, UNCONSTITU-
    TIONAL, 2004, The Disinformation
    Company, Documentary
Director, Producer, Writer, MAMA/M.A.M.A.,
    2003, Pyedog, Documentary
Director, Producer, Writer, THE JAUNDICED
    EYE, 1999, SomFord Entertainment,
    Documentary

Ana Marie de la Peña Portela

San Antonio, TX 78209
Tel 210-669-9935
Tel 212-313-6850
Email...............adep78209@yahoo.com
Web....................www.anadeportela.com

Manager: George & Liz Ozuna,
210-669-9935, cineman@ev1.net

Writer, I LIKE EUROPE AND EUROPE LIKES
    ME, 2003, Experimental
Writer, LAST TANGO IN SAN ANTONIO,
    2003, Ozuna Digital, Short
Writer, SHAVING FOR THE CITY, 2003,
    Ozuna Digital, Short

Deborah de la Torre*

Festival Director
Tulipanes Latino Art & Film Festival
Holland, MI 49423
Tel 616-355-2121
Fax 616-355-2123
Email ....info@tlaff.org
Web ....www.tulipanes.org

Margie de la Torre Aguirre*

Abrazo Productions
Yorba Linda, CA 92887
Email ....mareflections@aol.com

Mario F. de la Vega
Prickly Pear Productions
Studio City, CA 91604
Tel 818-985-2630
Email ....mariodlv@access1.net

Director, Producer, Writer, ROBBING PETER,
2004, Prickly Pear Productions, Feature

Dita de Leon*
Muevete Entertainment, Inc.
Beverly Hills, CA 90212
Tel 323-469-9978
Tel 973-484-5161
Email.................ditadeleon@yahoo.com
Web.....................www.DitadeLeon.com

Actor, ABSOLUTE TANGERINE, 2005,
Feature
Actor, EL VACILON, 2004, Feature
Writer, SEX SYMBOL DIVA, 2004, Stand Up
Comedy
Actor, AMOR A LA MEXICANA, 2003,
Feature
Actor, OUT OF BALANCE, 2003, Feature

Margo de Leon*
San Bernardino, CA 92411
Tel 909-381-6984
Email ....btr_p@hotmail.com

Perla de Leon*
Fotografica
New York, NY 10036
Tel 212-244-5182
Fax 212-244-5182
Email ....perlafotografica@aol.com

Director, Editor, Producer, Writer, LA CASITA,
2004, Short
Technical Consultant, ROSA & TJE EXECU-
TIONER, 2004, Feature

Nancy de los Santos*
GT Productions
Los Angeles, CA 90026
Tel 323-226-9256
Cell 213-926-4345
Fax 323-226-1066
Email ....LaNancyD@sbcglobal.net

Agent: Tanya Lopez, ICM,
310-550-4000, tlopezti@icmtalent.com

Producer, LALO GUERRERO: THE ORIGINAL
CHICANO, 2004, LPB, Documentary
Writer, AMERICAN FAMILY, 2002, PBS, TV
Series
Director, Writer, BRONZE SCREEN: ONE
HUNDRED YEARS OF THE LATINO IMAGE
IN AMERICAN CINEMA, 2002, Bronze
Screen Productions, Documentary
Writer, GOTTA KICK IT UP!, 2002, Disney
Channel, TV Movie
Writer, RESURRECTION BLVD., 2002,
Showtime, TV Series
Associate Producer, SELENA, 1997, Warner
Bros., Feature

Ron de Moraes
Beverly Hills, CA 90212

Agent: John Ferritere, WMA,
310-859-4000

Director, EMMY AWARDS PRE-SHOW, 2003,
Fox Film Corp., TV Special
Director, PRIMETIME CREATIVE ARTS EMMY
AWARDS, 2003, E! Entertainment
Television, TV Special
Director, 2002 WINTER OLYMPICS OPENING
& CLOSING CERMONIES & MEDAL CON-
CERTS, 2002, NBC, TV Special
Director, WORLD'S GREATEST COMMER-
CIALS, 2002, CBS, TV Special

Ivan de Paz
Manager
Ivan de Paz Management
Los Angeles, CA 90001
Tel 310-409-8638
Email ......ivan@de-paz-management.com

Alfredo de Villa*
Miami Beach, FL 33139
Tel 917-749-2244
Email ....bunuelhitch@earthlink.net

Agent: Stuart Manashil, UTA,
310-273-6700,
smanashil@unitedtalent.com

Director, Writer, ONE-NINE, 2005, Feature
Director, WASHINGTON HEIGHTS, 2002,
  Mac Releasing, Feature
Director, THE DOORMAN, 1999,
  Documentary
Director, NETO'S RUN, 1998, Atom Films,
  Short
Director, Producer, TV COMMERCIALS,
  1997-Present, Y&R, DDB, Commercial

Andre Degas*
Degasworks
New York, NY 10019
Tel 212-581-3950
Tel 212-245-7713
Email ....degasworks@mac.com

Dan del Campo
Publicist
401 Productions/DDC Publicity and
Communications
Los Angeles, CA 90036
Tel 310-314-2790
Fax 310-314-2790
Email ....dan@indiefilter.net

Publicist, HEALTHY LIVING, 2001, PBS
  Series, TV
Publicist, THE WOMAN CHASER, 2001,
  Patrick Warburton, Feature

Ron del Rio*
Manager
Gilbertson Kincaid
Santa Monica, CA 90401
Tel 310-393-8585
Email ....rdr1050@aol.com

Graciela del Toro*
J. Walter Thompson
Brooklyn, NY 11226
Tel 212-210-7284
Fax................................212.210.7520
Email ....chela@peopleweb.com

Guillermo del Toro
Austin, TX

Agent: Mike Simpson, WMA,
310-859-4000

Producer, CRONICAS, 2004, Palm Pictures,
  Feature
Director, Writer, HELLBOY, 2004, Columbia
  Pictures, Feature
Director, BLADE II, 2002, New Line Cinema,
  Feature
Producer, I MURDER SERIOUSLY, 2002,
  Magna Films S.L., Feature
Director, Writer, MIMIC, 1997, Dimension
  Films, Feature
Writer, CRONOS, 1993, October Films,
  Feature

Natasha del Toro*
New York, NY 10027
Tel 813-846-3768
Email ....ndelto@hotmail.com

Rafael del Toro*
Brooklyn, NY 11226
Tel 917-406-3320
Email ......brownbull@industryfreaks.com
Web ....www.brownbullfilms.com

Director, Writer, SIX FEET AND SEVEN MIN-
  UTES, 2005, Short
Editor, DOS MINUTOS, 2003, TuTV, TV
  Series
Editor, 25TH HOUR, 2002, Touchstone,
  Feature
Director, Editor, Writer, THE SILENCE
  BEFORE, 2002, NYU, Short
Director, Writer, MUST BE LOVE, 2001,
  NYU, Short

Zulma del Toro*
Miami, FL 33176
Tel 305-470-5897
Email ....zulydeltoro@aol.com

filmmakers

Andrew Delaplaine*
Shallow Beach Entertainment
Miami Beach, FL 33139
Tel 305-535-6522
Fax 305-868-4477
Email ....andrew@shallowbeach.tv
Web ....www.shallowbeach.tv

Director, MIDNIGHT NEWS, 2003, Short
Director, PRODUCT PLACEMENT, 2003,
   Short
Director, THE MORNING NEWS, 2003, Short

Gloribel Delgado*
San Juan, PR 00918
Tel 787-607-7380
Email.................gloribeld@hotmail.com

Joseph Delgado*
Columbia, SC 29210
Email.................jfdelgadoinsc@aol.com

Nicole Delgado*
Albany, NY 12210
Fax 646 328 0415
Email ....nicolececilia@hotmail.com

Nelson Denis*
New York, NY 10032
Tel 212-568-0230
Cell 917-325-0453
Email..............nelsondenis248@aol.com
Web...............www.voteformemovie.com

Director, Producer, Writer, VOTE FOR ME!,
   2002, Feature
Director, HOUND DOG, 1987, Short
Director, EAST MEETS WEST, 1986, Short

Marlene Dermer*
Festival Director
Los Angeles Latino International Film
Festival
Los Angeles, CA 90028
Tel 323-469-9066
Fax 323-469-9067
Email ....mdermer@earthlink.net

Attorney: Marcia Daley, 213-291-3101

Director, Producer, SE RESUELVE, 1993,
   Feature
Line Producer, INFERNO, 1992,
   Documentary
Associate Producer, SIN KLINE, 1991, Short

Alejandro Diaz
Cuentos del Pueblo Productions
Beverly Hills, CA 90213
Tel 323-462-6019
Email..cuentos_del_pueblo@hotmail.com
Web ....www.cuentosdelpueblo.com

Director, Writer, PAN DULCE Y CHOCOLATE,
   Short

Lucia Diaz*
Los Angeles, CA 90028
Email ....lucia@lamandinga.com

Ellie Diez*
Loisaida Cortos
New York, NY 10021
Tel 917-907-3745
Email ....loisaidacortos@yahoo.com
Web ....www.loisaidacortos.com

Alberto Dominguez*
Bronze Screen Productions
Glendale, CA 91206
Tel 818-662-8009
Fax 818-662-0109
Email.........hollywoodcom@earthlink.net

Director, Producer, THE BRONZE SCREEN:
   100 YEARS OF THE LATINO IMAGE IN
   AMERICAN CINEMA, 2002, Documentary

Juan M. Dominguez*
Bogota, NJ 07603
Email ....Juan.Dominguez@otis.com

Walter Dominguez*
Los Angeles, CA 90035
Tel 323-651-4695
Email ....shelwalt2001@yahoo.com

Alvaro Donado*
Workshop Entertainment
New York, NY 10024
Fax 212-866-6168
Email ....aDonado@
            workshopentertainment.com
Web ....www.workshopentertainment.com

Xochitl Dorsey*
Brooklyn, NY 11205
Tel 718-623-2690
Tel 917-584-7667
Email..........xochitl_dorsey@hotmail.com

Mario Dubovoy*
Aventura FIlms
Aventura, FL 33180
Tel 305-527-2404
Email ......mdubovoy@aventurafilms.com
Web ....www.aventurafilms.com

Director, Producer, LEO, 2004, Aventura
    Films, Documentary

Alexon Duprey*
Arte Del Tercer Mundo
Caguas, PR 00725
Tel 787-397-8021
Fax 787-703-4186
Email ....alexon_duprey@yahoo.com

Karina Duque*
Austin, TX 78703
Email ....empresskarina22@hotmail.com

Sandra Duque*
La Negrita Productions
New York, NY 10021
Tel 212-502-0316
Tel 347-739-1720
Fax 212-772-1506
Email..LaNegritaProductions@yahoo.com

Juan Carlos (JC) Duran*
Pepe & Elmer Media, Inc
Los Angeles, CA 90048
Tel 323-960-5520
Fax 323-960-4310
Email ....jcduran@pepeandelmer.com
Web ....www.pepeandelmer.com

Producer, UNTITLED REALITY SERIES,
    2005, Telemundo, TV Series
Producer, ELECTRONIC PRESS KITS, 2004,
    Varous Television Networks, EPK
Media Consultant, FOX TELEVISION, 2004,
    Fox Television, Media, Market
Media Consultant, LATV, 2004, LATV, Media,
    Market
Media Consultant, NBC, 2004, NBC, Media,
    Market
Producer, PRICE OF GLORY: BEHIND THE
    SCENES, 2000, New Line
    Cinema/Esparza-Katz Productions,
    TV Special

Keyla Echevarria*
KND Production Assistant
Curious Pictures
Bronx, NY 10473
Email ....keylaechevarria@yahoo.com
Web ....www.castlehp.com

Joe Eckardt*
Sherman Oaks, CA 91403
Tel 818-708-7166
Fax 212-315-5607
Email.....................joeeckardt@aol.com

Mylo Egipciaco*
Los Angeles, CA 90036
Tel 323-933-9294
Tel 212-737-4033
Cell 323-377-2811
Fax 323-933-9294
Email ....Mylodinprods@aol.com

Writer, DREAM WITH ANGELS, 2005,
    Mylodin Productions, Stage Play
Actor, SINGLE VALLEY, 1993, Continental
    TV, TV Soap Parody
Director, Producer, Writer, ETERNAL
    REGRESSION, 1991, Mylodin
    Productions, Short
Host, Writer, NEWSROOM, 1991, Continental
    TV, TV News

filmmakers

Roni Eguia Menendez

Narrow Bridge Films
Studio City, CA 91604
Tel 818-766-1582
Fax 818-766-1882
Email ..narrowbridgefilms@sbcglobal.net

Producer, HUNTING OF MAN, 2003, Feature
Producer, BAD SEED, 2001, New City
   Releasing, Feature
Producer, SCRAPBOOK, 1999, PorchLight
   Entertainment, Feature
Associate Producer, AFTER SUNSET: THE
   LIFE & TIMES OF THE DRIVE-IN THE-
   ATER, 1995, Moonshadow Entertainment,
   Documentary
Producer, REMEMBRANCES, 1995, Feature

Manuel Elgarresta*

Program Development
TV Hut
Miami Beach, FL 33140
Email ....mannye@bellsouth.net

Katrina Elias*

Jude Shaw Co.
North Hollywood, CA 91606
Tel 818-766-3766
Email ....kelias1056@aol.com

Writer, ABUELO'S LEGACY, 2001, Stage Play
Writer, DEAD HEAT FILM, 2001, Feature

Hector Elizondo

Shanti Productions
Sherman Oaks, CA 91403

*Manager: Teitelbaum Artists Group,
310-203-8000*

Actor, THE PRINCESS DIARIES 2: ROYAL
   ENGAGEMENT, 2004, Buena Vista ,
   Feature
Actor, WRONG TURN AT LUNGFISH, 2004,
   Play
Actor, BATMAN: MYSTERY OF THE BAT-
   WOMAN, 2003, Warner Bros., Video
Actor, MIRACLES, 2003, ABC, TV Series
Actor, HOW HIGH, 2001, Universal, Feature
Actor, TORTILLA SOUP, 2001, Samuel
   Goldwyn Films, Feature
Actor, PRETTY WOMAN, 1990, Buena Vista
   Pictures, Feature

Jesus "Chuy" Elizondo

Los Angeles, CA 90001
Tel 818-346-1672

Director of Photography, VIEW FROM THE
   SWING, 2000, Feature
Director of Photography, EVASIVE ACTION,
   1998, Hallmark Entertainment, Feature
Director of Photography (2nd Unit), SEPA-
   RATE LIVES, 1995, Trimark Pictures,
   Feature
Director of Photography, THE CISCO KID,
   1994, Turner Pictures, Feature

Maria Endara*

New York, NY 10009
Email.................ml_endara@yahoo.com

Edgar Endress

Media Artist, Assistant Professor
Morcor County Community College
Beach Haven, NJ 08008
Tel 609-494-6351
Tel......................609-586-4800 x3457
Email ....endresse@mccc.edu
Web ....www.eendress.com

Director, CONCRETE WALL, 2005,
   Experimental
Director, THE MAN WITH BAD LUCK, 2005,
   Experimental
Director, THE LURE OF GESTURES, 2002,
   Documentary
Director, THE MEMORY OF SNAILS, 2001,
   Experimental
Director, COMMUNICATING COMMUNITAS,
   2000, Documentary
Director, ELVIS HATES AMERICA, 2000,
   Experimental
Director, EXIT 6, 1999, Experimental

Carolina Escalante*

Service Coordinator
Youth Volunteer Corp.
Tucson, AZ 85750
Tel 520-881-3300
Fax 520-881-3366
Email ....cescalan@email.arizona.edu

Jaime Escallon*

Toronto, Ontario M4Y1R6 Canada
Tel 416-920-5497
Cell 416-838-6779
Email ..jaimeescallonburaglia@hotmail.com

Writer, HOPELESS, 2004, Tucan
   Productions, Feature
Director, Writer, ID, 2004, OMNITV,
   Documentary
Director, Writer, WELCOME, 2004, NFR,
   Short
Director, THE CAGE, 2003, Cara Col TV,
   TV Series
Director, Writer, MEN'S STORIES, 2002,
   Cara Col TV, TV Series

Geno Escarrega

Top Boss Productions, Inc.
Santa Monica, CA 90406
Tel 310-393-9308

Producer, PASADENA, 2001, Columbia
   TriStar, TV Series
Producer, CHINA BEACH, 1988, ABC, TV
   Series

Maria Escobedo*

Rain Forest Films Inc.
Great Neck, NY 11021
Tel 718-279-0273
Email ....rainforestfilms@netzero.com

Director, Writer, LA COCINA/THE KITCHEN,
   2005, Latino Public Broadcasting, TV
   Movie
Writer, BIOGRAPHY: DIEGO RIVERA, 2004,
   Biography Channel, TV Series
Writer, LAW & ORDER, 2004, Spec Script,
   TV Series
Writer, DONA ANA'S FUNERAL, 2002,
   Feature
Director, Writer, RUM AND COKE, 2000,
   Delta/MCI video, Feature

Moctesuma Esparza*

Maya Pictures
Los Angeles, CA 90017
Tel 310-281-3770
Fax 310-281-3777
Web ....www.maya-pictures.com

Executive Producer, GODS AND GENERALS,
   2003, Warner Bros., Feature
Executive Producer, PRICE OF GLORY, 2002,
   New Line Cinema, Feature
Executive Producer, INTRODUCING
   DOROTHY DANDRIDGE, 1999, HBO,
   Feature
Executive Producer, SELMA, LORD, SELMA,
   1999, Buena Vista Television, TV Movie
Executive Producer, BUTTER, 1998, Life
   Entertainment, Feature
Executive Producer, ROUGH RIDERS, 1997,
   TNT, TV Movie
Producer, SELENA, 1997, Warner Bros.,
   Feature
Producer, THE DISAPPEARANCE OF GARCIA
   LORCA, 1997, Columbia TriStar, Feature
Executive Producer, THE CISCO KID, 1994,
   Turner Pictures, TV Movie
Producer, GETTYSBURG, 1993, New Line
   Cinema, Feature

Phil Esparza

El Teatro Campesino
San Juan Bautista, CA 95045
Tel 831-623-2444
Email ....phil_esparza@csumb.edu
Web ....www.elteatrocampesino.com

Actor, THE CISCO KID, 1994, Turner
   Pictures, TV Movie
Executive Producer, LA PASTORELA, 1991,
   PBS, TV Movie
Associate Producer, ZOOT SUIT, 1982,
   Universal Pictures, Feature

Tonantzin Esparza*

Maya Pictures
Los Angeles, CA 90017
Tel 310-281-3770
Fax 310-281-3777
Email ....tonantzin_e@hotmail.com
Web ....www.maya-pictures.com

Manager: McCleod Management,
323-960-4356,
debbiemcleod@netzero.net

Associate Producer, CIRCUMSIZED CINEMA,
   2005, Si TV, TV Series
Actor, CHOLA THE URBAN EXPLORA, 2004,
   Si TV, TV Pilot
Actor, STRONG MEDICINE, 2004, Lifetime,
   TV Series

Actor, AMERICAN FAMILY, 2003, PBS, TV
Series
Actor, GEORGE LOPEZ, 2002, ABC/Warner
Bros., TV Series

Dolly Josette Espinal*
Manager of Development
Si TV
Los Angeles, CA 90065
Tel 323-256-8900
Tel 323-543-2763
Email ....despinal@sitv.com
Web ....www.sitv.com

Development Executive, BREAKFAST LUNCH
AND DINNER, 2004, Si TV, TV Series
Development Executive, CHOLA THE URBAN
EXPLORA, 2004, Si TV, TV Pilot
Producer, THE RUB, 2004, Si TV, TV Series

Alfonso Espinosa*
Carmona Entertainment
Los Angeles, CA 90022
Tel 323-721-FILM
Fax 323-728-4045
Web ....www.carmona-entertainment.com

Writer, GOD'S PENITENTIARY, 2004,
Carmona Entertainment Inc., Feature
Editor, ASI SE HACE, 2003, Channel 22, TV
Series
Editor, COMO TE VES, 2003, Channel 22, TV
Series
Editor, TRIBUNAL DEL PUEBLO, 2003,
Channel 22, TV Series
Producer, IN SEARCH OF AZTLAN, 2002,
Carmona Entertainment Inc., Documentary

Paul Espinosa*
Espinosa Productions
Scottsdale, AZ 85252
Tel 480-965-3635
Tel 480-965-5120
Fax 480-965-3421
Email ....espinosa@electriciti.com
Web ....www.EspinosaProductions.com

Producer, BEYOND THE DREAM, 2005, LPB,
Documentary
Producer, TACO SHOP POETS, 2004, PBS,
Documentary
Producer, VISIONES: LATINO ART &CUL-
TURE, 2004, PBS, Documentary

Producer, THE BORDER, 2000, PBS,
Documentary
Producer, THE U.S. - MEXICAN
WAR:1846-1848, 1998, PBS,
Documentary

Richard Espinosa
On Air Manager
Showtime Networks Inc.
New York, NY 10019
Tel 212-708-1600
Web ....www.sho.com

Carlos Espinoza*
Lynwood, CA 90262
Tel 323-632-3040
Email ....nito_ent03@yahoo.com

Production Assistant, HOW THE GARCIA
GIRLS SPENT THEIR SUMMER, 2003,
Loosely Based Pictures, LLC, Feature

Freddie Espinoza
West Coast Bureau Producer
Univision Network
Los Angeles, CA 90093
Tel 3110-348-3634
Web ....www.univision.net

Stephen Espinoza*
Attorney
Ziffren, Brittenham, Branca
Los Angeles, CA 90067
Tel 310-552-6506
Fax 310-553-7068
Email.............Stephene@ziffrenlaw.com

Trina Espinoza*
San Francisco, CA 94129
Email ....trina@theorphanage.com

Mario Esquer*
CTV Film and Video Production
Scottsdale, AZ 85253
Tel 480-483-8473
Email ....mario.esquer@
gcmail.maricopa.edu

Melinda Esquibel*
Mundo Maravilla
Beverly Hills, CA 90213
Tel 323-654-9874
Email ......melinda@mundomaravilla.com

Cari Esta-Albert*
Noon Attack
Los Angeles, CA 90035
Tel 310-278-3316
Email ....cea@noonattack.com

Executive Producer, LOVE IS STRANGE,
   1999, Lifetime Television, TV Movie
Producer, THE TRUTH ABOUT CATS &
   DOGS, 1996, 20th Century Fox, Feature
Executive Producer, HEART AND SOULS,
   1993, MCA/Universal Pictures, Feature

Natatcha Estebanez*
Belmont, MA 02478
Tel 617-484-1325
Tel 617-484-2383
Fax 617-484-2383
Email ....natatcha@aol.com
Web ....www.bluediner.com

Executive Producer, POSTCARDS FROM
   BUSTER, 2005, PBS, WGBH, TV Series
Director, Producer, Writer, BLUE DINER,
   2002, First Look Home Entertainment,
   Feature
Producer, Writer, BREAKTHROUGH: THE
   CHANGING FACE OF SCIENCE AMERICA,
   1996, Black Site Inc., Documentary

Ivelisse Estrada
Sr. VP of Corporate & Community
Relations
Univision Communications, Inc.
Los Angeles, CA 90067
Tel 310-348-3656
Web ....www.univision.net

Kevin Estrada*
Burbank, CA 91501
Tel 818-381-1025
Tel 818-607-6057
Cell 818-381-1025
Fax 267-375-2475
Email ....kevinestrada@sbcglobal.net
Web ....www.kevinestrada.com

Still Photographer, WU TANG CLAN - DISCI-
   PLES OF THE 36 CHAMBERS, 2004,
   Sanctuary Music Group, Music Video
Director, Editor, RAUL MALO - TODAY, 2003,
   Eske Entertainment, EPK
Executive Producer, SLAYER - SOUNDTRACK
   TO THE APOCALYPSE, 2003, Universal
   Music Group, Music Video
Still Photographer, SLAYER - SOUNDTRACK
   TO THE APOCALYPSE, 2003, Universal
   Music Group, Music Video
Director, Editor, Writer, IT'S NOT UNUSUAL,
   2001, Eske Entertainment, 16mm Short
   Film

Arlene Ahna Eyre*
Lomita, CA 90717
Email ....arlene_eyre@yahoo.com

Lisa Marie Fabrega*
Lethal Blossom Entertainment
Glen Ridge, NJ 07028
Email ....lafabrega@yahoo.com

Verena Faden*
Faden to Black Pictures
Miami, FL 33015
Tel 305-632-3113
Email ....cinemaddicta@aol.com
Web ....www.scenariosUSA.org

Videographer, ALL FALLS DOWN, 2004,
   Scenarios USA, Documentary
Director, Editor, Producer, Writer, DAMSEL IN
   DISTRESS, 2004, Short
Actor, Director, Writer, OLLIVES, 2004, Short
Director, Editor, Writer, SELF SABOTAGE,
   2003, Short
Writer, JUST LIKE YOU IMAGINED?, 2002,
   Scenarios USA, Short

filmmakers

Errol Falcon

Falcon Productions Inc.
Coral Gables, FL 33134
Tel 305-442-1318
Cell 786-457-8111
Fax 305-445-7432
Email ....falconfilm@aol.com

Director, Producer, LOS TEENS, 2003,
   Telemundo, TV Series
Director, Producer, RITMO LATINO AWARDS,
   2002, Telemundo, Musical Awards Show
Director, CINDY MARGOLIS SHOW, 2001,
   CBS, Eyemark, TV Pilot
Director, Producer, CORTE TROPICAL, 1994,
   Univision, TV Series
Director, SABADO GIGANTE, 1990,
   Univision, TV Variety

Daniel Faraldo

Imagen Entertainment
Burbank, CA 91505
Tel 818-845-1424
Fax 818-845-1113
Email............info@imagentertainment.tv
Web ....www.imagentertainment.tv

*Agent: Bobby Ball, Bobby Ball Talent
Agency, 818-506-8188*

Sebastian Feldman*

San Francisco, CA 94107
Tel 415-637-7139
Email ....sebas0710@yahoo.com
Web ....www.sevenrupies.com

Director, Editor, Producer, BOILERMAKERS,
   2004, Short
Equipment Coordinator, MISSION MOVIE,
   2003, Feature

Anna Felix

Felix Entertainment West
Whittier, CA 90601
Tel 562-705-3163
Cell ....fewc@thestudioshow.tv
Web ....www.thestudioshow.tv

Executive Producer, IN THE STUDIO 5,
   2004, TV Special
Executive Producer, IN THE STUDIO 3,
   2003, TV Special

Executive Producer, IN THE STUDIO 4,
   2003, TV Special
Executive Producer, IN THE STUDIO 2,
   2002, TV Special
Executive Producer, IN THE STUDIO PILOT,
   TV Special

Joao Fernandes

Los Angeles, CA 90001
Tel 323-664-8464
Email ....jferna2501@aol.com

Director of Photography, BETRAYAL, 2003,
   American World Pictures, Feature
Director of Photography, ONE MAN'S HERO,
   1999, MGM - Orion, Feature
Director, WALKER TEXAS RANGER, 1996,
   CBS, TV Series

Richard Fernandes

Los Angeles, CA 90001
Tel 888-688-9821
Email ....rick@fernandes.net

Director, Producer, THE PET PSYCHIC,
   2002, A & R Media Group, TV Series
Producer, BOOK OF POOH, 2001, Buena
   Vista Television, TV Series
Editor, TAINA, 2001, Nickelodeon Networks,
   TV Series
Director, BETWEEN THE LIONS, 2000,
   PBS/WBGH-Boston, TV Series
Producer, TAINA, 2000, Nickelodeon, TV
   Series
Director, BEAR IN THE BIG BLUE HOUSE,
   1997, Disney Channel, TV Series

Alejandro Fernandez*

Brooklyn, NY 11222
Email ....fernandezfilm@yahoo.com

Carlos Fernandez

President
Filmax International
Barcelona, 08908 SPAIN
Tel 34-9-33-36-85-55
Fax 34-9-32-63-08-24
Web ....www.filmaxinternational.com

Evelina Fernandez
Sleeping Giant Productions
Los Angeles, CA 90026
Tel 323-667-3390
Fax 323-887-9600
Email............SleepingGiantPro@aol.com
Web ....www.sleepinggiantpro.com

Agent: Jimmy Cota, The Artists Agency,
310-277-7779

Manager: Maggie Roithe,
310-876-1561

Writer, PREMEDITATION, 2004, Short
Writer, DEMENTIA, 2003, Latino Theatre
   Company, Stage Play
Actor, GABRIELA, 2001, Power Point Films,
   Feature
Producer, Writer, LUMINARIAS, 2000, New
   Latin Pictures, Feature

George E. Fernandez
Canopy Road Pictures, LLC
Tallahassee, FL 32309
Tel 305-972-6018
Fax 305-626-9711

Professor, CODED LANGUAGE, 2004, Short
Writer, POINT OF IMPACT, 1993, Vidmark
   Entertainment, Feature
Executive Producer, Writer, SHALLOW
   GRAVE, 1987, Feature
Executive Producer, Writer, CEASE FIRE,
   1985, Cineworld, Feature

Ilse Fernandez
Staff
Lion Television
New York, NY 10012
Tel 646-729-8482
Tel 212-533-5592
Email........................ifnyc@yahoo.com

Producer, PROS/CONS: THE GOOD, THE
   BAD, & THE UGLY, 2003, BBC, TV Series
Producer, THE SEQUOIA PRESIDENTIAL
   YACHT, 2002, History Channel,
   Documentary

Julio Fernandez
Chairman
Filmax International
Barcelona, 08908` SPAIN
Tel 34-9-33-36-85-55
Fax 34-9-32-63-08-24
Web ....www,filmaxinternational.com

Yvette Fernandez*
Cinecolores Productions
Toluca Lake, CA 91602
Tel 310-274-6588
Email..............cinecolores@hotmail.com

Israel Ferrer*
South Side Films
West Hollywood, CA 90048
Tel 310-276-9168
Email ....south.southfilms@gmail.com

Jaime Ferrer
Agent
Jaime Ferrar Agency (JFA)
Valley Village, CA 91607
Email ....jfatalent@sbcglobal.net

Marisa Ferrey
Los Angeles, CA 90025
Tel 310-966-9927
Cell 310-922-6794

2nd 2nd Assistant Director, SURVIVING
   CHRISTMAS, 2004, Columbia Pictures,
   Feature
2nd 2nd Assistant Director, DADDY DAY
   CARE, 2003, Columbia Pictures, Feature
2nd 2nd Assistant Director, AUSTIN POW-
   ERS IN GOLDMEMBER, 2002, New Line
   Cinema, Feature
2nd 2nd Assistant Director, SHOWTIME,
   2002, Warner Bros., Feature

Pablo Figueroa*
President
Cemi Circle Inc.
New York, NY 10011
Tel 212-243-4383
Email ....pfig@nyc.rr.com

Alicia Flores
LA TV
Los Angeles, CA 90064
Tel 310-943-5288
Fax 310-943-5299
Email ....alicia@latv.com
Web ....www.latv.com

Producer, LATV LIVE, 2005, LATV, TV
Line Producer, MEX 2 THE MAX, 2003,
    LATV, TV
Camera Assistant, KING OF THE MOON,
    2002, Short
Camera Assistant, PACO'S SUITCASE BOMB,
    2002, Short

Benny Flores
Benny Flores Creations
San Antonio, TX 78247
Tel 210-325-6724
Email ....bennyflorez@yahoo.com
Web.......................www.whatsuptv.com

Producer, WHATSUP TEXAS!, 2003, PBS, TV
    Special
Camera Operator, Producer, MAXIMUM OUT-
    DOORS, 2002, La Familia Network, TV
    Series

Claudia Flores*
Director of Operations
National Hispanic Media Coalition
Los Angeles, CA 90007
Tel 213-746-6988
Fax 213-746-1305
Email ....shadow021@yahoo.com
Web...............................www.nhmc.org

Media Advocate

Consuelo Flores
Diversity Department
Writers Guild of America, West
Los Angeles, CA 90048
Tel 323-782-4589
Fax 323-782-4807
Email ....cflores@wga.org
Web ....www.wga.org

Media Advocate

Korina Flores*
Production Dept.
Univision Network
Austin, TX 78756
Tel 512-533-2812
Email ....kflores@univision.net
Web ....www.univision.net

Norma Flores*
Public Relations
Musa Music Producciones
Irvine, CA 92614
Tel 786-390-0006
Fax 949-567-1818
Email..........normalflores@yahoo.com.mx

Lorena Flores Chatterjee*
Iventures
San Carlos, CA 94070
Tel 650-631-0000
Email..........lorenachatterjee@yahoo.com

Francisco Fonseca*
Olympia, WA 98501
Email ....intrepid@hotmail.com

Michael C. Fortuno*
Tucson, AZ 85749
Email ....astralstrider@hotmail.com

Cris (Cristóbal) Franco
Cris Franco Entertainment
Sherman Oaks, CA 91411-4060
Tel 818-642-0935
Tel 818-907-6456
Email..............CrisFrancoShow@aol.com
Web ....www.crisfranco.com

*Agent: Joan Messenger, Pinnacle Talent,
323-939-5440, joan@aef.com*

*Manager: Select Artists Limited,
818-382-4711,
slectartists@earthlink.net*

Actor, Segment Producer, Writer, LIFE &
    TIMES, 2004-2005, KCET, TV News
    Series

Actor, Writer, CALIFORNIA CONNECTED, 2003-2005, PBS - California, TV News Magazine
Host, Producer, Writer, THE CRIS FRANCO SHOW, 2003-2004, Cris Franco Entertainment, Sketch Comedy, Talk Show
Host, Producer, Writer, CAFÉ CALIFORNIA CLASSICS, 2001-2003, KCET, Sketch Comedy, Talk Show
Host, Writer, CAFÉ CALIFORNIA WITH CRIS FRANCO, 1999-2001, Cris Franco Entertainment, Sketch Comedy, Talk Show

Germaine Franco
Los Angeles, CA 90034
Tel 310-836-8499
Cell 310-985-8423
Email ....germainefranco@hotmail.com

Composer, CROSSINGS, 2003, Loyola Marymount University, Short
Production Assistant, GIGLI, 2003, Sony
Production Assistant, THE ITALIAN JOB, 2003, Paramount, Feature
Composer, REVELACCIONES, 1996, Cornell University, Documentary
Composer, LA CARPA, 1992, American Playhouse Theatre, TV Movie

Rami Frankl*
Hoboken West Digital Media
Sherman Oaks, CA 91403
Tel 818-380-8155
Fax 818-380-8134
Email ....rami@hobokenw.com
Web ....www.hobokenw.com

Juan Frausto*
Chicago, IL 60629
Email............ortamexfilms@hotmail.com

John Carlos Frey
Gatekeeper Productions
Los Angeles, CA 90069
Tel 323-656-1355
Fax 323-656-1619
Email ....Gatekeeperfilm@aol.com

Director, Writer, GATEKEEPER, 2002, Feature

Sonia Fritz*
Grupo Vanguardia
San Juan, PR 00914
Tel 787-268-0063
Fax 787-268-4379
Email ....sfritz@caribe.net
Web ....www.islafilms.com

Efrain Fuentes*
Director, Multicultural Programs
Walt Disney Company
Burbank, CA 91521
Tel 818-560-4264
Email ....efrain.fuentes@disney.com

Zetna Fuentes*
New York, NY 10009
Tel 212-254-8670
Cell 917-523-3288
Email ....zetna@nyc.rr.com

Producer, DIRTY WORKS, 2005, Villar-Hauser Theatre, Stage Play
Co-Producer, THE DV WORKSHOP, 2005, Arco Films, Series of Shorts
Director, Producer, Writer, ON AIR PROMOTIONS & PACKAGING, 2003, Arco Films for the Independent Film Channel, TV Special
Producer, THE MAKING OF CASA DE LOS BABYS, 2003, The Independent Film Channel, EPK

Donna Gaba
Agent
David Shapira & Associates
Encino, CA 91436
Tel 818-906-0322
Fax 818-783-2562

Nino Gabaldon*
Podemos Pictures
Los Angeles, CA 90038
Tel 323-769-7059
Cell 323-855-4416
Email ....mknfilms@earthlink.net
Web ....www.changethemove.com

Actor, SPLINTER, 2005, Produced by
Edward James Olmos, Feature
Actor, Director, CHANGE, 2004, Podemos
Pictures, Feature
Actor, PAN DULCE, 2004, 3rd Grade Teacher
Prod., Feature
Actor, HIGH, 2003, 180 Films, Short
Actor, TOMORROW, 2003, Wonderland Films,
Feature

Carolina Gaete*

Leadership Development Director of
Training
Public Allies
Chicago, IL 60623
Tel..........................312-422-7777 x13
Fax 312-422-7776
Email ....cgaete71@hotmail.com

Evy Ledesma Galán*

Galán Inc.
Austin, TX 78746
Tel 512-327-1333
Fax 512-327-1547
Email ....info@galaninc.com
Web..........................www.galaninc.com

Hector Galán*

Galán Inc.
Austin, TX 78746
Tel 512-327-1333
Fax 512-327-1547
Email ....galan@galaninc.com
Web..........................www.galaninc.com

Director, Producer, CINCO DE MAYO, 2004,
History Channel, Documentary
Executive Producer, VISIONES: LATINO ART
& CULTURE, 2004, PBS, Documentary
Producer, ACCORDION DREAMS, 2001,
PBS, Documentary Series
Producer, THE FORGOTTEN AMERICANS,
2000, PBS, Documentary
Producer, CHICANO! THE HISTORY OF THE
MEXICAN/AMERICAN CIVIL RIGHTS
MOVEMENT, 1996, PBS, Documentary
Producer, SONGS OF THE HOMELAND,
1995, PBS, Documentary
Producer, LOS MINEROS, 1991, PBS-The
American Experience, Documentary
Producer, VAQUERO: THE FORGOTTEN COW-
BOY, 1988, PBS, Documentary

Producer, ELEVEN 1 HR. EPISODES FOR
THE FRONTLINE SERIES, 1982-1994,
PBS-Frontline, Documentary

Kathryn F. Galán*

Executive Director
NALIP
Santa Monica, CA 90401
Tel 310-457-4445
Fax 310-395-8811
Email.....................nalip_kfg@msn.com
Web ....www.nalip.org

Executive Producer, EARLY BIRD SPECIAL,
2001, Early Bird Special LLC, Feature
Producer, FRENCH KISS, 1995, Twentieth
Century Fox, Feature
Producer, SQUANTO, 1994, Walt Disney
Company, Feature
Executive Producer, BECOMING COLETTE,
1992, CANAL+, Feature
Executive Producer, DAYBREAK, 1992, HBO,
Feature

Nely Galán

Galán Entertainment
Venice, CA 90291
Tel 310-823-2822
Fax 310-823-7361
Email ....ngalan@galanent.com
Web..........................www.galanent.com
Agent: Mark Itkin, WMA, 310-859-4000

Executive Producer, THE SWAN, 2004, Fox
Network, TV Series
Producer, LA CENICIENTA, 2003, Telemundo
Network, TV Series
Producer, VIVA VEGAS, 2000, Telemundo
Network, TV Series
Producer, LOS BELTRAN, 1999, Telemundo
Network, TV Series
Executive Producer, SOLO EN AMERICA,
Telemundo, TV Series

Esteban Galarce*

Hialeah, FL 33016
Tel 786-326-3272

Felipe Galindo*

New York, NY 10025
Tel 212-864-6648
Fax 212-316-1645
Email ....feggo@mail.com
Web...................www.felipegalindo.com

Director, Producer, SERENADE, 2002,
   Anmated Interstitial
Director, Producer, MANHATITLÁN CHRONI-
   CLES, 2000, Subcine, Animation Short
Director, Producer, SHORTS FOR MTV, 1993,
   Colossal Pictures, Animation Shorts
Director, Producer, FEGGORAMA, 1992,
   Animation Short

Dennis Gallegos*

Tepper Gallegos Casting
Los Angeles, CA 90004
Tel 323-469-3577

Casting Director, THE GLASS JAR, 1999,
   Sterling Pacific Films, Feature
Casting Director, TEAM KNIGHT RIDER,
   1997, Universal, TV
Casting Director, TWO BITS & PEPPER,
   1995, PM Entertainment, Feature

Jose Gallegos*

Production Senior Producer
Latin Media Ventures
New York, NY 10012
Tel 646-263-9093
Fax 212-812-7981
Email ....jose@lmvi.net
Web................................www.lmvi.net

Gia Galligani*

Producer
ABC
Los Angeles, CA 90049
Cell 310-497-8127
Email..............giagalligani@hotmail.com

Isabel Galvan*

Sherman Oaks, CA 91423
Tel 310-694-1315
Email ....isabel.galvan@my.brooks.edu

Co-Producer, BITTER CREEK, 2004, Alex
   Lane Productions, Short
Director, Writer, BLINDNESS, 2004, Vuela
   Alto Films, Short
Director, Writer, GRIS, 2004, Vuela Alto
   Films, Short
Producer, NO FUI YO, 2004, Nosotros
   Fulmos Films, Short
Director, Editor, Producer, THE OJAI RAPTOR
   CENTER, 2003, Galvan Bros. Productions,
   Documentary
Director, Producer, VENICE, 2003, Silver
   Chest Productions, Documentary

Kristin Elise Gamez*

Austin, TX 78751
Email ....kristin-g@mail.utexas.edu

Naiti Gamez*

Austin, TX 78722
Email ....marielita@earthlink.net

Mariana Garbagnati*

Research Associate
NALIP
Los Angeles, CA 90025
Tel 310-689-8643
Email ..marianagarbagnati@yahoo.com.ar

Albert Garcia*

San Antonio, TX 78201
Tel 210-737-2611

Alexis Garcia*

Attorney
Sheppard, Mullin, Richter & Hampton,
LLP
Los Angeles, CA 90067
Tel 310-228-3736
Fax 310-228-3936
Email ....agarcia@sheppardmullin.com
Web...............www.sheppardmullin.com

filmmakers

Ana Maria Garcia
Bayamon, PR 00956
Tel 787-731-7237
Email ....anamaria@yunque.net

Producer, LA OPERACIÓN, 1982, Cinema
Guild, Documentary

Andy Garcia
CineSon
Sherman Oaks, CA 91423
Tel 818-501-8246
Fax 818-501-3647
Web ....www.cineson.com

Agent: Clifford Stevens, Paradigm,
310-288-8000

Actor, Executive Producer, MODIGLIANI,
2004, Feature
Actor, OCEAN'S TWELVE, 2004, Warner
Bros., Feature
Actor, THE LAZARUS CHILD, 2004, Warner
Bros., Feature
Actor, Producer, THE LOST CITY, 2004,
Platinum Equity, Feature
Producer, THE MAN FROM THE ELYSIAN
FIELDS, 2001, Samuel Goldwyn Films,
Feature
Executive Producer, THE TIES THAT BIND,
2001, Universal Studios Home Video,
Feature
Producer, THE UNSAID, 2001, Universal
Studios Home Video, Feature
Executive Producer, THE ARTURO SAN-
DOVAL STORY, 2000, HBO, Feature
Producer, JUST THE TICKET, 1999, United
Artist, Feature
Executive Producer, SWING BOAT, 1999,
ABC, TV Movie

Brenda Garcia*
Newbury Park, CA 91320
Tel 310-413-8953
Email.............rotagirl123@hotmail.com

Cyndi Garcia*
Valencia, CA 91355
Email.....................cindytg@yahoo.com

Danielo Garcia*
Machine Rex Filmworks, Inc.
New York, NY 10040
Tel 917-584-2321
Email ....dbg@machinerex.com

Eric Garcia
Beverly Hills, CA 90212

Agent: Brian Lipson, Endeavor Talent
Agency, 310-248-2000

Co-Executive Producer, Writer, ANONYMOUS
REX, 2004, Book
Writer, MATCHSTICK MEN, 2003, Book

Eric Garcia
New Conception Films
Natalia, TX 78059
Tel 830-709-5481
Cell 830-200-9483

Director, Director of Photograhy, Producer,
Writer, THE NOVICE, 2004, Feature
Director, Producer, Writer, HUNTERS OF THE
DEAD, 2003, Short

Erick C. Garcia*
Research Associate
NALIP
Santa Monica, CA 90401
Tel 310-437-9230
Email....................erickgarcia@nalip.org

Janice Garcia*
Los Angeles, CA 90028
Tel 213-687-7771
Email ....comicrican333@yahoo.com

Jose Jesus JJ Garcia*
Bellaire, TX 77402
Tel 713-774-1292
Email ....hollywoodtexas@aol.com

Josie Garcia*
Los Angeles, CA 90015
Tel 213-368-8832
Email........................josiemg@aol.com

Julissa Garcia

Agent
William Morris Agency (WMA)
Beverly Hills, CA 90212
Tel 310-859-4000
Fax 310-859-4462
Web...............................www.wma.com

Manuel Ray Garcia*

Lone Stars Productions
Austin, TX 78758
Tel 512-835-5390
Email....................mray@lone-stars.com
Web ....www.lone-stars.com

Editor, Technical Director, DESDE AUSTIN, 2004, Univison Austin, TV Special
Director, JF QUE?, 2004, Promo
Still Photographer, Technician, LA PAS-TORELA, 2004, Austin Latino Theater Alliance, Stage Play
Co-Writer, Director, Producer, LAS CARPAS, 2003, Latino Public Broadcasting, Interstitials

Mike Garcia

Director, Drama Series
HBO Original Programming
Santa Monica, CA 90404
Tel 310-382-3000
Web ....www.hbo.com

Rafael Garcia*

Los Angeles, CA 90046
Tel 323-654-6135
Email..........................raf@elgarcia.com

Rodrigo Garcia

La Banda Films
Beverly Hills, CA 90210
Tel 310-858-7203
Web...................www.labandafilms.com

Agent: Adriana Alberghetti, Endeavor Talent Agency, 310-248-2000

Director, Writer, NINE LIVES, 2005, Mockingbird Productions, Feature
Director, FATHERS AND SONS, 2004, Mockingbird Pictures, Feature

Director, CARNIVALE, 2003, HBO, TV Series
Director, TEN TINY LOVE STORIES, 2001, Lios Gate Films Home Entertainment, Feature
Director of Photography, BODY SHOTS, 1999, New Line Cinema, Feature

Tadeo Garcia

Iconoclast Films
Email ....tadyg@aol.com

Director, Director of Photography, Editor, ON THE DOWNLOW, 2004, Feature

Victor Garcia

Los Angeles, CA 90036
Tel 818-560-1681
Email ....victoreligarcia@yahoo.com

Producer, EROSION, 2003, Dark Lantern Entertainment, Feature
Producer, THE LEGEND OF DIABLO, 2003, Spartan Entertainment , Feature
Producer, TEA WITH GRANDMA, 2002, Short
Producer, GIANT ROBO EPISODE II, Manga Entertainment
Producer, THE BOY IN THE BOX, Short

William Garcia*

Hollywood, FL 33023
Tel 954-437-6886
Fax 954-241-6768
Email ....dp4261@bellsouth.net
Web ....www.williamgarcia.com

Director of Photography, AREA 305 "DONDE ESTARA", 2003, Univision Records, Music Video
Director, LENNY KRAVITZ, 2003, Virgin Records, EPK
Director, OBIE "ANTE", 2003, Emi Latin, Music Video
Director of Photography, RED BIRD, 2003, Andromeda Productions, Short
Director, THE SOLDIER, 2003, Film Festival, Short
Director of Photography, MICHAEL JACKSON, 2002, Epic Records, Documentary

filmmakers

199

Georgina Garcia Riedel*
Loosely Based Pictures, LLC
Silverlake, CA 90026
Tel 323-810-2687
Tel 323-934-0947
Email ....griedel@hotmail.com

Director, Producer, Writer, HOW THE GARCIA
GIRLS SPENT THEIR SUMMER, 2004,
Feature
Director, Producer, Writer, ONE NIGHT IT
HAPPENDED, 2003, Short

Carolina Garcia-Aguilera
Miami Beach, FL 33109
Email ....4cubans@bellsouth.net

Writer, ES CUESTION DE SUERTE: UNA
NOVELA, 2004, Book
Writer, LUCK OF THE DRAW: A NOVEL,
2003, Book
Writer, ONE HOT SUMMER, 2003, Book
Writer, AGUAS SANGRIENTAS, 2002, Book
Writer, BLOODY SECRETS: A LUPE SOLANO
MYSTERY, 2002, Book
Writer, BITTER SUGAR: A LUPE SOLANO
MYSTERY, 2001, Book
Writer, HAVANA HEAT: A LUPE SOLANO
MYSTERY, 2001, Book
Writer, A MIRACLE IN PARADISE: A LUPE
SOLANO MYSTERY, 2000, Book
Writer, BLOODY SHAME: A LUPE SOLANO
MYSTERY, 1997, Book
Writer, BLOODY WATERS: A LUPE SOLANO
MYSTERY, 1997, Book

Anne Garcia-Romero
Santa Monica, CA 90405
Tel 310-314-1633
Email ....agaro@aol.com

*Manager: Marilyn Atlas Management,
310-278-5047*

Writer, DESERT LONGING OR LAS AVEN-
TURERAS, 2002, South Coast Repertory,
Stage Play
Writer, SANTA CONCEPCION, 1998,
NYSF/Public Theater, Stage Play

Irma Garcia-Sinclair
Syngarnicity
Alameda, CA 94501
Tel 510-522-1182
Fax 510-864-3222
Email ....newagecurandera@earthlink.net
Web ....www.cybertran.com

Agent: SYNGARNICITY, 510-864-3221

ADR Looping, AMERICAN FAMILY, 2004,
PBS, TV Series
ADR Looping, MAN ON FIRE, 2004, 20th
Century Fox, Feature
ADR Looping, SPANGLISH, 2004, Columbia
Pictures, Feature
ADR Looping, CARNIVALE, 2003, HBO, TV
Series
Actor, FIDEL, 2002, Showtime, Feature
Dialect Coach, ALL THE PRETTY HORSES,
2001, MCA/Universal, Feature
ADR Looping, MASK OF ZORRO, 2001,
MCA/Universal, Feature
Dialect Coach, 187, 1997, 20th Century Fox,
Feature
ADR Looping, DANCES WITH WOLVES,
1992, Warner Bros., Feature
Actor, JURY OF ONE, 1992, ABC, TV Series

Belinda Gardea*
Casting Director
Long Beach, CA 90809
Tel 323-896-2353
Email ....bgardea@aol.com

Casting Director, HOW THE GARCIA GIRLS
SPENT THEIR SUMMER, 2004, Loosely
Based Pictures, LLC, Feature
Casting Director, QUALITY OF LIFE, 2004,
Quality of Film LLC, Feature
Casting Director, LIVING THE LIFE, 2000,
Richs Productions, Feature
Casting Director, STAR MAPS, 1997, 20th
Century Fox, Feature

Lisa Garibay*
Los Angeles, CA 90027
Tel 213-840-3517
Fax 310-453-5258
Email ....lyg@thenitmustbetrue.com
Web ....www.thenitmustbetrue.com

Director, Producer, SISTERS Y SANTOS,
2005, Documentary

Writer, THE HARLOWES, 2005, TV Series
  Pilot
Music Supervisor, Producer, ROBBING
  PETER, 2004, Prickly Bear Productions,
  Feature

Juan C. Garza
Los Angeles, CA 90042
Tel 323-478-9505
Fax 323-478-9505
Email..............juancarlosgarza@usa.com

Editor, EYES, 2004, WB TV/ABC, TV Series
Editor, SIETE DIAS, 2004, Telecine, Feature
Editor, Title Design, THE HANDLER,
  2003-2004, Viacom/CBS, TV Series
Director, Producer, Writer, NEVER TRUST A
  SERIAL KILLER, 2002, Feature
Editor, RESURRECTION BLVD., 2000,
  Showtime, TV Series
Editor, THE PRINCESS AND THE BARIO
  BOY, 2000, Showtime, TV Movie

Mario Garza*
San Marcos, TX 78666
Tel 512-974-9778
Tel 512-393-3310
Cell 512-217-5417
Email ....Mario.Garza@centurytel.net
Web ....www.mariogarza.com

Victoria Garza*
ClearThought Productions LLC
Los Angeles, CA 90026
Tel 323-481-3128
Email victoria.garza@clearthoughtproduc-
tions.com

Lydia Garza-Marines*
Austin, TX 78735
Tel 512-223-7048
Email......................lr1069@txstate.edu

Melba Gasque*
Miami, FL 3317
Tel 305-438-4656

William Gastelum*
Groove Addicts
Los Angeles, CA 90066
Tel 310-572-4646
Email ....william@grooveaddicts.com

Michael Gavino*
Michael Gavino Productions
Lighthouse Point, FL 33064
Tel 954-941-1334
Cell 754-235-4170
Fax 954-941-1334
Email................meangavine@yahoo.com

Agent: Joyce Glusman, Martin &
Donalds, 954-921-2427,
mdtalent@bellsouth.net

Actor, MOTEL, 2004, Adrenaline Studios,
  Feature
Actor, MURDER BY THE BOOK, 2004, Lee
  Productions, Short
Writer, Actor, Producer, THE DEVIL AND THE
  GIRL, 2004, 4-Um Films, Short
Actor, BATMAN BEYOND, 2003-2004,
  Ultimate Vengeance Productions, Feature
Writer, Producer, THE ENCOUNTER, 2002,
  Movie Machine Productions, Short

Digna Gerena*
Executive Producer
Boston Latino
Boston, MA 02128
Tel 617-653-2389
Email ....digna.gerena@alum.bu.edu

Executive Producer, BOSTON LATINO, 2003,
  Boston Neighborhood Network TV, TV
  Special
Media Advocate, CONTRIBUTOR, 2003,
  Candela Magazine, Website
Media Advocate, THE LATINO FILM CON-
  SORTIUM, 2003, Strand Theatre Boston,
  Film Series

Mauricio Gerson
Sr. VP, Programming
Telemundo
Hialeah, FL 33010
Tel 305-884-8200
Fax 202-296-7908
Web ....www.telemundo.com

filmmakers

Monica Gil
Community Relations Executive
Telemundo
Glendale, CA 91201
Tel 818-502-5700
Email.......................v4m@hotmail.com

Guido Giordano
Agent
International Creative Management
(ICM)
Beverly Hills, CA 90211
Tel 310-550-4000
Email ....ggiordano@icmtalent.com
Web ....www.icmtalent.com

Jeff Gipson*
Festival Director
Cine Las Americas
Austin, TX 78767
Tel 512-841-5930
Email ....jeff@cinelasamericas.org
Web ....www.cinelasamericas.org

Executive Producer, SHE FLIES, 2005, Cine
   Las Americas, Short
Producer, STARGIRL, MIGUEL ALVAREZ,
   2005, Este Bandido, Short
Camera, Director, Editor, CIUDADANO,
   MANEJA BETO, 2004, Ear To The Rail,
   Music Video
Camera, Director, Editor, NEVAHEARD,
   ROMEO NAVARRO, 2004, BBoy City
   Production, Music Video

Sergio Giral*
Giral Media
Bay Harbor Island, FL 33154
Tel 305-864-8567
Cell 786-897-2422
Email.....................giralmedia@aol.com
Web ....www.giralmedia.com

Manager: Armando Dorrego,
304-864-8567, giralmedia@aol.com

Polita Glynn*
Surfside, FL 33154
Tel 305-868-0100
Email...................polita@the-beach.net

Producer, DRUM OF TIME, 2000, Short
Producer, BISCAYNE NATIONAL PARK:
   LEGACY OF ENVIRONMENTAL PIONEERS,
   1997, PBS, Documentary

Devora Gomez*
Dar Luz Films
Bellflower, CA 90706
Tel 562-804-4516
Fax 562-804-4573
Email.....................darluzfilm@aol.com

Magdalena Gomez*
Jaywalking
Springfield, MA 01108
Tel 413-731-7483
Email.......................lesgopro@rcn.com
Web ....www.amoxonica.com

Marisol Gomez*
New York, NY 10029
Email.........marisolgomez@earthlink.net

Mike Gomez*
El Monte, CA 91732
Tel 626-443-1837
Email ....creativemgo@adelphia.net
Web ....www.mikegomez.info

Actor, LUMINARIAS, 2000, New Latin
   Pictures, Feature
Actor, THE BIG LEBOWSKI, 1998, Gramercy
   Pictures, Feature
Actor, THE MILAGRO BEANFIELD WAR,
   1988, Universal Pictures, Feature
Actor, EL NORTE, 1984, Artisan
   Entertainment, Feature

Patricia Gomez
Producer
WMVS
Milwaukee, WI 53233
Tel 414-271-1036

Stephen Gomez*
Laguna Niguel, CA 92677
Email ....sjgomez_11@yahoo.com

Diana E. Gonzales
Producer
E! Entertainment
Los Angeles, CA 90066
Tel 310-709-6783
Email ....dgonzales@eentertainment.com

Producer, ACADEMY AWARDS 2003, 2003,
    E! Entertainment, TV Special
Producer, E! COMPANY MEETING, 2003, E!
    Entertainment, Event
Producer, GOLDEN GLOBES, 2003, E!
    Entertainment, TV Special

Elizabeth Gonzales
Menifee, CA 92584
Cell 951-238-0538
Email ....showliz@yahoo.com

Stage Manager, ALF'S HIT TALK SHOW,
    2004, KTLA Tribune Studios, TV Series
Stage Manager, THE RUB, 2004, Si TV,
    JAAM Productions, TV Series
Stage Manager, FULFILLMENT FUND
    AWARDS, 2003, SoapNet Cable, TV Series
Stage Manager, MTV - ROCK THE VOTE,
    2002, MTV Productions, TV Special

Olga Gonzales*
Chicago, IL 60626
Email ....olga01@ameritech.net

Richard Gonzales*
Farce Productions
Studio City, CA 91604
Tel 818-506-7424
Email ....driftwood14@earthlink.net

Vincent George Gonzales
Burbank, CA 91501
Tel 310-497-7793

2nd Assistant Director, MELVIN GOES TO
    DINNER, 2003, Sundance Channel,
    Feature
2nd Assistant Director, PEARL HARBOR,
    2001, Buena Vista International, Feature

2nd Assistant Director, RUSTIN, 2001,
    Vanguard Cinema, Feature
2nd Assistant Director, SIX FEET UNDER,
    2001, HBO, TV Series

A.P. Gonzalez*
Los Angeles, CA 90068
Tel 323-957-1936
Tel 310-825-0294
Fax 323-957-1938
Email ....apg@ucla.edu

Attorney: E. Barry Haldeman,
310-553-3610, bhaldeman@ggfirm.com

Director, SILENT CRISIS:DIABETES AMONG
    US, 2002, Discovery Health, Documentary
Director, FOTO NOVELAS: MANGAS, 1997,
    ITVS, TV Series
Director, TOGETHER AGAINST ABUSE,
    1990, PBS, Documentary

Al Gonzalez*
Vision Quest Entertainment
Burbank, CA 91505
Tel 818-842-2757
Email ....vqe@att.net
Web ....www.visionquestent.com

Carolina Gonzalez*
Daily News
Brooklyn, NY 11238
Tel 718-389-8541
Fax 212-643-7828
Email....................cgonza@earthlink.net

David Gonzalez
Palm City, FL 34990
Tel 954-427-2522
Tel 772-288-4381
Fax 954-427-3233
Email.....................gonzalezdj@aol.com

Director of Photography, FOR THE RECORD,
    GUAM IN WWII, 2004, ITVS, Documentary
Director of Photography, LOUIE: A SERIOUS
    COMEDY, 2004, Feature
Director of Photography, THE STATE OF THE
    TERRITORY: US-PUERTO RICO RELA-
    TIONS AT THE CROSSROADS, 2004,
    Polymorphous Pictures, Documentary

Frank Bennett Gonzalez

Senior Manager, Talent Development Programs
ABC Entertainment Television Group
Burbank, CA 91521
Tel 818-460-6452
Fax 818-460-5292
Email ....Frank.B.Gonzalez@abc.com
Web ....www.abcnewtalent.disney.com

Hector Gonzalez*

Executive Producer
PBS KUAT-TV
Tucson, AZ 85721
Tel 520-621-7368
Fax 520-621-3360
Email ....gonzalez@u.arizona.edu
Web...............................www.kuat.org

Producer, REFLEXIONES, 2003, PBS
    KUAT-TV, TV Series
Producer, ARIZONA ILLUSTRATED ,
    1980-2005, PBS KUAT-TV, TV Series

Irma Gonzalez*

Media Rare
Holland, MI 49423
Tel 616-886-0644
Email ....salsera616@yahoo.com

Javier Gonzalez*

Philadelphia, PA 19101
Tel 215-237-7951

Joe D. Gonzalez*

Director
Innerspace
San Juan, PR 00936-3212
Tel 787-731-1201
Tel 787-731-5233
Cell 787-717-2638
Fax 787-731-5233
Email.................joegonz@direcway.com

Jose Gonzalez

CEO
World Film Magic Distribution Corp.
Hollywood, CA 90038
Tel 323-785-2118
Web ....www.worldfilmmagic.com

Joseph Julian Gonzalez*

Simple Music Productions
San Gabriel, CA 91775
Tel 661-665-2226
Fax 661-665-2226
Email ....jjgonzalez@mac.com
Web ..www.simplemusicproductions.com

*Agent: John Temperau, Soundtrack
Music Associates, 310-724-5600,
teresa@soundtrk.com*

Composer, CONCIERTO PARA MARIACHI,
    2004
Composer, MISA AZTECA, 2004
Composer, VISIONES: LATINO ART &CUL-
    TURE, 2004, PBS, Documentary
Composer, RESURRECTION BLVD., 2002,
    Showtime, TV Series
Composer, PRICE OF GLORY, 2000, New
    Line Cinema, Feature
Composer, CURDLED, 1996, Miramax,
    Feature

Juan Gonzalez*

Arenas Entertainment
Beverly Hills, CA 90210
Tel 310-385-4434
Fax 310-385-4402
Email ....juan@arenasgroup.com

Julieta Gonzalez*

Tucson, AZ 85701
Tel 520-622-5340
Tel 520-626-4336
Cell 520-975-0809
Fax 520-740-0216
Email ....thepony@dakotacom.net
Web ....www.uanews.org

*Attorney: Susan Villarreal,
520-784-0604, scv@villarreallaw.com*

Writer, CLAUDIA'S FAMILY, 1995, Sonora
    Films, Feature

Juvencio Gonzalez*

Latino Media Alliance
Philadelphia, PA 19101
Tel 215-917-2291
Email ......juvencio.gonzalez@temple.edu

Maria Gonzalez*

Cranbury, NJ 08512
Email ....MG2ari@aol.com

Omar Eqequiel Gonzalez*

Los Angeles, CA 90048
Tel 800-786-0747
Email......................omar@calocine.com

Researcher, TEENS, 2001, WB, Documentary
Assistant to the Director, PRICE OF GLORY,
   2000, New Line Cinema, Feature
Director, Producer, Writer, ROQUE, 1996,
   Short
Director, Producer, Writer, EN LA DULCE
   SENSACION DE UN BESO MORDELON,
   1994, Short

Rafael Gonzalez*

Los Angeles, CA 90014
Email ....gonzraf@sbcglobal.net

Rosa Gonzalez

Culver City, CA
Tel 310-559-3928
Email...............prrosagonzalez@aol.com

Line Producer, ASTHMA: FIGHTING TO
   BREATHE, 2003, Discovery Health,
   Documentary
1st Assistant Director, BUBBA HO-TEP,
   2003, Vitagraph Films, LLC, Feature
Line Producer, SILENT CRISIS: DIABETES
   AMONG US, 2002, Discovery Health,
   Documentary

Sonia Gonzalez*

Chica Luna Productions
Los Angeles, CA 90026
Tel 213-250-7709
Email ....lasone189@aol.com
Web ....www.chicaluna.com

Director, BRAGGING RIGHTS, 2004, Chica
   Luna Productions, Documentary
Editor, NUYORICANS, 2002, PBS/Glazen
   Creative, Documentary
Writer, BODEGA DREAMS, 2000, Fox
   Searchlight, Feature
Director, DEBUTANTE, 2000, Short
Editor, EL CIRCULO VICIOSO, 1998, Ground
   Zero Entertainment, Feature
Editor, DESTINATION UNKNOWN, 1996,
   Ground Zero Entertainment, Feature

Victor Gonzalez

West Covina, CA 91790
Tel 626-858-9013
Email..............vgonzalez3@earthlink.net

Producer, VIVIR INTENTANDO, 2003, Buena
   Vista International, Feature
Director of Photography, INHERITANCE,
   2001, Argentina Video Home (AVH) ,
   Feature
Director of Photography, EL VISITANTE,
   1999, Líder Films S.A., Feature

Alejandro Gonzalez Iñarritu

Beverly Hills, CA 90212
Email ....backshopla@aol.com

*Agent: John Lesher, Endeavor Talent
Agency, 310-248-2000,
jlesher@endeavorla.com*

Executive Producer, NINE LIVES, 2005,
   Mockingbird Pictures, Feature
Director, PARIS, JE T'AIME, 2005, Feature
Director, 21 GRAMS, 2003, Focus Features,
   Feature
Director, Writer, AMORES PERROS, 2000,
   Lions Gate Films, Feature

Jackie Gonzalez-Carlos*

GonCa Entertainment Productions
Culver City, CA 90232
Tel 310-309-0901
Email ....GonCaProductions@Mail.com

Producer, 2FAST 2FURIOUS, 2003,
   Universal/Def Jam Recordings, VOD
Producer, 8 MILE VOD, 2003,
   Universal/Aftermath/Shady Records, DVD
Director, Executive Producer, INNER HEART,
   2003, GonCa Entertainment Productions,
   Documentary

Executive Producer, Director, MORNING
SHOW (IN PROGRESS), 2003, GonCa
Entertainment Productions, Documentary
Producer, WINDTALKERS DVD SPECIAL FEA-
TURES, 2002, MGM, DVD

Marina González-Palmier*

TexMex Tales, LLC
Los Angeles, CA 90068
Tel 323-969-1499
Fax 323-463-0331
Email ....whitelikemoon@aol.com
Web ....www.whitelikethemoon.com

Actress, CSI: MIAMI, 2004, TV Series
Actress, GENERAL HOSPITAL, 2004, Soap
Opera
Actress, RIVALS, 2004, Laguna Productions,
Amigo Films, Feature
Actress, TACO BENDER, 2004, Coppas
Films, Short
Actress, THE TRICK, 2004, Trick
Productions, Short
Actress, THREAT MATRIX, 2004, TV Series
Director, Writer, WHITE LIKE THE MOON,
2002, AFI/HBO, Short

Roberto F. Gonzalez-Rubio

Pasadena, CA 91103
Tel 626-791-6880
Cell 818-406-3095
Fax 626-791-7996

2nd Assistant Director, ALMOST A WOMAN,
2001, PBS, TV Movie
2nd Assistant Director, RESURRECTION
BLVD., 2001, Showtime, TV Series
2nd Assistant Director, PRISON LIFE, 2000,
Incarcerated Entertainment Productions,
Short
2nd 2nd Assistant Director, RESURRECTION
BLVD., 2000, Showtime, TV Series
2nd 2nd Assistant Director, THE BROTHERS
GARCIA, 2000, Nickelodeon, TV Series

Veronica Gonzalez-Rubio

Simi Valley, CA 93063
Tel 818-548-5877

1st Assistant Director, EVERYBODY LOVES
RAYMOND, 1999, CBS, TV Series
1st Assistant Director, KATIE JOPLIN, 1999,
Warner Bros., TV Series

2nd Assistant Director, HOPE & GLORIA,
1996, NBC, TV Series
2nd Assistant Director, NAKED GUN 2 1/2,
1991, Paramount Pictures, Feature

Maureen Gosling*

Intrepidas Productions
Oakland, CA 94609
Tel 510-595-7926
Email ....mgosling@igc.org
Web...............www.maureengosling.com

Director, Producer, BAMAKO CHIC, 2005,
Intrepidas Productions, Documentary
Co-Director, Co-Producer, NO MOUSE
MUSIC, 2005, Down Home Sisters
Productions, Documentary
Editor, HEART OF CONGO, 2004, Moira
Productions, Documentary
Editor, WAITING TO INHALE, 2004, Jed
Riffe Films, Documentary
Co-Producer, A'AI ETE AU BAL, 2003, Brazos
Films, Documentary
Co-Producer, CHULAS FRONTERAS, 2003,
Brazos Films, Documentary

Brian F. Grabski*

Willingboro, NJ 08046
Tel 609-835-6650
Email ....grabber_grab@yahoo.com

Erika O. Grediaga*

Santa Monica, CA 90403
Tel 310-968-9735
Fax 323-856-9253
Email ....egrediaga@hotmail.com

Writer, MIRROR WORLD, 2005, ABC/Disney,
Feature
Executive Producer, SOBA, 2004, Feature
Writer, TRATO HECHO, 2004, Univision, TV
Series
Director, Writer, ANIMA, 2003, AFI, Short
Post Production Coordinator, SOFIA, 2000,
Feature
Director, Writer, ADELA DESPIERTA,
DESPIERTA, 1997, Short

Michele Greene*
Requinto Productions
Los Angeles, CA 90048
Tel 310-278-5017
Email ....michelegreene@earthlink.net
Web ....www.michelegreen.com

Laura Greenlee*
Line Producer
Los Angeles, CA 90019
Email..............................lalag@nwc.net

Line Producer, THE MOGULS, 2005, New
    Market Films, Feature
Co-Producer, Line-Producer, JERSEY GIRL,
    2004, Miramax Films, Feature
Co-Producer, Line-Producer, JAY & SILENT
    BOB STRIKE BACK, 2001, Dimension
    Films, Feature
Co-Producer, THE DEEP END, 2001, 20th
    Century Fox, Feature
Co-Producer, DOGMA, 1999, Columbia
    TriStar, Feature
Line Producer, VERY BAD THINGS, 1998,
    PolyGram Entertainment, Feature

Evangeline Griego*
About Time Productions
Los Angeles, CA 90041
Tel 323-493-2790
Fax 323-982-1635
Email.....................abouttyme@aol.com

Producer, CALAVER HIGHWAY, 2004,
    Documentary
Line Producer, MY JOURNEY HOME, 2004,
    PBS/ Weta TV, Documentary
Co-Producer, THE NEW AMERICANS , 2004,
    PBS./ Kartemquin Films, Documentary
Director, Producer, BORDER
    VISIONS/VISIONES FRONTERIZOS, 2003,
    About Time Productions, Documentary
Director, Producer, PAÑO ARTE: IMAGES
    FROM INSIDE, 1997, About Time
    Productions, Documentary

Javier Grillo Marxuach
Los Angeles, CA 90048
Tel 323-782-4548

*Agent: Chris Silberman, Broder, Webb,
Chervin, Silbermann Agency,
310-281-3400*

Writer, JAKE 2.0, 2003, UPN, TV Series
Producer, JAKE 2.1, 2003, UPN, TV Series
Producer, Writer, BOOMTOWN, 2002,
    UPN/NBC, TV Series
Writer, THE DEAD ZONE, 2002, UPN and
    SciFi Channel, TV Series
Writer, LAW AND ORDER, 2001, NBC, TV
    Series

Michelle Guanca*
Latin American Video Archives
New York, NY 10014
Tel 212-243-4804
Fax 212-243-2007
Email ....mguanca@lavavideo.org
Web ....www.lavavideo.org

Junior Guapo
Los Angeles, CA 90007
Tel 323-414-2295
Email ....jguapo@onebox.com

Producer, PEPSI, AMERICAN EAGLE CLOTH-
    ING, 2003, Paradigm Independent,
    Commercial
Executive Producer, SCOUT, 2003, MGM,
    Feature-Animation
Producer, TRAUCO'S DAUGHTER, 2002,
    Short

Armando Guareño*
Executive Director
La Cinemafe Film Festival of New York
New York, NY 10027
Tel 212-281-5786
Cell 917-407-2375
Fax 212-281-5786
Email ....armando@lacinemafe.org
Web ....www.lacinemafe.org

Producer, RED PASSPORT, 2003, Pachuco
    Entertainment, Short
Production Consultant, MAESTRO, 2002,
    Short

filmmakers

Jay Guerra

San Pedro, CA 90731
Tel 310-548-5026
Fax 310-548-0432
Email ....jayguerra@earthlink.net

2nd Assistant Director, DRAGNET, 2003,
  ABC, TV Series
1st Assistant Director, RECYCLING SLO,
  2003, AFI, Feature
1st Assistant Director, CRAZY BEAUTIFUL,
  2001, Buena Vista Pictures, Feature
2nd Assistant Director, MURDER IN SMALL
  TOWN X, 2001, Fox Network, TV Series

Lucas Guerra

Creative Director
ARGUS
Boston, MA 02210
Tel 617-261-7676
Fax 617-261-7557
Email ....lucas@thinkargus.com
Web ....www.thinkargus.com

Graphic Designer

Luis Guerra*

Austin, TX 78704
Tel 512-443-0587
Email ....victorguerra@earthlink.net

Phillip V. Guerra*

Phillip Guerra Video
San Antonio, TX 78211
Tel 210-738-2727
Tel 210-677-9944
Cell 210-724-2727
Email ....paidagrand@aol.com
Web ....www.phillipguerra.com

Producer, COMEDY RIOTS COMEDY SERIES,
  1996, TV Series
Producer, YOU HEARD IT HERE, 1995,
  Documentary

Aurora Guerrero*

Los Angeles, CA 90026
Tel 323-669-6227

Claudine "Playful" Guerrero*

Promotions Street Teamer
100.3 The Beat
Los Angeles, CA 90005
Tel 213-713-1036
Email ....laplayful@comcast.net

Dan Guerrero

Los Angeles, CA 90036
Tel 323-822-1278
Email ....dan@danguerrero.com
Web ....www.danguerrero.com

Producer, Writer, NCLR ALMA AWARDS
  GALA, 2002, Live Event
Producer, AL DIA CON MARIA CONCHITA,
  1998, Telemundo Network, TV Show
Producer, LOCO SLAM, 1994, HBO, TV
  Series
Co-Producer, Writer, THE PAUL RODRIGUEZ
  SHOW, 1990-1994, Univision, TV Series

Luis Guerrero*

Executive Assistant
Maya Pictures
Los Angeles, CA 90017
Tel 310-281-3770
Fax 310-281-3777
Email ....luisg@mayacinemas.com
Web ....www.maya-pictures.com

Sergio Guerrero*

Indie Productions
Santa Monica, CA 90403
Tel 310-453-4340
Email ....indieye@verizon.net
Web ....www.frijolywood.com

Producer, Writer, A DAY WITHOUT A MEXI-
  CAN, 2004, Indieye Productions, Feature
Director, Writer, CONDORITO, 2004, World
  Editors Inc., TV Series, Animated
Director, CORONA IN CHINA, 2004, Quittani
  Producciones, Commercial
Director, JOB CORP, 2004, Indieye
  Productions, Commercial
Director, Producer, LATINOLOGUES DVD,
  2004, Sabrosa Entertainment, DVD Series

Kristy Guevara-Flanagan*

Vaquera Productions
Oakland, CA 94608
Tel 510-652-1770
Email ....kristy@agirlslife.org
Web...........................www.agirlslife.org

Co-Director, Co-Producer, BLOW THEM UP, 2000, Blackchair Films, Short
Director, Producer, EL CORRIDO DE CECILIA, 1999, New Day Films, Documentary

Adrian Guillen

Poetic Pictures
Palmdale, CA 93550
Tel 661-305-5807
Fax 661-947-3743
Email ....poeticpictures01@aol.com

Producer, HOMIES GRAVEYARD SHIFT, 2003, Belle Vista Pictures, Feature
Producer, ROUND TWO, 2003, Feature

Inez Guillen*

Guisando Productions
New York, NY 10025
Tel 212-316-0567
Tel 212-316-4142
Cell 646-321-2845
Email................tainaqt71@earthlink.net

Director, Producer, Writer, HOW BIG IS IT?, 2002, Short

Maritza Guimet*

FV Productions
Miami, FL 33172
Tel 303-559-7324
Email.........maritza@cpeproduction.com

Jason Gurvitz*

Green Dog Films
Beverly Hills, CA 90212
Cell 310-866-8128
Email ....jason@greendogfilms.com
Web..................www.greendogfilms.com

Manager: Fusion Management, 310-278-2812, rree@fusion-mgmt.com

Attorney: Amitesh Damodar, amiteshdamudar@sbcglobal.net

Producer, TLATELOLCO, 2006, Greed Dog/Calabartaz, Feature
Producer, LILY, 2005, Greed Dog Films, Feature
Producer, INTERNAL EXILE, 2003, Greed Dog Films, Documentary

Carla Gutierrez*

Los Angeles, CA 90048
Tel 650-906-7457
Email ....carlagu@earthlink.net

Editor, CIRCUMCISED CINEMA, 2004-2005, Si TV/Maya Pictures, TV Series
Second Editor, FALL OF FUJIMORI (SUNDANCE 2005), 2004, Stardust Pictures, Documentary
Editor, Producer, TIME LOST (IDA FINALIST, MILL VALLEY FESTIVAL 2004), 2004, Short
Editor, Producer, FIRST WORDS, 2003, Short
Associate Producer, LINEA DIRECTA, 2001-2002, Telemundo, TV Public Affairs Show

Carlos Gutierrez*

San Francisco, CA 94110
Email ....lemonsoda7@hotmail.com

Carlos Gutierrez*

Lazarus Productions, Inc.
New York, NY 10021
Tel 917-406-4400
Email ....cg536@nyu.edu

Charlotte Gutierrez

Cine Acción
San Francisco, CA 94103
Tel 415-553-8135
Fax 415-553-8137
Email ....info@CineAccion.com
Web ....www.cineaccion.com

Diego Gutierrez
Beverly Hills, CA 90212

Agent: Chris Harbert, CAA,
310-288-4545

Writer, JUDGING AMY, 2003, Fox/CBS, TV
  Series
Writer, KINGPIN, 2003, NBC/ Lions Gate
  Films, TV Movie
Writer, THE SHIELD, 2003, FX, TV Series
Writer, BUFFY THE VAMPIRE SLAYER,
  2001, UPN/20th Century Fox, TV Series

Eduardo Gutierrez*
West Islip, NY 11751
Tel 516-435-7043
Email ....edgutier@aol.com

Gary Michael Gutierrez
San Francisco, CA 94707
Tel........................415-788-7500 x235

Agent: Peter Turner, The Peter Turner
Agency, 310-315-4772

Special/Visual Effects, THE LIZZIE MCGUIRE
  MOVIE, 2003, Buena Vista Pictures,
  Feature
Special/Visual Effects, MAX Q, 1998, Buena
  Vista Pictures, TV Movie
Special/Visual Effects, JACK, 1996, Buena
  Vista Pictures, Feature
Special/Visual Effects, DRACULA, 1992,
  Columbia Pictures, Feature

Ricardo Adrian Guzman*
IT Media Creative Director
Saudi Aramco
Al Khobar, 31952 Saudi Arabia
Tel 966-3-874-8584
Email ....ricardo.guzman@aramco.com

Johnathan Gwyn*
Austin, TX 78660
Tel 512-252-3020
Fax 512-252-3020
Email ....worldwidefilm@gmail.com

Agent: Cynthia Robbins, Blvd. Talent,
512-458-2583

Actor, HOLY BEARS, 2004, The Motion Pixel
  Company, Animation Pilot
Director, KEEP IT REAL, 2004, Candy
  Coated Records, Music Video
Director, CONFESSION INVASION, 2003,
  Much Luvv Records, Music Video
Director, HIPPOCRIT, 2003, Da South
  Records, Music Video
Director, COTTON MOUTH, 2002, Madison
  Home Video, Feature

Leslie Haas*
Phoenix, AZ 85040
Tel 602-643-4281
Email ..lhaas@desertmountainmedia.com
Web ......www.DesertMountainMedia.com

Shelli Hall*
Executive Director
Tucson Film Office
Tucson, AZ 85701
Tel 520-770-2126
Fax 520-884-7804
Email ....shall@mtcvb.com

Matthew Handal*
Handal With Care Productions
New York, NY 10009
Tel 212-260-7702
Tel 212-505-5268
Cell 917-209-4242
Fax 212-260-7702
Email ....handalm@aol.com

Editor, LIZARD LICK, 2003, MTV, TV Series
Producer, ROCCO MORETTI: 1ST DAY;
  D-DAY, 2003, Short
Writer, VIAGRA SPOT, 2003, Commercial
Editor, WOMANDOCS, 2001, True Ent.,
  Documentary
Writer, NOWHERE MAN, 2000, Feature
Writer, BIRDS OF PREY, 1997, Feature
Editor, PARA VIVIR O MORIR, 1996, de la
  nada prods., Feature

Mary Harder*
Glorybridge Productions
San Antonio, TX 78251
Tel 210-684-1868
Email ....harderrlmo@aol.com

Lead, AN OLD BOLERO, 2004, Short
Extra, CRAZY LIFE, 2004, Short
Director, Producer, Writer, DISCOVERING
   JEWISH ROOTS, CULINARY ODYSSEY,
   2004, Documentary
Director, Co-Producer, LOGICAL LOVE, 2004,
   Short

Christy Haubegger*

Brand Marketing Agent
Creative Artists Agency (CAA)
Beverly Hills, CA 90212
Tel 310-288-4545
Fax 310-288-7681
Email.............chaubeggerasst@caa.com
Web ....www.caa.com

Executive Producer, SPANGLISH, 2004,
   Columbia Pictures, Feature
Associate Producer, CHASING PAPI, 2003,
   Twentieth Century Fox, Feature

Melchor B. Hawkins*

Kingsville, TX 78363
Tel 361-516-1810
Email ....the_thinking_man@hotmail.com

Salma Hayek

Ventanarosa Productions
Beverly Hills, CA 90212

Agent: Michelle Bohan, WMA,
310-859-4000

Manager: Evelyn O'Neil

Actor, ASK THE DUST, 2005, Paramount,
   Feature
Actor, BANDIDAS, 2005, Fox, Feature
Actor, AFTER THE SUNSET, 2004, New Line
   Cinema, Feature
Actor, SPY KIDS 3-D GAME OVER, 2004,
   Dimension Films, Feature
Actor, ONCE UPON A TIME IN MEXICO,
   2003, Dimension Films, Feature
Actor, Producer, FRIDA, 2002, Miramax
   Films, Feature
Director, Producer, THE MALDONADO MIRA-
   CLE, 2002, Showtime Networks Inc.,
   Feature

Jamie Hayes*

SDSU
San Diego, CA 92116
Tel 619-283-3895
Email ....jchayes@hotmail.com

Judy Hecht-Dumontet

Bel Air, CA 90077
Tel 818-783-9575
Fax 818-783-6603

Manager: Richard Schwartz
Management, 818-783-9575

Director, Writer, TORTILLA HEAVEN, 2005,
   Feature
Director, Producer, THE NOVICE, 1995,
   Feature
Associate Producer, AND THE VIOLINS
   STOPPED PLAYING, 1988, Orion, Feature

Juan Heinrich*

Tucson, AZ 85716
Tel 520-358-7769
Email ....beanmachine00@cox.net

Cristela Henriquez*

New York, NY 10028
Email.....................ink05@hotmail.com

Eric W. Henriquez

New York, NY 10128
Cell 917-374-2048
Email ....yohebaby@aol.com

2nd Assistant Director, IT RUNS IN THE
   FAMILY, 2003, MGM, Feature
2nd Assistant Director, BAD COMPANY,
   2002, Buena Vista Pictures, Feature
2nd Assistant Director, HACK, 2002, CBS,
   TV Series
2nd Assistant Director, BOILER ROOM,
   2000, New Line Cinema, Feature

Paula Heredia

Mamboreta, Inc.
New York, NY 10006
Tel 212-953-3564

Agent: Larry Garvin Management

filmmakers

Editor, IN MEMORIAM: NEW YORK CITY,
2002, HBO, Documentary
Director, THE PARIS REVIEW: EARLY CHAP-
TERS, 2001, Checkerboard Foundation,
Documentary
Editor, I REMEMBER ME, 2000, Zeitgeist
Films, Documentary
Director, THE COUPLE IN THE CAGE, 1997,
Maraboreta, Documentary
Editor, UNZIPPED, 1995, Miramax Films,
Documentary

Alma Mireya Hernandez*
Tucson, AZ 85719
Tel 520-861-4228
Email ....amh2@email.arizona.edu

Bel Hernandez*
Publisher/Editor-in-Chief
Latin Heat Entertainment
West Covina, CA 91793
Tel 310-464-5290
Fax 310-593-4065
Email............bhernandez@latinheat.com
Web ....www.latinheat.com

Christian Hernandez*
Sueños Entertainment, Inc
Venice, CA 90291
Tel 310-433-4140
Email ....chernandez@
                        mexicocitythemovie.com
Web ....www.mexicocitythemovie.com

Dan Hernandez*
Montebello, CA 90640
Tel 562 439-6901
Email ....Sptfishing@aol.com
Web ....www.sport-fishing.com

Dennis Hernandez*
Los Angeles, CA 90067
Tel 310-556-1444
Email ......dhernandez@lunaglushon.com
Web ....www.lunaglushon.com

Francisco Hernandez*
Smokin' Mirrors Productions
Los Angeles, CA 90027
Tel 323-906-2937
Cell 323-397-7508
Email ....fran2k@pacbell.net
Web ....www.smokinmirrors.net

Producer, HOMEBOY INDUSTRIES, 2004,
Smokin' Mirrors Productions, PSA
Director, PLANTA DE LOS PIES, 2004,
Quetzal Music, Music Video
Director, FUTURES TOO BRIGHT, 2003,
Smokin' Mirrors Productions, Music Video
Director, JAROCHO ELEGUA, 2002, Vangarde
Records, Music Video
Producer, PACO'S SUITCASE BOMB, 2002,
Fox Searchlab, Short

Helen Hernandez
President
Imagen Foundation
Encino, CA 91316
Tel 626-791-8140
Fax 626-791-5957
Email ....info@imagen.org
Web ....www.imagen.org

Media Advocate

Jorge Hernandez*
Los Angeles, CA 90049
Email ....ghernandez1997@aol.com

Lou Hernandez*
Fiddler Productions, Inc.
Naples, FL 34104
Tel............................239-435-1818 x1
Tel 239-793-2459
Cell 239-248-2493
Fax 239-649-4965
Email................Fiddlerpro@comcast.net
Web ....www.FiddlerProductions.com

Director, ONE EVENING, 2004, Fiddler
Productions Inc., Feature
Director, BAREFOOT WILLIAMS, 1999, Ten
Thousand Island Films, Short
Director, BLACK, 1999, Minnot Motion
Pictures, Short

Director, EDGE'S GIG, 1999, Fiddler
    Productions Inc., Short
Director, TACKLEBOX, 1999, Fiddler
    Productions, Short

Louis Hernandez
Public Relations
World Film Magic Distribution Corp.
Hollywood, CA 90038
Tel 323-785-2118
Web ....www.worldfilmmagic.com

Miguel Hernandez
Filmax International
Barcelona, 08908 SPAIN
Tel 34-9-33-36-85-55
Fax 34-9-32-63-08-24
Email ....m.yebra@filmax.com
Web ....www.filmaxinternational.com

Natalia Hernandez*
Writers Guild of America, East
Brooklyn, NY 11201
Email ....nhernandez@wgaeast.org

Peggy Hernandez*
Queen of Hearts Productions
Beverly Hills, CA 90210
Tel 310-385-8487
Email ....peggy_hernandez@msn.com

Roger Hernandez*
En Caliente Productions
San Antonio, TX 78205
Tel 210-223-8830
Fax 210-223-9900
Email ....encalientepro@msn.com

Rudy Hernandez*
Bakersfield, CA 93312
Tel 661-587-5893
Email.......................rmhactor@aol.com

Sandra Hernández*
Research & Development Specialist
Simi Valley, CA 93094
Email ....shernan@earthlink.net

Freelance Product Placement/Research & Dev
    Coord, CHROMIUMBLUE.COM,
    2001-2002, Zalman King Productions &
    Showtime, TV Series
Exec Asst/Prod Resources & Product
    Placement Coordinator, 2000-2001,
    Spelling Ent., Website, Prime Time TV
    Series
Casting Assistant, PASSIONS, 1999-2000,
    NBC Television, TV Series

Sharon Hernandez*
San Antonio, TX 78258
Tel 210-481-2300
Fax 210-481-2300
Email ....Beekeepersharon@yahoo.com

Susie Hernandez*
Station Relations Manager
Independent Television Service, ITVS
San Francisco, CA 94110
Tel.......................415-356-8383 x228
Cell 707-694-3360
Fax 415-356-8391
Email..............susie_hernandez@itvs.org

Station Relations Manager, INDEPENDENT
    LENS SERIES, 2002-2004, PBS & ITVS,
    Anthology Series
Executive Producer, INDEPENDENT LENS
    SERIES, 2002-2004, PBS & ITVS,
    Anthology Series

Veronica R. Hernandez*
Mirandez Productions
San Antonio, TX 78229
Tel 210-683-8780
Tel 210-573-2095
Email ....veronica@awave.com
Web............................www.awave.com

filmmakers

Rudy Hernandez, Jr.*
First Flight Pictures LTD
Key Biscayne, FL 33149
Tel 305-606-2129
Fax 305-261-8861
Email ..firstflightpictures2@hotmail.com

Director, Producer, ASÍ FUE, BABY, 2002,
  FFP, Documentary
Associate Producer, BABY FACE NELSON,
  2000, A&E Biography/Towers Productions,
  TV Special
Associate Producer, DOOMSDAY, 2000,
  Discovery Channel / Tower Productions, TV
  Special
Associate Producer, FRAMED, 2000, A&E
  American Justice / Towers Productions, TV
  Special

Wilfredo Hernandez Jr.*
Tripple H. Productions
Sayreville, NJ 08872
Tel 732-254-5285
Email ....stage73@optononline.net
Web ....www.tripleHproductions.com

Angel Hernandez Rivera*
New York, NY 11222
Tel 718-389-0351
Email ....dhs4474@hotmail.com

Mita Hernandez-Gosdin*
Summer Fling Productions
Austin, TX 78753
Tel 512-799-6687
Email ......SummerFling01@earthlink.net

Filly Herrarte-Colom*
San Francisco, CA 94115
Tel 415-336-2643
Email ....filmher@earthlink.net

Brenda Herrera
Director of Operations
Latin Heat Magazine
West Covina, CA 91793
Tel 310-464-5290
Tel 626-698-1038
Fax 310-593-4065
Email ....brenda@latinheat.com
Web ....www.latinheat.com

Media Advocate

Catherine Herrera*
Flor de Miel Films
San Francisco, CA 94110
Tel 415-240-3329
Tel 415-643-6893
Email ....mayanmx@att.net
Web ....www.gamerrera.com/transition

*Attorney: Brooke Oliver, 415-641-1116,
Brooke@artemama.com*

Associate Producer, BEYOND THE DREAM
  SERIES, PROGRAM: AGAINST THE
  GRAIN, 2004, Beyond the Dream, LLC,
  Documentary
Director, FROM THE SAME FAMILY: AN INTI-
  MATE VIEW OF GLOBALIZATION, 2004,
  Festival Distribution - BAVC, Documentary
Director, TRANSITION, 2003, Film Arts
  Foundation, Documentary
Producer, NEWS SEGMENTS, 1998,
  Canadian Broadcast Corporation,
  Documentary
Director, ALPHABET PEOPLE, 1992,
  Self-Distributed, Documentary

Fernando Herrera*
Pasadena, CA 90242
Tel 310-770-9770
Email ....nandofmvh@hotmail.com

Associate Producer, FAMILY FORENSICS,
  2004, Fox, TV Series
Assistant Editor, NANNY 911, 2004, Fox, TV
  Series
Associate Producer, TEMPTATION ISLAND,
  2003, Fox, TV Series
Producer, BET THE TRUCK, 2001, USC,
  Short
Editor, Producer, FORTUNE FISH, 2001,
  USC, Short

Jacob Herrera*
San Antonio, TX 78225
Tel 210-922-4251
Email...............nalip@jacobherrera.com

Miguel Herrera*
General Manager
Determined Management, LLC
Brooklyn, NY 11201
Tel 718-834-0644
Email..............miguelingotham@aol.com

Soledad Herrera*
Producer
SGM Records
Phoenix, AZ 85044
Tel 480-785-5917
Email ....soledad@sgmrecords.net

Director, Producer, NO PUEDO AMARTE,
   2004, SGM Records, Music Video
Director, Producer, REGRESA, 2004, SGM
   Records, Music Video
Producer, SI TU ESTUVIERAS AQUI, 2003,
   SGM Records, Music Video

Roberto Herrero*
Herrero Entertainment, LLC
Union, NJ 07083
Tel 212-946-5754
Email ..roberto@herreroentertainment.com

Mike Higuera
Cacho-Cacho Entertainment
La Tuna Canyon, CA 91352
Tel 818-504-0554
Fax 818-504-0556
Email ....mafigtree@cs.com

Director, VIVA VEGAS, 2000, Telemundo, TV
   Series
Director, LOS BELTRAN, 1999, Telemundo,
   TV Series
Director, HANG TIME, 1995, NBC, TV Series

Tina Huerta*
Tucson, AZ 85711
Email ....surealoutthere@yahoo.com

Jennie Hurtado*
New York, NY 10040
Email ....jhs5507@yahoo.com

Lena Hyde*
San Francisco, CA 94110
Email ....Lhyde@aol.com

Adriana Ibanez
Senior VP, Scheduling
Telemundo
Hialeah, FL 33010
Tel 305-884-8200
Email ....aibanez@telemundo.com
Web ....www.telemundo.com

Cristina Ibarra*
Subcine
New York, NY 10012
Tel 917-447-4498
Email..............cristinaibarra@yahoo.com
Web ....www.subcine.com

Director, Writer, LOVE & MONSTER TRUCKS,
   2005, Feature
Director, Producer, THE LAST CONQUISTA-
   DOR, 2005, PBS, Documentary
Director, Producer, AMNEZAC, 2004, Fulana,
   Short
Director, Producer, LUPE + JUANDI ON THE
   BLOCK, 2003, Fulana, Short
Director, Producer, GRANDMA'S HIP HOP,
   2002, Latino Public Broadcasting,
   Interstitial
Director, Producer, LATINO PLASTIC COVER,
   2001, Fulana, Short
Director, Producer, DIRTY LAUNDRY: A
   HOMEMADE TELENOVELA, 2000, PBS,
   Subcine, Short

John Ibarra*
Astoria, NY 11102
Tel 347-564-0743
Email ....john@bionic.tv

Leon Ichaso

Santa Monica, CA 90401

Agent: Jim Stein, Innovative Artists,
310-656-0400

Director, Writer, MONK, 2005, Greenestreet
Films Inc., Feature
Director, Writer, PINERO, 2001, Miramax,
Feature
Director, ALI: AN AMERICAN HERO, 2000,
Fox Network, TV Movie
Director, HENDRIX, 2000, MGM &
Showtime, TV Movie
Director, EXECUTION OF JUSTICE, 1999,
Showtime, TV Movie
Director, FREE OF EDEN, 1999, Showtime,
TV Movie
Writer, AZUCAR AMARGA, 1996, First Look
Pictures Releasing, Feature

Kathy Im*

Program Officer
The MacArthur Foundation
Chicago, IL 60603
Tel 312-726-8000
Fax 312-917-3693
Email ....kim@macfound.org

George Iniguez*

Rockport, TX 78382
Tel 361-563-9332

Jorge Insua

Agent
Creative Artists Agency (CAA)
Beverly Hills, CA 90212
Tel 310-288-4545
Email ....jinsua@caa.com
Web ....www.caa.com

Arturo Interian

VP, Production
Lifetime Networks
Los Angeles, CA 90067
Tel 310-556-7500
Email ....ainterian@lifetimetv.com
Web ....www.lifetimetv.com

Yvan Iturriaga*

Mun2 TV
Los Angeles, CA 90031
Cell 213-952-7652
Email ....cacique03@earthlink.net

Cameraman, THE ROOF, LA STREETS, LA
CONEXION, NO COVER, 2004-2005,
Perfect Image/Mun2, TV Series
Director of Phography, CITY OF
ANGELES-KRAZY RACE, 2004,
GreenHouse Creative Partnership, Music
Video
Director, Writer, Producer, DEEP INK-BOOK-
WORM BROWN, 2004, GreenHouse
Creative Partnership, Music Video
Director, Producer, Writer, CONTINUITY OF
PATHWAYS, 2003, Occidental College, LA,
Short
Director, Producer, Writer, OFFSIDES, 2003,
Occidental College, LA, Short

Raymundo Jacquez*

Hayward, CA 94544
Email ....mundo@chicanowarrior.com

Bill Jersey*

CEO
Quest Productions
Berkeley, CA 94710
Tel 510-548-0854
Fax 510-548-1824
Email ....bjersey@questprod.com

Director, Producer, THE MAKING OF
AMADEUS, 2002, Saul Zaentz Company,
Documentary
Director, Producer, THE RISE AND FALL OF
JIM CROW - "DON'T SHOUT TOO SOON",
2002, PBS, Documentary
Director, Producer, EVOLUTION - "WHAT
ABOUT GOD?", 2001, PBS, Documentary

Lillian Jiménez*

Latino Educational Media Center
Bronx, NY 10451
Tel 854-634-5251
Email ....Lilpiri@aol.com

Producer, ABRIENDO CAMINO, 2004, Latino
Educational Media Center, Documentary

Mercedes Jimenez-Ramirez*
Teaneck, NJ 07666
Tel 718.596.9937
Email ....jrmlatin@aol.com

Producer, BACK2 CALI, 2004, Documentary

Margarita Jimeno*
Belkaproduce
Booklyn, NY 11211
Email ....belkaproduce@hotmail.com
Web.........................www.telegrama.org

Producer, PERDER ES CUESTÍON DE
    MÉTODO, 2004, Feature
Director, Producer, ANAQUÍA EN LA ESTRA-
    DA, 2001, Music Video
Director, Producer, BIRD TIME, 2001, Short
Art Department, WASHINGTON HEIGHTS,
    2001, Feature
Director, Producer, THE SHAM, 1999, Short

Karen Johnson*
Dallas, TX 75252
Email ....goodmoviesent@aol.com

Producer, DOUBLE DARE, 2003, Goodmovies
    Entertainment, Documentary
Producer, PROSPECT, 2002, Feature
Co-Producer, TWICE UPON A YESTERDAY,
    1998, Trimark Pictures, Feature

Judi Jordan*
Divine Horizons Entertainment, Inc.
Venice, CA 90291
Tel 310-301-6618
Fax 310-876-2425
Email ....goldenfeather2000@yahoo.com
Web ....www.clubvidaloca.com

Producer, CLUB LA VIDA LOCA, 2005,
    Echelon Ent. Inc., Feature
Producer, TWIN FLAMES, 2002, Short

Otavio Juliano*
Interface Films
Los Angeles, CA 90024
Tel 310-801-4195
Email ....oajfree@hotmail.com

Director, THIRD WORLD CALIFORNIA, 2005,
    Documentary

Betty Kaplan
Luzadero, LLC
Los Angeles, CA 90004
Tel 323-654-8809
Fax 323-654 9179
Web ....www.bettykaplan.org

Agent: Micky Freiberg, 323-602-0330

Manager: Suzanna Camejo,
310-449-4064

Director, UNO, 2006, Feature
Writer, AZTEC EAGLE, 2005, Feature
Director, ALMOST A WOMAN, 2002, PBS, TV
    Movie
Director, THE DIVISION, 2001, Lifetime, TV
    Movie
Director, Writer, DONA BARBARA, 1998,
    Universal Pictures, Feature
Director, Writer, OF LOVE AND SHADOWS,
    1994, Miramax, Feature
Director, BOLIVAR, 1990, Venezolana de
    Television, TV Movie
Director, Writer, THE VIOLINIST, 1981, PBS,
    Short

Scott Kardel*
Assistant Counsel
Writers Guild of America, East
New York, NY 11231
Tel 212-767-7835
Fax 212-582-1909
Email ....skardel@wgaeast.org
Web ....www.wgaeast.org

Gary Keller*
Regents' Professor and Director
Hispanic Research Center/Arizona State
University
Tempe, AZ 85287
Tel 480-965-3990
Fax 480-965-0315
Email ....gary.keller@asu.edu

Bill Kersey*
Oro Valley, AZ 85737
Email ....wkersey@email.arizona.edu

Andy Kleinman*
Miami, FL 33131
Email ....andyk@andyk.net

Joleen Koehly*
Director of Planning & Evaluation
Digital Media Art College
Boca Raton, FL 33431
Tel ....561-391-1148 ext. 215
Fax 561-391-2489
Email ....jkoehly@dmac-edu.org

Production Designer, BAKER'S MEN, 2002,
Hyahr Films, Short
Production Designer, SLING SHOT, 2000,
IFAC, Short
Production Designer, YOUR EYES, 2000,
Namascar Films, Short

Cristina Kotz Cornejo*
Assistant Professor
Emerson College
Cambridge, MA 02138
Tel 617-824-8816
Fax 617-824-8816
Email ....info@wildwimminfilms.com
Web.............www.wildwimminfilms.com

Director, Editor, Writer, LA GUERRA QUE NO
FUE (THE WAR THAT NEVER WASO,
2004, Wild Wimmin Films, Short
Director, MI FAMILIA ARGENTINA, 2003,
Wild Wimmin Films, Documentary
Director, OCEAN WAVES, 2002, Wild
Wimmin Films, Short
Director, ERNESTO, 2000, Partnership for a
Drug Free America, Short
Director, Editor, THE APPOINTMENT, 1999,
Urban Entertainment, Short

Deborah Kravitz*
Still Photographer
Archive Studios
Tucson, AZ 85716
Tel 520-548-4118
Email ....silverdre@aol.com

Umesh Krishnan*
Monmouth, NJ 08852
Email....................tooncity@ureach.com

Robert Kubilos*
Hollywood, CA 90068
Tel 323-462-0112
Fax 323-464-3537
Email ....kubilos@earthlink.net

Joseph LaMorte
Ex-Bo Productions
New York, NY 10018
Tel 646-366-0018
Fax 212-921-0456
Email.......................exboprod@aol.com

Editor, Producer, LOVE AND LAUNDRY,
2004, Documentary
Executive Producer, WASHINGTON HEIGHTS,
2004, MAC Releasing, Documentary
Executive Producer, WHAT'S FOR DINNER?,
2004, Short
Executive Producer, DETAILS, 2000, HBO,
Short

Gloria LaMorte Herrera*
New York, NY 10018
Tel 646-366-0018
Fax 212-921-0456
Email.......................exboprod@aol.com

Editor, Producer, LOVE AND LAUNDRY,
2004, Documentary
Co-Producer, Production Manager, WASHING-
TON HEIGHTS, 2004, MAC Releasing,
Feature
Writer, WHAT'S FOR DINNER?, 2004, Short
Co-Producer, Writer, DETAILS, 2000, HBO,
Short

Mary Lampe*
Executive Director
SouthWest Alternative Media Project
(SWAMP)
Houston, TX 77006
Tel 713-522-8592
Fax 713-522-0953
Email ....mmlampe@swamp.org

Media Advocate

Carlos R. Lara*
Los Angeles, CA 90024
Email ....closlara@adelphia.net

Frances Lausell*
Isla Films
San Juan, PR 00913
Tel 787-268-0063
Cell 787-640-5290
Fax 787-268-4379
Email ....islafilms@coqui.net
Web ....www.islafilms.com

Producer, CARNIVALS OF THE CARIBBEAN, 2004, Documentary
Producer, TIBES CEREMONIAL PARK, 2004, Documentary
Producer, UNA HISTORIA COMUN, 2004, Feature
Producer, THE AMERICAN DREAM, 2003, Cinema Guild, Documentary
Producer, THE LOVELY FACES OF TITE CURET, 2003, Documentary
Producer, EL BESO, 2000, RGH Lions/Vanguard Int., Feature

Robert Leach*
Publisher
SCREEN Magazine
Chicago, IL 60610
Tel 312-640-0800
Fax 312-640-1928
Email ....publisher@screenmag.com

Rick Leal*
Arroyo Productions
Grand Prairie, TX 75050
Tel 972-986-3044
Cell 214-740-9372
Email ....rickleal60@aol.com

Segment Producer, VISIONES: LATINO ART & CULTURE, 2004, PBS, Documentary
Producer, Writer, AMERICA'S DEADLIEST STORM: GALVESTON ISLAND 1900, 2003, Documentary
Field Producer, TEXAS AND THE LATINO VOTE, 2000, Texas PBS/KERA-Galan Productions, Documentary
Associate Producer, US-MEXICAN WAR 1846-1848, 1998, PBS/KERA Dallas, Documentary
Producer, LITTLE MEXICO/EL BARRIO, 1997, KERA & WGBH (La Plaza), Documentary

Director, Producer, Segment, TAIWAN: THE NEW CHINA, 1994, PBS SECA Series/KMBH Harlingen, Texas, Documentary

Sophia Leang*
Bronx, NY 10458
Email..............sophia@carmona-inc.com
Web ....www.carmona-inc.com

Andy Lebron*
Bronx, NY 10475
Cell 917-544-0766
Fax 509-267-1841
Email................lebron1112@yahoo.com
Web ....www.latinoextra.com

John Leguizamo
Lower East Side Films
New York, NY 10014
Tel 212-966-0111
Email ....lesf@aol.com

Manager: 3 Arts Entertainment, 310-888-3200

Attorney: Hansen, Jacobsen, Teller, 310-271-8777

Actor, CRONICAS, 2004, Palm Pictures, Feature
Actor, Director, Executive Producer, Writer, UNDEFEATED, 2003, HBO, TV Movie
Actor, COLLATERAL DAMAGE, 2002, Warner Bros., Feature
Actor, Executive Producer, EMPIRE, 2002, Universal, Feature
Actor, Writer, SEXAHOLIC: A LOVE STORY, 2002, Cream Cheese Films, TV Special
Actor, Executive Producer, KING OF THE JUNGLE, 2001, Urbanworld Films, Feature
Actor , MOULIN ROUGUE, 2001, Fox, Feature
Co-Executive Producer, PIÑERO, 2001, Miramax, Feature
Actor, WHAT'S THE WORST THAT COULD HAPPEN, 2001, MGM, Feature
Actor, Writer, FREAK, 1998, HBO, TV Special

filmmakers

Duba Leibell*
Big Fish/Tall Tales
Miami Beach, FL 33139
Tel 305-582-6571
Email ....dubaleibell@aol.com

Chris Lemos*
Asst. to President & Vice Chairman of
Motion Picture Group
Paramount Pictures
Hollywood, CA 90038
Email ....chris_lemos@paramount.com

Asst. to Producer, THE STEPFORD WIVES,
  2004, Paramoung Pictures, Feature
Asst. to Producer, WITHOUT A PADDLE,
  2004, Paramount Pictures, Feature
Asst. to Producer, THE ITALIAN JOB, 2003,
  Paramount Pictures, Feature
Asst. to Producer, DOMESTIC DISTUR-
  BANCE, 2001, Paramount Pictures,
  Feature

Dennis Leoni**
Patagonia House
Valencia, CA 91385
Tel 661-254-0979
Fax 661-253-1763
Email.............PatagoniaHouse@aol.com

*Agent: Dennis Kim, The Rothman-Braecher
Agency, 310-247-9898,
dkim@rothmanbrecher.com*

*Attorney: Ziffren, Brittenham, Branca, Fisher,
310-552-6506, stephen@zbbfgs.com*

Executive Producer, Writer, BLACK & WHITE,
  2003, Showtime/ Patagonia House, TV
  Series Pilot
Executive Producer, Writer, ANGEL OF
  MERCY, 2002, NBC/ Patagonia House, TV
  Series Pilot
Director, Executive Producer, RESURREC-
  TION BLVD., 2000-2002, Showtime, TV
  Series
Executive Producer, MCKENNA, 1994, ABC,
  TV Series
Writer, COVINGTON CROSS, 1992, ABC, TV
  Series
Writer, THE COMMISH, 1991, ABC, TV
  Special
Executive Producer, THE GUARD, 1990,
  Showtime/ Patagonia House, TV Movie

Luisa Leschin
Beverly Hills, CA 90212

*Agent: Cori Wellins, WMA,
310-859-4000*

Co-Producer, GEORGE LOPEZ, 2003, ABC,
  TV Series
Writer, RESURRECTION BLVD., 2000,
  Viacom Productions Inc., TV Series

Diana Lesmez*
Caterpillar Jazz Entertainment
Los Angeles, CA 90025
Tel 310-820-2647
Fax 208-693-8252
Email ....dlesmez@caterpillarjazz.com
Web ....www.caterpillarjazz.com

Producer, CULTURE CLASH IN AMERICCA,
  2004, Arenas Entertainment, Feature
Producer, A SONG FOR HONEST ABE, 2002,
  SunriseWest Productions, Documentary
Producer, VARIOUS COMMERCIALS, 2001,
  Admark Group & Adobe Television,
  Advertising

Melissa Levine*
Los Angeles, CA 90048
Tel 310-274-4020
Cell 310-594-5503
Email ....Melissacandace@yahoo.com

David Levinson*
Boys and Girls Productions
Sherman Oaks, CA 91413
Tel 818-613-6117
Tel 818-905-6117
Email ....dlevinson@
                boysandgirlsproductions.com
Web....www.boysandgirlsproductions.com

Anna Leyva*
Executive Assistant/Jr. Manager
MBST Entertainment
Beverly Hills, CA 90210
Tel 310-385-1728
Cell 310-918-6003
Fax 310-385-1834
Email ....anna@mbst.com

Josef Manuel Liles*
Goleta, CA 93117
Tel 805-683-5884
Email ....jmliles@umail.ucsb.edu

James Lima
Beverly Hills, CA 90212

Agent: Steve Wohl, ICM,
310-550-4000, swohl@icmtalent.com

Attorney: Matthew Saver,
310-820-0202

Executive Producer, JOE MILLIONAIRE,
    2003, NBC, TV Series
Co-Producer, Director, THE SCARIEST
    PLACES ON EARTH, 2001, Fox Family
    Channel, TV Series
Director, BEHIND THE SCENES, 2000, Lions
    Share Pictures, Feature

Paul Lima*
North Hollywood, CA 91605
Email ....plima15@hotmail.com

Matías Lira*
PWI U.S.A
Santa Monica, CA 90401
Tel 310 587-2287
Fax 310 587-2504
Email....................mlira@pwimedia.com

Ruth Livier
Stevenson Ranch, CA 91381

Agent: Michael Wimer, CAA,
310-288-4545

Manager: Ellen Travis, 310-459-7274

Actor, CUP O' JOE, 2004, Hollywood Head,
    Short
Voice Over, KING OF THE HILL, 2003, 20th
    Century Fox TV, TV Movie
Actor, RESURRECTION BLVD., 2001-2002,
    Showtime, TV Series

Luis Llosa
Coastal Desert
Miami, FL 33149
Email ....lucholl@terra.com.pe

Agent: Michael Wimer, CAA,
310-288-4545, mwimer@caa.com

Director, Writer, THE FEAST OF THE GOAT,
    2005, Feature
Co-Producer, BIOGRAPHY OF MARIO VAR-
    GAS LLOSA, 2004, Documentary
Director, ANACONDA, 1997, Columbia
    TriStar, Feature
Writer, EL ANGEL VENGADOR, 1994, TV
    Movie
Producer, NEW CRIME CITY, 1994, Iguana
    Films, Feature
Director, THE SPECIALIST, 1994, Warner
    Bros., Feature
Producer, WATCHERS III, 1994,
    Concorde-New Horizons, Feature
Producer, EIGHT HUNDRED LEAGUES
    DOWN THE AMAZON, 1993,
    Concorde-New Horizons, Feature
Director, SNIPER, 1993, Tri Star Pictures,
    Feature

Benjamin Lobato*
Astoria, NY 11103
Tel 917-826-0474
Email ....bdlobato@earthlink.net

Director, Writer, NO IMPORTA, 2004, Music
    Video
Director, Writer, WOMB, 2004, In the
    Moment Productions, Music Video
Director, Writer, ORANGE, 2003, Short
Producer, Writer, PATHWAYS, 2002, Pima
    County Health Department, TV Special
Director, Writer, MARIPOSA CANYON, 2001,
    Short

Claudia Loewenstein*
2Chicas Productions
Dallas, TX 75230
Tel 214-373-1113
Fax 214-373-1114
Email ....dabronx101@aol.com
Web......www.SalsaCalientetheMovie.com

Efrain Logreira

Corte Hispana
Santa Monica, CA 90402
Tel 310-458-6998
Email ....efrem@cortehispana.com
Web....................www.cortehispana.com

Attorney: John Levine, 310-899-9408

Writer, MIRANDA'S RIGHTS, 2002,
   Independent, Edutainment
Producer, VIOLENCIA EN EL TRABAJO,
   2001, Independent, Educational/Industrial
Producer, BASTA YA DE ACOSARME, 2000,
   Independent, Educational/Industrial
Writer, NO... STOP HARASSING ME!, 2000,
   Industrial film, Edutainment
Composer, CENTILNELAS DEL SILENCIO,
   Independent, Short

Diana Logreira Campos*

Hispanic Information and
Telecommunication Network
New York, NY 10002
Tel 212-966-5660
Email....................brujadilc@yahoo.com

Rick Lombardo

Valencia, CA 91355
Tel 213-498-9468
Email ....rlombardo@mindspring.com

Producer, ACCESS HOLLYWOOD, 2004,
   NBC, TV Series
Producer, REAL TV, 2004, Paramount, TV
   Series
Producer, VIVIR INTENTANDO, 2003, Buena
   Vista International, Feature
Director, PLACES OF MYSTERY, 2000, The
   Discovery Network, TV Series

Julian Londono*

Houston, TX 77002
Tel 713-594-6502
Email ....julian_londono@hotmail.com

Director, Writer, FAILING TO ADJUST, 2002,
   Texas A&M University, Short
Director, Writer, THE EAGLE: LEARNING TO
   FLY AGAIN, 2001, Texas A&M University,
   Short

Gilda Longoria

San Antonio, TX 78217
Tel 210-650-9836
Tel 210-650-9836
Cell 210-887-0449
Fax 210-650-9836
Email ....longmag@sbcglobal.net

2nd Assistant Director, BROKEN SKY, 2003,
   PBS, TV Series
Producer, TEJANO MUSIC AWARDS, 2003,
   TTMA - PBS, TV Special
Producer, FAITH PLEASES GOD, 2002, La
   Familia Television, TV Series
Production Manager, GOD PLEASER, 2002,
   La Familia Television, TV Series
Production Manager, LATINO LAUGH FEST,
   2002, Si TV, TV Special

Marcie Longoria*

Executive Office Associate Director of
Community and Public Affairs
National Hispanic Institute
Maxwell, TX 78656
Tel 512-357-6137
Fax 512-357-2206
Email ....marsea32@yahoo.com
Web............................www.nhi-net.org

Media Advocate

Adam Lopez*

San Fernando, CA 91340
Tel 310-699-5444
Email ....adamlopez@nalip.info

Director, Writer, REAL WISDOM, 2003, Short
Director, Writer, SOUL FOOD, 2000, Short

Angel Dean Lopez*

c/o WGA
Los Angeles, CA 90048
Tel 323-821-4542
Email........................angeldean@att.net

Executive Story Editor, 10-8: OFFICERS ON
   DUTY, 2003, Buena Vista, TV Series
Executive Story Editor, LEAP YEARS, 2001,
   Showtime, TV Series
Writer, JUDGING AMY, 1999-2002, CBS, TV
   Series

Writer, BRIMSTONE, 1998, Fox Network, TV
Series
Writer, NEW YORK UNDERCOVER, 1994,
Fox Network, TV Series

Arthur Lopez*
A Media Vision
Staten Island, NY 10303
Tel 718-448-6395
Cell 347-423-2075
Email ....amediavision@aol.com

Associate Producer, Director of Photography,
LA CASITA, 2004, Short

Benjamin Lopez*
VientoFuego Productions
Tucson, AZ 85748
Tel 520-247-5520
Tel ....520-881-3300 ext. 111
Email.........benlopez@email.arizona.edu

Executive Producer, DUDEVISION, 2004,
Short
Producer, TUESDAY, 2004, Short
Actor, BORDER WARZ, 2003, Trinity Home
Entertainment, Feature
Production Assistant, HOW THE GARCIA
GIRLS SPENT THEIR SUMMER, 2003,
Feature
Producer, Writer, 500 YEARS OF CHICANO
HISTORY, 1998, Short

Carmen Lopez*
Wilton, CT 06897
Tel 203-858-6384
Fax 203-761-1574
Email ....blackandblue@optionline.net

Cynthia Lopez*
Vice President
P.O.V./American Documentary Inc.
New York, NY 10004
Tel 212-989-8121
Fax 212-727-0549
Email ....clopez@pov.org

Media Advocate

George Lopez
Encanto Enterprises, Inc.
Burbank, CA 91522
Tel 818-954-3332
Web ....www.georgelopez.com

Manager: Ron DeBlasio, 323-933-9977,
ron@sdmmusic.com

Actor, THE ADVENTURES OF SHARK BOY &
LAVA GIRL IN 3-D, 2005, Columbia
Pictures, Feature
Actor, NAUGHTY OR NICE, 2004, ABC, TV
Movie
Actor, TORTILLA HEAVEN, 2004, Feature
Producer, Writer, THE GEORGE LOPEZ
SHOW, 2003-2005, ABC, TV Series
Actor, FRANK MCKLUSKY, C.I., 2002, Buena
Vista Pictures, Feature
Actor, REAL WOMEN HAVE CURVES, 2002,
HBO, Feature
Actor, BREAD AND ROSES, 2000, Lions
Gate, Feature

Jessica Lopez*
Oxnard, CA 93033
Cell 805-701-3234
Email ....lowka1@hotmail.com

Attorney: Jeff Silberman,
310-282-8961

Writer, LOWRIDER VIDEO SERIES, 2002,
Video Series
Writer, LOWRIDER MAGAZINE, Magazine
Writer, NICKELODEON PRODUCTIONS,
Animation

Josefina Lopez*
Chispas Productions
Paris, France
Email ....chispasprods@hotmail.com
Web ....www.josefinalopez.com

Agent: Sean Davis, Phoenix Org.,
310-566-5085, sdavis@phoenixorg.com

Manager: Marilyn Atlas, 310-278-5047,
matlas704@yahoo.com

Writer, ADD ME TO THE PARTY, 2005,
Chispas Productions, Feature
Writer, LOLA GOES TO ROMA, 2005, Chispas
Productions, Feature
Director, Writer, BABY BOOM, 2004, Chispas
Productions, Short

filmmakers

Writer, AND BABY MAKES THREE, 2003,
  CBS/Atlantic Alliance, TV Movie
Writer, LOTERIA FOR JUAREZ, 2003, HBO,
  Feature
Writer, MACARTHUR PARK, 2003,
  Showtime, Feature
Writer, REAL WOMEN HAVE CURVES, 2002,
  HBO, Feature

Juan Jose Lopez*
Chicago, IL 60610
Tel 312-391-0369
Email..............j-lopez@northwestern.edu
Web ....www.jjpopp.com

Koryne Lopez*
Tucson, AZ 85705
Fax 520-573-6289
Email ....klopez18@yahoo.com

Paco López*
President
Animación Boricua Inc.
Carolina, PR 00999
Tel 787-604-4959
Email ....pacolopez@prtc.net
Web ....www.animacionboricua.com

Roberto Lopez*
Newark, NJ 07104
Tel 973-954-2490

Tania Lopez
Agent
International Creative Management
Beverly Hills, CA 90211
Tel 310-550-4322
Tel 310-540-4100
Email ....tlopez@icmtalent.com
Web ....www.icmtalent.com

Tery Lopez*
Maya Pictures
Los Angeles, CA 90017
Tel 310-281-3770
Fax 310-281-3777
Email.................rockenvivo@yahoo.com
Web ....www.maya-pictures.com

Victoria Lopez
Manager of Finance
HBO
New York, NY 10036
Tel 212-512-1000
Web ....www.hbo.com

Lalo Lopez Alcaraz
Pocho Productions
Los Angeles, CA 90063
Tel 562-907-1996
Email.......................pocho@pocho.com

Writer, PACO'S SUITCASE BOMB, 2002, Fox
  Searchlab, Short
Writer, TACO TRUCK: THE MOVIE, 2002,
  New Line, Feature

Alfredo Lopez-Brignoni*
Conquista Entertainment
Coral Gables, FL 33114
Tel 305-448-1518
Email...............alopezbrignoni@aol.com

Madeleine Lopez-Silvero
VP, Acquisitions
A&E Mundo History Channel
Miami, FL 33010
Tel 305-260-7577
Fax 305-260-0843

Teresa Lorenz*
Tucson, AZ 85719
Tel 818-657-0181
Email ....tlorenz@email.arizona.edu

Mariana Loterszpil*
Cap Fed ZZ, 1430 Argentina
Email ....dunedain@ciudad.com.ar

Roberto Lovato*
Los Angeles, CA 90026
Tel 213-250-4724
Email ....robvato@aol.com

Carrie Lozano*
Berkeley, CA 94702
Email ....carrloz@yahoo.com

Jorge Lozano
Festival Director
Alucine Toronto Film Festival
Toronto, Ontario M5T1P3 Canada
Tel 416-986-4989
Email ....info@alucinefestival.com
Web ....www.alucinefestival.com

Karla Lozano
Associate Manager
HBO Latino
New York, NY 10036
Tel 212-512-1750
Email ....karla.lozano@hbo.com
Web ....www.hbo.com

Monica Lozano
President
La Opinion
Los Angeles, CA 90028
Tel 213-896-2153
Email ......monica.lozano@laopinion.com

Emmanuel Lubezki
Los Angeles, CA 90028
Tel 323-460-4767
Fax 323-460-4804

Agent: Julia Kole, The Jacob & Kole Agency, 323-460-4767, thejkagency@hotmail.com

Director of Photography, MEXICO '68, 2006, Producciones Anhelp, Feature

Director of Photography, THE NEW WORLD, 2005, New Line Cinema, Feature
Director of Photography, LEMONY SNICKET'S A SERIES OF UNFORTUNATE EVENTS, 2004, Paramount Pictures, Feature
Associate Producer, Director of Photography, THE ASSASSINATION OF RICHARD NIXON, 2004, ThinkFilm Inc., Feature
Director of Photography, THE CAT IN THE HAT, 2003, Universal Pictures, Feature
Director of Photography, Y TU MAMA TAMBI-EN, 2001, MGM Home Entertainment, Feature

Daniel Lucio*
Miami, FL 33185
Email ....mlucio@bellsouth.net

Elmo Lugo*
Astrid Creative Endeavors, Inc.
Aventura, FL 33160
Tel 305-932-3643
Cell 786-683-0281
Email ....astrid_creative_endeavors@
yahoo.com
Web ....www.geocities.com/
astrid_creative_endeavors

Director, ETHAN'S PARABLES ON DVD: ETHAN & GOLIATH, 2003-2004, Alpha Omega Publications, Direct to DVD
Producer, NATIONAL PARKINSON'S FOUN-DATION: CARING VOICES SPANISH VIDEO, 2003-2004, National Parkinson's' Foundation, Educational Video
Camera, KOTO AND SHAKUHACHI CON-CERT, 2003, Florida Intl. University, Direct to DVD
Camera, TELEMAESTRO, 2002, Kellogg Foundation, Educational
Director, Writer, WCAA-FM NEW YORK, 2001, Hispanic Broadcasting Corp., On-Air Advertising
Producer, Writer, CELEBRACION NAVIDENA EN WALT DISNEY WORLD RESORT, 1999, ABC Radio Intl., National Radio Show

Fred Lugo*
Los Angeles, CA 90057
Fax 213-382-2162
Email ....flugo@latinotv.com

Elba Luis Lugo
MUVI Films
San Juan, PR 00901
Tel 787-729-9180

Producer, Writer, SIAN KA'AN, 2004, Feature
Producer, 12 HORAS, 2001, Manhattan
   Pictures International, Feature

Jesse Lujan*
Lockhart, TX 78644
Tel 512-554-2573
Email ....jlujan1200@yahoo.com

Rudy Luna*
Salt Lake City, UT 84101
Fax 801-972-9003
Email ....rudymoonluna@yahoo.com

Rocio Luquero*
Seattle, WA 98144
Tel 206-860-7891
Email ....rocioln@hotmail.com

Emilio Mabomar*
Long Island, NY 11101
Tel 718-786-0010
Tel 516-236-1690
Fax 718-482-8990
Email ....emilio@soundwriters.com
Web ....www.soundwriters.com

Vanessa Macedo*
Elizbaeth, NJ 07201
Tel 908-247-4402
Email ....vmacedo@eden.rutgers.edu

Grace Machado*
Vaya Productions, Inc.
Orlando, FL 32812
Email ....gmachado@aol.com

Paco Madden*
Washington, DC 20009
Tel 202-387-9173
Email ....Screen_Scribe@hotmail.com

Elsa Madrigal
Chicago, IL 60615
Tel 312-543-5495
Email ....elsamadrigal@aol.com

Producer, CALLA LA BOCA, 2003, Columbia
   College, Documentary

Yuri Makino*
Asst. Professor
Univ. of Arizona, Dept. of Media Arts
Tucson, AZ 85705
Tel 520-621-8974
Fax 520-621-9662
Email ....ymakino@u.arizona.edu
Web ....www.borderlinefilms.com

Azucena Maldonado*
Los Angeles, CA 90012
Fax 323 226-1066
Email......................azu@sbcglobal.net

Sonia Malfa-Clements*
Programs Director
AIVF
Brooklyn, NY 11215
Tel 718-809-6080
Tel 212-807-1400
Email ....soniamalfa@earthlink.net
Web ....www.aivf.org

Juan Mandelbaum*
President
Geovision
Watertown, MA 02472
Tel.......................617-926-5454 x104
Fax 617-926-5411
Email ....juanm@geovisiononline.com
Web ....www.geovisiononline.com

Director, Producer, A TASTE OF PASSOVER,
   1999, PBS/Geovision, TV Special
Director, Producer, POETRY HEAVEN, 1998,
   Films for Humanities, TV Series
Director, Producer, A NEW WORLD OF
   MUSIC, 1996, APS/Geovision,
   Documentary

Director, ANTI-SMOKING CAMPAIGN,
1994-2002, State of Massachusetts, PSA
Campaign
Director, Producer, CAETANO IN BAHIA,
1994, WGBH.Geovision, Documentary

Luis Mandoki
Santa Barbara, CA 93108

Agent: Mike Simpson, WMA,
310-859-4000

Director, Producer, ONE MORE DAY FOR
HIROSHIMA, 2005, Azucar Entertainment,
Feature
Producer, HEART OF THE ATOM, 2004, Wild
at Heart Films, Feature
Director, Producer, VOCES INOCENTES,
2004, 20th Century Fox, Feature
Producer, UTOPIA, 2003, SciFi Channel, TV
Series
Director, TRAPPED, 2002, Sony Pictures
Entertainment, Feature
Director, ANGEL EYES, 2001, Warner Bros.,
Feature
Director, AMAZING GRACE, 2000, Trimark
Pictures, Feature
Director, MESSAGE IN A BOTTLE, 1999,
1994, Feature
Director, WHEN A MAN LOVES A WOMAN,
1994, Buena Vista Pictures, Feature

José Carlos Mangual*
Santa Monica, CA 90403
Tel 310-393-8636
Fax 310-899-1598
Email ....mangual1@msn.com

Production Manager, CAYO, 2004,
Producciones Paractuar, Feature
Producer, HOW THE GARCIA GIRLS SPENT
THEIR SUMMER, 2004, Loosely Based
Pictures, LLC, Feature
Line Producer, JACK SATIN, 2004, Feature
Producer, ANIMA, 2003, AFI, Short
Production Coordinator, RAICES, 2000,
Documentary

Pancho Mansfield*
Sr. VP Development,
Original Programming
Showtime Networks
Los Angeles, CA 90024
Tel 310-234-5262
Fax 310-234-5389
Email ..pancho.mansfield@showtime.net

Ignacio Manubens*
Director of Development, Production &
Acquisitions
Arenas Entertainment
Beverly Hills, CA 90210
Tel 310-385-4476
Cell 310-384-9379
Fax 310-385-4402
Email ....ignacio@arenasgroup.com

Associate Producer, CULTURE CLASH IN
AMERICA, 2004, Arenas Entertainment,
Feature
Director, Editor, Producer, Writer, GIRLS
NEVER CALL, 2004, Overrated Movies,
Feature
Director, Producer, Writer, ONANISMO, 2004,
Overrated Movies, Short
Director, Editor, Producer, Writer, WHEELS,
2004, Canita Films, Short

Billy Marchese*
Venice, CA 90291
Email ....billy@dezartcinematic.com

Poli Marichal
Los Angeles, CA 90036
Tel 323-655-1275
Email ....rocopolis@earthlink.net

Animator, AMERICAN FAMILY, 2002, PBS,
TV Series
Director, Producer, SON AFROCARIBENO,
1998, Documentary
Producer, Writer, TODO CAMBIA, 1994,
Universal Pictures, Short

filmmakers

Cheech Marin

Culver City, CA 90232
Tel 415-271-1489
Fax 323-936-1696
Email ....jenna@forwardfilms.net

*Manager: Power Entertainment,
310-481-0004*

*Attorney: Weissman, Wolff, Bergman,
Coleman, 310-858-8777*

Actor, THE UNDERCLASSMAN, 2004,
Miramax, Feature
Actor, THE ORTEGAS, 2003, Fox Network,
TV Series
Writer, LAUGHING OUT LOUD: AMERICA'S
FUNNIEST COMEDIENS, 2001, TV
Special
Director, Writer, BORN IN EAST LA, 1987,
Universal Pictures, Feature
Director, GET OUT OF MY ROOM, 1985,
Feature
Writer, CHEECH AND CHONG'S THE CORSI-
CAN BROTHERS, 1984, MGM, Feature

Octavio Marin*

Signature Programs Director
NALIP
Santa Monica, CA 90401
Tel 310-395-8880
Cell 310-429-8351
Fax 310-395-8811
Email ....octavio@nalip.org
Web ....www.nalip.org

*Agent: Arlene Thorton & Associates,
818-760-6688*

Production Manager, HOW THE GARCIA
GIRLS SPENT THEIR SUMMER, 2005,
Loosely Based Pictures, LLC., Feature
Production Consultant, AMERICA 101, 2003,
Fobia Films, Feature
Production Associate, TEXAS RANGERS,
2001, Dimension Miramax, Feature
Production Associate, ONE MAN'S HERO,
1999, MGM - Orion, Feature
Production Supervisor, CAFÉ ARGENTINA,
1997, Crome Pictures, Short

Juan Marquez*

Casa Grande Films
Guaynabo, PR 00968
Tel 787-671-6391
Fax 787-781-6644
Email ....juan@cginteractive.com
Web ....www.casagrandefilms.com

Xavier Marrades Orga*

New York, NY 10003
Email ....xavs01@hotmail.com

Carmen Marron*

SparkHope Productions
Burbank, CA 91506
Tel 818-843-7047
Email ....carmen@spark-hope.com

Ivy Martin*

Account Executive
Time Warner Media Sales
Cypress, CA 90360
Tel 714-657-1084
Fax 714-657-1046

Alma Martinez*

Santa Cruz, CA 95064
Tel 831-459-4918
Fax 831-459-3553
Email ....almamar@ucsc.edu

*Agent: Dee Dee, JE Talent,
415-395-9475, DeeDee@jetalent.com*

Producer, CHICANO THEATRE IN AMERICA,
PART I, II, 1998, Stanford University
Television, Documentary

Angela Martinez*

Brooklyn, NY 11201
Tel 917-361-2424
Email ....bange@mindspring.com

Consulting Producer, I WAS A TEENAGE
FEMINIST, 2004, Trixie Films,
Documentary
Associate Producer, DEEP SEA DETECTIVE,
2003-2004, The History Channel, TV
Series

Assistant Producer, QUESTIONING FAIR, 2002, HBO/Cinemax, River Films, Documentary
Associate Producer, BRING NOMAD, 1998, Great Jones Productions, Feature

Beatriz "Vivi" Martinez*
Pasadena, CA 91102
Email ....vivimartinez@hotmail.com

Benito Martinez
Burbank, CA 91501
Tel 818-558-5677

Agent: SDB Partners, 310-785-0060

Actor, NEW SUIT, 2002, Trillon Entertainment, Feature
Actor, THE SHIELD, 2002, Columbia TriStar, TV Series
Actor, MI FAMILIA/MY FAMILY, 1995, New Line, Feature
Actor, OUTBREAK, 1995, Warner Home Video, Feature

Chuck Martinez
True Friend Productions
Santa Monica, CA 90406
Tel 310-230-9807
Email..............chuckmartinez@mac.com

Director, SUPERBOY, 1998, Viacom, TV Series
Director, THE EFFECTS OF MAGIC, 1998, The Discovery Network, TV Series
Director, NICE GIRLS DON'T EXPLODE, 1987, New World Home Video, Feature

Gerardo Vicente Martinez*
Cris Productions, Inc.
Los Angeles, CA 90034
Tel 310-497-4818
Fax 310-559-1951
Email ....CrisStudios@aol.com

Jesus Martinez*
Chicago, IL 60608
Tel 312-925-4436
Tel 312-733-1297
Cell 312-926-4436
Email ....Caifan002@aol.com

Post-Production Assistant, BUSCANDO A LETY, 2004, Dalia Productions, Feature
1st Assistant Director, ROMEO AND JULIET: A MODERN DAY STORY, 2004, Short
Production Assistant, WELCOME BACK TO THE BARRIO, 2004, Mindlight Films, Feature

Johnnie Martinez*
Los Angeles, CA 90007
Email ....jomar225@hotmail.com

Joselyn Martinez*
Bronx, NY 10471
Email ....joselynmartinez@aol.com

Phillipe Martinez
CEO
Bauer Martinez Studios
Largo, FL 33770
Tel 727-852-9939
Fax 727-852-9709
Email...................bmstudios1@aol.com
Web ......www.bauermartinezstudios.com

Producer, DOT. KILL, 2004, Feature
Producer, HOUSE OF NINE, 2004, Feature
Producer, MODIGLIANI, 2004, Feature

Richard Martinez*
Composer, Music Producer
Light Body Music, Inc.
Montrose, NY 10548
Tel 914-739-9410
Tel 914-739-7457
Cell 917-250-8241
Web ....www.lightbodymusic.com

Manager: Cristina Altieri-Martinez, 914-739-9410, cristina@lightbodymusic.com

Composer, HOWARD ZINN: YOU CAN'T BE NEUTRAL ON A MOVING TRAIN, 2004, First Run Features, Documentary
Additional Music, STILL DOING IT, 2004, Films Transit Int., Documentary
Music Producer, S.W.A.T, 2003, Columbia Pictures, Feature
Music Producer, FOR THE PEOPLE, 2002, Lifetime TV, TV Series
Music Producer, FRIDA, 2002, Miramax, Feature

Stephanie Martinez

Bayer Martinez Studios
Largo, FL 33770
Tel 727-852-9939
Fax 727-852-9709
Email...................bmstudios1@aol.com
Web ......www.bauermartinezstudios.com

Producer, MODIGLIANI, 2004, Feature
Producer, WAKE UP DEATH, 2004,
  Blockbuster, Feature
Co-Producer, CITIZEN VERDICT, 2003,
  Feature

José Martinez, Jr.*

Attorney
Martinez Law
Los Angeles, CA 90036
Tel 323-330-0505
Tel 212-566-4500
Fax 212-566-4542
Email....JoseMartinez@palmpictures.com

Barbara Martinez-Jitner

El Norte Productions
Culver City, CA 90232
Tel 310-244-2518
Email ....bmjelnorte@hotmail.com

Agent: Martha Luttrell, ICM,
310-550-4000

Producer, BORDERTOWN, 2005, MGM,
  Feature
Director, Executive Producer, Writer, AMERI-
  CAN FAMILY, 2002, Fox Television/PBS,
  TV Series
Producer, THE 20TH CENTURY: IN THE
  MELTING POT, 1999, Showtime, TV
  Special
Director, WHY DO FOOLS FALL IN LOVE,
  1998, Warner Bros., Feature
Second Unit Director, SELENA, 1997,
  Warner Home Video, Feature

Miguel Mas*

Mas & More Entertainment
Los Angeles, CA 90026
Tel 213-250-9162
Cell 323-365-5610
Fax 213-250-9162
Email ....mas@masandmore.com
Web ....www.masandmore.com

Manager: The Levin Agency,
323-653-7073,
levinagency@earthlink.net

Director, Writer, CIRCULOS, 2005, Mas &
  More Entertainment, Feature
Actor, Executive Producer, THE KING OF THE
  LIGHT HOUSE, 2005, Mas & More
  Entertainment, Play
Director, Writer, TRICKLE, 2005, Mas & More
  Entertainment, Feature
Actor, Director Executive Producer, Writer,
  2+2=5=1, 2004, Mas & More
  Entertainment, Short

Marta Masferrer*

Swandive Films, Inc
New York, NY 10012
Tel 917-554-2191
Tel 718-274-2855
Email.............mam@swandivefilms.com
Web ....www.swandivefilms.com

Editor, Producer, EL TIGRE, 2005, Swandive
  FIlms, Documentary
1st AD, ADI AND J, 2004, Cornwell
  Productions, Short
Director, Editor, Producer, BAD BEHAVIOUR,
  2004, Swandive Films, Short
Editor, 1st AD, BLIND DATE, 2004, Chica
  Luna Sol, Short
Editor, CONVERSE SNEAKERS, 2004,
  Hamill Productions, Spot
Editor, Producer, MOVE ON (7 SPOTS) FOR
  PRESIDENTIAL ELECTION, 2004,
  MoveOn.org, Spots

Angelica Mata*

Austin, TX 78705
Tel 832-868-6730
Email ....gellatx@hotmail.com

Bienvenida Matías*
New York, NY 10014
Tel....................212-807-1400 ext 224
Email ....beni@aivf.org

Producer, ABRIENDO CAMINO, 2004, Latino
   Educational Media Center, Documentary
Producer, FOR THE RECORD: GUAM IN
   WW II, 2004, Polymorphous Pictures, Inc.,
   Documentary
Educator, HUNTER COLLEGE, 2002, Film &
   Media Studies Dept., Portable Video
   Production
Director, HEART OF LOISAIDA, 1979,
   Reaven / Matias Productions, Documentary

Jessica Matluck*
EyesInfinite Productions
Brooklyn, NY 11222
Tel 718-813-2538
Email ....eyesinfinite@aol.com

Alex Matos*
GAD Films
San Juan, PR 00910
Tel 787-723-3440
Fax 787-723-3463
Email ....gadfilms@yahoo.com

Nicole Mattei*
368 Design
Newark, NJ 07102
Tel 973-328-7211
Email ....nicole@368design.com
Web www.368design.com

Web Developer

Drew Mayer-Oakes*
Convention & Visitors Bureau Film
Manager
City of San Antonio
San Antonio, TX 78205
Tel 210-207-6700
Fax 210-207-6843
Email ..dmayer-oakes@sanantoniovisit.com

Alonso Mayo*
Los Angeles, CA 90039
Tel 323-309-1036
Email ....afmayo@mac.com

Director, Writer, ANYONE, 2004, Esquire
   Celluloid Style, Short
Director, Writer, KEEPER OF THE PAST,
   2004, American Film Institute, Short
Director, Writer, WEDNESDAY AFTERNOON,
   2004, American Film Institute, Short
Director, Writer, SILENCIO, 2002, Manzana
   Azul, Short
Director, Writer, ALAS HUMANAS, 2001,
   Manzana Azul, Music Video

Sara Mayorga*
Los Angeles, CA 90019
Email ....mischow79@yahoo.com

Madeline Mazzaira*
Festival Coordinator
Miami Latin Film Festival
Miami, FL 33176
Tel 305-279-1809
Fax 305-279-1809
Email ....mmazaira@hispanicfilm.com
Web ....www.hispanicfillm.com

Eren McGinnis*
Dos Vatos Productions
Lexington, KY 40508
Tel 859-254-3928
Fax 859-254-3928
Email ....erenmcginnis@hotmail.com
Web..........................www.dosvatos.com

Producer, IMPRESARIO, 2002, Dos
   Vatos/KET, Documentary
Producer, BEYOND THE BORDER, 2001, Dos
   Vatos/ITVS/LPBP, Documentary
Producer, THE GIRL NEXT DOOR, 2000,
   Café Sisters/Indican, Feature
Producer, TOBACCO BLUES, 1998, Café
   Sisters/ITVS, TV Special

James McNamara
President-CEO
Telemundo
Hialeah, FL 33010
Tel 305-884-8200
Web ....www.telemundo.com

Marcos Meconi*
Cantina Films
Brooklyn, NY 11222
Tel 917-544-8398
Email ....marcos@cantinafilms.com

Agustin Medina*
Attorney of Counsel
Beltran & Medina
Los Angeles, CA 90012
Tel 213-580-0124
Cell 626-379-3516
Fax 213-580-0055
Email................agustm@beltranlaw.com

Dan Medina
Director of Operations & Sales
Wilshire Stages
Los Angeles, CA 90048
Tel 323-951-1700
Fax 323-951-1710
Email ....dmedina@wilshirestages.com
Web ....www.wilshirestages.com

Production Facilities & Services

Daniel Medina*
South Pasadena, CA 91030
Email ....monster613@aol.com

Hugo Medina*
Canoga Park, CA 91304
Tel 818-998-4481
Email ....hugomedina67@yahoo.com

Joey Medina*
Spank Monkey Productions
Pasadena, CA 91107
Tel 818-415-4434
Fax 626-797-5539
Email ....SpankMonkeyFilms@aol.com
Web ....www.elmatadorthemovie.com

Writer, CIRCUMCISED CINEMA, 2005, Si TV,
  TV Series
Host, Producer, LOCO COMEDY JAM, 2004,
  mun2, TV Series
Director, EL MATADOR, 2001, Feature
Producer, GAME SHOW NETWORK, 2000,
  Game Show Network, TV Series

Louis Medina*
Los Angeles, CA 90020
Tel 213-382-9512
Email ....futuromedina@netzero.net

Translator, ENGLISH/SPANISH/JAPANESE

Nellie Medina*
Futuri Entertainment
W. Hempstead, NY 11552
Tel 516-414-5312
Email ....futurientertainment@yahoo.com

Line Producer, FESTIVAL EXPRESS, 2004,
  Feature
Director, Producer, Writer, NOW WHAT?,
  2004, Short
Line Producer, CONCERT OF BANGLADESH,
  2003, Apple Corps LTD. UK., Documentary
Producer, HUNG-UP, 2003, Short
Line Producer, GULLY, 2002, Short
Producer, THE ICEMAN CONFESSES, 2002,
  HBO, TV Special
Producer, AUTOPSY SERIES, 2001-2002,
  HBO, TV Special

Armando Medrano*
South Texas Film
Brownsville, TX 78521
Tel 956-550-8076
Fax 956-550-8626
Email.......manager@southtexasfilm.com
Web ....www.southtexasfilm.com

Nick Medrano*
South Texas Film
Brownsville, TX 78521
Tel 956-550-8076
Fax 956-550-8626
Email ....nickm@7thcode.com
Web ....www.southtexasfilm.com

Louis Mejia
President
CEO TV News
Miami, FL 33143
Tel 786-268-2723
Fax 305-888-5161
Email ....lmejia@the-beach.net
Web ....www.ceotvnews.com

Attorney: Ozzie Torres

Executive Producer, Writer, TIMELESS SOUL, 2001, BKWSU, Short

Luis Mejia*
Miami, FL 33143
Tel 786-268-2723
Email ....cuscocondor@yahoo.com
Web...........................www.tribalink.org

Andrea Melendez*
Gaea Productions
Buda, TX 78610
Tel 512-295-8989
Email ....gaealies@hotmail.com

Producer, BLUEPRINT SCHOOLS, 2005, Social Education, Documentary
Producer, "J.F. QUE?", 2004, NALIP Austin Film Committee, 48 Hour Film Project
Producer, AFRICAN DIASPORA, 2001, UT Austin Research Channel Iniative, Documentary
Producer, PROGRAMME FOR BELIZE, 2001, UT Austin Research Channel Iniative, Documentary
Media Advocate
Educator, COMMUNICATION, CIVIL RIGHTS, VOTING RIGHTS FOR SOUTHWEST VOTER REGISTRATION AND EDUCATION PROJECT

Lawrence D. Melendez*
Tel 213-446-4519
Email ....scenicshops@yahoo.com
Web ....www.scenicshops.com

Art Director, 2004 SUMMER LIBRARY, 2004, Boffa Productions, Commercial
Production Design, SCRAMBLED EGGS, 2004, Glass Beach Entertainment, Short
Art Director, THE KUSTOMIZER, 2004, Discovery Channel, Documentary
Art Director, FREAK OF THE WEEK, 2003, LA Film Schools, TV Pilot
Production Design, SNACKERS, 2003, USC Film School, Short
Production Design, THE BUG MAN, 2003, Bugman Films, Short

Maria Meloni*
Miami, FL 33185
Tel 305-225-3808
Tel 305-970-0611
Cell 786-355-9190
Fax 305-225-3808
Email ....mariameloni@gmail.com

Location Manager, CUANDO LLORA EL CORAZON, 2004, FV Productions/Televisa, TV Series
Location Manager, INOCENTE DE TI, 2004, FV Productions/Televisa, TV Series
Location Manager, ANGEL REBELDE, 2003, FV Productions/Venevision, TV Series
Production Coordinator, "GIVING BACK" TIDE, 2002, CIC Films, Commercial
Location Manager, REBECA, 2002, Fonovideo/Venevision, TV Series
Production Coordinator, HEY MIAMI, 2001, Intraroyal, TV Series

Harry Mena*
Brooklyn, NY 11220
Tel 718-492-1214

Joey Mendez*
Lucky 13 Film & Video
Montebello, CA 90640
Tel 323-816-3237
Email ....joedez1@yahoo.com
Web www.lucky13filmandvideo.com

Von Marie Mendez*
Indigo Films
San Juan, PR 00927
Tel 787-531-4776
Fax 767-764-8548
Email .....vonmariemendez@hotmail.com

Ricardo Mendez Matta
Los Angeles, CA 90048
Tel 323-655-1275
Fax 323-655-8343
Email ....rocopolis@earthlink.net

Agent: Michael Sheehy, The Stone Manners Agency, 323-655-1313

1st Assistant Director, THE LOST CITY, 2004, Lions Gate Films, Feature
Director, THE DISTRICT, 2003, CBS, TV Series
Director, TOUCHED BY AN ANGEL, 2002, CBS, TV Series
Director, NASH BRIDGES, 2001, CBS, TV Series
1st Assistant Director, ALI: AN AMERICAN HERO , 2000, Fox , TV Movie
1st Assistant Director, BREAD AND ROSES, 2000, Lions Gate Films, Feature
1st Assistant Director, PRICE OF GLORY, 2000, New Line Cinema, Feature

Jim Mendiola*
Badass Pictures
Los Angeles, CA 90068
Tel 213-840-5396
Email ....hidalgo12@aol.com

Attorney: Loeb & Loeb, 310-282-2000, cemanuel@loeb.com

Director, Writer, SPEEDER KILLS, 2003, Feature
Director, Producer, Writer, COME AND TAKE IT DAY, 2002, ITVS, TV Movie
Director, Writer, PRETTY VACANT, 1996, Short

Alex Mendoza*
Mendoza & Associates
Temple City, CA 91780
Tel 626-614-8277
Cell 626-233-0066
Fax 626-447-0469
Email ....alexmend@aol.com
Web ....hometown.aol.com//alexmend/
AMAHomePage.html

Associate Producer, THE DEVIL INSIDE, 2005, Feature
Production Facilities & Services, Printing
Graphic Designer

Ashley Mendoza
New York, NY 10025
Tel 212-865-9227
Cell 917-859-6017
Email ....amfilm@mac.com

Associate Producer, Writer, DORA THE EXPLORER, 2001, Nickelodeon, TV Series, Animated

Edy Mendoza
Comedy Development Department
CBS
Los Angeles, CA 90035
Tel 323-575-4025
Email.........edith.mendoza@tvc.cbs.com

Linda Mendoza*
Sherman Oaks, CA 91401
Tel 818-981-4288

Agent: Andy Elkin, CAA, 310-288-4545

Manager: Blueprint, 323-330-0337

Director, CHASING PAPI, 2003, Fox 2000, Feature
Director, THE ORTEGAS (PILOT), 2003, Fox Network, TV Series
Director, A.U.S.A., 2002, Fox, NBC, TV Series
Director, GROUNDED FOR LIFE, 2001, Fox Network, TV Series
Director, THE BERNIE MAC SHOW, 2001, Fox Network, TV Series
Director, ALMA AWARDS, 2000, 1999, ABC, TV Series
Director, THE BROTHERS GARCIA, 2000, Si TV/Nickelodeon, TV Series

Roberto Mendoza

Quoddy Bay Productions
Orono, ME 04469
Tel 207-581-8817
Tel 207-581-8817
Email ....condorhombre@yahoo.com

Director, Editor, THE EARTH IS OUR MOTH-
ER, 1971, American Documentary Films,
Documentary
Director, Editor, Writer, NOTEBOOK, 1966,
Cinema 16, Short

Elisa Menendez*

Miami, FL 33175
Email.........madmadameb@hotmail.com

Joe Menendez

Beverly Hills, CA 90212

Agent: Raul Matteu, WMA,
305-938-2020

Producer, URBAN JUNGLE, 2004, Si TV, TV
Series
Director, Writer, HUNTING OF MAN, 2003,
Feature
Writer, LUIS, 2003, Fox, TV Series
Director, Writer, LORDS OF THE BARRIO,
2002, Spectrum Films, Feature
Director, THE BROTHERS GARCIA, 2001,
Nickelodeon, TV Series

Ramon Menendez

Santa Monica, CA 90401

Agent: Nancy Nigrosh, Innovative
Artists, 310-656-5142

Attorney: Mark Kalmansohn,
310-553-8833

Director, GOTTA KICK IT UP, 2002, The
Disney Channel, TV Movie
Writer, TORTILLA SOUP, 2001, Samuel
Goldwyn Company, Feature
Director, PERVERSIONS OF SCIENCE, 1997,
HBO, TV Movie
Director, TALES FROM THE CRYPT: THE
BRIBE, 1994, HBO, TV Series
Director, Writer, MONEY FOR NOTHING,
1993, Hollywood Pictures, Feature
Director, Writer, STAND AND DELIVER,
1988, Warner Bros., Feature

Jon Mercedes III*

Fiesta Studios
Hollywood, CA 90028
Tel 323-314-5647
Email ....jonwrites@hotmail.com

Manager: Mercedes Management

Associate Producer, CHASE, 1990, AIP,
Feature
Associate Producer, DEADLEY PREY, 1988,
AIP, Feature
Associate Producer, MAN KILLERS, 1987,
AIP, Feature
Manager

Rafael Merino*

Grupo Huracán
El Barrio, NY 10029
Tel 212-369-4261
Fax 212-202-3919
Email ....rmerino@grupohuracan.com
Web ....www.grupohuracan.com

Producer, DIO, NACION, NOSOTROS, 2004,
Cine Huracán, Trailer
Director, Producer, LIBORIO MATEO FEST,
2004, Cine Huracán, Documentary
Producer, LISTEN, MR. BLANCO..., 2004,
Cine Huracán, Feature
Director, Producer, PALENQUE PROJECT,
2004, Cine Huracán, Docmumentary
Director, Producer, JUST DO IT, PAPA, 1999,
Cine Huracán, Short

Humberto L. Meza*

Meza Productionz
Canoga Park, CA 91304
Tel 818-704-1752
Email ....mezaproductionz@yahoo.com
Web ....www.humbertosplace.com

Agent: Kay Billings, Chateau Billings,
323-965-5432,
chateaub@mindspring.com

Jean Meza*

Lawndale, CA 90260
Email....................jmeza1@hotmail.com

Leonardo Meza*

Arekita Productions
Los Alamitos, CA 90720
Tel 562-673-2022
Fax 562-598-9927
Email........................rafy@arekita.com

Omar Meza*

Vice President
Loiza Films
Los Angeles, CA 90007
Tel 213-289-4986
Email ....omeza@tmail.com

Executive Producer, GET TITO, 2005,
   Feature
Producer, SINK OR SWIM, 2003, Pilot
Manager

Rick Michaels*

Acquisition & Development VP
Blue Desert Entrtainment
Key Largo, FL 33037
Tel 305-453-9169
Fax 305-453-9169
Email...............pakaprod@bellsouth.net

Oralia Michel*

Pasadena, CA 91105
Tel 626-568-0902
Email ....oralia@ommpr.com

Miriam Millan*

Brooklyn, NY 11217
Tel 917-857-8331
Email ....mnmeditor@aol.com

Gene Raphael Miller*

New York, NY 10031
Tel 917-749-6639
Email...............grmiller@icarofilms.com
Web ....www.icarofilms.com

Joe Miraglilo

A-Wave Studios
San Antonio, TX 78229
Tel 210-573-2095
Email.......................awave@awave.com
Web...........................www.awave.com

Graphic Designer
Web Developer

Elisha Miranda*

Chica Luna Productions/ Chica Sol Films
New York, NY 10029
Tel 212-410-3544
Email ......elishamiranda@chicaluna.com
Web ....www.chicaluna.com

*Attorney: Innes Smolansky, Esq.,
Innes@filmlegal.com*

Director, BLIND DATE, 2003, Chica Sol
   Films, LLC/Student Academy Award Grant,
   Short
Writer, FOR THE LOVE OF PATRIA, 2003,
   Women Make Movies, Short
Producer, A-ALIKE, 2002, New Heritage
   Films/Middle Passage Filmworks, Short
Director, Producer, BAPTISM BY FIRE, 2002,
   Women Make Movies, Documentary
Director, Producer, CORPORATE DAWGZ,
   2002, DV Republic.com, Short

Nestor Miranda

Mira Productions
Los Angeles, CA 90045
Tel 310-621-5357
Email ....nesndi@yahoo.com

Director, Writer, AVENUE A, 2004, Fox
   Searchlight, Feature
Producer, BLAZIN', 2003, Ground Zero
   Entertainment, Feature
Director, Writer, SHIVER, 2003, Ground Zero
   Entertainment, Feature
Producer, ALONG FOR THE RIDE, 2000,
   BFF Entertainment, Feature
Director, Producer, Writer, DESTINATION
   UNKNOWN, 1997, Ground Zero
   Entertainment, Feature

Rhonda L. Mitrani*
The Florida Room
Miami Beach, FL 33139
Tel 305-582-7191
Fax 305-610-4564
Email ....rhonda@thefloridaroom.com
Web ....cubamiathefilm.com

Editor, THE SUITOR, 2001, Gigantic
  Pictures, TV Movie
Editor, HIT AND RUNWAY, 1999, Lot 47,
  Feature

Lilia Molina*
Glendale, CA 91201
Tel 818-469-2714
Email.................molinalilis@yahoo.com

Sergio Molina
Presidente, Commissioner
National Film Commission of Mexico
Mexico, DF 03300 Mexico
Tel 52-55-56-88-78-13
Fax 52-55-56-88-70-27
Email ....conafilm@prodigy.net.mx
Web ....www.conafilm.org.mx

Executive Producer, MI FAMILIA/MY FAMILY,
  1995, New Line Cinema, Feature
Writer, HOY NO CIRCULA, 1993, TV Series
Writer, EL JINETE DE LA DIVINA PROVIDEN-
  CIA, 1988, Feature
Writer, LOS PIRATAS, 1986, Feature

Julie Monroy*
Film Club/CSNU
Los Angeles, CA 90065
Tel 323-277-0421
Cell 323-350-2163
Email............julie_monroy@hotmail.com

Director, CENTRAL AMERICANS, FIRST
  GENERATIONS, 2001, Documentary
Executive Producer, SALVADORAN WOMEN
  AND THEIR RELIGION, 2001,
  Documentary
Director, HOMMIES UNIDOS, 2000,
  Documentary

Ricardo Montalban*
Nosotros
Hollywood, CA 90004
Tel 323-466-8566
Fax 323-466-8540
Email ....velascojjv@aol.com
Web ....www.nosotros.org

*Agent: Jerry Velasco, Velasco and
Associates, 323-466-8566*

Actor, SPY KIDS 3, 2003, Miramax, Feature
Actor, SPY KIDS 2, 2002, Miramax, Feature
Actor, CANNONBALL RUN 2, 1984, Warner
  Bros., Feature

Alberto Montero*
Yuma, AZ 85364
Tel 928-329-1052
Cell 928-503-2958
Email ....alberto_monterojr@hotmail.com

Actor, HOW THE GARCIA GIRLS SPENT
  THEIR SUMMER, 2005, Loosely Based
  Pictures, LLC, Feature
Actor, CEASAR AND CLEOPATRA, 2004,
  Arizona Western College, Play
Actor, ON THE CUTTING ROOM FLOOR,
  2004, Skinny Bones Production, Feature

Melissa Montero*
Woodhaven, NY 11421
Email..............zoemontero@hotmail.com

Producer, OUR WOMEN, OUR STRUGGLE,
  2004, Documentary

John Montoya
His Panic Endeavors
Lancaster, CA 93534
Tel 661-886-0967
Email ....johnmontoya55@yahoo.com

*Attorney: Leif Reinstein, Bloom, Hergott
and Diemer, 310-859-6800,
lwr@bhdllp.com*

Director, BORN 2B GANGSTAZ?, 2003,
  Documentary
Director, Director of Photography, INTRODUC-
  ING LEANDRO FELIPE, 2003,
  Documentary

filmmakers

Producer, BOOK WARS, 2000, Avatar,
    Documentary
Director of Photography, Producer, LIVE
    NUDE GIRLS UNITE!, 2000, First Run
    Features, Documentary

Richard Montoya
Los Angeles, CA 90001
Tel 213-447-0538
Web ....www.cultureclash.com

*Manager: Ivan de Paz Management,
310-409-8638*

Actor, Co-Executive Producer, Writer, CUL-
    TURE CLASH IN AMERICCA , 2004,
    Arenas Entertainment, Feature
Actor, Writer, CHAVEZ RAVINE, 2003, Mark
    Taper Forum, Stage Play
Actor, Writer, NUYORICAN STORIES, 1999,
    INTAR, Stage Play

Scott Montoya
Payaso Entertainment
Hollywood, CA 90038
Tel 323-956-3822
Fax 323-862-2148

Producer, ROBIN HOODZ, 2005, Feature
Executive Producer, THE ORIGINAL LATIN
    DIVAS OF COMEDY, 2005, Paramount,
    Feature
Executive Producer, THE ORIGINAL LATIN
    KINGS OF COMEDY, 2002, Paramount,
    Feature
Co-Producer, IDIOTS AND ARMADILLOS,
    1998, Feature

Danny Mora*
Los Angeles, CA 90010
Tel 310-802-1753
Email.....................drsusane@msn.com

Felix Mora*
Hispanos en Canada
Richmond Hill, Ontario L4S-2E1 Canada
Tel 905-770 4645
Email ....felix.mora@rogers.com

Abie Morales*
Tucson, AZ 85712
Email.................abie@abiemorales.com

Carla P. Morales*
Philadelphia, PA 19131
Tel 215-473-1556
Email ....carlapharaoh62@aol.com

Christina "Herricane" Morales*
Philadelphia, PA 19131
Tel 267-252-7320
Email ....herricane62@aol.com

Rosalinda Morales
FarMore Casting and Prod.
Los Angeles, CA 90001
Tel 213-840-4738
Fax 530-325-4738

Casting Supervisor, EL PADRINO, 2004, El
    Padrino, LLC, Feature
Casting Director, WHITE LIKE THE MOON,
    2002, AFI, Short
Casting Director, BREAD AND ROSES, 2000,
    Lions Gate Films, Feature
Casting Director, REYES Y REY, 1998, TV
    Series

Sylvia Morales*
Los Angeles, CA 90066
Email.............smorales88@comcast.net

*Agent: Ronny Lief, Contemporary Artists
Ltd., 310-395-1800*

Director, RESURRECTION BLVD. , 2000,
    Showtime, TV Series
Producer, TELL ME AGAIN...WHAT'S LOVE,
    1998, PBS, TV Series
Director, REYES Y REY, 1995, Telemundo
    Network, TV Series
Producer, CHICANO! THE MEXICAN AMERI-
    CAN CIVIL RIGHTS MOVEMENT, 1994,
    PBS, TV Series
Producer, THE FAITH EVEN TO THE FIRE,
    1990, PBS, TV Series

Alex Moreno*
Marketing Director
Creative Industry Handbook
Toluca Lake, CA 91602
Tel 818-752-3200
Cell 818-968-9444
Fax 818-752-3220
Email ....alex@creativehandbook.com
Web ....www.creativehandbook.com

Graphic Designer
Production Facilities & Services

Mylene Moreno
Souvenir Pictures
Los Angeles, CA 90046
Tel 323-512-4678
Fax 323-512-4679
Email ....mylenem@earthlink.net

Director, TRUE HEARTED VIXENS, 2001,
   POV, Documentary
Producer, CORMAC'S TRASH, 1999, Short
Director, Producer, CHICANO! EPISODE,
   1996, PBS/KCET, Documentary

Bob Morones
Universal City, CA 91602
Tel 323-465-8110

Casting Director, KINGPIN, 2003, NBC, TV
   Series
Casting Director, RESURRECTION BLVD.,
   2002, Showtime, TV Series
Casting Director, DEAD IN THE WEST, 2000,
   Razorwire Pictures, Feature
Casting Director, ROMERO, 1989, Four
   Square, Feature

Tomas Aceves Mournian*
Los Angeles, CA 90046
Tel 323-654-6341
Email ....iamthos1@aol.com

Producer, Writer, AMERICAN ODYSSEY,
   2005, Documentary
Writer, SEDUCTION OF JOEY FABULOUS,
   2005, Stage Play
Producer, Writer, HIDING OUT, 2002, MTV,
   Equality Rocks, Short

Maria Muñoz*
Ph.D. Candidate
UCLA's Critical Studies Program in the
Film, TV and Digital Media Dept.
San Pedro, CA 90731
Tel 310-548-0894
Email ....munozchacon@hotmail.com

Robert Muñoz
Director of Business Development
New Line Cinema
Los Angeles, CA 90048
Tel 310-854-5811
Web ....www.newlinecinema.com

Summer Joy Muñoz-Main*
Tica Productions
Malibu, CA 90265
Tel 310-733-8422
Cell 917-401-2628
Fax 310-457-6118
Email.............sjm@ticaproductions.com
Web ....www.ticaproductions.com

Producer, JUST A GIRL, 2005, Desert Flower,
   Tica Productions, Short
Director, Producer, LA CERCA, 2005, Tica
   Productions, Short
Producer, SWAN DIVE, 2004, Voyager Films,
   Tica Productions, Short

Jose Manuel Murillo*
Membership Coordinator
NALIP
Santa Monica, CA 90401
Tel 310-395-8880
Fax 310-395-8811
Email.................membership@nalip.org
Web ....www.nalip.org

Co-Producer, FIREPUSSY, 2003, Short
Director, Producer, Writer, CROSSROADS,
   2002, Short
Director, Producer, Writer,
   GREENPEACE.COM, 2002, PSA
Director, Producer, Writer, RUN ROSA RUN,
   2002, Short

filmmakers

Maria Murillo*
Cine Chatota
Eagle Rock, CA 90041
Tel 323-578-3294
Email ....lachatota@earthlink.net

Richard A. Murray Jr.*
Production Manager
Landmark K Productions
Philadelphia, PA 19144
Tel 215-991-5915
Fax 215-844-8551
Email ....plarite06@comcast.net

Joaquin Murrieta*
Rancho Cucamonga, CA 91730
Tel 323-819-0042
Email ....immurrieta@aol.com

Peter Murrieta
Tel 818-954-4255
Email ....candyb32@yahoo.com

Agent: Ted Miller, CAA, 310-288-4545

Producer, ALL ABOUT THE ANDERSONS,
   2003, Warner Bros. Television Network, TV
   Series
Writer, R3, 2003, Sony Pictures
   Entertainment, Documentary
Producer, Writer, GREETINGS FROM TUC-
   SON, 2002, Warner Bros. Television
   Network, TV Series
Writer, THREE SISTERS, 2001, NBC, TV
   Series
Writer, JESSE, 1998, NBC, TV Series

Kimberly Myers*
Maya Pictures
Los Angeles, CA 90017
Tel 310-281-3770
Fax 310-281-3777
Web ....www.maya-pictures.com

Producer, PASSION, 1996, PBS, TV Movie
Producer, JACOB, 1994, TNT, TV Movie
Producer, MIDNIGHT'S CHILD, 1992, The
   Polone Company, TV Movie
Executive Producer, LA PASTORELA, 1991,
   PBS, TV Movie

Executive Producer, THE LOST LANGUAGE
   OF CRANES, 1991, BBC, TV Movie
Executive Producer, UNCLE VANYA, 1991,
   WNET New York, TV Movie
Executive Producer, HAMLET, 1990, PBS, TV
   Movie

Mateo-Erique Nagassi*
Cinema Sol Productions
Los Angeles, CA 90078
Tel 323-350-6149
Fax 714-549-5170
Web ....www.onthelowmovie.com

Executive Producer, ON THE LOW, 2004,
   Cinema Soul Production, Torch Light
   Media, Short

Monica Nanez*
San Francisco, CA 94112
Tel 415-846-6938
Email ....monanez@sbcglobal.net

Producer, DIRTY LAUNDRY, 2000, Short

Gerardo Naranjo
Perro Negro Productions
Los Angeles, CA 90007
Tel 323-661-0977

Director, MALA CHANCE, 2003, Feature
Director, THE LAST ATTACK OF THE BEAST,
   2002, AFI, Short

Michael Narvaez
I Believe in America Productions, LLC.
Bronx, NY 10463
Tel 917-519-9600
Fax 718-432-2827
Email ....michael.narvaez@verizon.net

*Manager: LaSalle Management
Group, 212-541-4444,
lillian@lasallemangementgroup.com*

Producer, Writer, I BELIEVE IN AMERICA,
   2004, IBIA, LLC, Feature
Actor, FUNNY VALENTINE, 2003, Feature
Actor, MAID IN MANHATTAN, 2002, US
   Studio, Feature

Nicole Natale*
Starving Monkey Productions
Chandler, AZ 85246
Email ....Nicole@starvingmonkey.com

Antonia Nava
Senior Vice President of Sales and
Co-Production
Filmax International
Barcelona, 08908 SPAIN
Tel 34-9-33-36-85-55
Fax 34-9-32-63-08-24
Web ....www.filmaxinternational.com

Gregory Nava
El Norte Productions
Culver City, CA 90232
Tel 310-244-2518

Agent: Martha Luttrell, ICM,
310-550-4000

Director, Producer, BORDERTOWN, 2005,
　　MGM, Feature
Executive Producer, KILLING PABLO, 2005,
　　Dreamworks, Paramount, Feature
Director, Executive Producer, Writer, AMERI-
　　CAN FAMILY, 2002-2004, PBS, TV Series
Writer, FRIDA, 2002, Miramax, Feature
Producer, Director, 20TH CENTURY: AMERI-
　　CAN TAPESTRY, 1999, Showtime, TV
　　Movie, Documentary
Director, Writer, SELENA, 1997, Warner
　　Bros., Feature

Lisa Navarrete**
Communications Director
National Council of La Raza
Washington, DC 20036
Tel 202-785-1670
Fax 202-776-1792
Email ....lnavarrete@nclr.org
Web ....www.nclr.org

Media Advocate

Angela Michelle Navarro*
Tucson, AZ 85716
Email ....m_xel@yahoo.com

Bertha Navarro
Mexico City, DF 11560 Mexico
Email ....tequila_gang@terra.com.mx

Producer, CRONICAS, 2004, Palm Pictiures,
　　Feature
Producer, I MURDER SERIOUSLY, 2002,
　　Manga Films S.L., Feature
Producer, LOCO FEVER, 2001, Altavista
　　Films, Feature
Executive Producer, THE DEVIL'S BACK-
　　BONE, 2001, Sony Pictues Classics,
　　Feature
Producer, UN EMBRUJO, 1998, Salamandra
　　Producciones, Feature
Co-Producer, MEN WITH GUNS, 1997,
　　Anarchist's Convention Films, Feature
Producer, DE TRIPAS, CORAZEÓN, 1996,
　　Short
Producer, CRONOS, 1993, October Films,
　　Feature
Executive Producer, CABEZA DE VACA,
　　1991, Concorde Pictures, Feature
Producer, EL NORTE, 1983, Artisan
　　Entertainment, Feature

Chris Navarro*
San Marcos, TX 78666
Email ....johny_paiyaso@yahoo.com

Guillermo Navarro
Los Angeles, CA 90035
Tel 818-865-0227
Email ....aceimage@aol.com

Agent: Robin Sheldon, Jane Prosuit,
Lyon Sheldon Prosnit Agency,
310-652-8778, lsagency@aol.com

Director of Photography, ZATHURA, 2005,
　　Columbia Pictures, Feature
Director of Photography, HELLBOY, 2004,
　　Columbia Pictures, Lawrence Gordon
　　Productions, Feature
Director of Photography, IMAGINING
　　ARGENTINA, 2003, Arenas Entertainment,
　　Feature
Director of Photography, BROKEN SILENCE,
　　2001, Altavista Films, Oriafilms S.L.,
　　Feature
Director of Photography, SPY KIDS, 2001,
　　Dimension Films, Feature
Director of Photography, THE DEVILS BACK-
　　BONE, 2001, Sony Pictures Classics,
　　Feature

Jesus Nebot*
Zokalo Entertainment
Los Angeles, CA 90047
Tel 310-295-0000
Email ....jesus@zokalo.com
Web ....www.zokalo.com

Agent: Joel Kleinman, BKI,
323-874-9800

Actor, ARRESTED DEVELOPMENT, 2004,
 Fox, TV Series
Actor, LAS PUERTAS DE LA NOCHE, 2004,
 TVE (SPAIN), Feature
Director, Producer, TEA WITH JESUS, 2004,
 Public Access TV, TV Series
Actor, BOOMTOWN, 2003, NBC, TV Series
Actor, Director, Producer, Writer, NO TURN-
 ING BACK, 2002, Zocalo Ent., Universal,
 Feature
Actor, NYPD BLUE, 2000, ABC, TV Series

Pepper Negron*
Purple Velvet Productions
Jersey City, NJ 07307
Tel 201-555-4114
Email....pepper_photography@yahoo.com
Web..........................www.purplevp.com

Director, Producer, BEAUTY, 2004, HBO,
 Short
Director, Producer, Writer, TWO GUNS & A
 BAG OF SANDWICHES, 2003, Short
Director, Producer, Writer, MASTER & SER-
 VANT, 2001, Short

Frances Negron-Muntaner*
Polymorphous Pictures
New York, NY 10027
Tel 212-222-4134
Tel 305-724-6630
Email ....bikbaporub@aol.com

Director, Producer, FOR THE RECORD,
 GUAM IN WWII, 2005, ITVS, Documentary
Director, Producer, Writer, REGARDING
 VIEQUES, 2005, Polymorphous Pictures,
 Documentary
Director, Producer, Writer, PUERTO RICAN
 ID, 1996, ITVS, PSA
Director, Producer, Writer, BRINCANDO EL
 CHARCO: PORTRAIT OF A PUERTO
 RICAN, 1994, Women Make Movies,
 Documentary

Director, Producer, Writer, LATINOS UNIDOS,
 1994, Congreso de Latinos Unidos, PSA
Director, Producer, Writer, AIDS IN THE
 BARIO: ESO NO ME PASA A MÍ, 1990,
 AIDS Film Initiative, PSA

Lazara Nelson*
New York, NY 10040
Tel ....
Fax 212-568-5784
Email............lazaranelson@earthlink.net

Andres Nicolini*
New York, NY 10040
Tel 212-928-0097
Email ....andresnicolini@yahoo.com
Web ....www.andresnicolini.com

Sound, FILM SCHOOL, 2004, Independent
 Film Channel, Documentary
Director, Writer, RENDEZVOUS, 2004, Short
Sound, RIKER'S ISLAND HIGH SCHOOL,
 2004, Showtime, Documentary
Sound, HOUSTON ANIMAL COPS, 2003,
 Discover Channel: Animal Planet,
 Documentary
Producer, IGGY & ANTJUAN: A LIFE IN
 PROGRESS, 2001, PBS WYBE-35
 Philadelphia, Documentary
Director, Writer, BECOMING AMERICA,
 2000, Winner Best Film New York City
 Visions, Short

Gustavo Nieto-Roa*
Centauro Comunicaciones
Miami, FL 33166
Tel 305-436-1159
Fax 305-433-0974
Email.................gustavo@centauro.com
Web..........................www.centauro.com

Producer, Director, LIANA IN BODY AND
 SOUL, 2002, Centauro Communicaciones,
 Short
Producer, Director, MARIA SOLEDAD, 1994,
 Ecuavisa, Soap Opera
Producer, Director, CAIN, 1984, Focine,
 Feature
Producer, Director, LATIN IMMIGRANT,
 1980, Centauro Films, Feature
Producer, Director, TAXISTA MILLONARIO,
 1976, Centauro Films, Feature

Bill Nieves*

New York, NY 10024
Tel 212-724-2087
Tel 845-876-7032
Cell 917-334-1554
Fax 212-724-2111
Email........muchovideo@mindspring.com

Director, Producer, HISPANICS TODAY, 2002,
    Syndicated, Weekly Newsmagazine
Segment Producer, RIPLEY'S BELIEVE IT OR
    NOT, 1998-2002, Sony/Synd, TV Series
Director, ENTERTAINMENT TONIGHT,
    1987-2002, Paramount/Synd., TV Series
Producer, CBS NEWS (NY), 1982-1987, CBS
    News, Network News
Director, Producer, SIN NEWS, 1980-1982,
    SIN (Univision), Network News
Director, Producer, KDTV, SF, 1975-1980,
    KDTV (Univision), News, Public Affairs,
    Commericials

Danny Nieves

VP and General Manager
Premiere Films Inc.
San Juan, PR 00909
Tel 787-724-0762
Fax 787-723-4562
Email......dnieves@premierefilmsinc.com
Web..............www.premierefilmsinc.com

Nestor Nieves

Executive Vice President, International
Releasing
New Line Cinema
Los Angeles, CA 90048
Tel 310-854-5811
Fax 310-659-2459
Web ....www.newlinecinema.com

Alex Nogales*

President
National Hispanic Media Coalition
Los Angeles, CA 90007
Tel 213-746-6988
Fax 213-746-1305
Email ....nhmc@azteca.net
Web............................www.nhmc.com

Media Advocate

Maximo Norat*

New York, NY 10001
Tel 646-336-0832
Email ....mxnrt@aol.com

Dr. Chon Noriega*

Director and Professor
UCLA Chicano Studies Research Center
Los Angeles, CA 90095
Tel 310-206-0714
Fax 323-660-9302
Email ....Cnoriega@ucla.edu
Web ....www.chicano.ucla.edu

Board Member, ITVS, 2001-2007
Author, SHOT IN AMERICA: TELEVISION,
    THE STATE, AND THE RISE OF CHICANO
    CINEMA, 2000, University of Minesota
    Press
Educator, UCLA Department of Film,
    Television and Digital Media
Media Advocate

Julio Noriega

Film & Video Division Director
Venevision International
Coral Gables, FL 33134
Tel 305-442-3411
Fax 305-448-4762
Web ....www.venevisioninternational.com

Emanuel Nuñez

Agent
Creative Artists Agency (CAA)
Beverly Hills, CA 90212
Tel 310-288-4545
Fax 310-288-4800
Email...........................enunez@caa.com
Web ....www.caa.com

Frank Nuñez
Little Boyz Dreams
Vista, CA 92084
Tel 760-758-7389
Fax 760-758-7389
Email ....nunezfrank@hotmail.com

Director, Producer, 187 SHADOW LANE,
    2003, Spartan/El Matador, Feature
Director, Producer, DIABLO, 2003, Feature
Writer, JAIL CELL, 2003, Short

Nick Nuñez*
New York, NY 10019
Email ....nigunu@aol.com

Lorenzo O'Brien
Copal Productions
Pasadena, CA 91105
Tel 213-709-0527
Email ....lobrien@gte.net

Co-Producer, THE LOST CITY, 2004, Lions
    Gate, Feature
Co-Producer, Writer, AMERICAN FAMILY,
    2003, PBS, TV Series
Producer, NEVER TRUST A SERIAL KILLER,
    2002, Feature
Producer, PILGRIM, 2000, Lions Gate Films
    Home Entertainment, Feature

Jose Luis Obregozo*
Brooklyn, NY 11215
Tel 718-399-3116
Email ....jlorbe@hotmail.com
Web ....www.orbeworld.com

Director, Producer, Writer, MARYANN, 2002,
    Short
Producer, THE CLOSED DOOR, 1997, Short

Chemen Ochoa*
Santa Fe, NM 87508
Tel 505-466-2311
Fax 505-466-2319

Key 2nd Assistant Director, IN FROM THE
    NIGHT, 2004, Hallmark Hall of Fame
    McGee St. Prods., MOW
1st Assistant Director, 2nd Unit NM Shoot,
    THE LONGEST YARD, 2004, Paramount,
    Feature

2nd Assistant Director, AROUND THE BEND,
    2003, Warner Independent, Feature
2nd 2nd Assistant Director, THE MISSING,
    2003, Revolution Studios, Imagine
    Entertainment, Feature
2nd Assistant Director, BLIND HORIZON,
    2002-2003, Nu Image, Feature
2nd 2nd Assistant Director, SUSPECT ZERO,
    2002, Cruise/Wagner Intermedia, Feature
1st Assisant Director, 2nd Unit, SELENA,
    1996, Warner Bros, Feature

Kaaren F. Ochoa
Albiquiu, NM 87510
Tel 505-685-4242
Email ....kaarenochoa@aol.com

Assistant Director, WAR STORIES, 2003,
    20th Century Fox, Television
1st Assistant Director, WHILE OLEANDER,
    2002, Warner Bros., Feature
Production Manager, PROOF OF LIFE, 2000,
    Warner Bros., Feature
1st Assistant Director, SELENA, 1997,
    Warner Bros., Feature
1st Assistant Director, GETTYSBURG, 1993,
    New Line Cinema, Feature

Antonio Ogaz*
Ogaz Entertainment Productions
Duarte, CA 91010 USA/Mexico
Tel 626-354-1961
Cell 626-354-1961
Email............ogazproductions@msn.com

*Agent: Jon Mercedes, Mercedes
Management, 323-314-5647,
jonwrites@yahoo.com*

Floor Director, TRATO HECHO, 2004-2005,
    El TRATO INC/Univision Television Group,
    TV Series
Videographer, HEY PANCHO: THE LIFE AND
    TIMES OF RICHARD GONZALEZ, 2004,
    Spike TV, Documentary
Director, Supervising Producer, INTEGRATED
    WASTE MEDIA OUTREACH
    CAMPAIGN-CITY OF BALDWIN PARK,
    2004, Ogaz Productions,
    Industrial/Educational Videos
Director, Producer, LOS GUEROS GRILL
    SUNDY BRUNCH 2:30 SPOTS, 2004,
    Ogaz Entertainment Productions,
    Commercials

Paul Ohnersorgen*
Los Angeles, CA 90027
Tel 310-435-4201
Email ....ajnaone@netzero.net

Alberto Ojeda*
Tucson, AZ 85730
Email......................Boxster66@aol.com

Francisco Olea
CFO
World Film Magic Distribution Corp.
Hollywood, CA 90038
Tel 323-785-2118
Web ....www.worldfilmmagic.com

Jorge Oliver
Professor, SFSU
Cherubim Productions
San Francisco, CA 94102
Tel 415-255-2454
Email ....joliver_stl@yahoo.com

Editor, LA PASPORTO AL LA TUTA MONDO,
   2002, Montell and Associates, TV
Editor, TIMBRELS AND TORAHS, 2000,
   Montell and Associates, Documentary
   Short
Director, PRIDE IN PUERTO RICO, 1999,
   Frameline Distribution, Documentary Short

Javier Olivera
Pachamama Films, LLC.
Los Angeles, CA 90068
Tel 323-871-1055
Cell 323-447-7185
Email ....pachamamafilms@aol.com

Director, AL FILO DE LA LEY , 2004,
   Univision, TV Series
Director, Writer, EL CAMINO, 2000, Tercer
   Milenio, Condor Media (USA), Feature

Edward James Olmos
Olmos Productions
Burbank, CA 91521
Tel 818-560-8651
Fax 818-560-8655
Email ....olmosonline@earthlink.net

Agent: Steve Tellez, CAA,
310-288-4545

Actor, Producer, SPLINTER, 2005, Feature
Actor, BATTLE STAR GALACTICA, 2004,
   SciFi Channel, TV Series
Actor (voice), THE BATMAN , 2004, Warner
   Bros., Animated TV Series
Actor, AMERICAN FAMILY, 2002 -2004,
   PBS, TV Series
Actor, Director, Producer, JACK AND MARI-
   LYN, 2002, Olmos Productions, Florida
   Studios, Feature
Producer, AMERICANOS: LATINO LIFE IN
   THE UNITED STATES, 2000, Olmos
   Productions, Documentary
Actor, SELENA, 1997, Warner Bros., Feature
Actor, MY FAMILY, 1995, New Line Cinema,
   Feature
Director, Producer, AMERICAN ME, 1992,
   Universal Pictures, Feature
Actor, STAND AND DELIVER, 1988, Warner
   Bros., Feature

Daniela Ontiveros*
Tucson, AZ 85701
Tel 520-792-9171
Email ....danielao@email.arizona.edu

Andrew Orci
Maya Pictures
Los Angeles, CA 90017
Tel 310-281-3770
Fax 310-281-3777
Web ....www.maya-pictures.com

Delia Orjuela*
Senior Director of Latin Music
BMI
Los Angeles, CA 90069
Tel 310-289-6345
Email.......................dorjuela@bmi.com
Web ....www.bmi.com

filmmakers

Sierra Ornelas
Tucson, AZ 85712
Tel 520-327-3852
Email ....jetagarlo@aol.com

Production Assistant, HOW THE GARCIA
GIRLS SPENT THEIR SUMMER, 2005,
Loosely Based Pictures, LLC., Feature

Paulette Orona*
Pacific Palisades, CA 90270
Email ....paulettemaria@hotmail.com

Roberta Orona-Cordova*
Professor
CSUN Alzada Productions
Winnetka, CA 91306
Tel 818-677-6818
Email...............roberta.orona@csun.edu

José Orraca-Brandenberger*
Creative Consultant
San Juan, PR 00901-1114
Tel 787-724-0213
Email ....pepeorraca@aol.com

Director, SIEMPRE TE AMARE, 2003,
Univision Puerto Rico, TV Movie
Director, Writer, Producer, PUNTO 45, 2001,
Premier Films, Feature
Director, Writer, Producer, CALLANDO
AMORES, 1997, Ateneo Puertorriqueño,
TV Movie
Director, Producer, INSOLITO, 1989-1990,
WAPA-TV, TV Series

Lourdes Ortega*
Publicist
Ortega Public Relations
Redondo Beach, CA 90277
Tel 310-316-3313
Cell 310-592-8530
Email ....lourdes@ortegapr.com
Web ....www.ortegapr.com

Publicist, FARMINGVILLE, 2004, PBS/
Camino Bluff Productions, Documentary
Publicist, SPLINTER, 2004, Feature
Publicist, THE WHITE HORSE IS DEAD,
2004, Blue Cactus Pictures, Feature
Publicist, TITO PUENTE JR., 2004, Muscian

Publicist, VISIONES: LATINO ART & CUL-
TURE, 2004, PBS, Documentary
Publicist, SCREEN ACTORS GUILD FOUN-
DATION, 2003-2005, Non Profit media
outreach
Publicist, LATINO PUBLIC BROADCASTING,
2003-2004, PBS/APT, 26+ hours of pro-
gramming
Publicist, NALIP, 2002-2005, Conference
IV-VI media outreach

David Ortiz*
Creative Executive
Warner Bros.
Burbank, CA 91522
Tel 818-954-6223
Email ....David.Ortiz@warnerbros.com

Ivan Ortiz*
Cine del Caribe
San Juan, PR 00915
Tel 787-769-8016
Email ....ivandariel@mindspring.com

Luis Ortiz
Program Manager
Latino Public Broadcasting
Los Angeles, CA 90028
Tel 323-466-7110
Fax 323-466-7521
Email.......................luis.ortiz@lpbp.org
Web ....www.lpbp.org

Michael Ortiz*
Tucson, AZ 85746
Tel 520-490-6101

Yazmin Ortiz*
Blind Ambition Films
Venice, CA 90294
Tel 323-460-2846
Email ....BAF@ureach.com
Web www.geocities.com/yazzie2000/
blindambitionfilms.html

Manager: Richard Rodriguez,
323-460-2846

Director, EL BAILE, 2003, Short

Gissele Ospina
Director of Hispanic Talent Division
The Green Agency, Inc.
Miami Beach, CA 33139
Tel 305-532-9225
Fax 305-532-9334
Email..............gissele@greenagency.com

Gigi Otero*
Gigi Otero Public Relations
Studio City, CA 91604
Tel 818-752-2151
Fax 818-752-2171
Email ....go@gopr.biz

Nelly Otsu*
San Diego, CA 92122
Email ....mysticgini@hotmail.com

Horacio Oyhanarte*
Dospelnacs
Los Angeles, CA 90049
Tel 310-476-3849
Fax 310-476-3849
Email ....horacio@dospelnacs.com

Antone Pagán*
The New Family Theatre
New York, NY 10108
Tel 212-459-1910
Cell 917-337-0164
Fax 212-459-1910
Email ....familywarrior@aol.com

Producer, Actor, SHORT EYES, 2005, Silent
    Warrior, New Family Thr, Broadway Revival
Co-Producer, 18B JUSTICE, 2004, Silent
    Warrior, Documentary
Actor, ALL MY CHILDREN, 2004, ABC
    Daytime, Soap Opera
Producer, THE DIE-IT, 2004, Silent Warrior,
    Zen Chango Arte, Short
Producer, Actor, THE STARSEED INCIDENT,
    2004, Silent Warrior, Experiemental,
    Animation

Edwin Pagan*
Pagan Images, Inc.
New York, NY 10009
Tel 917-653-2273
Email ....paganimage@aol.com
Web ....www.pagan-images.com

Line Producer, BEAUTY, 2004, Purple Velvet
    Productions, Short
Writer, BIG BROTHER HERESY, 2004, Pagan
    Images, Short
Director of Photography, FOR THE RECORD:
    GUAM AND WORLD WAR II, 2004,
    Polymorphous Pictures, Inc.
Line Producer, RENDEZVOUS, 2004, Nicolini
    Films, Short
Director of Photography, TWO GUNS AND A
    BAG OF SANDWICHES, 2004, Purple
    Velvet Productions, Short
Director of Photography, WHAT'S FOR DIN-
    NER, 2004, Exbo Productions, Short
Media Advocate

Carolina Paiz*
Hollywood, CA 90028
Tel 310-927-5291
Email ....carolina@yahoo.com

Lawrence Palomo*
San Marcos, CA 92069
Tel 805-587-4711
Email ....lpalomo@prodigy.net

Mercedes Palomo
Pigeon Productions
Miami, FL 33145
Tel 305-856-2929
Fax 305-858-0357
Email ....mercedes@pigeonprod.com
Web ....www.pigeonprod.com

Production Facilities & Services

Ari Palos
Dos Vatos Productions
Tucson, AZ 85719
Tel 520-325-0307

Director, IMPRESSARIO, 2001, PBS,
    Documentary

Director, KENTUCKY THEATER, 2000, Dos
  Vatos Productions, Documentary
Director of Photography, OKIE NOODLING,
  2000, Little League Pictures, Documentary

Robert Parada
Angelinos Productions
Pacoima, CA 91331
Tel 818-796-1779
Cell 818-216-8323
Fax 818-686-6009
Email ....angelinosprods@cs.com

Producer, THE BLUES, 2002, Ground Zero
  Entertainment, Feature
Producer, HUSTLAS, 2000, Maverick
  Entertainment, Feature
Producer, HUSTLAS, 1999, Maverick
  Entertainment, Feature

Rey Parla*
First Flight Pictures
Miami, FL 33172
Tel 718-522-5835
Email ....nalipmiami@hotmail.com

Arturo Parra*
PKB Productions
Houston, TX 77015
Tel 713-453-8419
Tel 832-483-4301
Fax 713-330-3394
Email ....aparra@lidmagazine.com

*Manager: Gerardo Parra, 832-496-2986,
gparrajr@lidmagazine.com*

Assistant Director, "LOCOS", 2004, Feature
Assistant Director, LOTERIA, 2004, Short
Camera Operator, CAPS-MF-ONE, 2003,
  Commercial
Camera Operator, DJ DIRTY HANDS, 2003,
  Commercial

George Parra
Malibu, CA 90265
Email.......................h2oparra@aol.com

Co-Producer, SIDEWAYS, 2004, Fox
  Searchlight Pictures, Feature
1st Assistant Director, LEGALLY BLOND 2:
  RED, WHITE & BLONDE, 2003, MGM,
  Feature

1st Assistant Director, MALIBU'S MOST
  WANTED, 2003, Warner Bros., Feature
1st Assistant Director, ABOUT SCHMIDT,
  2002, New Line Cinema, Feature
1st Assistant Director, XXX, 2002, Columbia
  TriStar, Feature

Eric Partida*
Whittier, CA 90601
Tel 626-893-1726
Email ....ericpartida@hotmail.com

Jose Luis Partida
Grupo Vida
Dallas, TX 75219
Email..............Joseluis@grupovida-tv.org
Web ....www.grupovida-tv.org

Producer, AIDS NATIONAL, PSA
Producer, DENNY'S NATIONAL COMMER-
  CIAL SPOTS, Commercial
Producer, DENNY'S NATIONAL PROMOTION,
  Commercial
Executive Producer, LAS VEGAS HEALTH
  (CERO HUMO CAMPAIGN)
Director, MI HIJO MI HIJA AMOR,
  Documentary

Lionel Pasamonte
Executive Producer
LATV
Venice, CA 90291
Tel 310-745-1575
Tel 310-943-5288
Email ....maxpasa1@aol.com

Producer, LATV LIVE, 2003, LATV, TV Series
Producer, ALMA AWARDS SHOW, 2002,
  ABC, TV Special

Antonio Pelaez*
MediaQuest
Zapopan, Jalisco 45019 Mexico
Tel 33-38-32-04-97
Cell 0-44-33-31-91-90-44
Fax 52-33-38-32-04-97
Email ....apelaez@cybercable.net.mx

Producer, Writer, Director, CUANDO LAS
  COSAS SUCEDEN, 2005, Feature
Producer, Writer, Director, XPLORANDO,
  2002, Disney, TV Series

Producer, Writer, Director, EL MILAGRO DE
LAS ROSAS, 2001, TV Special
Producer, Writer, Director, GUADALUPE,
2000, Role Entertainment, Documentary

Laura Pelaez*

MediaQuest
Zapopan, Jalisco 45019 Mexico
Tel 52-33-3832-0497
Cell.........................52-33-3832-9045
Fax 52-33-3832-0497
Email ....xplorando@yahoo.com

Producer, CUANDO LAS COSAS SUCEDEN,
2005, Feature
Producer, LA ROSA AZUL, 2004, Feature
Producer, TUMBAS, 2004, Feature
Producer, VITAMINCEA, 2004, TV Mexico,
Advertising
Producer, XPLORANDO, 2001-2002, TV
Series
Producer, EL MILAGRO DE LAS ROSAS,
1999, Short

Carlos Pelayo*

SDSU
San Diego, CA 92114
Tel 619-263-4171
Email ....clos98@yahoo.com
Web ....www.lokoartz.com

Jaime Pelayo*

Florycanto Productions
West Hollywood, CA 90048
Tel 323-651-2697
Fax 323-375-0251
Email ....jaimepelayo@hotmail.com

Dora Peña*

San Antonio, TX 78249
Tel 210-694-4677
Cell 210-723-6992
Email ....doralpena@hotmail.com

Director, Producer, CRAZY LIFE, 2004, Short
Producer, TEXAS GIRLS, 2003, Music Video
Director, Producer, Writer, THE DIRECTOR,
2002, LPB, Interstitial
Director, Producer, CAPSULED IN TIME,
2001, Documentary

Elizabeth Peña

Fletcher and Phil Inc.
Los Angeles, CA 90025
Fax 310-455-3439

Agent: Susie Tobin, Paradigm,
310-277-4400

Actor, HOW THE GARCIA GIRLS SPENT
THEIR SUMMER, 2004, Loosely Based
Pictures LLC., Feature
Actor, THE DEAD HOLLYWOOD MOMS SOCI-
ETY, 2004, Hallmark, TV Movie
Actor, TORTILLA SOUP, 2001, Samuel
Goldwyn Films, Feature
Actor, Director, RESURRECTION BLVD.,
2000, Showtime, TV Series
Director, THE BROTHERS GARCIA, 2000,
Nickelodeon, TV Series

Sandra Peña*

Pocha Productions
Santa Ana, CA 92701
Tel 714-998-6018
Tel 714-417-0073
Email........................pochioux@aol.com

Steven Peña*

Montebello Entertainment
Los Angeles, CA 90025
Tel 213 596-5798
Email ....steve@
montebelloentertainment.com

Jeff Penichet*

President
Bilingual Educational Services, Inc.
Los Angeles, CA 90007
Tel 213-749-6213
Fax 213-749-1820
Email ....filmdoer@aol.com

Luis Peraza

Senior VP, Acquisitions
HBO Latin America
Coral Gables, FL 33134
Tel 305-648-8100

Juaquin Perea*
Lakewood, CA 90713
Tel 562-787-5629
Email.....................mrjp49@yahoo.com

Louis E. Perego Moreno*
Skyline Features
New York, NY 10014
Tel 212-956-7771
Cell 917-535-4333
Fax 212-956-3115
Email ....SkyFeature@aol.com

*Attorney: Fernando Ramirez, Eaq.,
212-254-4010, framirezlaw@msn.com*

Casting Director, Field Producer, Director of
    Photography, MOMS GO ON STRIKE,
    2005, Lion Television/A & E, Documentary
Casting Director, 15: QUINCEAÑERA, 2004,
    HBO, Documentary
Casting Director, BRIDESMAIDS, 2004, Lion
    Television/TLC, Documentary
Producer, 30X30: FATHERLESSNESS, 2001,
    HBO, Documentary
Producer, 30X30: LATINAS PROVING THEM-
    SELVES, 2000, HBO Family, Documentary
Producer, 30X30: WHAT'S COOKING IN NEW
    YORK?, 2000, HBO Family, Documentary

Sylvia Perel*
Festival Director
Latino Film Festival of San Francisco
Bay Area
San Rafael, CA 94901
Tel 415-454-4039
Email ....info@latinofilmfestival.org
Web...............www.latinofilmfestival.org

Rene Pereyra
Los Angeles, CA 90064
Tel 310-397-1656
Email....................palmiro200@aol.com

Director, PEDRO PARAMO, 2003, Mexican
    Embassy, Stage Play
Director, REGRESO A CASA, 2000, Short
Director, KENNEDY'S CHILDREN, 1998,
    Actors Studio NY, Stage Play

Annie Perez
Miami-Dade Mayor's Office for Film &
Entertaimment
Miami, FL 33128
Tel 305-375-3288
Web...........................www.filmiami.org

Anthony Perez
Ground Zero Entertainment
Los Angeles, CA 90045
Tel 310-665-0074
Web.................www.groundzeroent.com

Chris Perez*
Captiva Group, Inc.
San Marcos, TX 78666
Tel 512-805-9072
Email ....cperez@captivagroup.com

Daniel Perez*
Mental Pictures, Inc.
Brookeville, MD 20833
Tel 301-502-9698
Fax 310-570-7608

Dianna Pérez*
InnerSpark
S. Pasadena, CA 91030
Tel 805-732-9698
Tel 310-979-0010
Email ....carcahadas@yahoo.com

Emily Perez
Los Angeles, CA 90064
Tel 310-804-7479
Fax 310-446-6258
Email ....em_perez@comcast.net

Producer, COMODYNES, 2003, Rebel Zone
    Films, Commercial
Producer, POWERADE: BOY BATTLE, 2003,
    Xeno Films, Commercial
Producer, THE AFFIDAVIT, 2003, Blue Fox
    Media, Short
Producer, COPPER WOMAN, 1994, IFP
    Project Involve, Feature

Hugo Perez*

Brooklyn, NY 11215
Tel 917-279-4846
Email ....hugo@aya.yale.edu

Jack Perez

Manager: Principal Entertainment,
310-446-1466

Director, WILD THINGS 2, 2004, Columbia
    Pictures, Home VIdeo
Director, Writer, MONSTER ISLAND, 2003,
    MTV Films, Feature
Second Unit Director, LIKE MIKE, 2002,
    20th Century Fox, Feature
Director, THE BIG EMPTY, 2001, Hollywood
    Home Video, Feature

Jessica Perez*

Moxie Firecracker Films
Brooklyn, NY 11217
Tel 718-230-5111
Fax 718-230-5999
Email ....jperez@moxiefirecracker.com

Leo Perez*

Chief Operating Officer
Si TV
Los Angeles, CA 90065
Tel 323-256-8900
Email ....lperez@sitv.com
Web ....www.sitv.com

Marilyn Perez*

New York, NY 10011
Tel 212-353-1111
Cell 917-538-2276
Fax 212-995-0426
Email ....mperez@marilynperez.com

Producer, PEACE IN THE 21ST CENTURY-AN
    IMPERATIVE FOR SURVIVAL, 2003, Third
    World Newsreel, Educational/Industrial
Writer, SMOKESCREEN (TRAILER), 2002,
    Studio 1101, Promotional Trailer
Producer, THE RETURN OF THE DIVAS,
    2002, The Gabriel Project, Documentary
    Short
Director, Producer, Writer, WOES, FOES &
    HEROES, 2001, LAVA, The Gabriel
    Project, Documentary

Director, Writer, JULIA VALDEZ-ONE CUBAN
    ARTIST, 1999, The Gabriel Project,
    Documentary
Director, VIRTUAL REALITIES/REALIDADES
    VIRTUALES, 1997, The Gabriel Project,
    Documentary

Patrick Perez*

Migrant Filmworks
Los Angeles, CA 90029
Tel 323-660-3437
Cell 213-926-6571
Email ....pperez2000@yahoo.com
Web ....www.migrantfilmworks.com

Producer, CHICANO ROCK, 2004, Wilkman
    Productions, PBS, Documentary
Director, Editor, FOGATA, 2003, Mayaque
    Music, Music Video
Director, BENNY THE MUTE, 2002, Indie,
    Short
Director, SHORT CHANGED, 1999, (untitled)
    inc., Short

Paul Perez

Advent Entertainment
Pasadena, CA 91107
Tel 626-575-7176

Script Supervisor, PEOPLES, 2004, Strictly
    Kings Productions, Feature

Robert Perez*

Migrant Filmworks
Los Angeles, CA 90029
Tel 310-748-4839
Email ....robperez@yahoo.com

Rosana Perez*

Los Angeles, CA 90018
Email.........rosana_perez01@excite.com

Sandra Perez*

Yonkers, NY 10701
Tel 347-224-7742
Email ....sandra@luztirada.com

Media Advocate

Jesse Perez Antigua*
Bronx, NY 10462
Tel 347-293-6892
Email ....yessenia@optonline.net

Maria Perez Brown*
Dorado Entertainment, Inc.
New York, NY 10019
Tel 212-654-6716
Email ....maria.perez@nick.com

Agent: Raul Matteu, WMA,
305-938-2020

Attorney: Miller & Pliakas, LLP,
310-860-1515

Executive Producer, ALL TOGETHER NOW,
2004, Nickelodeon, Pilot
Executive Producer, Writer, AM I CRAZY?,
2004, Touchtone, Pilot Script
Executive Producer, ZWOOSH, 2004,
Nickelodeon, Pilot
Executive Producer, Writer, ORTIZ & ORTIZ,
2003, Touchtone/CBS, Pilot Script
Executive Producer, Writer, DERRICK &
ISABEL, 2002, Touchtone, Pilot Script
Director, Executive Producer, TAINA, 2000,
Nickelodeon, TV Series
Executive Producer, GULLAH, GULLAH
ISLAND, 1994, Nickelodeon, TV Series

Dan Perez de la Garza*
Astoria, NY 11102
Tel 917-855-1150
Email ..danperezdelagarza@earthlink.net

Xavier Perez Grobet
Email.....................grobetx@laamc.com

Director of Photograpy, MONSTER HOUSE,
2006, Sony Pictures Entertainment,
Feature
Director of Photograpy, NINE LIVES, 2005,
Mockingbird Pictures, Feature
Director of Photography, CHASING PAPI,
2003, 20th Century Fox, Feature
Director of Photography, LUCIA, LUCIA, 2003,
Fox Searchlight, Feature
Director of Photograpy, TORTILLA SOUP,
2001, Samuel Goldwyn Films, Feature

Ivonne Pérez Montijo*
Frog Girl Productions
Valley Village, CA 91607
Tel 818-509-8856
Fax 818-509-0248
Email ....IvonnePMontijo@aol.com
Web ....www.froggirlproductions.com

Agent: Samantha Botana, The Samantha
Group, 626-683-2444

Producer, Writer, JUAN Y ROSA, LA VIRGEN
& FLAN, 2001, Stage Play
Producer, SKIP TRACER, 1997, Maverick
Arts, Short
Producer, Writer, DESEO, Coqui Productions,
Short

Lisandro Perez-Rey*
Gato Films
Miami, FL 33137
Tel 305-724-6373
Email ....gatoflix@yahoo.com

Director, Producer, LA FABRI-K (THE CUBAN
HIP HOP FACTORY), 2004, Gato Films,
Documentary
Director, Producer, MAS ALLA DEL MAR
(BEYOND THE SEA), 2003, Gato Films,
Documentary

Luis Perez-Tolon*
Festival Seminar Coordinator
Miami International Festival
Miami, FL 33132
Tel 305-237-7908
Fax 305-237-7344
Email ....LPerezTo@mdc.edu
Web ....www.miamifilmfestival.com

Quincy Perkins*
Los Angeles, CA 90027
Tel 213-841-9796
Email ....quincyperkins@hotmail.com

Ted Perkins-Lopez*
A La Conquista de Hollywood
Los Angeles, CA 90064
Tel 310-508-3902
Cell 310-508-3902
Email ....tedplopez@comcast.net
Web ......www.conquistadehollywood.com
Agent: Broder/Chervin
Manager: Underground Management
Attorney: Rob Syzmanski

Cesar Peschiera*
Film Production Coordinator
Packair Airfreight, Inc.
Los Angeles, CA 90045
Tel 310-337-0529
Tel 310-337-9993
Cell 310-261-7629
Fax 310-337-0669
Email ....filmlocations@packair.com
Web...........................www.packair.com

International Forwarding/Customs Broker
Production Facilities & Services

Giugliana Pessagno*
Miramar, FL 33029
Tel 786-206-0026

Joseph D. Peters*
Renaissance Productions, Ltd
San Dimas, CA 91773
Tel 909-394-1931
Fax 909-394-0430
Email ....jpeters@josephdpeters.com
Web ....www.josephdpeters.com

Director, Producer, Writer, WHEN AUTUMN
   COMES, 2003, Short
Director, Producer, Writer, EMOTIONS, 1999,
   Short
Director, Producer, Writer, RACHEL, 1995,
   Short
Director, Producer, Writer, ESKIMO ICE
   CREAM SHOES, 1990, Short

Mario Picayo*
New York, NY 10024
Email ....gycultura@aol.com

Miguel Picker
Artmedia
New York, NY 10013
Tel 212-343-2281
Cell 617-733-8202
Email ....miguel@miguelpicker.com
Web....................www.miguelpicker.com

Director, Editor, Producer, BEYOND GOOD
   AND EVIL, 2003, Media Education
   Foundation, Documentary
Director, Editor, Producer, MICKEY MOUSE
   MONOPOLY, 2001, Media Education
   Foundation, Documentary
Director, Editor, Producer, FRANCISCO
   MENDEZ, 1998, Documentary

Rachel Pineda*
Studio Technician
ESPN
Plainville, CT 06062
Tel 860-766-2000
Cell 210-885-7606
Email ....reedsucker@yahoo.com

Writer, X GAMES, 2004, EXPN.com, Website
Production Assistant, THIS IS SPORTS CEN-
   TER, 2003, ESPN, TV Series

Carlos F. Pinero
Burbank, CA 91501
Email...............tyranny2k@earthlink.net

1st Assistant Director, SWEET FRIGGIN'
   DAISIES, 2002, Feature
2nd Assistant Director, BARB WIRE, 1996,
   Gramercy Pictures, Feature
2nd Assistant Director, CLEAR AND PRE-
   SENT DANGER, 1994, Paramount,
   Feature
1st Assistant Director, FRIENDS, 1994, NBC,
   TV Series

Jorge Pinos
Agent
William Morris Agency (WMA)
Beverly Hills, CA 90212
Tel 310-859-4000
Fax 310-248-5954
Web...............................www.wma.com

filmmakers

Haley Pinyerd*
Tucson, AZ 85705
Email............pinyerd@email.arizona.edu

Felix Pire*
Hollywood, CA 90068
Tel 323-882-6523
Cell 323-823-1971
Email.............................fpire@aol.com
Web www.artsalumni.net/awardee89/
bios/PireFelix.html

Writer, THE ORIGINS OF HAPPINESS IN
LATIN, 2003, Arizona Theatre Company &
Off-Off B'way, Stage Play
Director, NEW MILLENNIUM PROJECT,
2001, Perfomed at L.A.'s Levantine
Center, Stage Play
Actor, DEAR GOD, 1996, Paramount
Pictures, Feature
Actor, IT'S MY PARTY, 1996, MGM/UA,
Feature
Actor, 12 MONKEYS, 1995, Universal
Studios, Feature

Tony Plana
Los Angeles, CA 90067
*Agent: Debbie Kline, Paradigm,
310-277-4400*

Actor, FIDEL, 2002, Showtime, TV Movie
Director, GREETINGS FROM TUCSON, 2002,
Warner Bros., TV Series
Actor, HALF PAST DEAD, 2002, Sony
Pictures Entertainment, Feature
Actor, VEGAS, CITY OF DREAMS, 2001,
DMG Entertainment, Feature
Director, RESURRECTION BLVD., 2000,
Showtime, TV Series
Director, THE BROTHERS GARCIA, 2000,
Nickelodeon, TV Series
Director, THE PRINCESS AND THE BARRIO
BOY, 2000, Showtime, TV Movie
Director, A MILLION TO JUAN, 1994, Sam
Goldwyn Entertainment, Feature

Begonya Plaza*
Izar Productions
New York, NY 10011
Tel 212-463-0197
Cell 310-279-2981
Email ......begonya@izarproductions.com
Web ....www.izarproductions.com

*Agent: Jaime Ferrar Agency,
818-506-8311*

*Attorney: Don Erik Franzen,
310-785-1710*

Actor, MEDIUM, 2005, NBC, TV Series
Director, Editor, Producer, Writer, SOUVENIR
VIEWS, 2003, Big Film Shorts,
Documentary
Director, Editor, Writer, GERNIKA LIVES,
1999, Short

Paulina Plazas*
Milford, CT 06460
Tel 203-910-3105
Email ....paulaplazas@hotmail.com
Web ....www.plazafilms.com

Erin Ploss-Campoamor*
Venice, CA 90291
Tel 310-305-4614
Email ....www.americanita.com
Web ....erin@americanita.com

Director, Writer, LA AMERICANITA, 2001,
Short

Ximena Ponce
Bay Harbor, FL 33154
Tel 305-866-5247
Cell 786-252-6607
Email....................xime999@yahoo.com

Director, Producer, Writer, BESAME MUCHO,
2002, Short

Anna M. Poore-Cordova*
Vice President
Film Look Inc.
Burbank, CA 91504
Tel 818-845-9200
Cell 818-521-5891
Fax 818-845-9238
Email ....anna@filmlook.com
Web ....www.filmlook.com

David Porras*
Brooklyn, NY 11211
Email ....ddporras@mac.com

Paulina Porter*
Montebello, CA 90640
Cell 619-279-3715
Email ....pporter@usc.edu

Lourdes Portillo*
Xochitl Film and Video
San Francisco, CA 94110
Tel 415-642-1614
Email.......................lportillo@mac.com
Web.................www.lourdesportillo.com

*Attorney: Michael Donaldson,
310-273-8394*

Director, MISSING YOUNG WOMEN, 2001,
  Balcony Releasing, Documentary
Director, SENORITA EXTRAVIADA, 2001,
  Balcony Releasing, Documentary
Director, CORPUS, 1999, Xochitl Film and
  Video, Documentary
Director, EL DIABLO NUNCA DUERME,
  1996, ITVS, Documentary
Director, SOMETIMES MY FEET GO NUMB,
  1996, Frame Line, Documentary
Director, THE DAYS OF THE DEAD, 1989,
  Documentary
Director, LAS MADRES DE LA PLAZA DE
  MAYO, 1985, First Run Features,
  Documentary

David Portorreal*
West Hollywood, CA 90046
Cell 310-560-0133
Email ....dportorreal@yahoo.com

Co-Producer, MEANS TO AN END, 2003,
  Short
Producer, MAGIC IN MOTION, 2002, Short
Editor, AN ESSENTIAL ELEMENT, 2000,
  Short
Writer, Director, CHERRY PICKIN', 2000,
  Short
Producer, GRIPOLOGY, 2000, Short
Editor, ON POINTS, 2000, Short

Mitchell Posada*
Board Member
IIFF
San Francisco, CA 94117
Tel 510-610-9295
Email ....mitchposada@filmfinancing.org
Web ....www.filmfinancing.org

Carolina Posse*
Producer, Sales Agent
Wright Brothers Photoplay
Chicago, IL 60615
Tel 773-358-5020
Email............posse_carolina@yahoo.com
Web ....www.wbphotoplay.com

Sales Agent, HOT CHILI, 2004, Wright
  Brothers Photoplay, Short
Voice Over, PEDRO ALONZO LOPEZ, 2004,
  Twoer Productions, A & E, Biography,
  Documentary TV
Associate Producer, THE QUIET, 2004,
  Wright Brothers Photoplay, Feature
Sales Agent, DULCES SUEÑOS, 2003,
  Esteban Gaggino, Short Animation
Sales Agent, GLORY DAYS, 2003, Wright
  Brothers Photoplay, Documentary
Voice Over, THE LIFE OF PABLO ESCOBAR,
  2003, Tower Productions, A & E,
  Documentary TV
Associate Producer, CHANGING MAN, 2002,
  Wright Brothers Photoplay, Feature

filmmakers

Susie Potter*
Potter Ruiz Productions Inc.
Arlington, MA 02474
Tel 781-646-3454
Email....................susie@potterruiz.com
Web ....PotterRuiz.com

Veronica Potter*
Mirandez Productions
San Antonio, TX 78216
Tel 210-683-8780
Email ....veronica@awave.com

Santiago Pozo
CEO
Arenas Entertainment
Beverly Hills, CA 90210
Tel 310-385-4401
Fax 310-385-4402
Email ....ceooffice@arenasgroup.com
Web ....www.arenasgroup.com

Executive Producer, CULTURE CLASH IN
   AMERICCA, 2004, Arenas Entertainment,
   Feature
Producer, IMAGINING ARGENTINA, 2003,
   Arenas Entertainment, Feature
Producer, EMPIRE, 2002, Arenas
   Entertainment, Feature
Executive Producer, THE LAST HARVEST,
   1992, Arenas Entertainment, Feature
Director, LOS PRIMEROS METRO, 1985,
   Feature
Manager

Francesca Prada*
Diana Films
San Francisco, CA 94110
Tel 415-826-2444
Tel 415-378-8658
Email ....Dianafilms@aol.com

Anayansi Prado*
Impacto Films
Los Angeles, CA 90026
Tel 323-251-7787
Email ....impactofilms@hotmail.com
Web ....www.ImpactoFilms.com

2nd Unit Director of Photography, BEYOND
   THE DREAM, 2004-2005, PBS,
   Documentary
Director, Producer, Writer, MAID IN AMERI-
   CA, 2004, Impacto Films, Documentary
Director, Co-Producer, IMMIGRANT WORK-
   ERS FREEDOM RIDE, 2003, AFL-CIO,
   Documentary
Consulting Producer, LETTERS FROM THE
   OTHER SIDE, 2003, Documentary

Henry K. Priest*
Festival Director
American Latino Film Festival
West Hollywood, CA 90046
Tel 213-739-3385
Email.............coachpriest@hotmail.com

Technical Director, LATINOLOGUES, 2004,
   Rick Najera Productions, Play
Producer, LOS FELIZ POETRY SLAM, 2004,
   Live Event
Casting Director, LOWRIDER PROJECT,
   2004, Maverick Ent./Lionsgate Ent.,
   Feature
Producer, NOSOTROS RADIO AD, 2004,
   www.CRNlive.com, Radio Commercial
Producer, SUNDAY EVENING HAIRCUT,
   2004, Boricua Films, Short
Casting Director, NIKE COMMERCIAL, 2003,
   TV Commercial
Executive Producer, UNDERDOG, 2003, Si
   TV, Short
Producer, URBAN GRAFFITI, 2003, Boricua
   Films, Pilot

Freddie Prinze Jr.
Beverly Hills, CA 90211
*Agent: Eddie Yablans, ICM,
310-550-4000*

Actor, SCOOBY DOO I, II, 2002, Warner
   Bros., Feature
Actor, HEAD OVER HEELS, 2001,
   MCA/Universal, Feature
Actor, SUMMER CATCH, 2001, Warner Bros.,
   Feature
Actor, BOYS AND GIRLS, 2000, Dimension
   Films, Feature
Actor, SHE'S ALL THAT, 1999, Miramax
   Films, Feature

Pablo Proenza*
Mare's Hoof Productions, LLC
Venice, CA 90291
Tel 310-305-4614
Fax 310-943-3359
Email..............pablo@pabloproenza.com
Web ....www.pabloproenz.com

Jon Proudstar*
Proudstar Productions
Tucson, AZ 85714
Tel 520-808-2388
Email............jonproudstar@hotmail.com

Felipe Pruneda Sentíes*
Middlebury, VT 05753
Tel 802-443-4286
Email ....fpruneda@middlebury.edu

Anthony Puente*
Poca Madre Films
Long Beach, CA 90807
Tel 562-618-6078
Email.......................apuente@ucla.edu

Nick Puga
Agent
Arts & Letters Management
Los Angeles, CA 90046
Tel 323-883-1070
Fax 323-883-1067

Raul Puig
Post Urban Productions
Miami, FL 33156
Tel 305-670-9859
Email...............raulapuig@bellsouth.net

Producer, CURDLED, 1996, Miramax Films,
    Feature

Ernesto Quintero*
Higher Ground Entertainment
Los Angeles, CA 90032
Tel 323-286-2011
Fax 323-225-1353
Email...................EQFBHE@yahoo.com
Web.......................FourBrownHats.com

Producer, HEY PANCHO; WARRIOR OF THE
    COURT, 2004, Spike TV, Higher Ground
    Entertainment, Documentary
Producer, VETERANOS: A LEGACY OF
    VALOR, 2004, EQ Productions, Short
Producer, THE LAST ANGRY BROWN HAT,
    1995-2002, Four Brown Hats
    Entertainment, Stage Play

Gabriela Quiros*
Azul Films
Albany, CA 94706
Tel 510-527-3103
Fax 510-527-3103
Email.........azulproductions@yahoo.com

Associate Producer, Assistant Editor, BLOOD-
    LINES, 2003, Backbone Media,
    Documentary
Assistant Editor, SENORITA EXTRAVIADA,
    2001, Xochitl Films, Documentary
Associate Producer, Assistant Editor,
    SECRETS OF THE SAT, 1999, Frontline,
    PBS, Documentary
Producer, Director, Editor, TANGO 73: A BUS
    RIDER'S DIARY, 1998, New Day Films,
    Documentary

Cate Rachford*
Vision Quest Entertainment
Burbank, CA 91505
Tel 818-842-2757
Email.......................catieford@aol.com
Web ....www.visionquestent.com

Susan Racho
Glendale, CA 91206
Tel 818-551-9619
Fax 818-551-9619
Email ....sracho@msn.com

Director, Producer, THE BRONZE SCREEN:
    100 YEARS OF THE LATINO IMAGE IN
    AMERICAN CINEMA, 2002, Documentary

Mike Racioppo*

Nouveau Media Corp.
Staten Island, NY 10310
Tel 973-258-1781
Email ....mraci@webcastingmedia.com
Web ....www.modelnouveau.com

Producer, BACKHOE, 2004, Nouveau Media
    Corp, Short
Producer, TUNNEL SOUND, 2003, Nouvea
    Media Corp, Documentary
Producer, CITY UNDER FIRE, 2001, City of
    New York, Documentary
Producer, FDTV, 2001, City of New York,
    Documentary
Producer, HIGH RISE, 2000, Crosswalks
    Productions, PSA
Producer, KIDS 4 SAFETY, 2000, Board of
    Education, PSA
Graphic Designer

Faith Radle*

Los Angeles, CA 90026
Tel 213-975-9277
Email ....FaithRadle@aol.com

Associate Producer, Editor, CINCO DE MAYO,
    2004, History Channel, Documentary
Editor, VISIONES: LATINO ART & CULTURE,
    2004, PBS, Documentary
Producer, SPEEDER KILLS, 2003, Badass
    Pictures, Feature
Associate Producer, VOICES FROM TEXAS,
    2003, Cinema Guild, Documentary
Postproduction Supervisor, COME AND TAKE
    IT DAY, 2001, ITVS, Feature

Sunny Raina*

Pasadena, CA 91106
Tel 323-788-5800
Email ....sunnyquepaso@aol.com
Web ....www.sunnyraina.com

Daniela Ramirez*

Malinche Productions
Oxnard, CA 93030
Tel 805-486-6138
Email ..malincheproductions@hotmail.com
Web ....www.malincheproductions.com

Director, Editor, Producer, IWIGIRA: THE
    FINAL BREATH, 2001, Documentary
Director, Editor, Producer, RUNNERS OF THE
    WIND, 2001, Documentary

Fernando Ramirez*

Attorney
New York, NY 10003
Tel 212-254-4010
Fax 212-254-0104
Email ....framirezlaw@msn.com

Ingrid Ramirez*

San Juan, 00920 Puerto Rico
Email ....ingridn_rd@yahoo.com

Irma Ramirez*

Pasadena, CA 91104
Tel 626-390-0528
Email ....irmaramz@charter.net

Joe Ramirez*

Nacovision
Tucson, AZ 85745
Tel 520-979-0517
Cell 520-979-0517
Email ....UberjoeR@aol.com

Director, Producer, Writer, SUEÑOS LATINOS,
    2004, Telemundo, TV Series
Director, Talent, Videographer, EN VIVO,
    1995-1997, Telemundo, TV Special

Mario Ramirez*
Jakmar Entertainment
Toluca Lake, CA 91610
Tel 818-761-5725
Fax 818-761-5725
Email ....mario@marioramirez.com
Web ....www.marioramirez.com

Agent: Innovative Artists,
310-656-0400

Director of Photography, CROSSING FRON-
  TIERS, 2005, Documentary
Director, Producer, Writer, LA VERDADERA
  HISTORIA DE SERGIO, 2005, Vulcano
  Productions, Documentary
Actor, Director, Writer, ATRAPAMOS A BIN
  LADEN, 2004, Venevision, Documentary

Rick Ramirez*
Vice President, Emerging Markets
Fox Entertainment Group, Inc.
Los Angeles, CA 90035
Tel 310-369-5047
Fax 310-969-0210
Email....................rick.ramirez@fox.com

Margarita Ramon*
Film & Sound Commissioner
Yukon Film & Sound Commission
Whitehorse, Yukon Y1A 1Z9 Canada
Tel 867-667-5400
Fax 867-393-7040
Email ....margarita.ramon@gov.yk.ca
Web ....www.reelyukon.com

Director, MARIA DEL MAR BONET, 2003,
  CBC Canada, Radio Documentary
Director, POWER MAPPING, 1998, Telelatino
  TV, Documentary
Writer, GIOCCO LOCO, 1992, Telelatino
  Network TV, TV Series
Writer, NOVEDADES, 1992, CFMTV, TV
  Series
Director, CHINA AFTER TIANNOMEN
  SQUARE, 1991, BCTV, TV Series
Writer, ULTIMA HORA, 1988, CFMTV -
  Ontario/New York State, TV Series

Alfredo Ramos
Los Angeles, CA 90027
Tel 213-262-0051

Executive Producer, SUCKERS, 2001,
  Ground Zero Entertainment, Video

Ana Ramos*
WNET
New York, NY 10001
Tel 212-560-2984
Email ....ramosa@thirteen.org

Lise Ramos*
Creative Director
NY Squadron Productions Inc.
New York, NY 10036
Tel 212-245-1950
Tel 212-245-1980
Fax 212-245-1990
Email ..info@nysquadronproductions.com
Web ....www.nysquadronproductions.com

Nina Ramos*
San Francisco, CA 94114
Tel 415-305-8537
Email ....ninar@pobox.com

Victor Ramos*
Providence, RI 02907
Tel 401-440-2844
Email.......................vicramos@aol.com

Erica Rangel*
Chicago, IL 60643
Email.................erica81@sbcglobal.net

Stephanie Rauber
Rauber Filmworks
New York, NY 10019
Tel 212-529-9711

Director, DEMYSTIFYING THE DEMON,
  2004, Documentary

Rafael Rebollar*

Mexico City, DF 10910 Mexico
Email ......huaxolotl2002@yahoo.com.mx
Web ....www.afromexico.org

Victoria Regina*

Podemos Pictures
Hollywood, CA 90028
Tel 323-769-7059
Email ....info@victoriaregina.com
Web ....www.victoriaregina.com

*Manager: Midwest Talent Management,
818-765-3785,
betty@midwesttalent.com*

Actor, Producer, CHANGE, 2004, Podemos
  Pictures, Feature
Actor, DAVID & DEE, 2004, Johnathan Vara,
  Director, Short
Actor, LATIN LOVER, 2004, Aaron Behl,
  Short
Actor, PAN DULCE, 2004, 3rd Grade Teacher
  Productions, Feature
Actor, WEDNESDAY AFTERNOON, 2004,
  Alonso F. Mayo Drive, Short
Actor, LOCO LOVE, 2003, Artisan, Feature
Web Developer

Harrison Reiner*

Staff Story Analyst
CBS
Email......................hreinercbs@aol.com

Educator

Travis R. Rendon*

Converse, TX 78109
Tel 210-828-4909
Email......trx@rasquacheproductions.com
Web ......www.rasquacheproductions.com

Victora Rene*

Houston, TX 77277
Email ....torarenee@aol.com

Nikkolas Rey*

Agent, Principal
Alvarado Rey Agency
Los Angeles, CA 90048
Tel 323-655-7978
Fax 323-655-2777
Email ....nikkolas@alvaradorey.com
Web ....www.alvaradorey.com

Arnie Reyes*

The Reyes Law Firm P.C.
Austin, TX 78746
Tel 512-495-9380
Email..............arnie3@reyeslawfirm.com
Web ....www.reyeskawfirm.com

Attorney, Director, Producer, Writer, STICKS
  & STONES, 2005, Short
Attorney, Producer, BUNNY & CLYDO, 2004,
  Short
Director, Producer, SLIM & SHORTY VS.
  EVIL, 2004, Short
Director, DEADSTOCK, 2003, Short
Director, Writer, I'M FOR REAL DUDE, 2003,
  Short
Director, Producer, Writer, ROBBIE
  RODRIGUEZ' 10 MIN FILM SCHOOL,
  2003, Short
Director, Producer, Writer, THE DIARY, 2002,
  Short

Franc Reyes

Loiza Films
New York, NY 10001

*Manager: Nine Yards Entertainment,
310-289-1088*

Director, Writer, THE SETUP, 2005, RKO,
  Feature
Director, Writer, CERAMIC LIFE, 2004,
  Universal Pictures, Feature
Director, Writer, EMPIRE, 2002, Universal
  Pictures, Feature

Jorge Reyes
Beverly Hills, CA 90212

Agent: Tracy Murray, CAA,
310-288-4545

Creator, Co-Executive, Producer, Writer,
  KEVIN HILL, 2004, UPN, TV Series
Writer, RESCUE 77, 2000, Warner Bros. YV,
  TV Series
Writer, RESURRECTION BLVD., 2000,
  Viacom Production Inc., TV Series
Writer, NEW YORK UNDERCOVER, 1994,
  Fox TV, TV Series

Leo Reyes*
Madwolf Productions
Schertz, TX 78154
Tel 210-658-3035
Cell 210-885-1734
Email ....dusty-roads@earthlink.net
Web ....www.leoreyes.com

Producer, COMMUNITY VARIETY SHOW,
  2004, Time Warner Cable, Public Acces,
  TV Variety Show
Graphic Designer

Rose Reyes*
Austin, TX 78735
Email..............rose_reyes@sbcglobal.net

Ruperto Reyes*
Artistic Director
Teatro Vivo
Austin, TX 78703
Tel 512-474-6379
Cell 512-970-7016
Email ....rupertreyes@yahoo.com

Executive Producer, Writer, JF QUE?, 2004,
  Short
Actor, MISS CONGENIALITY, 2000, Warner
  Bros., Feature
Actor, OFFICE SPACE, 1999, 20th Century
  Fox, Feature

Leonardo Ricagni*
Los Angeles, CA 90027
Tel 917-225-0141
Fax 323-660-1520
Email..........................lricagni@aol.com

Ramon Ricard
New York, NY 10040
Tel 212-923-6106
Email..................sabadofilms@mac.com

Director, SABADO MORNING, 2002, Sabado
  Films, Short
Line Producer, THE GOTHIC LINE, 2001, Hit
  and Run, Feature
Director, COJUNTOS ANTIBALAS MUSIC
  VIDEO, 1999, The Family Productions,
  Music Video
Line Producer, SUNSHINE DELI AND GRO-
  CERY, 1999, Feature

Gizella Richardson*
Stockton, CA 95209
Tel 209-478-8619
Email ....richardson2n2@cs.com

Franklyn G. Richardz*
Los Angeles, CA 90002
Tel 323-249-9797
Email ....canislupusprods@yahoo.com

Diana Rico*
Mermaid Moon Productions
Venice, CA 90291
Tel 310-823-9496
Cell 310-428-4412
Fax 310-823-9496
Email ....dianarico@earthlink.net

Writer, A&E BIOGRAPHY, 2004, A&E, TV
  Series
Post-Producer, Writer, HOW DO I LOOK?,
  2004, Style Network, TV Series
Post Producer, Story Editor, URBAN JUNGLE,
  2004, SiTV, TV Series
Director, Producer, Writer, IT'S GOOD TO BE
  ..., 2003, E! Entertainment Television, TV
  Series
Director, Producer, Writer, E! TRUE HOLLY-
  WOOD STORY, 2002, E! Entertainment
  Television, TV Series
Producer, ROYALTY A-Z, 2002, E!
  Entertainment Television, TV Series

Jed Riffe*

Jed Riffe Films
Berkeley, CA 94710
Tel 510-845-2044
Email ....jed@beyondthedream.org

Diana Rios*

Associate Professor of Communication
Sciences and Latino Studies
University of Connecticut
Storrs, CT 06269
Tel 860-486-3187
Fax 860-486-2906
Email ....diana.rios@uconn.edu

Jonisha Rios*

Hollywood, CA 90078
Tel 323-244-9608
Email ....baezent@yahoo.com

Co-Host, THE DROP, 2004, Si TV, TV Series
Producer, CHICLE, 2002, Baez
   Entertainment, TV Special
Producer, NUDE IN NEW YORK, 2000,
   Producers' Club, Stage Play

Marcial Rios

Santa Ana, CA 92701
Tel 714-227-6080
Email ....marcialrios@hotmail.com

Director, Producer, Writer, LA TIERRA DEL
   DOLOR, 2003, Short
Director, Writer, UNFORGIVING DREAM,
   2002, Short
Director, Writer, ICE CREAM MAKES THINGS
   BETTER, 2001, Short

Ricardo Rios*

Chicago, IL 60611
Tel 773-398-5517
Fax 773-271-2718
Email ....rick@subliminalpictures.net

Raul Rios-Diaz*

San Juan, PR 00936
Tel 787-781-6416
Email ....alt165@prtc.net

Alexander Rivas

Port S. Lucie, FL 34983
Tel 772-873-1073
Tel 772-370-8966
Cell 772-370-0909
Email ....pascui@argentina.com
Web ....www.el-sereno.com.ar

Director, Editor, EL SERENO, 2004, Short
Director, Editor, MALAMADRE, 2004, Stage
   Play
Associate Director, Editor, ECLIPSE, 2003,
   Short
Sound, INDOCUMENTADOS, 2002, Feature
Graphic Designer

Pascui Rivas

Cordoba, NY 5000 Argentina
Tel 11-54-351-4815677
Email ....pascui@argentina.com
Web ....www.el-sereno.com.ar

Director, EL SERENO, 2004, Short
Sound, LA CIUDAD DE LOS HOMBRES LAC-
   TANTES, 2001, Short
Sound, EL MEDICO RURAL, 2000, Short

Alex Rivera*

Journeyman Productions
New York, NY 10012
Tel 212-253-6273
Email......................alex@alexrivera.com
Web ....www.subcine.com

Producer, VISIONES: LATINO ART & CUL-
   TURE, 2004, PBS, Documentary
Director, Producer, THE SIXTH SECTION,
   2003, POV/American Documentary,
   Documentary
Director, ANIMAQUILADORA/WHY
   CYBRACEROS?, 1997, Third World News
   reel, Mockumentary
Director, Producer, PAPAPAPA, 1997, Third
   World Newsreel, Documentary

Angel Rivera*
National Director of Affirmative Action
and Diversity
Screen Actors Guild
Hollywood, CA 90036
Tel 323-954-1663
Email ....arivera@sag.org
Web................................www.SAG.org

Media Advocate

Bunnie Rivera*
QuuQuui Films, LLC
Los Angeles, CA 90005
Tel 949-306-1103
Fax 213-252-1765
Email ....quuquui@yahoo.com

Carmen Rivera*
Brooklyn, NY 11206
Email......................Carmyn33@aol.com

Caty Rivera*
Delegate
San Sebastian International Film
Festival
Los Angeles, CA 90025
Cell 310-245-4040
Email ....catyrivera@aol.com
Web ....www.sansebastianfestival.com

Isabel Rivera
RiverFish Productions
New York, NY 10009
Tel 212-489-9781
Email....irivera@riverfishproductions.com
Web..........www.riverfishproductions.com

Creator, Executive Producer, LATIN ACCESS,
   2002, NBC, TV Series
Executive Producer, NEW YORK MAGAZINE
   AWARDS SHOW, 2001, NBC, TV Special
Executive Producer, PUERTO RICAN DAY
   PARADE, 2000, NBC, TV Special

Jose Rivera
Los Angeles, CA 90212
Agent: Shana Eddy, UTA, 310-273-6700
Manager: Neverland Films,
310-772-0008

Writer, THE MOTORCYCLE DIARIES, 2004,
   Southfork Pictures, Feature
Writer, SHADOW REALM, 2002, Si FI
   Channel, TV Movie
Writer, NIGHT VISIONS, 2001, Warner Bros.
   Television, TV Series
Writer, THE JUNGLE BOOK: MOWGLI'S
   STORY, 1998, Buena Vista, Home Video
Creator, Producer, Writer, EERIE, INDIANA,
   1992, NBC, TV Series

Miguel Rivera*
Bronx, NY 0451
Tel 917-653-6794
Email ....mr991@columbia.edu

Rey Rivera*
Los Angeles, CA 90027
Tel 323-445-7643
Email ....reyo@yahoo.com

Ted Rivera*
Los Gatos, CA 95032
Tel 408-354-9048

Alicia Rivera Frankl*
Hoboken West Digital Media
Sherman Oaks, CA 91403
Tel 818-380-8155
Fax 818-380-8134
Email ....alicia@hobokenw.com
Web ....www.hobokenw.com

Production Manager, ASTHMA: FIGHTING TO
   BREATHE, 2003, Discovery Health,
   Documentary
Production Manager, CRISIS DIABETES
   AMONG US, 2002, Discovery Health,
   Documentary
Production Manager, D.R.E.A.M TEAM,
   1999, Fremantle Group, Documentary
Line Producer, Production Manager, THE
   MASK OF ZORRO, 1998, Columbia
   Pictures, Feature

filmmakers

Jesus "Chuchi" Rivero*
Moonwater Pictures
Miami, FL 33173
Tel 305-582-9996
Fax 305-412-7812
Email ....info@moonwaterpictures.com
Web ....www.moonwaterpictures.com

Bernardo Riveros*
Toronto, Ontario, M3C1L8 Canada
Tel 416-704-4157
Email ....bernie@ilac.com

Sandra Roa*
Flushing, NY 11355
Email ....scrphoto@earthlink.net

Henry Robles*
Los Angeles, CA 90019
Tel 323-936-3656
Fax 323-931-3523
Email...............texmex12@earthlink.net

Agent: Jay Gassner, UTA,
310-273-6700

Staff Writer, COLD CASE, 2004, CBS
    Television, TV Series

Veronica Robles
Orale con Veronica
Chelsea, MA 02150
Tel 617-884-2136
Tel 727-944-5544
Email..........contact@veronicarobles.com
Web................www.veronicarobles.com

Producer, ORALE CON VERONICA, 2002,
    Cuenca Vision & Public Access TV, TV
    Series
Producer, MARIACHI / CONTINENTE, 1999,
    Cuenca Vision MA, TV Special
Producer, MEXICO MAGIA Y PASION, 1999,
    Thalia Spanish Theater, Stage Play

Christopher Rodarte*
La Llorona Productions
Tucson, AZ 85711
Tel 520-326-7163

Victor Rodarte*
Sahuarita, AZ 85629
Tel 520-398-6288
Email ....VRodarte@longrealty.com

Alex Rodriguez*
Public Relations
VirtualHispanic
Santa Barbara, CA 93105
Tel 805-964-9393
Fax 805-964-9398
Email ....alex@virtualhispanic.com
Web ....www.VirtualHispanic.com

Media Advocate

Alfredo Rodriguez*
Westlake Village, CA 91361
Email ....alrod_la@hotmail.com

Baldemar Rodriguez*
Adelante Studios
Pasadena, TX 77501
Tel 713-477-9446
Email ....baldemarrodriguez@mail.com

Carolina Rodriguez
Screen Actors Guild, Florida Branch
Miami, FL 33156
Tel 305-670-7677
Fax 305-670-1813
Email ....carodriguez@sag.org
Web ....www.sag.org

Danilo Rodriguez*
Head of Research
Cinetic Media
New York, NY 10001
Tel 212-204-7979
Fax 212-204-7980
Email..............danilo@cineticmedia.com
Web....................www.cineticmedia.com

Danny Rodriguez*
Bellavic Entertainment
Burbank, CA 91506
Tel 818-371-3414
Fax 310-410-3003
Email ..dannyrodriguez03@sbcglobal.net
Web ......www.bellavic-entertainment.com

Executive Producer, THE DEVIL INSIDE,
   2005, Bellavic Entertainment, Feature
Producer, HUSTLAS, 2003, Maverick,
   Feature
Producer, THE BLUES, 2003, Sony Red
   Distribution, Feature
Executive Producer, MISERY LOVE COMPA-
   NY, 2000, York Entertainment, Feature

Felix Rodriguez*
Brooklyn, NY 11217
Email ....felix.rodriguez@citigroup.com
Web ....www.ajamuproductions.com

Producer, LA BRUJA, 2004, Documentary

Grisel Rodriguez*
Cedar Park, TX 78613
Tel 512-426-7360
Email ....grisel43@hotmail.com

Harry Rodriguez*
New York, NY 10013
Email................samrodfilmsny@aol.com

Horacio Rodriguez*
Los Angeles, CA 90067
Tel 310-968-3758
Email....................horaciordz@mac.com

James P. Rodriguez*
San Antonio, TX 78201
Tel 210-341-8490
Cell 210-386-8490
Email ....jimpatro@yahoo.com

Director of Photography, CRAZY LIFE, 2004,
   Jadoigze Services Inc., Short
Director of Photography, HERITAGE, 2004,
   TV Series

Producer, Director, LIVING ADVENTURES,
   2004, TV Series
Director of Photography, OBATALA, 2004,
   Aveneaux Films, Short

Jorge Rodriguez*
Worldwide Distribution & Latin American
Sales Manager
Taffy Entertainment
Los Angeles, CA 90006
Tel 323-734-2309
Fax 323-734-2309
Email..........jdrgonzalezzzz@hotmail.com

Post Production Assistant, GREEN DRAGON,
   2001, Franchise Pictures, Feature
Director, Producer, Writer, MACARTHUR
   PARK, 2001, Cine Real Pictures, Short
Assistant Editor, ZIG ZAG, 2001, Franchise
   Pictures, Feature

Jose Luis Rodriguez
President
Hispanic Information Television Network
New York, NY 10013
Tel 212-966-5660
Fax 212-966-5725

Luis Rodriguez*
Odessa, TX 79765
Email ....lrod42@yahoo.com

Maria Teresa Rodriguez*
Pata de Perros Productions
Philadelphia, PA 19147
Tel 215-467-4417
Email ....patadeperroprod@aol.com

Co-Producer, Director, MIRROR DANCE,
   2005, PBS/ITVS, Documentary
Co-Producer, Director, UNDER NEW MAN-
   AGEMENT, 2003, WYBE-TV, Documentary
Director, GED CONNECTION: READING
   SERIES (6X30), 2001, PBS, Educational
Director, Producer, FROM HERE TO THERE,
   1998, Pata de Perros Productions,
   Documentary
Director, Producer, MORNINGTIDE, 1993,
   Pade de Perros Productions, Short

Maria Elena Rodriguez

Chairperson
Hispanic Academy of Media Arts and
Sciences
New York, NY 10163
Fax 212-686-7030

Molly Robin Rodriguez

Northridge, CA 91325
Tel 818-320-0123
Email.................mollyrobin@yahoo.com

2nd 2nd Assistant Director, KINGPIN, 2003,
Bravo, TV Series
2nd 2nd Assistant Director, 15 MINUTES,
2001, New Line Cinema, Feature
2nd 2nd Assistant Director, RESURRECTION
BLVD., 2000, Showtime, TV Series
Associate Producer, STRAIGHT RIGHT, 2000,
Allengate Film Group, Feature

Nestor N. Rodriguez*

Avant Garde Entertainment, LLC
Riverdale, NY 10463
Tel 718-543-9238
Email ....RainmakerNYC@aol.com

Producer, MALEDETTA PRIMAVERA, 2001,
Short

Noell Rodriguez*

Tucson, AZ 85704
Email ....noellrodriguez@yahoo.com

Paul Rodriguez

Rodriguez Entertainment
Los Angeles, CA 90067
Tel 323-459-0578
Web ....www.paulrodriguez.com

*Agent: Chris Smith, ICM,
310-550-4000*

Actor, CLOUD NINE, 2005, Frozen Films
Inc., Feature
Actor, THE WORLD'S FASTEST INDIAN,
2005, Feature
Actor, A CINDERELLA STORY, 2004, Warner
Bros, Feature

Producer, THE ORIGINAL LATIN KINGS OF
COMEDY, 2002, Paramount Pictures, TV
Special
Actor, ALI, 2001, Columbia Pictures, Feature
Actor , TORTILLA SOUP, 2001, Samuel
Goldwyn Films, Feature
Actor, PRICE OF GLORY, 2000, New Line
Cinema, Feature
Director, A MILLION TO JUAN, 1994,
Samuel Goldwyn Company, Feature

Paul Rodriguez

Senior Vice President
Wilshire Stages
Los Angeles, CA 90048
Tel 323-951-1700
Tel 323-302-0210
Fax 323-951-1710
Email ......prodriguez@wilshirestages.com
Web ....www.wilshirestages.com

Production Facilities & Post Sound

Phillip Rodriguez

Los Angeles, CA 90086
Tel 323-481-4634
Email ....ba433@lafn.org
Web ....www.cityprojects.net

Director, Producer, LOS ANGELES NOW,
2004, Documentary

Rebecca Rodriguez*

La Center, WA 98629
Email ..rebeccarodriguez@mindspring.com
Web ....www.luckyheadfilms.com

Richard Rodriguez

Executive Director
National Hispanic Foundation for the
Arts
Washington, DC 20007
Tel 202-293-8330
Fax 202-965-5252
Email ....rrodriguez@HispanicArts.org
Web ....www.HispanicArts.org

Media Advocate

Robert Rodriguez

Los Hooligans Productions
Austin, TX 78701
Tel 512-443-3713
Web ....www.loshooligans.com

Agent: Robert Newman, ICM,
310-550-4000,
rnewman@icmtalent.com

Composer, Director, Director of Photography,
  Editor, Producer, Writer, SIN CITY, 2005,
  Dimension Films, Feature
Director, Editor, Producer, Writer, THE
  ADVENTURES OF SHARK BOY & LAVA
  GIRL IN 3-D, 2005, Columbia TriStar,
  Feature
Director, Writer, ONCE UPON A TIME IN
  MEXICO, 2003, Sony Pictures
  Entertainment, Feature
Director, SPY KIDS 3-D: GAME OVER, 2003,
  Miramax, Feature
Writer, SPY KIDS, 2001, Miramax, Feature
Executive Producer, FROM DUSK TILL DAWN
  3: THE HANGMAN'S DAUGHTER, 2000,
  Buena Vista Home Video, Feature
Executive Producer, FROM DUSK TILL DAWN
  2: TEXAS BLOOD MONEY, 1999,
  Dimension Films, Feature
Executive Producer, FROM DUSK TILL
  DAWN, 1996, Dimension Films, Feature
Writer, DESPERADO, 1995, Columbia
  Pictures, Feature
Director, EL MARIACHI, 1992, Columbia
  Pictures, Feature

Pilar Rodriguez-Aranda*

Anarca Films
Santa Fe, NM 87505
Tel 505-986-0642
Cell 505-501-0277
Email.................pilar@anarcafilms.com
Web ....www.anarcafilms.com

Director, BORDER SHE IS, 2001, Iron
  Communications, Canada, Short
Director, EL GUAJOLOTE, 2000, Iron
  Communications, Canada, Short
Director, THE IDEA WE LIVE IN, 1991,
  Women Make Movies, Short

Lupe Rodriguez-Haas*

A La Brava Entertainment
Torrance, CA 90501
Tel 213-300-8431
Email ....lupers@earthlink.net

Producer, BE A VJ CONTEST, 2004, KJLA,
  TV Series
Producer, LA TV HOLIDAY MOVIE SPECIAL,
  2004, KJLA, TV Series
Segment Producer, LA TV LIVE, 2004, KJLA,
  TV Series
Director, Writer, DAYDREAM BELIEVER,
  2002, A La Brava Entertainment, Short
Director, Writer, WHERE YA FROM?, 2000, A
  La Brava Entertainment, Short

Roy M. Rodriguez-Padron*

Miami, FL 33145
Tel 305-798-0854
Email ....soybomb72@hotmail.com

Ingrid Rojas*

Brooklyn, NY 11238
Tel 917-592-7481
Email ....indierojas@yahoo.com

Associate Producer, BREAKING VEGAS,
  2005, History Channel, Documentary
Associate Producer, LA LUPE: A MIRROR OF
  THE TIMES, 2005, Documentary
Director, LEGALLY BLIND, 2005,
  Documentary

Evelyn Rojo*

Northridge, CA 91330
Tel 818-677-0414
Email..............crashdowncafe@msn.com

Freya Rojo*

Glendale, CA 91202
Email ....freyarojo@yahoo.com

filmmakers

Sylvie Rokab*
In the Light Productions, Inc.
Coral Gables, FL 33146
Tel 305-663-4647
Email..sylvie@in-the-lightproduction.com
Web ....www.in-the-light.com

Director, Director of Photography, Producer,
   IN THE LIGHT, 2003, Innermotion,
   Documentary
Director of Photography, Commercials

Jon Roman*
Brooklyn, NY 11211
Email ....Jroman222@aol.com

Phil Roman*
Phil Roman Entertainment
Burbank, CA 91505
Tel 818-985-1200
Fax 818-985-2668
Email......................phil@romanent.com
Web ....www.philromanent.com

Director, Executive Producer, GRANDMA GOT
   RUN OVER BY A REINDEER, 2000,
   Warner Home Video, TV Movie, Animated
Executive Producer, KING OF THE HILL,
   1997, Twentieth Century Fox, TV Series,
   Animated
Executive Producer, THE MAGIC PEARL,
   1997, ABC Television, TV Movie, Animated
Executive Producer, BRUNO THE KID, 1996,
   Vitello Productions, TV Series, Animated
Executive Producer, C-BEAR AND JAMAL,
   1996, Xenon Entertainment Group, TV
   Series, Animated
Director, TOM AND JERRY - THE MOVIE,
   1993, Miramax, Feature, Animated
Director, Executive Producer, GARFIELD'S
   THANKSGIVING, 1989, CBS, TV Movie,
   Animated

Aldo Romero*
Symbiotic Productions
Ozone Park, NY 11416
Tel 718-296-5617
Email.............................ar826@att.net
Web ....www.symbioticfilm.com

Diana Romero*
President
I-Media Entertainment
Chicago, IL 60610
Tel 312-654-0684
Email.................gypsyfilms@yahoo.com

Elaine Romero*
Tucson, AZ 85705
Tel 520-624-7669
Cell 917-640-7027
Fax 520-624-7669
Email..........................erome1@aol.com
Web....................www.elaineromero.com

*Agent: Mark Subias, Mark Christian
Subias Agency,
marksubias@earthlink.net*

Director, Producer, FIDELITY, 2004, Short
Writer, THE FAMILY JEWEL, 2002, Silver
   Penny Productions, Short
Co-Producer, Writer, DREAM FRIEND, 2001,
   Dream Friend Productions, Short

Guiomar Romero*
Tucson, AZ 85716
Tel 520-320-1236
Fax 520-320-1216
Email ....romerogg@aol.com

Kiley Romero*
Tucson, AZ 85748
Tel 520-885-9365
Email ....kileyromero@yahoo.com

Ross Romero*
Anaheim, CA 92805
Tel 714-917-2045
Email ....ltnent@yahoo.com

Luis Carlos Romero-Davis*
Nogales, AZ 85621
Email ......FenceProductions@yahoo.com

Yolanda Romersa*

La Paloma Productions, LLC
Los Angeles, CA 90010
Tel 818-437-5737
Email ....yolanda@palomatheplay.com

Victor Rosa*

Bag of Beans Productions
Burlington, NJ 08016
Tel 804-366-7556
Tel 609-387-2386
Email ....vrosa@rcn.com

Rafael Rosado*

Columbus, OH 43085
Tel 614-291-2668
Email ....rrosado@columbus.rr.com

Storyboard Artist, BABY LOONEY TUNES,
  2002, Warner Bros. Animation, TV Series,
  Animated
Storyboard Artist, STUART LITTLE, 2002,
  Sony Animation, TV Series, Animated
Storyboard Artist, TEENAGE MUTANT NINJA
  TURTLES, 2002, 4 Kids Productions, TV
  Series, Animated
Director, Producer, THE TORTURED CLOWN,
  2001, Sundance Channel, Short
Director, Producer, MEN IN BLACK: THE
  ANIMATED SERIES, 1998, Sony
  Animation/Columbia, TV Series, Animated
Director, Producer, EXTREME GHOST-
  BUSTERS, 1997, Sony
  Animation/Columbia, TV Series, Animated

Sonia Rosario

Vice President of Production
Home Vision Entertainment
Chicago, IL 60640
Tel 778-878-2600
Fax 773-878-8406
Email ....info@homevision.com
Web ....www.homevision.com

Co-Producer, EVERY CHILD IS BORN A
  POET, 2002, Feature
Supervising Producer, THE PUZZLE PLACE,
  1994, KCET, TV Series
Producer, BIG BIRD IN JAPAN, 1991, PBS,
  TV Movie

Robert G. Rose*

President
AIM Tell-A-Vision
New York, NY 10003
Tel 212-627-3192
Fax 212-255-9232
Email ....info@aimtv.tv
Web ....www.aimtv.tv

Executive Producer, AMERICAN LATINO TV,
  2004, AIM-TV Dist., TV Series
Executive Producer, LATINATION, 2004,
  AIM-TV Dist, TV Series
Executive Producer, SONIDOS, 2003, AIM-TV
  Dist, TV Series
Executive Producer, URBAN LATINO TV,
  2001, AIM-TV Dist., TV Series

Cyn Cañal Rossi

Partner
Cynalex Productions, LLC
New York, NY 10021
Tel 212-207-4740
Fax 212-207-4709
Email ....cyn4cynalexprods@aol.com
Web ....www.cynalexproductions.com

Producer, A NIGHT TO FORGET, 2003, Stage
  Play
Producer, CHOPPING, 2002, Stage Play
Producer, Writer, RHYTHM OF THE SAINTS,
  2002, Feature

Fernanda Rossi*

New York, NY 10001
Tel 212-249-2017
Email ....info@documentarydoctor.com
Web ....www.documentarydoctor.com

Editor, THE LIFE JACKET IS UNDER YOUR
  SEAT, 2002, Mojo Films
Producer, Writer, INVENTING A GIRL, 2000,
  Documentary
Producer, Writer, ON THE EDGE, 2000,
  Documentary

filmmakers

Lydia Rousey*

LunaCproductions
Austin, TX 78753
Tel 512-223-7048
Fax 512-223-7833
Email ....lydia_rousey@hotmail.com

Bernardo Ruiz*

New York, NY 10001
Tel 347-385-6875
Email...........bernardo@bernardoruiz.net

Director, Writer, THE DEVIL'S TWILIGHT,
 2003, WNET, Short
Co-Producer, THE SIXTH SECTION, 2003,
 POV, Documentary

Fernando Ruiz*

Creative Director
Potter Ruiz Productions Inc.
Arlington, MA 02474
Tel 781-646-3454
Email ....potterruiz@aol.com
Web ....www.potterruiz.com

Jose Luis Ruiz

Green Dot Films
Santa Monica, CA 90401
Tel 310-656-4900
Fax 310-656-0444
Email ....mail@greendotfilms.com
Web ....www.greendotfilms.com

Director, UNA MUJER PROHIBIDA, 1974,
 Imperial Films, Feature
Producer, CRIMEN DE DOBLE FILO, 1965,
 C.B. Films, Feature

Juan Ruiz Anchía

Beverly Hills, CA 90212

Agent: David Gersh, The Gersh Agency,
310-274-6611

Director of Phtography, INNOCENT VOICES,
 2004, A Band Apart, Feature
Director of Phtography, SPARTAN, 2004,
 Warner Bros, Franchise Pictures, Feature
Director of Phtography, CONFIDENCE, 2003,
 Lions Gate Films, Ignite Entertainment,
 Feature

Director of Phtography, OFF THE MAP, 2003,
 Manhattan Pictures International, Feature
Director of Phtography, NO GOOD DEAD,
 2002, MAC Releasing, Seven Arts
 Pictrues, Feature

Nicole Sacker*

Cocky Rapscallions
Los Angeles, CA 90064
Tel 310-473-8297
Email ....nsacker@comcast.net
Web ....www.nicolesacker.com

Director, LIVING TOGETHER, 2005, TV Pilot
Director, Producer, Writer, THE DUEL, 2004,
 Britshort Ltd., Short
Director, Writer, Producer, MUNCHIES, 2000,
 Short

Gustavo Sagastume*

VP, Programming
Public Broadcasting Service
Alexandria, PA 22314
Tel 703-739-8474
Fax 703-739-8440
Email ....gsagastume@pbs.org
Web ....www.pbs.org

Stephanie Saint Sanchez*

Chicago, IL 60622
Tel 713-868-9827

Director, Producer, LA LLORONA, 2004,
 Short

Richard Saiz*

Programming Manager
ITVS
San Francisco, CA 94110
Tel 415-356-8383
Fax 415-356-8391
Email ....richard_saiz@itvs.org
Web ....www.itvs.org

Abel Salas*
Membership, Registration Coordinator
NATPE
Los Angeles, CA 90036
Tel 310-453-4440
Fax 310-453-5258
Email ....abel@natpe.org
Web................................www.natpe.org

Carolina Salas*
New York, NY 10027
Tel 212-853-1384
Cell 917-816-6375
Email ....ys2076@columbia.edu

Marconi Salazar*
Sueños Entertainment
Los Angeles, CA 90019
Tel 310-497-9616
Email msalazar@mexicocitythemovie.com

Ralph Salazar*
Vamos Productions
Riviera, TX 78379
Tel 361-595-5205

Michelle Salcedo
Brooklyn, NY 11201
Tel 718-246-8180
Cell 917-842-6415
Email ......michellesalcedo@earthlink.net

Editor, A BABY STORY, 2003, TLC, TV Movie
Director, A DONDE VA VICENTE? WHERE IS
    VINCENT GOING?, 2003, Documentary
Editor, MAKING THE BAND 2, 2003, MTV
    Networks, TV Series
Editor, WHAT NOT TO WEAR, 2003, The
    Learning Channel, TV Special

Manny Saldivar*
Anaheim, CA 92805
Tel 714-778-0138
Email ....mannysaldivar@yahoo.com

Martin Salinas
Santa Monica, CA 90401

*Agent: Nancy Nigrosh, Innovative
Artists, 310-656-0400*

Associate Producer, Writer, NICOTINA, 2003,
    Artisan Entertainment, Altavista Films,
    Feature
Writer, VAN VAN, LET'S PARTY, 2001, Arca
    Difusa, Documentary
Writer, FINAL MINUTE, 2000, Borensztein
    TV, TV Series

Ric Salinas
Los Angeles, CA 90067
Web ....www.cultureclash.com

*Manager: Ivan de Paz Management,
310-409-8638,
ivan@de-paz-management.com*

Actor, Writer, CHAVEZ RAVINE, 2003, Mark
    Taper Forum, Stage Play
Actor, Writer, NUYORICAN STORIES, 1999,
    INTAR, Stage Play
Actor , MI VIDA LOCA, 1994, Sony Pictures,
    Feature
Actor, Writer, RADIO MAMBO, 1993, INTAR,
    Stage Play

Rogelio & Rachel Salinas*
Odyssey DVD and Video Productions
San Antonio, TX 78205
Tel 210-710-0842
Tel 210-543-2458
Email ....odysseydvd@hotmail.com

Actor, Director, Editor, VOICES, 2003,
    Odyssey DVD & Video Productions, Music
    Video
Actor, Director, Editor, Music Supervisor,
    DISCO COPS 2, 2002, Salinas/Garcia
    Productions, Short
Actor, Director, Editor, Music Supervisor, LIFE
    OR DEATH, 1998, Salinas/Garcia
    Productions, Short

filmmakers

Xaviar C. Salinas

Three Moons Entertainment, Inc.
Los Angeles, CA 90028
Tel 323-890-1969
Email....................treslunas3@aol.com

Executive Producer, A TITAN IN THE RING,
2002, Feature
Executive Producer, EL BESO QUE ME
DISTE, 2000, Vanguard International
Cinema, Feature
Manager

Walter Salles

Beverly Hills, CA 90212

*Agent: John Lesher, Endeavor Talent
Agency, 310-248-2000*

Director, DARK WATER, 2005, Buenavista
Pictures, Feature
Producer, HERMANAS, 2005, Buenavista
Pictures, Feature
Director, THE MOTORCYCLE DIARIES, 2004,
Focus Features, Feature
Co-Producer, CITY OF GOD, 2002, Miramax
Films, Feature
Producer, MADAME SATÃ , 2002, Wellspring
Media, Feature
Director, Writer, BEHIND THE SUN, 2001,
Miramax Films, Feature
Director, Writer , CENTRAL STATION, 1998,
Sony Pictures Classic, Feature
Director, Writer , PRIMEIRO DIA, O, 1998,
WinStar Cinema, Feature
Director, Editor, Writer, TERRA
ESTRANGEIRA, 1996, Videofilmes
Productions, Feature
Director, A GRANDE ARTE , 1991, Miramax
Films, Feature

Calogero Salvo*

CS Productions, LLC
New York, NY 10011
Tel 212-691-8305
Fax 212-691-8305
Email ....call4cs@aol.com

Valerie Samaniego-Finch*

San Antonio, TX 78232
Email ....mauitx@hotmail.com

Marise Samitier*

Caelus Cinema
Los Angeles, CA 90026
Tel 213-250-3955
Fax 323-665-2192
Email ....ms@caelus.net

Writer, Director, APARTMENT 427, 2003,
Short
Writer, Director, THE RETURN OF REASON,
2000, Short
Writer, Director, THE VIRGIN, 1999, Short
Writer, Director, BAZAAR, 1997, Short
Writer, Director, THE RING, 1995, Short

Jinny Sample*

Willingboro, NJ 08046
Tel 609-835-6650
Fax 609-835-9591
Email ....starsartis@comcast.net
Web ....www.starsandartists.com

Carlos San Miguel

Los Angeles, CA 90066
Tel ....310-391 -7623
Email ....latinoactor@hotmail.com

*Agent: Samantha Botana, The Samantha
Group, 626-683-2444*

Producer, BRAINPEOPLE (BY JOSÉ RIVERA),
2004, Lee Strasberg Theater, Stage Play
Actor, Associate Producer, HER HUSBAND?,
2004, New York Film Academy, Short
Actor, Associate Producer, LOST LIVES,
2004, New York Film Academy, Short

Carla Sanchez*

Coral Gables, FL 33146
Email ....promo@carlasanchez.net
Web ....www.carlasanchez.net

Carlos Sanchez

Marketing Director, Latin America
Warner Home Video
Burbank, CA 91522
Tel 818-954-6000
Web ....www.warnerbros.com

Happy Sanchez
Latin Soul Syndicate
San Angelmo, CA 94960
Tel 415-482-6063
Email ....happysanchez@aol.com

Music Placement, MALCOM IN THE MIDDLE, 2004, TV
Music Placement, THE WHOLE TEN YARDS, 2004, Warner Bros., Feature
Music Placement, THE REAL WORLD PARIS, 2003, MTV, TV
Music Placement, THIRD ROCK FROM THE SUN, 2003, TV

Karen Sanchez*
Brooklyn, NY 11221
Email ....KS_ML2003@yahoo.com

Marta Sanchez*
Kalpullitlal Teca Medra Projects
San Francisco, CA 94112
Tel 415-307-3397
Fax 415-587-3492
Email...........marzinasanchez@msn.com

Martha Sanchez
Theatrical and International Sales Manager
Women Make Movies
New York, NY 10013
Tel 212-925-0606
Fax 212-925-2052
Email ....msanchez@wmm.com
Web ....www.wmm.com

Ralph Sanchez
Executive
Nickelodeon Animation Development
Burbank, CA 91502
Tel 818-736-3000

Veronica Sanchez
Commerce City, CO 80022
Tel 303-668-9325
Cell 303-668-9325
Email.................sanchezvp@yahoo.com

1st Assistant Director, Producer, Production Manager, SEX & ALCOHOL, 2003, Short
1st Assistant Director, Producer, YOUR MOVE, 2003, Short
Producer, LIMBO, 2002, Short
Production Manager, LOVE WON'T DIE, 2002, Music Video

Elvira Sanchez de Malicki*
Facets Productions Inc.
Toronto, Ontario M9B5C4 Canada
Tel 416-621-0470
Email ....elvira@malicki.ca

Milcha Sanchez Scott
New Yok, NY 10001

Agent: WMA, 212-586-5100

Writer, ROOSTERS, 1993, Olmos Productions/American Playhouse, Feature

Roberto Jose Sanchez-Santos*
Ponce, PR 00732
Tel 939-644-1366

Carlos Sandoval*
Camino Bluff Productions, Inc.
New York, NY 10025
Tel 631-267-6565

Director, Producer, Writer, FARMINGVILLE, 2004, P.O.V., Documentary

George James Sandoval*
West End Productions
Ojai, CA 93030
Tel 805-240-9496
Fax 805-240-9464
Email ....geosand@westendprod.com
Web ....www.westendprod.com

Sinnel Sandoval*
Balthazar Films
Flushing, NY 11385
Tel 917-403-0926
Email ....sinsandoval@hotmail.com

Dario Sanmiguel*
Arc Angel Pictures
San Francisco, CA 94102
Tel 415-505-8723
Email ....dariodirdp@earthlink.net
Web ....www.dariosanmiguel.com

Attorney: Jody Weiner, 415-921-2042

Elena Santaballa
Culver City, CA 90231
Tel 310-839-3349
Tel 310-576-3252
Fax 310-839-0525
Email ....esantaballa@zworg.com

1st Assistant Director, EVERYBODY LOVES
   RAYMOND, 1998, CBS, TV Series
2nd Assistant Director, SPORTSNIGHT,
   1998, ABC, TV Series
1st Assistant Director, FIRED UP, 1997,
   NBC, TV Series

Paul Santana
Agent
Agency for the Performing Arts
Los Angeles, CA 90069
Tel 310-273-0744
Fax 310-888-4242

Alex Santiago*
San Juan, PR 00907
Tel 787-644-3195
Email........................premisas@prtc.net

Marco Santiago*
Volarefilms LLC
Phoenix, AZ 85044
Tel 480-229-3143
Fax 623-321-1584
Email ....msantiago@volarefilms.com
Web ....www.volarefilms.com

Milton Santiago*
Miami, FL 33143
Email...............invictusfilm@yahoo.com

Myra Santiago*
Producer
Si TV
Los Angeles, CA 90028
Tel 323-256-8900
Email......myrasantiago1972@yahoo.com

Ray Santisteban*
Nantes Films
San Antonio, TX 78210
Tel 210-534-1919
Email ....nantes67@aol.com

Producer, POSTCARDS FROM BUSTER,
   2005, PBS, WGBH, TV Series
Director, Editor, VOICES FROM TEXAS,
   2003, Cinema Guild, Nantes Films,
   Documentary
Editor, MY WEST SIDE, 2001, Nantes Films,
   Documentary Short
Director, TEXAS CONJUNTO: MUSIC OF THE
   PEOPLE, 2000, Guadalupe Cultural Arts
   Center, Documentary Short
Associate Producer, CHICANO: HISTORY OF
   THE MEXICAN AMERICAN CIVIL RIGHTS
   MOVEMENT, 1996, Galan Productions,
   Documentary
Director, NUYORICAN POETS CAFE, 1994,
   Nantes Films, Documentary Short
Associate Producer, PASSIN' IT ON, 1992,
   First Run/Icarus Films, TV Series

Manny Santos
MIKAVI Productions, Inc
New York, NY 10128
Tel 212-348-9419
Cell 347-524-5345
Email ....mikavi@mikavi.com
Web ....www.mikavi.com

Director, NOTICIAS 41 UNIVISION, 2001,
   Univision Network, TV Series
Producer, AQUI Y AHORA, 2000, Univision
   Network, TV Series
Producer, DE LA SALLE, 2000, NBC, Feature
Producer, HISPANIC BUSINESS TODAY,
   2000, NBC, TV Series

Aurora Sarabia*
Chicana Rasquatchi Productions
Berkeley, CA 94704
Tel 510-649-8539
Email ......filmgoddess2001@yahoo.com

Actress, Animator, Director, Editor, Writer,
CHISMOSA Y MANTECA EN JEALOUSY,
2004, Short
Sound, DEAD REVENGE, 2003, Short
Script Supervisor, BAMPINAY, 2002, I Don't
Care Productions, Short
Animator, THE MONEY PIG, 2001, Banda
Productions, Short
Director, DELTA DREAMS, 2000,
Documentary

Cristina Saralegui
"Cristina"
Miami, FL 33172
Tel 305-538-9074

*Agent: Jorge Insua, CAA,
310-288-4545*

Executive Producer, A QUE NO TE ATREVES,
1999, Univision Network, TV Series
Executive Producer, Talk Show Host, EL
SHOW DE CRISTINA, 1989-2004,
Univision Network, TV Series

Stephen Sariñana-Lampson*
Cine Coyote Films
Los Angeles, CA 90031
Tel 323-222-7595
Fax 323-221-5067
Email ......stephen@thecoyotestudio.com

Director, Producer, FOUR DAYS IN BARRAN-
QUILLA, 2004, CineCoyote Films,
Documentary
Graphic Designer

Guillermo Sauceda*
Coral Gables, FL 33146
Tel 305-607-1852

Nancy Savoca
Beverly Hills, CA 90211

Agent: Ben Smith, ICM, 310-550-4000

Director, Writer, DIRT, 2003, Mac Releasing,
Feature
Director, RENO: REBEL WITHOUT A PAUSE,
2002, Seventh Arts Releasing,
Documentary
Director, THE MIND OF THE MARRIED MAN,
2001, HBO, TV Series
Director, Writer, THE 24 HOUR WOMAN,
1999, Artisan Entertainment, Feature
Director, THIRD WATCH: KNOW THYSELF,
1999, NBC/ John Wells Productions, TV
Series

John Scheiber*
Brownsville, TX 78520
Fax 956 544-5561
Email ....nik4s@hotmail.com
Web ....www.southtexasfilm.com

Adam Schlachter*
Los Angeles, CA 90068
Tel 323-708-1452
Email................adimafilm@hotmail.com
Web ....www.palmarejofilms.com

Writer, Producer, STRAY BULLET, 2006,
Feature
Director, Writer, PALMAREJO: MY BACKYARD
WAS A MOUNTAIN, 2005, Hypnotic Films,
Short
Director, Writer, CAUTION TO THE WIND,
2004, AFI, Short
Director, MARTY'S LIQUOR STOP, 2004, AFI,
Short

Mark Schreiber*
Venice, CA 90291
Tel 310-396-2144
Email ....markschreiber@excite.com

James Scurlock*
Trueworks, Inc.
Venice, CA 90291
Tel 310-488-9598
Email ....jjames@trueoworks.us

Ramiro Segovia*
Hollywood, CA 90078
Email............................miro@nalip.info

Patricio Serna
Pakidermo Films
San Pedro Garza Garcia, 66297 Mexico
Email ....patricio@pakidermo.com
Web ....www.pakidermo.com

*Agent: Elyse Scherz, Endeavor Talent
Agency, 310-248-2000*

Writer, BAILEN 58, 2003, Short
Actor, Director, Writer, MATING CALL, 2003,
   Short
Director, Writer, CHUPACABRAS, 2002,
   Short
Actor, Director, Writer, TROMBA D'ORO,
   2002, Short

Jason Serrone*
Palmdale, CA 93590
Tel 323-371-3331

Joan Shigekawa*
Program Officer
The Rockefeller Foundation
New York, NY 10018
Tel 212-869-8500
Fax 212-764-3468
Web ....www.rockfound.org

Jack Siegel*
Secret Fortress, Inc.
Los Angeles, CA 90029
Tel 323-662-3778
Email................jack@secretfortress.com
Web ....www.secretfortress.com

Robert Sierra*
Los Angeles, CA 90014
Email ....oregelfilms@aol.com

Antonio J. Sifre Seín*
Toro, Colón, Mullet, Rivera & Sifre,
P.S.C.
San Juan, PR 00918
Tel 787-751-8999
Tel 787-763-7760
Email ....ajsifre@tcmrslaw.com

Herbert Siguenza
Culture Clash
Los Angeles, CA 90067
Web ....www.cultureclash.com

*Manager: Ivan de Paz, Arenas
Entertainment, 310-385-4401*

Actor, Writer, CHAVEZ RAVINE, 2003, Mark
   Taper Forum, Stage Play
Producer, Writer, THE MOVIE PITCH, 2003,
   Arekita Productions, Feature
Actor, Writer, NUYORICAN STORIES, 1999,
   INTAR, Stage Play
Actor, STAR MAPS, 1997, 20th Century Fox,
   Feature
Actor, Writer, RADIO MAMBO, 1993, INTAR,
   Stage Play

Gail Silva*
President
Film Arts Foundation
San Francisco, CA 94103
Tel ....415-552-8760 ext. 315
Fax 415-552-0882
Email ....gails@filmarts.org
Web ....www.filmarts.org

Media Advocate

Mark Silverstein*
Sound Recordist
Observar
Phoenix, AZ 85014
Tel 602-277-7156
Email.................observar@earthlink.net
Web...........................www.observar.net

Chris Sisneros*
Tucson, AZ 84518
Email ....cnerojr@yahoo.com

Nicolas Smirnoff*
Prensario
Buenos Aires, Argentina
Tel 54-11-4924-7908
Email ....nicolas5@ba.net

Samantha Smith*
Picollina Productions
Georgetown, TX 78626
Tel 512-841-5930
Tel 512-797-6694
Fax 512-385-2398
Email ....cine@texas.net

Graphic Designer

Jimmy Smits
Los Angeles, CA 90212

Agent: Joe Coen, CAA, 310-288-4545

Manager: Brillstein-Grey Entertainment, 310-275-6135

Actor, LACKAWANNA BLUES, 2005, HBO, TV Movie
Actor, STAR WARS EPISODE III: RETURN OF THE SITH, 2005, 20th Century Fox, Feature
Actor , WEST WING, 2004-2005, Warner Bros., TV Series
Actor, STAR WARS EPISODE II: ATTACK OF THE CLONES, 2002, 20th Century Fox, Feature
Actor, PRICE OF GLORY, 2000, New Line Cinema, Feature
Actor, MI FAMILIA/MY FAMILY, 1995, New Line, Feature
Actor, NYPD BLUE, 1994-98, 20th Century Fox, TV Series
Actor, LA LAW, 1986-91, 20th Century Fox, TV Series

Roberto Sneider
La Banda Films
Beverly Hills, CA 90211
Tel 310-858-7204
Email ....roberto@labandafilms.com
Web....................www.labandafilms.com

Producer, FRIDA, 2002, Miramax, Feature
Director, Producer, Writer, DOS CRIMENES, 1995, Behavior, Feature

Dulce Solis*
San Diego, CA 92104
Email ....dulcesact@yahoo.com

Daniel Somarriba*
Washigton D.C., DC 20008
Tel 202-342-1924
Email ....danielart80@yahoo.com

Antonio Sosa
Vice President
Warner Home Entertainment
Burbank, CA 91522
Tel 818-977-1313
Email ......antonio.sosa@warnerbros.com
Web ....www.warnerbros.com

Irene Sosa*
Jersey City, NJ 07302
Tel 201-792-5004
Email ....IreneSosa@aol.com

Camera, Director, Editor, Producer, SHOP-PING TO BELONG, 2005, Documentary
Producer, Editor, NANCY SPERO VIDEO ANTHOLOGY, 2004, Centro Galego de Arte Contemporanea, Anthology
Camerica, Director, Editor, Producer, PLAYING WITH LIGHTS, 2003, Irene Sosa, Documentary
Camerica, Director, Editor, Producer, SEXUAL EXILES, 1999, Free Speech TV, Documentary

Orlando Sosa*
Creative VP Creative Director
Bromley Communications
Key Biscayne, FL 33149
Tel 304-858-9495
Fax 305-854-3656
Email ....orlisosa@hotmail.com

Rosario Sotelo*
San Francisco, CA 94108
Tel 415-260-7903
Email.................sotelo24@hotmail.com

Director, FABRICATION, 2003, Short

Luis Soto

Cool Moss, Inc.
Los Angeles, CA 90028
Tel 323-969-9313

Manager: Nick Mechanic,
310-741-1966

Producer, VIETNAM WAR STORY: THE LAST
 DAYS, 1989, HBO, Feature
Producer, THE HOUSE OF RAMON IGLESIA,
 1986, PBS, TV Movie
Producer, THE EQUALIZER, 1985, CBS, TV
 Series
Director, FAME, 1982, NBC, TV Series

Carolina Sotola*

Jersey City, NJ 07306
Email ....csotola@yahoo.com

Alison Sotomayor*

Santa Monica, CA 90405
Tel 310-901-5939
Fax 562-402-8701
Email ....fiztek@aol.com

Chris Spirito*

asfilms
Tucson, AZ 85737
Tel 520-975-7637
Email ....cspirito@asfilms.com

Gustavo Stebner*

Stebner Studios
New York, NY 10001
Tel 646-271-7750
Email ....gs@stebnerstudios.com
Web ....www.stebnerstudios.com

Director, PELOTAS, 2005, Diamante
 Pictures, Feature
Writer, FEMMES DE BERLIN, 2004, Feature
Director, Producer, THE DARK MAGIC SHOW,
 2003-2004, The Magic of Rolando
 Medina, Documentary
Director, CHAQUETA, 2003, Aveneaux Films,
 Short
Director, THE AIR HOCKEY AFFAIR, 2002,
 Aveneaux Films, Short
Producer, A SU SALUD, 2000-2003,
 Univision, TV Series

Yamila Sterling*

Woodhaven, NY 11421
Tel 718-296-1976
Email ....ysterlin@hunter.cuny.edu

James Stevens-Arce*

Stevens/Palmer Creative Services, Inc.
San Juan, PR 00926-6129
Tel 787-720-6003
Tel 787-272-5730
Cell 787-720-6003
Email ....jstevens@prdigital.com
Web ....www.stevens-arce.com

Agent: Dan Hooker, Ashley Grayson
Literary Agency, 310-514-0267,
Dan_Hooker@hotmail.com

Writer, Actor, Co-Executive Producer,
 Co-Director, SOULS, 2005, Viguié Films,
 Short
Actor, CAYO, 2004, Producciones Paractuar,
 Feature
Actor, SEX, FOOD AND GUAGUANCO, 2004,
 Jotaerre Productions, Feature
Director, THEY'RE PLAYING OUR SONG,
 1981, Civic Theatre of San Juan, Stage
 Play
Writer, WHAT IS A PUERTO RICAN?, 1976,
 Connecticut Public Television, TV Series

Herta Suarez*

Director of Special Projects
AFTRA
Hollywood, CA 33020
Tel 954-920-2476
Fax 954-920-2560
Email ....hsuarez@aftra.com
Web ....www.aftra.org

Media Advocate

Rosanne Sweeney*

Tucson, AZ 85711
Email ....rosannesweeney@cox.net

Elizabeth Szekeresh*

Huntington Beach, CA 92648
Tel 714-856-7933
Email ....besobandit@yahoo.com

Gabriela Tagliavini

Venus Films
Los Angeles, CA 90201
Tel 310-717-1907
Cell 310-717-1907
Email ....gabbo_t@yahoo.com

*Agent: Carlos Carreras, UTA,
310-273-6700*

Manager: Todd Sharp, 323-558-0818

*Attorney: Todd Rubinstein,
310-319-3907*

Director, 30 DAYS UNTIL I'M FAMOUS,
   2004, VH1, TV Movie
Director, LADIES NIGHT, 2003,
   Disney/Buena Vista International, Feature
Director, Writer, THE WOMAN EVERY MAN
   WANTS, 2001, Independent, Feature

Monica Taher*

Los Angeles, CA 90036
Tel 323-634-2025
Email ....taher@glaad.org

Olga Talavera de Magana*

Del Rio, TX 78840
Tel 830-774-4288
Email...............yogaolga@delriolive.com

Dalia Tapia*

Dalia's Production Inc.
Chicago, IL 60608
Tel 773-847-3278
Cell 773-719-2543
Email................daliatapia@hotmail.com

Director, Producer, BUSCANDO A LETI,
   2005, Featrure
Director, Producer, CAMINO-PATH, 2004,
   Short
Director, Producer, ELLA, 2004, Short
Director, Producer, BUSCANDO A LETY,
   2001, Short

Miguel Tejada-Flores

Beverly Hills, CA 90211

*Agent: Mark Marshak, The
Marshak/Zachary Co., 310-358-3191,
alan@themzco.com*

Writer, WORST CASE SCENARIO, 2005,
   Feature
Writer, RUTTWEILER, 2004, Feature
Writer, BEYOND RE-ANIMATOR, 2003, Lions
   Gate Films, Feature
Writer, DARKNESS, 2002, Dimension Films,
   Feature
Writer, FAUST, 2001, TriMark Video, Feature
Writer, THE TIES THAT BIND, 2001,
   Universal Pictures, Feature

Rick Tejada-Flores*

Paradigm Productions
Berkeley, CA 94702
Tel 510-653-1250
Fax 510-848-5795
Email ......grtf@paradigmproductions.org
Web.........www.paradigmproductions.org

Director, NUESTRO HIJOS, 2005,
   Documentary
Director, Producer, Writer, RACE IS THE
   PLACE, 2005, Paradigm Productions,
   KERA Dallas Productions, Documentary
Director, Producer, Writer, THE GOOD WAR
   AND THOSE WHO REFUSED TO FIGHT IT,
   2000, ITVS, Documentary
Producer, NASCI MULHER NEGRA, 1999,
   Documentary
Director, Producer, Writer, THE FIGHT IN
   THE FIELDS, 1997, ITVS, Documentary

Sandra Tellado*

Mancha 'e Platano Productions
Torrance, CA 90504
Tel 310-515-6205
Tel 310-283-7289
Email ....sandratellado@hotmail.com

Raymond Telles*
Partner
Paradigm Productions
Berkeley, CA 94710
Tel 510-883-9814
Cell 510-912-6391
Fax 510-848-5795
Email........................Rto2900@aol.com
Web ....www.paradigmproductions.com

Director, Producer, RACE IS THE PLACE,
2004, Paradigm & KERA TV, Documentary
Director, Producer, CRITICAL CHOICES,
2003, NBC, Documentary
Director, Producer, MEMORIALS, 2002, ABC
Nightline, Documentary
Director, Producer, MIRACLE BABIES, 2002,
NBC, Documentary
Director, Producer, LIFE 360, 2001-2002,
PBS & ABC, Documentary
Director, Producer, EYE ON THE UNIVERSE,
2001, Discovery Networks Intl.,
Documentary
Director, Producer, THE FIGHT IN THE
FIELDS, 1997, Cinema Guild/Paradigm,
Documentary

Rick Telles
North Hollywood, CA 91601
Tel 818-288-1072
Email..........................rdtelles@aol.com
*Agent: Neil Stearns, Don Buchwald &
Associates, 323-655-7400*

Consultant Producer, BATTLE FOR OZ FEST,
2004, MTV, TV Series
Executive Producer, SURREAL LIFE SEASON
3, 4, 2004, VH1, TV Series
Executive Producer, HITCHHIKER CHRONI-
CLES, 2003, FX, TV Series
Executive Producer, NEXT ACTION STAR,
2003, NBC, TV Series
Executive Producer, SURF GIRLS, 2003,
MTV, TV Series
Executive Producer, SURREAL LIFE, 2002 ,
Warner Bros., TV Series

Steve Tellez
Agent
Creative Artists Agency (CAA)
Beverly Hills, CA 90212
Tel 310-288-4545
Fax 310-288-4800
Email ....stellez@caa.com
Web ....www.caa.com

Max Terronez*
Exposure Plus Enterprises
Pasadena, CA 91107
Tel 626-229-0353
Fax 626-229-0353
Email ....max@exposureplus.org
Web ....www.exposureplus.org

Mary Ann Thyken*
Director of Production
Independent Television Service
Walnut Creek, CA 94596
Tel........................415-356-8383 x249
Email ....maryann_thyken@itvs.org
Web ....www.itvs.org

David Ticotin
Calabasas, CA 91301
Tel 818-889-7768
Fax 818-889-7768
Email ....dnaticotin@aol.com

1st Assistant Director, HIDALGO, 2004,
Buena Vista Pictures, Feature
1st Assistant Director, THE CHRONICLES OF
RIDDICK, 2004, Universal Pictures,
Feature
2nd Assistant Director, COLLATERAL DAM-
AGE, 2002, Warner Bros., Feature

Candido Tirado*
Brooklyn, NY 11231
Tel 718-855-5117
Email ....ctasterisk@aol.com

Frances Tobler

AAA Studio Rentals
Los Angeles, CA 90004
Tel 323-751-4812
Fax 323-751-2415
Email......................aaarentals@aol.com
Web ....www.aaarentals.com

Production Services & Rentals

Lawrence Toledo*

Hope Street Productions
Tucson, AZ 85719-2369
Tel 520-319-2613
Cell 520-444-8523
Fax 520-327-7672
Email.................hsp2@mindspring.com
Web ....www.runninatmidnite.com

Producer, RUNNIN' AT MIDNITE, 2002,
Interaction Entertainment, Feature

Pablo Toledo*

Tucson, AZ 85719
Tel 520-319-2613
Cell 310-754-9725
Fax 520-327-7725
Web ....www.runninatmidnite.com

Director, Writer, RUNNIN' AT MIDNIGHT,
2002, Hope Street Productions, Feature

Mike Tolleson*

Attorney
Tolleson & Associates
Austin, TX 78702
Tel 512-480-8822
Fax 512-479-6212
Email...............mike@miketolleson.com

Michael Toribio*

GT Pictures/La Cinemafe Film Festival
Rockaway Park, NY 11694
Tel 917-662-1286
Tel 212-281-5786
Cell 917-662-1286
Fax 718-318-9085
Email........Bambinotoribio@hotmail.com
Web.......................www.lacinemafe.org

Armando Torres*

Music Composer
Alhambra, CA 91803
Tel 626-281-3621
Cell 626-524-8132
Email...........bondagemusic@yahoo.com
Web ....www.armando-torrres.com

Arranger, Orchestrator, Conductor, BENITO,
2004, Raul Portillo, Musical Short
Contributing Composer, Music Editor, HEY
PANCHO, THE LIFE AND TIMES OF
RICHARD ALONZO GONZALES, 2004,
Esparza/Katz, Higher Ground
Entertainment, Olmos Productions,
Documentary
Composer, LEAVE IT IN THE CAR, 2004,
Alex Torres, Short
Composer, TAXCO RESTAURANT, 2004, Alex
Torres, TV Commercial
Composer, UNSPOKEN, 2004, Temah
Nelson, Animated Short

Benjamin N. Torres*

Total AXIS
Beverly Hills, CA 90212
Tel 888-465-5488
Email ....info@totalaxis.com
Web........................www.totalaxis.com

David M. Torres*

Austin, TX 78704
Tel 512-448-5414
Email ....austinights@aol.com
Web........................www.austinights.tv

Fabiola Torres*

Ethnic Studies Professor
Glendale Community College
Glendale, CA 91208
Tel.................818-240-1000 ext 3940
Tel 323-953-2904
Fax 818-677-7578
Email ....cyberfabi@netscape.net
Web ....fabiolatorres@mac.com

Director, Producer, AMERICAN: QUOTE
UNQUOTE, 2004, Glendale Community
College, Instructional Video

Producer, "LISTEN TO THE MUSIC" FEAT.
RICHARD HUMPTY VISSION, 2004,
Solmatic Records, Music Video
Co-Producer, "MAKIN' NOISE", 2003-2004,
Darus Productions/Journeys, Music Video

Fina Torres
Beverly Hills, CA 90211

Agent: Rene Tab, ICM, 310-550-4000

Director, Executive Producer, WOMAN ON
TOP, 2000, Fox Searchlight Pictures,
Feature
Director, Producer, Writer, CELESTIAL
CLOCKWORK, 1995, October Films,
Bastille Films, Feature
Director, Producer, Writer, ORIANA, 1985,
Facets Video, Avion Productions, Feature

Jackie Torres*
Jackmar Entertainment
Toluca Lake, CA 91610
Tel 818-761-5725
Fax 818-761-5725
Email ....jackmar@jackietorres.com

Director, CROSSING FRONTIERS, 2005,
Jakmar Entertainment, Short
Writer, ATRAPAMOS BIN LADEN, 2004,
Jakmar Entertainment, Feature
Director, EAST LA KING, 2004, Amigo Films,
Feature
Director, Producer, Writer, THE PRICE OF
THE AMERICAN DREAM, 2002, Amigo
Films, Feature

Noemi Torres*
Beverly Hills, CA 90212
Tel 310-286-1107
Email...............exito98155@yahoo.com
Web ....www.co-locations.com

Roselly A. Torres-Rojas*
Latin American Video Archives
New York, NY 10014
Tel 212-243-4804
Fax 212-243-2007
Email ....rosellytorres@lavavideo.org
Web ....www.lavavideo.org

Andres Torres-Vives*
Santa Monica, CA 90404
Tel 310-666-7362
Email ....atorresv@ucla.edu

Frida Torresblanco
New York, NY 10013
Tel 212-219-7610
Fax 212-601-5916
Email ....frida_torresblanco@hotmail.com

Executive Producer, CRONICAS, 2004, Palm
Pictures, Feature
Executive Producer, THE ASSASSINATION
OF RICHARD NIXON, 2004, ThinkFilm
Inc., Feature
Pre-Production Supervisor, THE DANCER
UPSTAIRS, 2002, Fox Searchlight
Pictuers, Feature
Executive Producer, GAUDI AFTERNOON,
2001, filmauro Distribuzione, Feature
Line Producer, MERRY CHRISTMAS, 2001,
Lolafilms Distribution, Feature

Oskar Toruno*
West Covina, CA 91790
Tel 323-547-3687
Email...............oskartoruno@yahoo.com

Joseph Tovares
WGBH-TV
Belmont, MA 02478
Tel 617-300-5965
Tel 617-489-3710
Cell 617-803-3176
Fax 617-254-7535
Email ....joseph_tovares@comcast.net

Director, REMEMBER THE ALAMO, 2004,
PBS, Documentary
Director, Writer, THE ZOOT SUIT RIOTS,
2002, PBS, Documentary
Executive Producer, LA PLAZA, 2000-2004,
PBS, TV Series
Director, Writer, BREAKTHROUGH: THE
CHANGING FACE OF SCIENCE IN AMERI-
CA, 1996, PBS, Documentary

Bill Traut*
Pacific Palisades, CA 90272
Tel 310-459-2559
Email ....bill@opendoormanagement.com
Web ......www.opendorrmanagement.com

Jesús Salvador Treviño*
Barrio Dog Productions
Los Angeles, CA 90041
Email ....chuytrevino@earthlink.net
Web.....................www.chuytrevino.com

Agent: Jeffrey Wise, WMA,
310-859-4126

Director, CROSSING JORDAN, 2004, NBC,
　TV Series
Director, TRU CALLING, 2004, Fox Network,
　TV Series
Director, THE O.C., 2003, Fox Network, TV
　Series
Director, THE COURT, 2002, ABC, TV Series
Director, RESURRECTION BLVD., 2000,
　Showtime, TV Series
Director, THIRD WATCH, 1999, NBC, TV
　Series

Ela Troyano*
New York, NY 10009
Tel 212-979-0135
Tel 212-529-5976
Email ....etroyano@aol.com

Director, Producer, LA LUPE, 2004, ITVS,
　Documentary
Director, DELTA, 1997, Strand Releasing,
　Feature
Director, Writer, LATIN BOYS GO TO HELL,
　1997, Strand Releasing, Feature

Charley Trujillo
San Jose, CA 95112
Tel 408-947-0958
Fax 408-279-6381
Email ....chusmahouse@earthlink.net

Director, 3 SOLDADOS: CHICANOS IN VIET-
　NAM, 2002, PBS, Documentary

Susana Tubert
New York, NY 10011
Tel 212-691-3587
Cell 917-292-2361
Fax 212-229-2379
Email....................susanat725@aol.com
Web ..www.susanatubertproductions.com

Attorney: Roger Arar, Loeb & Loeb,
212-407-4906, rarar@loeb.com

Director, Producer, Writer, GYPSY GIRL,
　2003, Short
Director, 4 GUYS NAMED JOSE... AND UNA
　MUJER NAMED MARIA!, 2000, Stage Play
Director, THE GUIDING LIGHT, SEGMENT
　DIR., 2000, CBS, TV Series

William Tucker*
Blackwood, NJ 08012
Tel 856-228-3432
Fax 856-964-2920
Email ....wtucker3290@comcast.net

Joui Turandot*
San Francisco, CA 94115
Email ....joitt@hotmail.com

Donna Umali*
Sampaguita Productions
Orange, CA 92867
Tel 206-818-6176
Email ....lildonna@hotmail.com

Director, REALITY CHECK, 2004, Chapman
　University School of Film and Television,
　Short

Pepe Urquijo*
Bandido Productions
San Francisco, CA 94102
Tel 415-550-9093
Email ....pepe@pepelicula.com
Web ....www.pepelicula.com

Producer, ATREVATE, 2003, Music Video
Producer, FRUIT OF LABOR, 2003, Feature
Producer, PIMPIN FRUIT, 2003, Short
Producer, EVERYDAY EASTLAKE, 2001,
　Short

filmmakers

Producer, BECA DE GILAS: REBECA'S
STORY, 1999, Subcine.com, Documentary
Producer, ALGUN DIA, 1998, Subcine.com,
Short

Dawn Valadez*
Vaquera Films
San Leandro, CA 94577
Tel 510-326-0309
Cell..same
Email ....dawn@agirlslife.org
Web............................www.agirlslife.org

Attorney: Alan Korn, aakorn@igc.org

Director, Producer, A GIRL'S LIFE, 2005,
Documentary
Director, Producer, CONFIDENT PARENTING,
1991, SFDPH, Industrials
Director, Producer, HIJAS DE RAMONA,
1989, Cine Accion, Documentary

John Valadez*
Valadez Inc.
Dix Hills, NY 11746
Tel 516-810-7238
Email ....johnjvaladez@aol.com
Web ....www.valadez.tv

Director, Producer, Writer, THE HEAD OF
JOAQUIN MURRIETA, 2006, LPB,
Documentary
Director, Producer, THE LAST CONQUISTA-
DOR, 2006, PBS, Documentary
Director, Producer, Writer, HIGH STAKES
TESTING, 2005, CNN, Documentary
Segment Writer, Director, BEYOND BROWN:
PURSUING THE PROMISE, 2004, PBS,
Documentary
Segment Producer, VISIONES: LATINO ARTS
&CULTURE, 2004, PBS, Documentary
Director, Producer, MATTERS OF RACE: THE
DIVIDE, 2003, PBS, Documentary

Marta Valadez*
San Antonio, TX 78250
Tel 210-522-1869
Email ....valadez_marta@netzero.net

David C. Valdes**
Tarzana, CA 91335
Email.................Summermagi@aol.com

*Attorney: Lichter, Grossman, Nichols,
Adler, Inc., 310-205-6999*

Producer, OPEN RANGE, 2003, Buena Vista
Pictures, Feature
Producer, TIME MACHINE, 2002, Warner
Bros., Feature
Producer, THE GREEN MILE, 1999, Warner
Bros., Feature
Producer, TURBULENCE, 1997, MGM,
Feature
Producer, STARS FELL ON HENRIETTA,
1995, Warner Bros., Feature
Executive Producer, IN THE LINE OF FIRE,
1993, Columbia TriStar, Feature
Executive Producer, UNFORGIVEN, 1992,
Warner Home Video, Feature
Producer, THE ROOKIE, 1990, Warner Bros.,
Feature
Executive Producer, WHITE HUNTER, BLACK
HEART, 1990, Warner Bros., Feature

Leslie Valdes
Walsh/Valdes Productions Inc.
Santa Monica, CA 90403
Cell 310-428-6596
Fax 310-587-1538
Email................alphabest@earthlink.net

*Agent: Angela Cheng Caplan, Cheng
Caplan Company Inc., 323-993-1988,
angela@chengcaplanco.com*

*Attorney: Fred D. Toczek, Nelson Felker
LLP, 310-441-8000*

Writer, HANDY MANNY, 2005, Disney
Television, TV Series, Animated
Co-creater, Writer, SHIN SHIN, 2005, Disney
Television, TV Series, Animated
Writer, THE BACKYARDIGANS, 2004,
Nickelodeon, TV Series, Animated
Writer, RUBBADUBBERS, 2003-2004,
Simon Spotlight, Books
Writer, DORA THE EXPLORER, 2002-2004,
Simon Spotlight, Book Series
Writer, DORA THE EXPLORER, 1999-2004,
Nickelodeon, TV Series, Animated

Anahuac Valdez*
Chicanos on the Run Productions
San Juan Bautista, CA 95045
Tel 831-623-2444
Fax 831-623-4127
Email ......anahuac_valdez@hotmail.com

Blanca Valdez
Blanca Valdez Casting
West Hollywood, CA 90046
Tel 323-876-5700
Fax 323-876-5297

Casting Director, Producer, EAST SIDE
STORY, 2005, Feature
Casting Director, VIVA VEGAS, 2000,
Telemundo Network, TV Series
Casting Director, LOS BELTRAN, 1999,
Telemundo Networks, TV Series

Jeff Valdez**
Chairman
Si TV
Los Angeles, CA 90065
Tel 323-256-8900
Fax 323-256-9888
Web ....www.sitv.com

Executive Producer, ACROSS THE HALL,
2004, Si TV, TV Series
Executive Producer, THE DROP, 2004, Si TV,
TV Series
Executive Producer, THE RUB, 2004, Si TV,
TV Series
Executive Producer, URBAN JUNGLE, 2004,
Si TV, TV Series
Executive Producer, Writer, THE BROTHERS
GARCIA, 2000-2004, Nickelodeon, TV
Series
Producer, Writer, CAFE OLE', 1997, Si TV, TV
Series
Producer, Writer, FUNNY IS FUNNY, 1997,
Galavision Television, TV Series
Producer, LATINO LAUGH FESTIVAL, 1997,
Showtime & Comedy Central, TV Special

Luis Valdez
Artistic Director
El Teatro Campesino
San Juan Bautista, CA 95045
Tel 831-623-2444
Email..........luis@elteatrocampesino.com
Web ....www.elteatrocampesino.com

*Agent: Joan Scott, Paradigm,
323-866-0900*

Director, Writer, THE CISCO KID, 1994,
Esparza/ Katz Productions, Feature
Director, Writer, LA PASTORELA, 1991,
Richard Soto Productions, TV Series
Director, Writer, LA BAMBA, 1987, Columbia
Pictures, Feature
Director, CHICANO STORY, 1982, Feature
Director, ZOOT SUIT, 1982, Universal
Pictures, Feature

Lupe Valdez*
Anteros Films
Austin, TX 78704
Email ....keiser_lupe@yahoo.com

Maria Valdez*
La Puente, CA 91746
Tel 818-980-0203
Email...............maria@mariavaldez.com

Actor, Producer, MOMMY, HOW MUCH DO
YOU MAKE AN HOUR?, 2005, Short

Ann Marie Valdivia*
Tucson, AZ 85711
Email ....annavaldivia@yahoo.com

Mabel Valdiviezo*
Bay Area Video Coalition
San Francisco, CA 94109
Tel 415-614-9697
Email.....................haikufilms@aol.com
Web.................www.soledadforever.com

Editor, FRUIT OF LABOR, 2003, Bandido
Productions, Documentary
Editor, GOOD MORNING MS. KELLEY!,
2001, Hybrid Productions, Documentary
Director, Editor, THE WATER'S MUSE, 2000,
Matahari Films, Short
Educator

filmmakers

Maribel Valdiviezo*
San Francisco, CA 94133
Tel 415-788-2230
Email ....matahripost@aol.com

Hanley Valentin*
North Hollywood, CA 91607
Tel 818-769-6364
Email ....etsee1@yahoo.com

Pablo Valentin*
Artesia, CA 90701
Email ......PanamaMaverick@hotmail.com

Jose Luis Valenzuela
Sleeping Giant Productions
Los Angeles, CA 90022
Tel 310-206-7291
Email ....SleepingGiantPro@aol.com

Director, Producer, LUMINARIAS, 2000, New
    Latin Pictures, Feature

Yvette Valenzuela*
San Diego, CA 92101
Tel 619-851-5627
Email ....evesandiego@hotmail.com

Christian van Oordt*
Marina del Rey, CA 90292
Email ..christianvanoordt@global.t-bird.edu

Deon Van Rooyen*
San Antonio, TX 78258
Tel 210-479-9234
Cell 210-846-2768
Email ....vanroogena@yahoo.com

Director, Writer, TKO, 2004, Short

Ethan Van Thillo*
Festival Director
San Diego Latino Film Festival
San Diego, CA 92102
Tel 619-230-1938
Email ....ethan@mediaartscenter.org
Web ....www.mediaartscenter.org

Myra Varadi*
Pigeon Post Films
Rego Park, NY 11374
Tel 718-459-7229
Fax 212-496-0047
Email ....myravaradi@aol.com

Laura Varela*
San Antonio Films
San Antonio, TX 78221
Tel 210-226-5307
Tel 210-977-8567
Cell 210-842-3787
Email ....ixcheli@aol.com

Director, Producer, AS LONG AS I REMEM-
    BER: AMERICAN VETERANOS, 2004, San
    Antonio Filmmakers, Documentary
Producer, TEXAS MAJORITY MINORITY,
    2004, Swell Cinema Anne Lewis
    Productions, Documentary
Associate Producer, A SLIGHT DISCOMFORT,
    2002, Potential Productions, Experimental
Transportation Coordinator, EVANHAND,
    2001, Cypress Films, Feature
Associate Producer, IMMIGRANT STORIES
    OF SURVIVAL, 2001, Political Asylum
    Project Austin, Educational
Director, Producer, HISTORIA-TEATRO
    HUMANIDAD, 2000, Teatro Humanidad,
    Industrial, Educational

Rosadel Varela
New York, NY 10001
Email ....varelar@noujaimfilms.com

Producer, CONTROL ROOM, 2004, Magnolia
    Pictures, Documentary
DGA Trainee, LAW AND ORDER, 2001, NBC,
    TV Series
DGA Trainee, RIDING IN CARS WITH BOYS,
    2001, Columbia Pictures, Feature
DGA Trainee, SEX AND THE CITY, 2000,
    HBO, TV Series

DGA Trainee, SHAFT, 2000, Paramount
   Pictures, Feature
Producer, 1996-1998, MTV News and Docs,
   TV Series

Adolfo Vargas*
SteamVision
Pomona, CA 91768
Tel 909-979-6309
Fax 909-979-6304
Email..............arvargas@csupomona.edu
Web ....www.video.csupomona.edu

Director, Producer, YANOMAMI, 1992, Video
   Project, Documentary
Director, Producer, EL ESPEJO, 1990, PBS,
   Documentary
Producer, Writer, INFINITY FACTORY, 1990,
   PBS, TV Series
Director, LATINO NAVAL OFFICERS, 1990,
   U.S. Navy, Documentary

Adrian Vargas*
Casa Vargas Productions
San Jose, CA 95116
Tel 408-314-2284
Email ....info@casa-vargas.com

Benjamin Vargas*
Santa Monica, CA 90404
Tel 310-453-2315

Pepe Vargas
Festival Director
Chicago International Latino Film
Festival
Chicago, IL 60605
Tel 312-413-1330
Tel 312-344-8030
Email ....pvargas@latinoculturalcenter.org
Web ....www.latinoculturalcenter.org

Rosie Vargas Goldberg*
Whatever Films, Inc.
Chicago, IL 60614
Tel 773-296-1139
Tel 312-909-1139
Email ....rosie@whateverfilms.com
Web ....www.whateverfilms.com

Co-Producer, I'M A FEMALE SEEKING A
   MALE, 2005, New Horizon Entertainment,
   Stage Play
Executive Producer, HOPELESS, 2004,
   Feature

Emmanuel Vargas-Ocasio*
San Juan, PR 00907
Tel 787-671-9808
Email ....emmisgroup@yahoo.com

Carlos Anibal Vazquez*
San Juan, PR 00911
Email.................carlosanibalV@aol.com

Gustavo Vazquez*
San Francisco, CA 94112
Tel 415-585-6984
Email ....gustavo@exploratorium.edu

Tontxi Vazquez*
Executive Director
Stooppix
London, SE41QX England
Tel 44-02-08-69-96-700
Email ....sarumsircle@yahoo.com
Web........................www.stoppix.free.fr

Producer, OUR VOICE, 2003, MGV
   Productions, Short
Producer, RIFTS, 2003, Short
Production Assistant, ACTS OF WORSHIP,
   2002, Manifesto Films, Feature
Producer, DEVRY INSTITUTE, 2001, Brown
   Advertising, Commericial
Producer, CHARCOAL, 2000, UB
   Productions, Short
Production Assistant, PERFUME, 2000,
   Manifesto Films/ Lions Gate, Feature

Astrid M. Vega*

Astrid Creative Endeavors, Inc.
Aventura, FL 33160
Tel 305-932-3643
Cell 305-776-2819
Fax 305-932-3643
Email ....acenalip@yahoo.com
Web ....www.geocities.com/
astrid_creative_endeavors

Art Direction, ETHAN'S PARABLES ON DVD:
ETHAN & GOLIATH, 2004, Alpha Omega
Publications, Direct to DVD
Assistant Producer, Coordinator, LINDSEY
HOPKINS TECHNICAL EDUCATION CEN-
TER, 2004, Jill Beach Productions,
Promotional Video
Translator, Writer, SUPER SPLASH WATER-
PARK, 2003, Super Splash Waterpark,
Edinburg, TX, Radio & TV Advertising
Writer, AL ROJO VIVO, 2002, Telemundo,
NBC, TV Show

Carmen Vega*

Los Angeles, CA 90006
Tel 213-694-2032
Email ....Cvpoema@hotmail.com

Mirtha Vega*

Aeria-Vega Productions, LLC
Sausalito, CA 94966
Tel 415-892-4790
Fax 415-892-4790
Email ....eaglesoar_prod@hotmail.com

Director, TRYST, 2003, Feature

Yvette Vega*

Yvette Vega Productions
Island Park, NY 11558
Tel 516-526-3077
Email ....reelcelebrities@aol.com
Web ....www.reelcelebrities.tv

Producer, IN SEARCH OF MY CULTURAL
HEROES, 2003, Latin USA Film Festival,
Documentary
Producer, REEL CELEBRITIES, 2003,
www.reelcelebrities.tv, TV Special
Producer, MY ANGEL ANGELICA, 2002,
Tribeca Film Center, Short

Diego Velasco*

Subcultura
Hollywood, CA 90028
Tel 323-462-1432
Cell 310-927-5291
Email ....diego@subcultura.tv
Web ....www.subcultura.tv

Director, Writer, DAY - SHIFT, 2005, Fox
Searchlab, Short
Director, Writer, LOOKING FOR CHARITY,
2002, Short
Director, FRUTISIMA, 2001, Commercial
Director, NESTLE VXLA, 2001, Commercial
Director, PLANETA DE SEIS, 2001, Televen
(Venezuela), TV Series
Director, Writer, CEDULA CIUDADANO,
2000, HBO, Atom Films, Short

Jerry Velasco*

President
Nosotros
Hollywood, CA 90004
Tel 323-466-8566
Fax 323-466-8540
Email ....velascojgv@aol.com

Award Shows
Media Advocate
Actor

Marlene Velasco

Programming Coordinator
ITVS
San Francisco, CA 94110
Tel........................415-356-8383 x232
Fax 415-356-8391
Email ....marlene_velasco@itvs.org
Web ....www.itvs.org

Aram Velazquez*

Miami, FL 33186
Cell 786-295-8727
Email.....................eramix@eramix.com
Web ....www.eramix.com

Director, Editor, OMISSION, 2004, Eramix
Productions Inc., Feature
Graphic Designer

Laura Velez
Director
Puerto Rico Film Commision
Hato Rey, PR 00918
Tel......................787-758-4747 x2251
Tel 787-754-7110
Fax 787-756-5706
Email ....lavelez@pridco.com
Web ....www.puertoricofilm.com

Cristina Venegas*
Professor
University of California, Santa Barbara
Santa Barbara, CA 93106
Tel 805-563-4506
Email ......venegas@filmstudies.ucsb.edu

Jorge Vergara
Apuesta Pictures
Los Angeles, CA 90048
Tel 323-936-2110
Fax 323-525-2721
Email ....victorguerra@earthlink.net

Producer, MEXICO '68, 2005, Feature
Producer, CRONICAS, 2004, Palm Pictures,
   Feature
Producer, ASSASSINATION OF RICHARD
   NIXON, 2003, Focus, Feature
Producer, AND YOUR MOTHER TOO, 2001,
   MGM, Feature
Producer, THE DEVIL'S BACKBONE, 2001,
   Columbia TriStar Home Entertainment,
   Feature

Christina Vergara-Andrews*
Ozark Productions
Los Angeles, CA 90034
Tel 310-836-6356
Email ....CVergaraAndrews@aol.com

Jose Vicuña
President
Plural Entertainment
Madrid, 28013 Spain
Tel 34-91-515-9280
Fax 34-91-515-9140
Email.................jvicuna@pluralent.com

Camilo Vila*
Venice, CA 90291
Tel 310-396-4301
Email ....olimac@comcast.net

Director, 18 WHEELS OF JUSTICE, 2000,
   Stu Segall Productions Inc., TV Series
Director, RESURRECTION BLVD., 2000,
   Showtime, TV Series
Director, UNLAWFUL PASSAGE, 1994,
   Seban Entertainment, Feature
Director, OPTIONS, 1988, Vestron Pictures,
   Feature
Director, THE UNHOLY, 1988, Vestron
   Pictures, Feature

Irene Vilar*
Evergreen, CO 80439
Tel 303-697-7724
Tel 303-697-7724
Email ....americas@uwpress.wisc.edu
Web ....www.wisc.edu/wisconsinpress

Miguel Villafañe*
JKL Films
San Juan, PR 00923
Tel 787-753-1881
Email ....jmv333@aol.com

Ligiah Villalobos
Jalapeno Films
West Hollywood, CA 90046

Agent: WMA, 310-859-4000

Writer, GO, DIEGO GO!, 2005, Nickelodeon,
   TV Series
Producer, Writer, ONE WORLD, 2001,
   Documentary
Co-Producer, DANCING IN SEPTEMBER,
   2000, HBO, Feature
Writer, ED, 2000, NBC, TV Series

filmmakers

Reynaldo Villalobos
Santa Barbara, CA 93101
Tel 805-745-8784
Fax 805-745-8804
Email ....debsamuel@aol.com

Director of Photography, SPLINTER, 2005,
Stonehenge Productions, Feature
Director of Photography, JACK AND MARI-
LYN, 2002, Feature
Director of Photography, JUWANNA MANN,
2002, Warner Bros., Feature
Director of Photography, WELCOME TO
AMERICA, 2002, Risk Entertainment,
Feature
Director of Photography, NOT ANOTHER
TEEN MOVIE, 2001, Columbia Pictures,
Feature

Luis Villanueva
President
Venevision International
Coral Gables, FL 33134
Tel 305-442-3411
Fax 305-448-4762
Web ....www.venevisioninternational.com

Raymond Villareal*
San Antonio, TX 78245
Email ....rv5555@yahoo.com

Alicia Villarreal*
Vamos Productions
Riviera, TX 78379
Tel 361-595-5205

Roberto Villarreal*
Vamos Productions
Riviera, TX 78379
Tel 361-595-5205

Viviane Vives*
Barcelona Films
Austin, TX 78704
Cell 512-443-5643
Fax 512-443-5143
Email ....vvv@barcelonafilms.com
Web ....www.barcelonafilms.com

Associate Producer, DEAR PILLOW, 2004,
Switch Film, Feature
Director, CHISHOLM TRAIL, 2002, Barcelona
Films, Documentary
Director, BRAVTON FIELD, 2001, Barcelona
Films, Documentary

Vlamyr Vizcaya*
The Latino Group, El Tuerto Pictures
New York, NY 10002
Tel 212-475-6601
Tel 310-593-4606
Fax 877-764-4783
Email ....Vlamyr@TheLatinoGroup.com
Web ....www.thelatinogroup.com

Director, ESTE AMOR, 2005, Music Video
Writer, NO WAY JÓSE, 2005, El Tuerto
Pictures, Feature
2nd Unit Director, Producer, VIOLET OF A
THOUSAND COLORS, 2005, The Latino
Group, Feature
Director, Writer, OUT OF LOVE - A VIDEO
DIARY, 2004, El Tuerto Pictures, The
Latino Group, Feature
Director, TEATRO SEA, 2004, The Latino
Group, TV Commercial
Editor, Producer, LA INDIA, 2003, The Latino
Group, Short

Kristine Wallis
Agent
The Wallis Agency
Burbank, CA 91505
Tel 818-953-4848
Fax 818-845-2437
Email.................info@wallisagency.com
Web ....www.wallisagency.com

Jennifer Warren*
Evergreen, CO 80439
Email ....benjean2@earthlink.net

Kirk Whisler*
President
Latino Print Network
Carlsbad, CA 92008
Tel 760-434-7474
Email..........................kirk@whisler.com
Web ....www.latinoprintnetwork.com

Hispanic Marketing Consultant, AMERICAN
ME, 1992, Universal, Feature
Media Director, STAND AND DELIVER, 1988,
Warner Bros., Feature
Media Director, BALLAD OF GREGORIO
CORTEZ, 1983, Embassy Pictures, Feature

Cheryl Williams*
ReArt Consultant
New York, NY 10023
Tel 212-969-0440
Email ....neptuneprods@hotmail.com

Michael Wimer
Agent
Creative Artists Agency (CAA)
Beverly Hills, CA 90212
Tel 310-288-4545
Fax 310-288-4800
Email ....mwimer@caa.com
Web ....www.caa.com

Peggy Wintermute
Agent
Wintermute Talent Agency
Beverly Hills, CA 90210
Tel 310-385-8487
Email ....pwintermute@arrow.com

Matt Wolf*
Acuna Entertainment
Sherman Oaks, CA 91423
Tel 818-501-1072
Email......matt@acunaentertainment.com

Manager

Alex Wolfe*
Mambo Media
Brooklyn, NY 11211
Tel 718-388-0350
Email........alex@santodomingoblues.com
Web ....www.santodomingoblues.com

Director, Writer, ROCK EN ESPANOL, 2005,
Arenas Entertainment, Feature
Director, Producer, SANTO DOMING BLUES:
LOS TIGUERES DE LA BACHATA, 2005,
Empire Pictures, Documentary
Director of Photography, Producer, REAL
WEDDING FROM KNOT, 2004, Oxygen
Media, TV Show
Producer, THE FIRST 48, 2004, A & E, TV
Program
Producer, TROVADOR, 2003, WNET Public
TV, Feature
Director, Producer, OFF THE CHARTS, 2002,
WNET Public TV, TV Segment

Ginny Wolnowics*
Cosmoflix
Sunny Isles Beach, CA 33160
Tel 786-286-6669
Cell...same
Fax 305-947-4549
Email ....Ginnydom@aol.com

US Locations Manager, AMERICA, 2004, TV
Globo, TV Series
Location Manager, OOWIE MUSIC VIDEO,
2004, BRK Entertainment, Music Video
Production Manager, PEPSI MUSICA, 2004,
Forti Layne, TV Series
US Locations Manager, WRP, 2004, WRP, TV
Series
Production Manager, Location Manager, FILO
DE LA LEY, 2003, Plural Entertainment,
TV Series Pilot

Vince Wright*
Infinity Unltd. Productions/Wright Films
buellton, CA 93427
Tel 805-688-4691
Cell 805-245-0157
Email........wrightfilms@macconnect.com
Web ....www.wrightfilms.com

Producer, Director, Unit Photography, WEL-
COME HOME EDDY, 2004, Landmark
Productions, Short

filmmakers

Writer, JOB CAST, 2000-2004, NJN Public TV, TV Series
Host, Producer, JOBCAST, 2000-2004, Non Public TV, TV Series
Writer, CLASSROOM CLOSE UP, 1997-2000, NJEA, Fox 29, UPN 9, TV Series
Host, Producer, CLASSROOM CLOSE UP, NJ, 1997-2000, NJEA, Fox 29, UPN9, TV Series

Karin Yanes*
Tucson, AZ 85745
Email ....kty@email.arizona.edu

Yvette Yates
Payaso Entertainment
Hollywood, CA 90038
Tel 323-956-3822
Fax 323-862-2148
Email ....yvettey@usa.net
Web ....www.payasoentertainment.com

Producer, SHRINKING SANTA FE, 2005, Feature
Producer, THE ORIGINAL LATIN DIVAS OF COMEDY, 2005, Concert Film
Producer, WARRIORS SONG, 2005, Feature

Christopher Ybarra*
Aurora, CO 80013
Tel 303-918-2592

Edgar Ybarra*
Tucson, AZ 85746
Email.................jan0194@hotmail.com

Edward Ybarra*
Sierra Cinema
Bonita, CA 91908
Tel 619-472-2830
Cell 619-890-9748
Fax 619-472-2830
Email ....eywriter@juno.com

Director, Writer, BROTHER M, 2004, Documentary
Camera, MAJOR LEAGUE BASEBALL, 2004, ESPN & Local San Diego, Live Event
Director, Writer, BREAK!, 2003, Short

Camera, ATLANTA OLYMPIC GAMES, 1998, All Olympic Broadcasting, Live Event
Camera, WORLD BASKETBALL CHAMP., 1998, Turner Network Sports, Live Event

Raquel Ybes*
Miami, FL 33145
Tel 305-856-2929
Email.........................rapyl@yahoo.com

Gabriela Yepes*
Austin, TX 78751
Email ....buenagaby@mail.utexas.edy

Raquel Yepes*
Buresa Media
Miami, FL 33145
Tel 305-856-2929
Cell 786-303-6193
Fax 305-858-0357
Email.........................rapyl@yahoo.com
Web....................www.buresamedia.com

Production Coordinator Manager, TODOBEBE, 2004/2003, Telemundo Network, TV Special
Associate Producer, SOMOS, 2004/2002, Bures Media, Documentary
Production Coordinator Manager, DELICIOSO, 2004, Cosmopolitan Channel, TV Special
Co-Producer, FURIAS DE LAS BESTIAS, 2004, Bures Media/Television De Galicia TVG (Espana), Documentary
Production Coordinator, SEXY BRASIL, 2004, Pigeon Production/Getty Imagen Bank, Stock Footage
Production Coordinator, Researcher, DISCOVERY HEALTH CAPSULES, 2003, Discovery Network Latin America, 3MIN Capsulas

Craig Young*
Brooklyn, NY 11211
Email ....grendelent@aol.com

Guillermina Zabala

San Antonio, TX 78209
Tel 210-822-0534
Cell 323-691-0927
Email ....guillita@aol.com

Director, Editor, UN TANGO PARA EL EXILIO, 2005, Cine del Sur, Documentary
Editor, CHALINO SANCHEZ, UNA VIDA DE PELIGROS, 2004, Image Entertainment, Documentary DVD
Editor, KORDAVISION, 2004, Halo Group, Documentary
Editor, LA CONEXION (MUN2), 2004, Pefect Image, TV Program

Alex Zacarias*

3N Productions, LLC
Greenbay, WI 54302
Tel 920-468-7564
Cell 920-265-0011
Fax 920-465-1788
Email ....alexzacarias@hotmail.com

Director, Producer, COLORS OF SUCCESS, 2994, 3N Productions, PSA
Director, Producer, ANGELS IN HEARTLAND, 2004, 3N Productions, Documentary
Producer, TALK, 2004, 3N Producitons, PSA
Editor, CAN YOU SEE MY PAIN, 2002, Wisconsin Public TV, Documentary
Editor, Producer, CULTURAL HORIZONS OF WI, 2002, Wisconsin Public TV, TV Series

Juan Carlos Zaldivar

90 Miles, LLC
Miami, FL 33139
Tel 305-532-8110
Email ....jucamaza@aol.com

Producer, ONCE THERE WAS A COUNTRY: REVISITING HAITI, 2005, Longstocking Productions, Documentary
Director, Producer, SOLDIERS PAY, 2004, Cinema Libre, Documentary
Director, Producer, 90 MILES, 2003, POV, Documentary
Director, STORY OF THE RED ROSE, 1998, Feature
Director, PALINGENESIS, 1989, Feature

Del Zamora

Los Angeles, CA
Tel 213-387-1315
Email ....delzamora@hotmail.com

Director, Writer, CHANNEL 0, 1999, Pocho Productions, TV Series
Director, Writer, FRIDA KAHLO IN THE CASA AZUL, 1996, Rampage Productions, Short
Producer, I'LL BE HOME FOR CHRISTMAS, 1991, Universal Pictures, Feature

Thomas Zamora*

Los Angeles, CA 90007
Tel 213-700-9179
Email ....tomzamora@hotmail.com

Patricia Zapata*

San Antonio, TX 78229
Tel 210-615-6540
Email ....pzapata@
     texasindependentfilmmakers.org

Gloria Susan Zarate*

Alhambra, CA 91803
Tel 626-536-4609
Email ....glorie2g@aol.com

Director, Producer, Writer, CLIPPING OF FLOWERS, 2004, Short

Jacqueline Zepeda*

San Antonio, TX 78212
Tel 305-532-8110
Email........jacqueline.zepeda@trinity.edu

Nicole Zepeda*

San Juan, TX 78705
Tel 956-460-4095
Tel 956-781-6226
Email......nicole.zepeda@mail.utexas.edu

Art Department, Script Supervisor, DOT, 2004, Burnt Orange Productions, Feature
Art Department, Script Supervisor, HARVEST OF REDEMPTION, 2004, Virtual Productions, Feature
Writer, NIGHTMARE ON AIDS STREET, 2004, Scenarios USA, Short

filmmakers

Production Assistant, TOOTHPASTE, 2004,
    Scenarios USA, Short
Script Supervisor, ENTRE DOS TIERRAS,
    2002, Raymond Lopez, Short

Tony Zertuche*

Brooklyn, NY 11201
Tel 212-714-3113
Cell 917-971-1607
Email ....tony.zertuche@hotmail.com

Monica Zevallos

Account Executive Latin Market
Ascent Media
Santa Monica, CA 91404
Tel 310-434-6529
Cell 323-547-0337
Fax 310-434-6511
Email ....mzevallos@ascentmedia.com

Esteban Zul*

Pocho Productions
Los Angeles, CA 90027
Fax 213-380-0378
Email ....badoso@aol.com

Writer, PACO'S SUITCASE BOMB, 2002, Fox
    Searchlab, Short
Writer, TACO TRUCK: THE MOVIE, 2002,
    New Line, Feature

Marcos Zurinaga

Miramar Films
Beverly Hills, CA 90212
Tel 787-753-1935

Executive Producer, MODIGLIANI, 2004,
    Feature
Director, Producer, CON LA MUSICA POR
    DENTRO, 1999, Documentary
Director, Producer, ROMANCE DEL CUM-
    BANCHERO, 1998, Documentary
Director, AL COMPAS DE UN SENTIMIENTO,
    1996, Documentary
Director, Producer, Writer, TANGO BAR,
    1988, Manley Films/Beco Films, Feature

Pedro Zurita

Executive Director
Videoteca del Sur
New York, NY 10009
Tel 212-674-5405
Fax 212-614-0464
Email....................VidelSur.96@aol.com

National Association of Latino Independent Producers

production
resources

courtesy of the
Hollywood Creative Directory

STUDIOS

The Walt Disney Company
500 S. Buena Vista St.
Burbank, CA 91521
Phone   818-560-1000
www.disney.com

DreamWorks SKG
1000 Flower St.
Glendale, CA 91201
Phone   818-695-5000
www.dreamworks.com

Metro-Goldwyn-Mayer (MGM)
10250 Constellation Blvd.
Los Angeles, CA 90067
Phone   310-449-3000
www.mgm.com

Miramax Films
New York
375 Greenwich St.
New York, NY 10013-2338
Phone   212-941-3800

Los Angeles
8439 Sunset Blvd.
West Hollywood, CA 90069
Phone 323-822-4100
www.miramax.com

New Line Cinema
116 N. Robertson Blvd., Ste. 200
Los Angeles, CA 90048
Phone   310-854-5811
www.newline.com

Paramount Pictures
5555 Melrose Ave.
Los Angeles, CA 90038-3197
Phone   323-956-5000
www.paramount.com

Sony Pictures Entertainment
10202 W. Washington Blvd.
Culver City, CA 90232-3195
Phone   310-244-4000
www.sony.com

Twentieth Century Fox
10201 W. Pico Blvd.
Los Angeles, CA 90035
Phone   310-369-1000
         310-FOX-INFO
www.foxstudios.com

Universal Pictures
100 Universal City Plaza
Universal City, CA 91608-1085
Phone   818-777-1000
www.universalstudios.com

Warner Bros.
4000 Warner Blvd.
Burbank, CA 91522-0001
Phone   818-954-6000
www.warnerbros.com

NETWORKS AND MAJOR CABLE CHANNELS

ABC
500 S. Buena Vista St.
Burbank, CA 91521
Phone   818-460-7777
www.abc.com

CBS
7800 Beverly Blvd.
Los Angeles, CA 90036-2188
Phone   323-575-2345
www.cbs.com

Fox
10201 W. Pico Blvd.
Los Angeles, CA 90035
Phone   310-369-1000
www.fox.com

HBO
1100 Avenue of the Americas
New York, NY 10036
Phone   212-512-1000
www.hbo.com

NBC
3000 W. Alameda Ave.
Burbank, CA 91523-0001
Phone   818-840-4444
www.nbc.com

PBS
1320 Braddock Pl.
Alexandria, VA 22314-1698
Phone   703-739-5000
www.pbs.org

Showtime
1633 Broadway
New York, NY 10019
Phone   212-708-1600
www.sho.com

UPN
11800 Wilshire Blvd.
Los Angeles, CA 90025
Phone   310-575-7000
www.upn.com

The WB Television Network
4000 Warner Blvd., Bldg. 34-R
Burbank, CA 91522-0001
Phone   818-977-5000
www.thewb.com

STATE FILM COMMISSIONS

ALABAMA
Alabama Film Office
401 Adams Ave., Ste. 630
Montgomery, AL 36104
Phone   334-242-4195
Fax   334-242-2077
www.alabamafilm.org
Brenda Hobbie – Film Office Coordinator

ALASKA
Alaska Film Program
550 W. Seventh Ave., Ste. 1770
Anchorage, AK 99501-3510
Phone   907-269-8190
Fax   907-269-8125
www.alaskafilm.org
Shelley James - Director

ARIZONA
Arizona Film Commission
1700 W. Washington St., Ste. 220
Phoenix, AZ 85007
Phone   602-771-1193
            800-523-6695
Fax   602-771-1211
www.azcommerce.com
Harry Tate - Director

ARKANSAS
Arkansas Film Office
One Capitol Mall, Ste. 4B-505
Little Rock, AR 72201
Phone   501-682-7676
Fax   501-682-3456
www.1-800-arkansas.com
Joe Glass - Film Commissioner

CALIFORNIA
California Film Commission
7080 Hollywood Blvd., Ste. 900
Hollywood, CA 90028
Phone   323-860-2960
            800-858-4749
Fax   323-860-2972
www.film.ca.gov
Amy Lemish - Director

COLORADO
Colorado Film Commission
1625 Broadway, Ste. 1700
Denver, CO 80202
Phone   303-620-4500
www.coloradofilm.org

production resources

CONNECTICUT

**Connecticut Film, Video &
Media Office**
805 Brook St., Bldg. 4
Rocky Hill, CT 06067
Phone　860-571-7130
　　　　800-392-2122
Fax　　860-721-7088
www.ctfilm.com
Guy Ortoleva - Executive Director

DELAWARE

Delaware Film Office
Delaware Tourism Office
99 Kings Highway
Dover, DE 19901
Phone　800-447-8846
　　　　302-739-4271
Fax　　302-739-5749
www.state.de.us/dedo
Cheryl Heiks - Film Office Coordinator

DISTRICT OF COLUMBIA

**Office of Motion Picture & TV
Development**
441 4th St. NW, Ste. 760N
Washington, DC 20001
Phone　202-727-6608
Fax　　202-727-3246
www.film.dc.gov
Crystal Palmer - Director

FLORIDA

**Governor's Office of Film &
Entertainment**
Executive Office of the Governor
400 S. Monroe St., Ste. 2002
Tallahassee, FL 32399-0001
Phone　850-410-4765
　　　　877-352-3456
　　　　818-508-7772 (LA Office)
Fax　　850-410-4770
www.filminflorida.com
Susan Albershardt – Film Commissioner

GEORGIA

**Georgia Film, Video &
Music Department**
75 Fifth St. NW, Ste. 1200
Atlanta, GA 30308
Phone　404-962-4052
Fax　　404-962-4053
www.georgia.org
Greg Torre - Director

HAWAII

**Hawaii Film Office
(State of Hawaii)**
250 S. Hotel St., 5th Fl.
Honolulu, HI 96813
Phone　808-586-2570
Fax　　808-586-2572
Email　info@hawaiifilmoffice.com
www.hawaiifilmoffice.com
Donne Dawson – Film Commissioner

**Maui County Film Office
(Islands of Maui, Molokai, Lanai)**
200 S. High St., 6th Fl.
Wailuku, HI 96793
Phone　808-270-7415
Fax　　808-270-7995
Email　info@filmmaui.com
www.filmmaui.com
Benita Brazier - Film Commissioner

**Honolulu Film Office
(Island of Oahu)**
530 S. King St., Rm. 306
Honolulu, HI 96813
Phone:　808-527-6108
Fax:　　808-527-6102
Email　info@filmhonolulu.com
www.filmhonolulu.com
*Walea Constantinau – Film
Commissioner*

production resources

Kauai Film Commision
(Island of Kauai)
4444 Rice St., Ste, 200
Lihue, HI 96766
Phone   808-241-6386
Fax   808-241-6399
Email   info@filmkauai.com
www.filmkauai.com
Tiffani Lizama – Film Commissioner

Big Island Film Office
(Island of Hawaii)
25 Aupuni St., Rm 219
Hilo, HI 96720
Phone   808-326-2663
Fax   808-935-1205
Email   film@bigisland.com
www.filmbigisland.com
Marilyn Killeri – Film Commissioner

IDAHO

Idaho Film Bureau
700 W. State St.
PO Box 83720
Boise, ID 83720-0093
Phone   208-334-2470
            800-942-8338
Fax   208-334-2631
www.filmidaho.com
Peg Owens - Director

ILLINOIS

Illinois Film Office
100 W. Randolph, Ste. 3-400
Chicago, IL 60601
Phone   312-814-3600
Fax   312-814-8874
www.filmillinois.state.il.us
Brenda Sexton – Film Commissioner

INDIANA

Indiana Film Commission
Indiana Department of Commerce
1 N. Capitol Ave., Ste. 700
Indianapolis, IN 46204-2288
Phone   317-232-8829
Fax   317-233-6887
www.filmindiana.com
Jane Rulon - Director

IOWA

Iowa Film Office
200 E. Grand Ave.
Des Moines, IA 50309
Phone   515-242-4726
Fax   515-242-4718
www.filmiowa.com
Tom Wheeler - Contact

KANSAS

Kansas Film Commission
1000 SW Jackson, Ste. 100
Topeka, KS 66612
Phone   785-296-4927
            888-701-FILM
Fax   785-296-3490
Email   pjasso@kansascommerce.com
www.filmkansas.com
Peter Jasso - Film Commissioner

KENTUCKY

Kentucky Film Commission
500 Mero St.
2200 Capitol Plaza Tower
Frankfort, KY 40601
Phone   502-564-3456
            800-345-6591
Fax   502-564-7588
www.kyfilmoffice.com
Todd Cassidy - Director

LOUISIANA

**Louisiana Governor's Office of
Film & TV Development**
800 Distributors Row, Ste. 101
Harahan, LA 70123
Phone   504-736-7280
Fax   504-736-7287
www.lafilm.org
Mark Smith - Film Commissioner

MAINE

Maine Film Office
59 State House Station
Augusta, ME 04333
Phone   207-624-7631
Fax   207-287-8070
www.filminmaine.com
Lea Girardin - Director

MARYLAND

Maryland Film Office
217 E. Redwood St.
Baltimore, MD 21202
Phone   410-767-6340
               800-333-6632
               410-767-0067 (Hotline)
Fax   410-333-0044
Email   filminfo@marylandfilm.org
www.marylandfilm.org
Jack Gerbes - Director

MASSACHUSETTS

**Massachusetts Sports & Entertainment
Commission**
One Fleet Center Pl., Ste. 200
Boston, MA 02114
Phone   617-624-1237
Fax   617-624-1239
Email   info@masportsandfilm.org
www.masportsandfilm.org
Mark R. Drago – President

MICHIGAN

Michigan Film Office
702 W. Kalamazoo St.
Lansing, MI 48915
Phone   517-373-0638
               800-477-3456
Fax   517-241-2930
www.michigan.gov/filmoffice
Janet Lockwood - Director

MINNESOTA

Minnesota Film & TV Board
401 N. Third St., Ste. 460
Minneapolis, MN 55401
Phone   612-332-6493
Fax   612-332-3735
www.mnfilm.org
Craig Rice - Executive Director

MISSISSIPPI

Mississippi Film Office
PO Box 849
Jackson, MS 39205
Phone   601-359-3297
Fax   601-359-5048
www.visitmississippi.org/film
Ward Emling - Manager

MISSOURI

Missouri Film Commission
301 W. High St., Ste. 720
PO Box 118
Jefferson City, MO 65102
Phone   573-751-9050
Fax   573-522-1719
www.mofilm.org
Jerry Jones - Director

production resources

MONTANA

Montana Film Office
301 S. Park Ave.
Helena, MT 59620
Phone   406-841-2876
          800-553-4563
Fax   406-841-2877
www.montanafilm.com
Sten Iversen - Director

NEBRASKA

Nebraska Film Office
PO Box 94666
301 Centennial Mall South, 4th Fl.
Lincoln, NE 68509-4666
Phone   402-471-3680
          800-228-6505
Fax   402-471-3365
www.filmnebraska.org
Laurie J. Richards - Nebraska Film Officer

NEVADA

Nevada Film Office
555 E. Washington Ave., Ste. 5400
Las Vegas, NV 89101
Phone   702-486-2711
          877-638-3456
Fax   702-486-2712
Email   lvnfo@bizopp.state.nv.us
www.nevadafilm.com
Charles Geocaris - Director

NEW HAMPSHIRE

New Hampshire Film & Television Office
172 Pembroke Rd.
PO Box 1856
Concord, NH 03302-1856
Phone   603-271-2665
Fax   603-271-6870
www.filmnh.org

NEW JERSEY

New Jersey Motion Picture & Television Commission
153 Halsey St., 5th Fl.
PO Box 47023
Newark, NJ 07101
Phone   973-648-6279
Fax   973-648-7350
www.njfilm.org
Joseph Friedman - Executive Director

NEW MEXICO

New Mexico Film Office
1100 St. Francis Dr., Ste. 1200
Santa Fe, NM 87505
Phone   505-827-9810
          800-545-9871
Fax   505-827-9799
www.nmfilm.com
Lisa Strout - Director

NEW YORK

New York State Governor's Office for Motion Picture & Television Department
633 Third Ave., 33rd Fl.
New York, NY 10017
Phone   212-803-2330
Fax   212-803-2339
www.nylovesfilm.com/index.asp
Pat Swinney Kaufman - Deputy Commissioner/Director

New York City Mayor's Office of Film, Theatre & Broadcasting
1697 Broadway, Ste. 602
New York, NY 10019
Phone   212-489-6710
Fax   212-307-6237
Email   info@film.nyc.gov
www.nyc.gov/film
Katherine Oliver - Commissioner

NORTH CAROLINA
North Carolina Film Office
4324 Mail Service Center
Raleigh, NC 27699-4324
Phone   919-733-9900
          800-232-9227
Fax   919-715-0151
www.ncfilm.com
Bill Arnold – Film Commissioner

NORTH DAKOTA
North Dakota Film Commission
1600 E. Century Ave., Ste. 2
Bismarck, ND 58503
Phone   701-328-2525
Fax   701-328-4878
www.ndtourism.com
Sara Otte Coleman – Film Commissioner

OHIO
Ohio Film Commission
77 S. High St., 29th Fl.
Columbus, OH 43215
Phone   614-466-2284
          800-230-3523
Fax   614-466-6744
www.ohiofilm.com
Steve Cover - State Film Commissioner

OKLAHOMA
Oklahoma Film Commission
15 N. Robinson, Ste. 802
Oklahoma City, OK 73102
Phone   405-522-6760
          800-766-3456
Fax   405-522-0656
www.oklahomafilm.org
Dino Lalli - Director

OREGON
Oregon Film & Video Office
One World Trade Center
121 SW Salmon St., Ste. 1205
Portland, OR 97204
Phone   503-229-5832
Fax   503-229-6869
www.oregonfilm.org
Veronica Rinard - Executive Director

PENNSYLVANIA
Pennsylvania Film Office
Commonwealth Keystone Bldg.
400 North St., 4th Fl.
Harrisburg, PA 17120-0225
Phone   717-783-3456
Fax   717-787-0687
www.filminpa.com
Jane Shecter - Director

PUERTO RICO
Puerto Rico Film Commission
355 F.D. Roosevelt Ave., Ste. 106
Hato Rey, PR 00918
Phone   787-754-7110
          787-758-4747, x2251
Fax   787-756-5706
www.puertoricofilm.com
Laura A. Velez - Executive Director

RHODE ISLAND
**Rhode Island Film &
TV Office**
RI Economic Development Corporation
One W. Exchange St.
Providence, RI 02903
Phone   401-222-2601
Fax   401-273-8270
www.rifilm.com
Rick Smith - Director

production resources

SOUTH CAROLINA
South Carolina Film Commission
1201 Main St., Ste. 1600
Columbia, SC 29201
Phone   803-737-0490
Fax   803-737-3104
Email   scfilmoffice@sccommerce.com
www.filmsc.com
Jeff Monks – Film Commissioner

SOUTH DAKOTA
South Dakota Film Office
711 E. Wells Ave.
Pierre, SD 57501
Phone   605-773-3301
Fax   605-773-3256
www.filmsd.com
Chris Hull - Manager

TENNESSEE
**Tennessee Film, Entertainment &
Music Commission**
312 Eighth Avenue N.,
Tennessee Tower, 9th Fl.
Nashville, TN 37243
Phone   615-741-3456
             877-818-3456
Fax   615-741-5554
www.filmtennessee.com
David Bennett - Executive Director

TEXAS
Texas Film Commission
PO Box 13246
Austin, TX 78711
Phone   512-463-9200
Fax   512-463-4114
www.texasfilmcommission.com
Tom Copeland - Director

UTAH
Utah Film Commission
324 S. State St., Ste. 500
Salt Lake City, UT 84111
Phone   801-538-8740
             800-453-8824
Fax   801-538-8746
www.film.utah.org
Leigh von der Esch - Executive Director

VERMONT
Vermont Film Commission
10 Baldwin St., Drawer #33
Montpelier, VT 05633-2001
Phone   802-828-3618
Fax   802-828-0607
www.vermontfilm.com
Danis Regal - Executive Director

VIRGINIA
Virginia Film Office
901 E. Byrd St.
Richmond, VA 23219-4048
Phone   804-371-8204
             800-854-6233
Fax   804-371-8177
www.film.virginia.org
Rita McClenny - Director

WASHINGTON
Washington State Film Office
2001 Sixth Ave., Ste. 2600
Seattle, WA 98121
Phone   206-256-6151
Fax   206-256-6154
www.filmwashington.com
Suzy Kellett - Director

WEST VIRGINIA

West Virginia Film Office
c/o West Virginia Division of Tourism
90 MacCorkle Ave. SW
South Charleston, WV 25303
Phone   304-558-2200
          800-225-5982
Fax   304-558-0108
www.wvdo.org
Pamela Haynes - Director

WISCONSIN

Wisconsin Film Office
201 W. Washington Ave., 2nd Fl.
Madison, WI 53703
Phone   800-345-6947
Fax   608-266-3403
www.filmwisconsin.org
Sarah Klavas - Director, Marketing

WYOMING

Wyoming Film Office
I-25 @ College Dr.
Cheyenne, WY 82002
Phone   307-777-3400
          800-458-6657
Fax   307-777-2877
www.wyomingfilm.org
Michell Phelan - Manager

INTERNATIONAL FILM COMMISSIONS

AUSTRALIA

AusFILM
2049 Century Plaza East, 19th Fl.
Los Angeles, CA 90067
Phone   310-229-4833
Fax   310-277-2258
Email   tracey.montgomery@
         austrade.gov.au
www.ausfilm.com.au
Tracey Montgomery – Film Commissioner, L.A.

Melbourne Film Office
GPO Box 4361
Melbourne, Victoria 3001
Australia
Phone   61-3-9660-3240
Fax   61-3-9660-3201
www.film.vic.gov.au/info
Caroline Pitcher – General Manager

New South Wales Film & Television Office
Level 7, 157 Liverpool St.
Sydney, New South Wales 2001
Australia
Phone   61-2-9264-6400
Fax   61-2-9264-4388
www.fto.nsw.gov.au
Garry Brennan – Film Commissioner

Pacific Film & Television Commission
Level 15, 111 George St.
Brisbane, Queensland 4000
Australia
Phone   61-7-3224-4114
Fax   61-7-3224-6717
www.pftc.com.au
Kylie Cross - Contact

South Australian Film Corporation
3 Butler Dr., Hendon Common
Hendon, South Australia 5014
Australia
Phone   61-8-8348-9300
Fax   61-8-8347-0385
Email   safilm@safilm.com.au
www.safilm.com.au
Nadine Hewson – Promotions & Media Liaison Officer

production resources

CANADA

Alberta Film Commission
5th Fl., Commerce Pl.
10155 – 102 St.
Edmonton, Alberta
T5J 4L6 Canada
Phone   780-422-8584
Fax   780-422-8582
www.albertafilm.ca
Dan Chugg – Film Commissioner

British Columbia Film Commision
201-865 Hornby St.
Vancouver, British Columbia
V6Z 2G3 Canada
Phone   604-660-2732
Fax   604-660-4790
www.bcfilm.bc.ca
Susan Croome – Film Commissioner

Thompson-Nicola Film Commission
300-465 Victoria St.
Kamloops, British Columbia
V2C 2A9 Canada
Phone   250-377-8673
Toll Free BC 1-877-377-8673
Fax   250-372-5048
Cell   250-319-6211
Email   vweller@tnrd.bc.ca
www.tnrd.bc.ca
*Victoria Weller – Executive Director of
Film*

Montréal Film & TV Commission
303 Notre-Dame Street East, 6th Fl.
Montréal, Québec H2Y 3Y8 Canada
Phone   514-872-2883
Fax   514-872-3409
www.montrealfilm.com
Daniel Bissonnette – Film Commissioner

Toronto Film & Television Office
Toronto City Hall
100 Queen Street West,
Main Fl., West Side
Toronto, Ontario M5H 2N2 Canada
Phone   416-392-7570
Fax   416-392-0675
www.torontofilm.permits.com
www.toronto.ca/tfto
*Rhonda Silverstone – Film
Commissioner*

FRANCE

Commission Nationale du Film France
30, Avenue de Messine
Paris 75008 France
Phone   33-1-5383-9898
Fax   33-1-5383-9899
www.filmfrance.com
Benoit Caron – Executive Director

GERMANY

Berlin Brandenburg Film Commission
August-Bebel-Str. 26-53
Potsdam-Babelsberg D-14482 Germany
Phone   49-331-743-8730
Fax   49-331-743-8799
www.filmboard.de
Christiane Raab – Film Commissioner

ITALY

Italian Film Commission
1801 Avenue of the Stars, Ste. 700
Los Angeles, CA 90067
Phone   323-879-0950
Fax   310-203-8335
www.filminginitaly.com
*Fortunato Celi Zullo – Film
Commissioner*

NEW ZEALAND
Film New Zealand
23 Frederick St.
PO Box 24142
Wellington, New Zealand
Phone   64-4-385-0766
Fax   64-4-384-5840
Eamil   info@filmnz.org.nz
www.filmnz.com
Judith McCann - CEO

UNITED KINGDOM
British Film Commission
10 Little Portland St.
London W1W 7JG UK
Phone   44-020-7861-7860
Fax   44-020-7861-7864
Wmail   info@ukfilmcouncil-us.org
www.ukfilmcouncil-us.org
www.bfc.co.uk
Steve Norris – Film Commissioner

London Film Commission
20 Euston Centre
London NW1 3JH UK
Phone   44-020-7387-8787
Fax   44-020-7387-8788
www.london-film.co.uk
Sue Hayes – Film Commissioner

UK Film Council, U.S.
8533 Melrose Ave., Ste. C
Los Angeles, CA 90060
Phone   310-652-6169
Fax   310-652-6232
Email   film@ukfilmcouncil-usa.org
www.britfilmusa.com
Susna Finalyson-Stich – Director

GUILDS, UNIONS, AND ASSOCIATIONS

Academy of Motion Picture Arts and Sciences (AMPAS)
www.oscars.org
Honorary organization of motion picture professionals founded to advance the arts and sciences of motion pictures.
8949 Wilshire Blvd.
Beverly Hills, CA 90211-1972
Phone   310-247-3000
Fax   310-859-9351
            310-859-9619

Academy of Television Arts & Sciences (ATAS)
www.emmys.tv
Nonprofit corporation for the advancement of telecommunications arts and sciences.
5220 Lankershim Blvd.
North Hollywood, CA 91601
Phone   818-754-2800
Fax   818-761-2827

Academy Players Directory
www.playersdirectory.com
Print and online casting directories.
1313 N. Vine St.
Hollywood, CA 90028
Phone   310-247-3058
Fax   310-550-5034
Email   players@oscars.org
Su Hyatt – Associate Editor

Actors' Equity Association (AEA)
www.actorsequity.org
Labor union representing US actors and stage managers working in the professional theater.

Chicago
125 S. Clark St., Ste. 1500
Chicago, IL 60603
Phone   312-641-0393
Fax   312-641-6365

Los Angeles
Museum Square
5757 Wilshire Blvd., Ste. 1
Los Angeles, CA 90036
Phone　323-634-1750
Fax　　323-634-1777

Orlando
10319 Orangewood Blvd.
Orlando, FL 32821
Phone　407-345-8600
Fax　　407-345-1522

New York
National Headquarters
165 W. 46th St., 15th Fl.
New York, NY 10036
Phone　212-869-8530
Fax　　212-719-9815

San Francisco
350 Sansome St., Ste. 900
San Francisco, CA 94104
Phone　415-391-3838
Fax　　415-391-0102

Actors' Fund of America
www.actorsfund.org
Nonprofit organization providing for the social welfare of entertainment professionals.

Chicago
203 N. Wabash Ave., Ste. 2104
Chicago, IL 60601
Phone　312-372-0989
Fax　　312-372-0272

Los Angeles
5757 Wilshire Blvd., Ste. 400
Los Angeles, CA 90036
Phone　323-933-9244
Fax　　323-933-7615

New York
729 Seventh Ave., 10th Fl.
New York, NY 10019
Phone　212-221-7300
Fax　　212-764-0238

Actors' Work Program
www.actorsfund.org
Career counseling for members of the Actors' Fund of America.

Los Angeles
5757 Wilshire Blvd., Ste. 400
Los Angeles, CA 90036
Phone　323-933-9244
Fax　　323-933-7615

New York
729 Seventh Ave.
New York, NY 10019
Phone　212-354-5480
Fax　　212-921-4295

Alliance of Canadian Cinema, Television & Radio Artists (ACTRA)
www.actra.ca
Labor union founded to negotiate, safeguard, and promote the professional rights of Canadian performers working in film, television, video, and all recorded media.
625 Church St., 3rd Fl.
Toronto, Ontario M4Y 2G1 Canada
Phone　800-387-3516
　　　　416-489-1311
Fax　　416-489-8076

Alliance of Motion Picture & Television Producers (AMPTP)
www.amptp.org
Trade association involved with labor issues within the motion picture and television industries.
15503 Ventura Blvd.
Encino, CA 91436
Phone　818-995-3600
Fax　　818-382-1793

American Cinema Editors (ACE)
www.ace-filmeditors.org
*Honorary society made up of editors
deemed to be outstanding in their field.*
100 Universal City Plaza,
Bldg. 2282, Rm. 234
Universal City, CA 91608
Phone   818-777-2900
Fax   818-733-5023

American Cinematheque at the Egyptian & Aero Theatres
www.egyptiantheatre.com
www.americancinematheque.com
*Nonprofit cultural arts organization
programming specialty film series at
the Egyptian Theatre.*
1800 N. Highland Ave., Ste. 717
Hollywood, CA 90028
Phone   323-461-2020
       323-466-3456
      (24-hour recorded information)
Fax   323-461-9737
*Margot Gerber – Marketing & Publicity
Manager*

American Federation of Film Producers (AFFP)
www.filmfederation.com
*Trade organization of creative
professionals committed to excellence
in filmmaking.*
3000 W. Alameda Ave., Ste. 1585
Burbank, CA 91523
Phone   818-840-4924

American Federation of Musicians (AFM)
www.afm.org
*Labor union representing professional
musicians.*
Los Angeles
3550 Wilshire Blvd., Ste. 1900
Los Angeles, CA 90010
Phone   213-251-4510
Fax   213-251-4520

New York
1501 Broadway, Ste. 600
New York, NY 10036
Phone   212-869-1330
Fax   212-764-6134

American Federation of Television & Radio Artists (AFTRA)
www.aftra.org
*Labor organization representing
broadcast performers.*
Los Angeles
5757 Wilshire Blvd., Ste. 900
Los Angeles, CA 90036
Phone   323-634-8100
Fax   323-634-8126
Christopher de Haven - Contact
New York
260 Madison Ave., 7th Fl.
New York, NY 10016
Phone   212-532-0800
Fax   212-532-2242

American Film Institute (AFI)
www.afi.com
*Organization dedicated to preserving
and advancing the art of the moving
image through events, exhibitions
and education.*
Los Angeles
2021 N. Western Ave.
Los Angeles, CA 90027
Phone   323-856-7600
Fax   323-467-4578
Washington, DC
The John F. Kennedy Center for the
Performing Arts
Washington, DC 20566
Phone   202-833-2348
Fax   202-659-1970

production resources

American Guild of Musical Artists (AGMA)

www.musicalartists.org
Union representing classical artists, opera singers, ballet dancers, stage managers, and stage directors.
1430 Broadway, 14th Fl.
New York, NY 10018
Phone   212-265-3687
Fax   212-262-9088

American Guild of Variety Artists (AGVA)

Labor union representing performers in Broadway, off-Broadway, and cabaret productions, as well as theme park and nightclub performers.

Los Angeles
4741 Laurel Canyon Blvd., Ste. 208
North Hollywood, CA 91607
Phone   818-508-9984
Fax   818-508-3029

New York
363 Seventh Ave., 17th Fl.
New York, NY 10001
Phone   212-675-1003
Fax   212-633-0097

American Humane Association (AHA)

www.ahafilm.org
www.americanhumane.org/film
Watchdog organization dedicated to preventing cruelty to animal actors performing in films and television.
Western Regional Office
Film and Television Unit
15366 Dickens St.
Sherman Oaks, CA 91403
Phone   818-501-0123
          800-677-3420 (Hotline)
Fax   818-501-8725

American Screenwriters Association (ASA)

www.goasa.com
Nonprofit organization promoting and encouraging the art of screenwriting as well as the support and advancement of screenwriters.
269 S. Beverly Dr., Ste. 2600
Beverly Hills, CA 90212-3807
Phone   866-265-9091

American Society of Cinematographers (ASC)

www.theasc.com
Union representing professional cinematographers, dedicated to improving the quality of motion picture presentation.
1782 N. Orange Dr.
Hollywood, CA 90028
Phone   323-969-4333
          800-448-0145
Fax   323-882-6391

American Society of Composers, Authors & Publishers (ASCAP)

www.ascap.com
Performing rights organization representing composers, lyricists, songwriters, and music publishers.

Los Angeles
7920 W. Sunset Blvd., 3rd Fl.
Los Angeles, CA 90046
Phone   323-883-1000
Fax   323-883-1049

Nashville
2 Music Square West
Nashville, TN 37203
Phone   615-742-5000
Fax   615-742-5020

New York
One Lincoln Plaza
New York, NY 10023
Phone   212-621-6000
Fax   212-724-9064

American Society of Journalists & Authors (ASJA)
www.asja.org
Organization of independent nonfiction writers.
1501 Broadway, Ste. 302
New York, NY 10036
Phone   212-997-0947
Fax   212-768-7414

American Society of Media Photographers (ASMP)
www.asmp.org
Trade organization dedicated to protecting and promoting the interests and high professional standards of photographers whose work is for publication.
150 N. Second St.
Philadelphia, PA 19106
Phone   215-451-2767
Fax   215-451-0880

American Women in Radio & Television, Inc. (AWRT)
www.awrt.org
National organization supporting the advancement of women in the communications industry.
8405 Greensboro Dr., Ste. 800
McLean, VA 22102
Phone   703-506-3290
Fax   703-506-3266

Art Directors Guild & Scenic, Title and Graphic Artists
www.ialocal800.org
Organization representing production designers, art directors, assitant art directors and scenic, title and graphic designers.
Local 800 I.A.T.S.E.
11969 Ventura Blvd., Ste. 200
Studio City, CA 91604
Phone   818-762-9995
Fax: 818-762-9997
Lydia Zimmer – Office Manager

Association of Film Commissioners International (AFCI)
www.afci.org
Organization providing representation and support to member film commissions.
314 N. Main, Ste. 308
Helena, MT 59601
Phone   406-495-8040
(LA)   323-462-6092
Fax   406-495-8039
(LA)   323-462-6091
Email   info@afci.org
Bill Lindstrom - CEO

Association of Independent Commercial Producers (AICP)
www.aicp.com
Organization representing interests of US companies that specialize in producing commercials in various media (film, video, Internet, etc.) for advertisers and agencies.

Los Angeles
650 N. Bronson Ave., Ste. 223B
Los Angeles, CA 90004
Phone   323-960-4763
Fax   323-960-4766
Farah Fima – Office Manager

New York
3 W. 18th St., 5th Fl.
New York, NY 10011
Phone   212-929-3000
Fax   212-929-3359

Association of Independent Video and Filmmakers (AIVF)
www.aivf.org
Nonprofit membership organization serving local and international film and videomakers, including documentarians and experimental artists.
304 Hudson St., 6th Fl.
New York, NY 10013
Phone   212-807-1400
Fax   212-463-8519
Email   info@aivf.org
Bo Mehrad – Info Services Director

production resources

Association of Talent Agents (ATA)
www.agentassociation.com
Nonprofit trade association for talent agencies representing clients in the motion picture and television industries, as well as literary, theater, radio, and commercial clients.
9255 Sunset Blvd., Ste. 930
Los Angeles, CA 90069
Phone   310-274-0628
Fax   310-274-5063
Shellie Jetton – Administrative Director

The Authors Guild
www.authorsguild.org
Society dedicated to advocacy for fair compensation, free speech, and copyright protection for published authors.
31 E. 28th St., 10th Fl.
New York, NY 10016
Phone   212-563-5904
Fax   212-564-5363

The Black Filmmaker Foundation (BFF)
www.dvrepublic.org
Nonprofit organization of emerging Black filmmakers.
670 Broadway, Ste. 300
New York, NY 10012
Phone   212-253-1690
Fax   212-253-1689

Breakdown Services
www.breakdownservices.com
Communications network and casting system providing integrated tools for casting directors and talent representatives, as well as casting information for actors.

Los Angeles
2140 Cotner Ave.
Los Angeles, CA 90025
Phone   310-276-9166

New York
Phone   212-869-2003

Vancouver
Phone   604-943-7100

Broadcast Music, Inc. (BMI)
www.bmi.com
Nonprofit performing rights organization of songwriters, composers and music publishers.

Los Angeles
8730 Sunset Blvd., 3rd Fl. West
West Hollywood, CA 90069-2211
Phone   310-659-9109
Fax   310-657-6947

Nashville
10 Music Square East
Nashville, TN 37203-4399
Phone   615-401-2000
Fax   615-401-2707

New York
320 W. 57th St.
New York, NY 10019
Phone   212-586-2000
Fax   212-489-2368

California Arts Council (CAC)
www.cac.ca.gov
State organization encouraging artistic awareness, expression, and participation reflecting California's diverse cultures.
1300 I St., Ste. 930
Sacramento, CA 95814
Phone   916-322-6555
          800-201-6201
Fax   916-322-6575
Adam Gottlieb – Communications Director

Casting Society of America (CSA)

www.castingsociety.com
Trade organization of professional film and television casting directors.

Los Angeles
606 N. Larchmont Blvd., Ste. 4B
Los Angeles, CA 90004-1309
Phone   323-463-1925
Fax   323-463-5753
Larry Raab – Office Manager

New York
C/O Bernard Telsey
145 W. 28th St., Ste. 12F
New York, NY 10001
Phone   212-868-1260
Fax   212-868-1261

Cinewomen

www.cinewomen.org
Nonprofit organization dedicated to supporting the advancement of women within the motion picture industry.

Los Angeles
9903 Santa Monica Blvd., Ste. 461
Beverly Hills, CA 90212
Phone   310-855-8720

New York
PO Box 1477, Cooper Station
New York, NY 10276
Phone   212-604-4264

Clear, Inc.

www.clearinc.org
Organization of clearance and research professionals working in the film, television, and multimedia industries.
PO Box 628
Burbank, CA 91503-0628
Fax   413-647-3380

Commercial Casting Directors Association (CCDA)

Organization dedicated to providing a level of professionalism for casting directors within the commercial industry.
c/o Jeff Gerard @ Chelsea Studios
11530 Ventura Blvd.
Studio City, CA 91604
Phone 818-782-9900

Costume Designers Guild (CDG)

www.costumedesignersguild.com
Union representing motion picture, television, and commercial costume designers. Promotes research, artistry and technical expertise in the field of film and television costume design.
4730 Woodman Ave., Ste. 430
Sherman Oaks, CA 91423
Phone 818-905-1557
Fax   818-905-1560
Email   cdgia@earthlink.net
James J. Casey, Jr. – Executive Director

Directors Guild of America (DGA)

www.dga.org
Labor union representing film and television directors, unit production managers, first assistant directors, second assistant directors, technical coordinators, tape associate directors, stage managers and production associates.

Chicago
400 N. Michigan Ave., Ste. 307
Chicago, IL 60611
Phone 888-600-6975
         312-644-5050
Fax   312-644-5776

Los Angeles
7920 Sunset Blvd.
Los Angeles, CA 90046
Phone 800-421-4173
         310-289-2000 (Main Line)
         323-851-3671 (Agency Listing)
Fax   310-289-2029

production resources

New York
110 W. 57th St.
New York, NY 10019
Phone   800-356-3754
        212-581-0370
Fax   212-581-1441

The Dramatists Guild of America, Inc.
www.dramaguild.com
Professional association of playwrights, composers and lyricists.
1501 Broadway, Ste. 701
New York, NY 10036
Phone   212-398-9366
Fax   212-944-0420

Filmmakers Alliance
www.filmmakersalliance.com
Nonprofit collective of independent filmmakers.
453 S. Spring St.
Los Angeles, CA 90013
Phone   213-228-1152
Fax   213-228-1156

Hispanic Organization of Latin Actors (HOLA)
www.hellohola.org
Arts service organization committed to projecting Hispanic artists and their culture into the mainstream of Anglo-American industry and culture.
107 Suffolk St., Ste. 302
New York, NY 10002
Phone   212-253-1015
Fax   212-253-9651
Email   holagram@hellohola.org
Manny Alfaro – Executive Director

Hollywood Radio & Television Society (HRTS)
www.hrts-iba.org
Nonprofit organization made up of West Coast executives from the entertainment (and ancillary) industries, providing mentoring and scholarship programs as well as networking opportunities. Sponsors The International Broadcasting (& Cable) Awards.
13701 Riverside Dr., Ste. 205
Sherman Oaks, CA 91423
Phone   818-789-1182
Fax   818-789-1210

Horror Writers Association
www.horror.org
Worldwide organization of horror and dark fantasy writers and publishing professionals.
PO Box 50577
Palo Alto, CA 94303
Phone   650-322-4610

The Humanitas Prize
www.humanitasprize.org
Prestigious prizes awarded to film and television writers whose produced scripts communicate values which most enrich the human person.
17575 Pacific Coast Highway
PO Box 861
Pacific Palisades, CA 90272
Phone   310-454-8769
Fax   310-459-6549
Email   humanitasmail@aol.com
Enio Sevilla – General Manager

Independent Feature Project (IFP)
www.ifp.org
Nonprofit service organization providing resources and information for independent filmmakers and industry professionals.

Chicago
33 E. Congress Parkway, Ste. 505
Chicago, IL 60605
Phone   312-435-1825
Fax   312-435-1828

Los Angeles (IFP/W)
8750 Wilshire Blvd., 2nd Fl.
Beverly Hills, CA 90211
Phone   310-432-1200
Fax   310-432-1203

Miami
210 Second St.
Miami Beach, FL 33139
Phone   305-538-8242

Minneapolis
401 N. Third St., Ste. 450
Minneapolis, MN 55401
Phone   612-338-0871
Fax   612-338-4747

New York
104 W. 29th St., 12th Fl.
New York, NY 10001-5310
Phone   212-465-8200
Fax   212-465-8525

Independent Film & Television Alliance (IFTA)
www.ifta-online.org
Trade association for the independent film and television industries.
10850 Wilshire Blvd., 9th Fl.
Los Angeles, CA 90024-4321
Phone   310-446-1000
Fax   310-446-1600
Jean Prewitt - President

International Alliance of Theatrical Stage Employees (IATSE)
www.iatse.lm.com
Union representing technicians, artisans and craftpersons in the entertainment industry including live theater, film and television production and trade shows.

Los Angeles
10045 Riverside Dr.
Toluca Lake, CA 91602
Phone   818-980-3499
Fax   818-980-3496

New York
1430 Broadway, 20th Fl.
New York, NY 10018
Phone   212-730-1770
Fax   212-730-7809
        212-921-7699

International Press Academy
www.pressacademy.com
Association of professional entertainment journalists.
9601 Wilshire Blvd., Ste. 755
Beverly Hills, CA 90210
Phone   310-550-8209
Fax   310-550-0420
Mirjana Van Blaricom - President

Motion Picture Association of America (MPAA)
www.mpaa.org
Trade association for the US motion picture, home video and television industries.
15503 Ventura Blvd.
Encino, CA 91436
Phone   818-995-6600
Fax   818-382-1799

Motion Picture Editors Guild
www.editorsguild.com
Union representing motion picture, television, and commercial editors, sound technicians and projectionists and story analysts.

Chicago
6317 N. Northwest Highway
Chicago, IL 60631
Phone   773-594-6598
        888-594-6734
Fax   773-594-6599

Los Angeles
7715 Sunset Blvd., Ste. 200
Hollywood, CA 90046
Phone   323-876-4770
Fax   323-876-0861

production resources

New York
165 W. 46th St., Ste. 900
New York, NY 10036
Phone   212-302-0700
Fax   212-302-1091

Multicultural Motion Picture Association (MMPA)

www.diversityawards.org
Association promoting and encouraging diversity of ideas, cultures and perspectives in film; sponsor of the annual Diversity Awards.
9244 Wilshire Blvd.
Beverly Hills, CA 90212
Phone   310-285-9743
Fax   310-285-9770

Music Managers Forum (MMF)

www.mmfus.org
Organization dedicated to furthering the interests of managers and their artists in all fields of the music industry including live performance and recording and publishing matters.
PO Box 444, Village Station
New York, NY 10014
Phone   212-213-8787
Fax   212-213-9797

Music Video Production Association (MVPA)

www.mvpa.com
Nonprofit trade organization made up of music video production and post production companies, as well as editors, directors, producers, cinematographers, choreographers, script supervisors, computer animators and make-up artists involved in the production of music videos.
201 N. Occidental Blvd., Bldg. 7, Unit B
Los Angeles, CA 90026
Phone   213-387-1590
Fax   213-385-9507
info@mvpa.com
Andrea Clark – Executive Director

Mystery Writers of America (MWA)

www.mysterywriters.org
Organization of published mystery authors, editors, screenwriters, and other professionals in the field. Sponsors symposia, conferences and The Edgar Awards.
17 E. 47th St., 6th Fl.
New York, NY 10017
Phone   212-888-8171
Fax   212-888-8107

Nashville Association of Talent Directors (NATD)

www.n-a-t-d.com
Professional entertainment organization comprised of industry professionals involved in all aspects of the music and entertainment industries.
PO Box 23903
Nashville, TN 37202-3903
Phone   615-662-2200 (x*410)

National Association of Latino Independent Producers (NALIP)

www.nalip.org
Organization of independent Latin film producers.

Los Angeles
1323 Lincoln Blvd., Suite 220
Santa Monica, CA 90401
Phone   310-395-8880
Fax   310-395-8811

New York
c/o P.O.V.
32 Broadway, Fl. 14
New York, NY 10004
Phone   646-336-6333
Fax   212-989-8230

National Academy of Recording Arts & Sciences (NARAS)

www.grammy.com
Organization dedicated to improving the quality of life and cultural condition for musicians, producers, and other recording professionals. Provides outreach, professional development, cultural enrichment, education and human services programs. Sponsors the Grammy Awards.
The Recording Academy
3402 Pico Blvd.
Santa Monica, CA 90405
Phone   310-392-3777
Fax   310-399-3090

National Association of Television Program Executives (NATPE)

www.natpe.org
www.natpeonline.com
Nonprofit association of business professionals who create, develop and distribute content.
2425 Olympic Blvd., Ste. 600E
Santa Monica, CA 90404
Phone   310-453-4440
Fax   310-453-5258

National Conference of Personal Managers (NCOPM)

www.ncopm.com
Association for the advancement of personal managers and their clients.

Palm Desert
PO Box 609
Palm Desert, CA 92261-0609
Phone   760-200-5892
Fax   760-200-5896

New York
41 W. 56th St.
New York, NY 10019
Phone   212-582-1940
Fax   212-582-1942

National Council of La Raza (NCLR)

www.nclr.org
Private, nonprofit, nonpartisan, tax-exempt organization dedicated, in part, to promoting fair, accurate, and balanced portrayals of Latinos in film, television and music. Sponsor of the ALMA Awards.
1111 19th St., Ste. 1000
Washington, DC 20036
Phone   202-785-1670
Fax   202-785-7620

National Music Publishing Association (NMPA)

www.nmpa.org
Organization dedicated to interpreting copyright law, educating the public about licensing, safeguarding the interests of American music publishers, and protecting music copyright across all media and national boundaries.
475 Park Avenue South, 29th Fl.
New York, NY 10016-6901
Phone   646-742-1651
Fax   646-742-1779

Nosotros

www.nosotros.org
Organization established to improve the image of Latinos/Hispanics as they are portrayed in the entertainment industry, both in front of and behind the camera, as well as to expand employment opportunities within the entertainment industry. Sponsor of The Golden Eagle Awards.
650 N. Bronson Ave., Ste. 102
Hollywood, CA 90004
Phone   323-466-8566
Fax   323-466-8540

production resources

The Organization of Black Screenwriters, Inc.
www.obswriter.com
Nonprofit organization developing and supporting Black screenwriters.
1968 W. Adams Blvd.
Los Angeles, CA 90018
Phone   323-735-2050
Fax   323-735-2051

PEN
www.pen.org
Nonprofit organization made up of poets, playwrights, essayists, novelists, television writers, screenwriters, critics, historians, editors, journalists, and translators. Dedicated to protecting the rights of writers around the world, to stimulate interest in the written word and to foster a vital literary community.
Pen American Center
568 Broadway, 4th Fl.
New York, NY 10012-3225
Phone   212-334-1660
Fax   212-334-2181

Producers Guild of America (PGA)
www.producersguild.org
Organization representing the interests of all members of the producing team.
8530 Wilshire Blvd., Ste. 450
Beverly Hills, CA 90211
Phone   310-358-9020
Fax   310-358-9520

Recording Musicians Association (RMA)
www.rmala.org
Nonprofit organization of studio musicians and composers.
817 Vine St., Ste. 209
Hollywood, CA 90038-3716
Phone   323-462-4762
Fax   323-462-2406
Ximena Marin – Executive Administrator

Romance Writers of America (RWA)
www.rwanational.org
National nonprofit genre writers' association providing networking and support to published and aspiring romance writers.
16000 Stuebner Airline, Ste. 140
Spring, TX 77379
Phone   832-712-5200
Fax   832-717-5201

Screen Actors Guild (SAG)
www.sag.org
www.castsag.org - Member Contact Information
Union representing actors in feature films, short films and digital projects.

Los Angeles
5757 Wilshire Blvd.
Los Angeles, CA 90036
Phone   323-954-1600
(Main Line)
  323-549-6858
(Commercial/Infomercials/ Industrial/Education)
  323-549-6811
(Production Services-Extras)
  323-549-6864
(Music Entertainment Contracts)
  323-549-6835
(Television Contracts)
  323-549-6828
(Theatrical Motion Pictures)
  323-549-6737
(Actors to Locate)
  323-549-6644
(Affirmative Action)
  323-549-6745
(Agency/Agent Contracts)
  323-549-6540
(Casting Seminars & Showcase Info)
  323-549-6755
(Dues Information)
  323-549-6773
(Emergency Fund)
  323-549-6627
(Legal Affairs)
  323-549-6778
(Membership Services)

323-549-6769
(New Memberships)

323-549-6505
(Residuals)

800-205-7716
(Residuals)

323-549-6869
(Signatory Records)

818-954-9400
(SAG Pension & Health)

323-549-6855
(Stunts/Safety)

323-549-6023
(SAG Jobs Hotline)

323-549-6639
(Young Performers/Coogan Law)

Fax　　323-549-6603

New York
360 Madison Ave., 12th Fl.
New York, NY 10017
Phone　212-944-1030
(Main Line)
　　　　212-944-6715
(TTY Line)
Fax　　212-944-6774

Scriptwriters Network
www.scriptwritersnetwork.com
Organization providing information and career counseling for film and television writers.
11684 Ventura Blvd., Ste. 508
Studio City, CA 91604
Phone　323-848-9477

SESAC
www.sesac.com
Nonprofit performing rights organization of songwriters, composers and music publishers.

Los Angeles
501 Santa Monica Blvd., Ste. 450
Santa Monica, CA 90401-2430
Phone　310-393-9671
Fax　　310-393-6497

Nashville
55 Music Square East
Nashville, TN 37203
Phone　615-320-0055
Fax　　615-329-9627

New York
152 W. 57th St., 57th Fl.
New York, NY 10019
Phone　212-586-3450
Fax　　212-489-5699

Society of Children's Book Writers & Illustrators (SCBWI)
www.scbwi.org
Professional organization of writers and illustrators of children's books.
8271 Beverly Blvd.
Los Angeles, CA 90048
Phone　323-782-1010
Fax　　323-782-1892

Society of Composers & Lyricists
www.filmscore.org
Nonprofit volunteer organization advancing the professional interests of lyricists and composers of film and television music.
400 S. Beverly Dr., Ste. 214
Beverly Hills, CA 90212
Phone　310-281-2812
Fax　　310-284-4861

Society of Illustrators (SOI)
www.societyillustrators.org
Society made up of professional illustrators, art directors, art buyers, creative supervisors, instructors and publishers, dedicated to the well-being of individual illustrators and the industry of illustration.
128 E. 63rd St.
New York, NY 10021-7303
Phone　212-838-2560
Fax　　212-838-2561

production resources

Society of Operating Cameramen (SOC)

www.soc.org
Organization promoting excellence in the fields of camera operation and the allied camera crafts.
PO Box 2006
Toluca Lake, CA 91610
Phone   818-382-7070

Society of Stage Directors & Choreographers (SSDC)

www.ssdc.org
Union representing directors and choreographers of Broadway national tours, regional theater, dinner theater and summer stock, as well as choreographers for motion pictures, television, and music videos.
1501 Broadway, Ste. 1701
New York, NY 10036-5653
Phone   212-391-1070
Fax   212-302-6195

Stunts-Ability, Inc.

www.stuntsability.com
Nonprofit organization training amputees and other disabled persons for stunts, acting, and effects for the entertainment industry.
PO Box 600711
San Diego, CA 92160-0711
Phone   619-542-7730
Fax   619-542-7731

Talent Managers Association (TMA)

www.talentmanagers.org
Nonprofit organization designed to establish credibilty for the profession of talent management.
4804 Laurel Canyon Blvd., Ste. 611
Valley Village, CA 91607
Phone   310-205-8495
Fax   818-765-2903
Betty McCormick Aggas – Contact

Women In Film (WIF)

www.wif.org
Organization dedicated to empowering, promoting and nurturing women in the film and television industries.
8857 W. Olympic Blvd., Ste. 201
Beverly Hills, CA 90211
Phone   310-657-5144
Fax   310-657-5154

Women's Image Network (WIN)

www.winfemme.com
Not-for-profit corporation encouraging positive portrayals of women in theater, television, and film.
2118 Wilshire Blvd., Ste. 144
Santa Monica, CA 90403
Phone   310-229-5365

Writers Guild of America (WGA)

Union representing writers in the motion pictures, broadcast, cable and new technologies industries.

Los Angeles (WGAW)
www.wga.org
7000 W. Third St.
Los Angeles, CA 90048-4329
Phone   323-951-4000 (Main Line)
            323-782-4502 (Agency Listing)
Fax   323-782-4800

New York (WGAE)
www.wgaeast.org
555 W. 57th St., Ste. 1230
New York, NY 10019
Phone   212-767-7800
Fax   212-582-1909

production resources

LIBRARIES AND MUSEUMS

Academy of Motion Picture Arts & Sciences - Margaret Herrick Library
www.oscars.org
Extensive and comprehensive research and reference collections documenting film as an art form and an industry.
333 S. La Cienega Blvd.
Beverly Hills, CA 90211
Phone   310-247-3000 (Main Line)
         310-247-3020 (Reference)
Fax   310-657-9351

American Museum of Moving Images
www.ammi.org
Permanent collection of moving image artifacts.
35th Ave. At 36th St.
Astoria, NY 11106
Phone   718-784-4520
Fax   718-784-4681

The Library of Moving Images, Inc.
www.libraryofmovingimages.com
Independent film archives including 19th Century experimental film footage, silent film footage, 20th Century newsreel footage, short subjects, education and industrial films, classic documentaries, vintage cartoons and home movies.
6671 Sunset Blvd., Bungalow 1581
Hollywood, CA 90028
Phone   323-469-7499
Fax   323-469-7559

Los Angeles Public Library – Frances Howard Goldwyn/ Hollywood Regional Branch Library
www.lapl.org
Extensive collection documenting the entertainment industry including scripts, posters, and photographs.
1623 N. Ivar Ave.
Los Angeles, CA 90028
Phone   323-856-8260
Fax   323-467-5707

Museum of Television & Radio
www.mtr.org
Extensive collection of television and radio programming.

Los Angeles
465 N. Beverly Dr.
Beverly Hills, CA 90210
Phone   310-786-1000
Fax   310-786-1086

New York
25 W. 52nd St.
New York, NY 10019
Phone   212-621-6600
Fax   212-621-6700

New York Public Library for the Performing Arts
www.nypl.org
Extensive combination of circulating, reference and rare archival collections in the performing arts.
40 Lincoln Center Plaza
New York, NY 10023-7498
Phone   212-870-1630

Writers Guild Foundation Library
www.wga.org
Collection dedicated to the art, craft, and history of writing for motion pictures, radio, television and new media. Open to the public and Guild members.
7000 W. Third St.
Los Angeles, CA 90048-4329
Phone   323-782-4544
Fax   323-782-4695

production resources

National Association of Latino Independent Producers

index of
NALIP
members

Luis Cady Abarca	212-529-3977
Carlos Abascal	954-217-5300
Damian Acevedo	818-481-2979
Martin Acevedo	macevedo@txlawyerscommittee.org
Stephen Acevedo	Sacevedo@aol.com
Belinda Acosta	512-653-3918
John Acosta	john_direct@hotmail.com
Marvin Acuña	310-828-0209
Ricardo Acuña	323-478-1928
Sergio Aguero	310-820-2111
Maria Agui-Carter	617-429-1258
Carlos Aguilar	angelsoverhavana@msn.com
Claire Aguilar	415-356-8383
Gustavo Aguilar	512-327-1333
Corey Aguirre	714-777-6810
Jorge Aguirre	212-477-3143
Margarita D. Aguirre	714-777-6810
Luis Aira	323-851-6145
Carlos Albert	818-764-6534
Magdalena Albizu	718-622-0083
Russell Alexander-Orozco	323-666-0690
Fabio Alexandre da Silva	fabio.alexandre@tvglobo.com.br
Frank Algarin	212-222-9206
Natalia Almada	718-782-4501
Iris Almaraz	iris@bdfilms.biz
Raquel Almazan	305-527-3395
Maxim Almenas	917-714-6708
Diane Almodovar	305-266-3636
German Alonso	626-524-4445
Pedro Alonso	562-861-6927
Elvia Alvarado	626-441-9016
Patricia Alvarado-Nuñez	617-300-2289
Gina Amador	818-668-2030
Daniel Anaya	323-550-8610
Mario Anaya	213-388-8695
Rafael Andreu	305-532-1575
Cruz Angeles	718-252-1272
Emilia Anguita Huerta	305-662-6298
Kary Antholis	310-382-3255
Jorge Luis Aquino Calo	787-466-2948
Charles Aragon	760-749-2017
Frank Aragon	323-707-2964
Oriana Aragon	760-747-9111
Alfonso Arambula	305-761-9862
Olga Arana	310-393-8636
Jesse Aranda	310-480-6028
José Araujo	718-768-0358
Leslie Arcia	305-586-8777
Roberto Arevalo	404-651-0574
Edward Luis Arguelles	323-257-1540
Fidel Arizmendi	213-248-0581
Eddie T. Arnold	202-637-2063 x6124
Marisa Aronoff	310-369-0034
Janis Astor del Valle	917-529-5290
Monica Aswani	monica@blueelephant.tv
Marilyn R. Atlas	310-278-5047
Magi Avila	323-833-8761
Nicolas Aznarez	323-951-4477
Andre Baca	415-613-3726

Shawna Baca	310-980-8906
Evelyn Badia	917-539-1677
Michael Baez	818-901-9081
Dan Baker	705-327-9059
Mario Balibrera	310-390-7817
Charisma Baltodano	Charizb@aol.com
Marcos Baraibar	512-736-2753
Trina Bardusco	347-837-1542
Eduardo Barraza	619-733-3329
Ruben Barrera	361-595-5205
Pablo Barrios	pbarrios2783@netscape.net
Frank Barron	949-222-4411
Joe Basquez	512-219-0174
Carmen Bautista	cb1218@yahoo.com
José Bayona	347-351-0207
Veronica Bellver	54-11-47-42-44-76
Mary Beltran	608-262-8788
Salvador Benavides	323-665-6102
Daniel Bernardi	480-727-8588
María Berns	915-833-0421
Jennifer Berry	303-786-7600
Rudy Beserra	rbeserra@na.ko.com
Nelson Betancourt	407-273-4079
Maria Bird-Pico	mbird@sanjuanstar.net
Angelo Bolanos	973-904-006
Jorge Bonamino	305-788-2326
Blanca Bonilla	617-524-8154
Maria Piedad Bonilla	310-358-1943
Josefina Bonilla-Ruiz	617-821-1615
Margarita Borda	305-667-4887
Eddie Borges	eddieborges@hotmail.com
Jesse Borrego	323-464-0870
Victor Bowleg	520-740-5779
Cynthia Braden	cynthiabraden@hotmail.com
James Brennan	310-259-0646
Pablo Bressan	305-458-0197
Evelyn Brito	617-670-9094
Abraham Alfonso Brown	310-829-3948
Bette Brown	281-988-8888
Georgia Brown-Quiñones	214-855-1297
Adrian Brunello	agentbrunello@hotmail.com
Cynthia Buchanan	830-876-3034
Maria Bures	305-856-2929
Raza Burgee	310-842-5583
Ernie Bustamante	ermie.bustamante@tvbyfox.com
Alberto Caballero	310-854-6518
Kirk Cabezas	818-998-3707
Mayra Cabrera	cricketg@att.net
Juan Caceres	212-491-3892
Al Cadena	bigfilfy@yahoo.com
Nora Cadena	512-380-0229
Elizabeth Caldas	212-788-7816
Carolyn Caldera	323-906-9500
Elizabeth Calienes	calienes@sakonline.com
Deborah Calla	310-392-3775
Cecilia Camacho	562-928-7942
Celia Camacho	562-869-6000
Ray Camacho	310-308-8031
Félix Leo Campos	718-842-4460

331

National Association of Latino Independent Producers

index by craft

1st Assistant Director
Michael Baez
Elvira Carrizal
Fernando Alberto Castroman
Maria Elena Chavez
Jaime Escallon
Elizabeth Gonzales
Rosa Gonzalez
Veronica Gonzalez-Rubio
Jay Guerra
Jesus Martinez
Marta Masferrer
Ricardo Mendez Matta
Chemen Ochoa
Kaaren F. Ochoa
Antonio Ogaz
Arturo Parra
George Parra
Carlos F. Pinero
Veronica Sanchez
Elena Santaballa
David Ticotin

2nd Assistant Director
Iris Almaraz
Valintino Costa
Elizabeth Gonzales
Vincent George Gonzales
Roberto F. Gonzalez-Rubio
Veronica Gonzalez-Rubio
Jay Guerra
Eric W. Henriquez
Gilda Longoria
Maria Meloni
Chemen Ochoa
George Parra
Carlos F. Pinero
Molly Robin Rodriguez
Elena Santaballa
David Ticotin
Fabiola Torres

2nd 2nd Assistant Director
Michael Baez
Maria Elena Chavez
Valintino Costa
Marisa Ferrey
Elizabeth Gonzales
Roberto F. Gonzalez-Rubio
Chemen Ochoa
Rafael Rosado

Acting Coach
Russell Alexander-Orozco
Raquel Almazan
Juliette Carrillo
Otavio Juliano
Victoria Regina
Carlos San Miguel

Actor
Carlos Albert
Raquel Almazan
Frank Aragon
Yareli Arizmendi
Janis Astor del Valle
Magi Avila
Antonio Banderas
Salvador Benavides
Jesse Borrego
Yvonne Caro Caro
Marisa Castaneda
Manuel Ceballos
Monique Gabriela Curnen
Angel David
Ana Marie de la Peña Portela
Dita de Leon
Mylo Egipciaco
Katrina Elias
Hector Elizondo
Phil Esparza
Tonantzin Esparza
Verena Faden
Evelina Fernandez
Nino Gabaldon
Andy Garcia
Irma Garcia-Sinclair
Michael Gavino
Mike Gomez
Marina González-Palmier
Salma Hayek
Yvan Iturriaga
John Leguizamo
Dennis Leoni
Ruth Livier
George Lopez
Josefina Lopez
Elmo Lugo
Cheech Marin
Joey Medina
Alberto Montero
Richard Montoya
Michael Narvaez
Jesus Nebot
Edward James Olmos

Antone Pagán
Elizabeth Peña
Patrick Perez
Ivonne Pérez Montijo
Felix Pire
Tony Plana
Begonya Plaza
Henry K. Priest
Freddie Prinze Jr.
Mario Ramirez
Victoria Regina
Ruperto Reyes
Paul Rodriguez
Rogelio & Rachel Salinas
Carlos San Miguel
Cristina Saralegui
Patricio Serna
Jimmy Smits
James Stevens-Arce
Jackie Torres
Leslie Valdes
Maria Valdez
Jerry Velasco
Christina Vergara-Andrews
Yvette Yates

ADR Looping
Carolina Posse
Carlos San Miguel
James Stevens-Arce

Agent
Carlos Alvarado
Michael Camacho
Carlos Carreras
Nancy Chaidez
Jaime Ferrer
Donna Gaba
Julissa Garcia
Guido Giordano
Christy Haubegger
Jorge Insua
Tania Lopez
Emanuel Nuñez
Gissele Ospina
Jorge Pinos
Nick Puga
Nikkolas Rey
Paul Santana
Steve Tellez
Kristine Wallis
Michael Wimer
Peggy Wintermute

Animator
Rafael Andreu
Felipe Galindo
Paco López
Phil Roman
Rafael Rosado
Aurora Sarabia

Art Department
Samuel Cordoba
Margarita Jimeno
Lawrence D. Melendez
Nicole Zepeda

Associate Producer
Magdalena Albizu
Natalia Almada
Maxim Almenas
Guillermo Arriaga
Shawna Baca
Jellybean Benitez
Carolyn Caldera
Félix Leo Campos
Phil Esparza
Judy Hecht-Dumontet
Rudy Hernandez, Jr.
Catherine Herrera
Rick Leal
Angela Martinez
Jon Mercedes III
Carolina Posse
Gabriela Quiros
Faith Radle
Molly Robin Rodriguez
Ingrid Rojas
Martin Salinas
Carlos San Miguel
Ray Santisteban
Laura Varela
Viviane Vives
Raquel Yepes

Attorney
Marcia L. Daley
Stephen Espinoza
Alexis Garcia
José Martinez, Jr.
Agustin Medina
Raul Puig
Fernando Ramirez
Arnie Reyes
Mike Tolleson

Award Shows
Russell Alexander-Orozco
Shawna Baca
Salvador Benavides
David Chavez
Errol Falcon
Diana E. Gonzales
Dan Guerrero
Brenda Herrera
Lionel Pasamonte
Jerry Velasco

Camera Assistant
Magdalena Albizu
Mike Racioppo
James P. Rodriguez
Marise Samitier
Carlos San Miguel
Edward Ybarra

Camera Operator
Damian Acevedo
Maxim Almenas
Michael Baez
Almudena Carracedo
Carlos Castañeda
Roger Castillo
David Cortez
Kaye Cruz
Rene Simon Cruz
Alicia Flores
Jeff Gipson
Soledad Herrera
Yvan Iturriaga
Arthur Lopez
Elmo Lugo
Rafael Merino
Bill Nieves
Antonio Ogaz
Arturo Parra
Mike Racioppo
James P. Rodriguez
Marise Samitier
Daniel Somarriba
Irene Sosa
Edward Ybarra
Guillermina Zabala
Alex Zacarias

Casting Director
Trina Bardusco
Maria Piedad Bonilla
Carmen Cuba
Dennis Gallegos
Belinda Gardea
Rosalinda Morales
Bob Morones
Louis E. Perego Moreno
Henry K. Priest
Carlos San Miguel
Blanca Valdez

Caterer
Lori Cordova

Co-Producer
Patricia Alvarado-Nuñez
Rafael Andreu
Isaac Artenstein
Jellybean Benitez
Paul F. Cajero
Natalie Chaidez
Zetna Fuentes
Isabel Galvan
Maureen Gosling
Laura Greenlee
Evangeline Griego
Dan Guerrero
Kristy Guevara-Flanagan
Mary Harder
Karen Johnson
Gloria LaMorte Herrera
Luisa Leschin
James Lima
Luis Llosa
Stephanie Martinez
Scott Montoya
Jose Manuel Murillo
Bertha Navarro
Lorenzo O'Brien
George Parra
David Portorreal
Anayansi Prado
Maria Teresa Rodriguez
Elaine Romero
Sonia Rosario
Walter Salles
Fabiola Torres
Rosie Vargas Goldberg
Ligiah Villalobos
Raquel Yepes

Composer
Gina Amador
Alejandro Amenabar
Joe Basquez
Federico Chavez Blanco
Joseph Julian Gonzalez
Richard Martinez
Happy Sanchez
Armando Torres

Costume Designer
Salvador Benavides
Joleen Koehly
Nicole Zepeda

Customs Broker
Cesar Peschiera

Dialect Coach
Maria Piedad Bonilla

Director, Commercial
Luis Aira
Evelyn Badia
Sergio Guerrero
Elmo Lugo
Antonio Ogaz
Pablo Toledo
Tontxi Vazquez
Diego Velasco

Director, Documentary
Maria Agui-Carter
Russell Alexander-Orozco
Natalia Almada
Patricia Alvarado-Nuñez
Louis Alvarez
Emilia Anguita Huerta
José Araujo
Luis Argueta
Trina Bardusco
Marta Bautis
Gabriela Bohm
Carlos Bolado
Margarita Borda
Frank Borres
Maria Bures
Nora Cadena
Deborah Calla
Almudena Carracedo
Elvira Carrizal
Carlos Castañeda

Roger Castillo
Maria Elena Chavez
Barbara Guadalupe Bustillos
  Cogswell
Maria Elena Cortinas
Rene Simon Cruz
Patricia Cunliffe
Carlos de Jesus
Nonny de la Peña
Alfredo de Villa
Alberto Dominguez
Mario Dubovoy
Jaime Escallon
Hector Galán
Lisa Garibay
Jeff Gipson
A.P. Gonzalez
Sonia Gonzalez
Maureen Gosling
Evangeline Griego
Armando Guareño
Kristy Guevara-Flanagan
Jason Gurvitz
Rudy Hernandez, Jr.
Catherine Herrera
Cristina Ibarra
Bill Jersey
Margarita Jimeno
Otavio Juliano
Cristina Kotz Cornejo
Rick Leal
Adam Lopez
Elmo Lugo
Juan Mandelbaum
Alma Martinez
Angela Martinez
Marta Masferrer
Andrea Melendez
Rafael Merino
John Montoya
Sylvia Morales
Jesus Nebot
Frances Negron-Muntaner
Andres Nicolini
Antonio Ogaz
José Orraca-Brandenberger
Jose Luis Partida
Antonio Pelaez
Marilyn Perez
Patrick Perez
Lisandro Perez-Rey
Miguel Picker
Begonya Plaza

Lourdes Portillo
Anayansi Prado
Gabriela Quiros
Mike Racioppo
Daniela Ramirez
Mario Ramirez
Diana Rico
Alex Rivera
Maria Teresa Rodriguez
Phillip Rodriguez
Sylvie Rokab
Fernanda Rossi
Bernardo Ruiz
Ray Santisteban
Aurora Sarabia
Stephen Sariñana-Lampson
Nancy Savoca
Irene Sosa
Gustavo Stebner
Dalia Tapia
Rick Tejada-Flores
Raymond Telles
Joseph Tovares
Ela Troyano
Dawn Valadez
John Valadez
Laura Varela
Adolfo Vargas
Ligiah Villalobos
Viviane Vives
Guillermina Zabala
Alex Zacarias
Juan Carlos Zaldivar
Marcos Zurinaga

Director, Documentary Short
Maria Agui-Carter
Russell Alexander-Orozco
Natalia Almada
Patricia Alvarado-Nuñez
Louis Alvarez
Edward Luis Arguelles
Janis Astor del Valle
Evelyn Badia
Trina Bardusco
Marta Bautis
Frank Borres
Elvira Carrizal
Carlos Castañeda
Marisa Castaneda
Maria Elena Chavez
Patricia Cunliffe
Carlos de Jesus

index by craft

Mario Dubovoy
Verena Faden
Hector Galán
Isabel Galvan
A.P. Gonzalez
Maureen Gosling
Kristy Guevara-Flanagan
Carla Gutierrez
Mary Harder
Rudy Hernandez, Jr.
Catherine Herrera
Margarita Jimeno
Rick Leal
Elmo Lugo
Juan Mandelbaum
Alma Martinez
Marta Masferrer
Bienvenida Matias
Andrea Melendez
Rafael Merino
Andres Nicolini
Jose Luis Partida
Dora Peña
Marilyn Perez
Patrick Perez
Lisandro Perez-Rey
Lourdes Portillo
Anayansi Prado
Gabriela Quiros
Mike Racioppo
Daniela Ramirez
Alex Rivera
Maria Teresa Rodriguez
Ingrid Rojas
Sylvie Rokab
Fernanda Rossi
Ray Santisteban
Stephen Sariñana-Lampson
Rick Tejada-Flores
Raymond Telles
Joseph Tovares
Ela Troyano
Dawn Valadez
John Valadez
Adolfo Vargas
Ligiah Villalobos
Vince Wright
Edward Ybarra
Marcos Zurinaga

Director, Experimental
Russell Alexander-Orozco
Natalia Almada
Raquel Almazan
Roger Castillo
Barbara Guadalupe Bustillos
  Cogswell
David Cortez
Patricia Cunliffe
Carlos de Jesus
Edgar Endress
Catherine Herrera
Soledad Herrera
Margarita Jimeno
Benjamin Lobato
Andrea Melendez
Lisandro Perez-Rey
Arnie Reyes
Guillermina Zabala

Director, Feature
Alejandro Agresti
Maria Agui-Carter
Luis Aira
Alejandro Amenabar
Frank Aragon
Alfonso Arau
Sergio Arau
José Araujo
Luis Argueta
Miguel Arteta
Carlos Avila
Michael Baez
Antonio Banderas
José Bayona
Carlos Bolado
Alberto Caballero
Juan Jose Campanella
Patricia Cardoso
Salvador Carrasco
Manuel Correa
Rene Simon Cruz
Alfonso Cuaron
Michael Cuesta
Mario F. de la Vega
Alfredo de Villa
Guillermo del Toro
Marlene Dermer
Maria Escobedo
Natatcha Estebanez
John Carlos Frey
Rodrigo Garcia
Tadeo Garcia

Georgina Garcia Riedel
Juan C. Garza
Alejandro Gonzalez Iñarritu
Armando Guareño
Johnathan Gwyn
Salma Hayek
Judy Hecht-Dumontet
Lou Hernandez
Leon Ichaso
Margarita Jimeno
Betty Kaplan
Luis Llosa
Josefina Lopez
Luis Mandoki
Ignacio Manubens
Cheech Marin
Chuck Martinez
Barbara Martinez-Jitner
Miguel Mas
Marta Masferrer
Joey Medina
Jim Mendiola
Linda Mendoza
Joe Menendez
Ramon Menendez
Rafael Merino
Nestor Miranda
Gerardo Naranjo
Gregory Nava
Jesus Nebot
Gustavo Nieto-Roa
Frank Nuñez
Javier Olivera
José Orraca-Brandenberger
Elizabeth Peña
Jack Perez
Patrick Perez
Tony Plana
Mike Racioppo
Franc Reyes
Robert Rodriguez
Jose Luis Ruiz
Walter Salles
Nancy Savoca
Adam Schlachter
Gustavo Stebner
Gabriela Tagliavini
Dalia Tapia
Pablo Toledo
Fina Torres
Jackie Torres
Joseph Tovares
Ela Troyano

Jeff Valdez
Luis Valdez
Jose Luis Valenzuela
Mirtha Vega
Aram Velazquez
Camilo Vila
Vlamyr Vizcaya
Juan Carlos Zaldivar
Del Zamora
Marcos Zurinaga

Director, Feature, Animated
Phil Roman

Director, Interstitial
Russell Alexander-Orozco
Maria Bures
Zetna Fuentes
Felipe Galindo
Manuel Ray Garcia
Cristina Ibarra
Marta Masferrer

Director, Mockumentary
Russell Alexander-Orozco
Patricia Cunliffe
Antonio Ogaz

Director, Music Video
Luis Aira
Maxim Almenas
Rafael Andreu
Michael Baez
Mike & Gibby Cevallos
Barbara Guadalupe Bustillos
  Cogswell
Maria Elena Cortinas
Patricia Cunliffe
Kevin Estrada
Jeff Gipson
Johnathan Gwyn
Francisco Hernandez
Soledad Herrera
Yvan Iturriaga
Margarita Jimeno
Benjamin Lobato
Miguel Mas
Alonso Mayo
Patrick Perez
Mike Racioppo
Ramon Ricard
Rogelio & Rachel Salinas

Vlamyr Vizcaya
Vince Wright

Director, PSA
Luis Aira
Russell Alexander-Orozco
Emilia Anguita Huerta
Edward Luis Arguelles
Michael Baez
Maria Bures
Elvira Carrizal
Carlos Castañeda
Roger Castillo
Maria Elena Cortinas
Patricia Cunliffe
Carlos de Jesus
Jeff Gipson
Elmo Lugo
Juan Mandelbaum
Marta Masferrer
Andrea Melendez
Jesus Nebot
Antonio Ogaz
Miguel Picker
Pablo Toledo
Astrid M. Vega
Alex Zacarias

Director, Radio Documentary
Russell Alexander-Orozco
Barbara Guadalupe Bustillos
  Cogswell
Patricia Cunliffe
Elmo Lugo
Laura Varela

Director, Second Unit
Emilia Anguita Huerta
Margarita Jimeno
Barbara Martinez-Jitner
Marta Masferrer
Chemen Ochoa
Vlamyr Vizcaya
Vince Wright

Director, Short
Jorge Aguirre
Carlos Albert
Russell Alexander-Orozco
Natalia Almada
Iris Almaraz
German Alonso

Rafael Andreu
Cruz Angeles
Emilia Anguita Huerta
Edward Luis Arguelles
Janis Astor del Valle
Shawna Baca
Evelyn Badia
Michael Baez
Salvador Benavides
María Berns
Maria Bures
Juan Caceres
Julissa Carmona
Juliette Carrillo
Elvira Carrizal
José Casado
Carlos Castañeda
Marisa Castaneda
Diana Contreras
Manuel Correa
Maria Elena Cortinas
Patricia Cunliffe
Carlos de Jesus
Perla de Leon
Rafael del Toro
Andrew Delaplaine
Nelson Denis
Mylo Egipciaco
Edgar Endress
Jaime Escallon
Kevin Estrada
Verena Faden
Felipe Galindo
Isabel Galvan
Georgina Garcia Riedel
Michael Gavino
A.P. Gonzalez
Omar Eqequiel Gonzalez
Sonia Gonzalez
Marina González-Palmier
Erika O. Grediaga
Mary Harder
Lou Hernandez
Fernando Herrera
Cristina Ibarra
Yvan Iturriaga
Margarita Jimeno
Betty Kaplan
Cristina Kotz Cornejo
Joseph LaMorte
Gloria LaMorte Herrera
Benjamin Lobato
Julian Londono

Adam Lopez
Josefina Lopez
Ignacio Manubens
Jesus Martinez
Miguel Mas
Marta Masferrer
Alonso Mayo
Andrea Melendez
Jim Mendiola
Elisha Miranda
Summer Joy Muñoz-Main
Gerardo Naranjo
Gustavo Nieto-Roa
Yazmin Ortiz
Joseph D. Peters
Begonya Plaza
David Portorreal
Mike Racioppo
Arnie Reyes
Ramon Ricard
Alexander Rivas
Jorge Rodriguez
Maria Teresa Rodriguez
Pilar Rodriguez-Aranda
Lupe Rodriguez-Haas
Elaine Romero
Nicole Sacker
Stephanie Saint Sanchez
Rogelio & Rachel Salinas
Marise Samitier
Aurora Sarabia
Adam Schlachter
Patricio Serna
Gustavo Stebner
James Stevens-Arce
Dalia Tapia
Pablo Toledo
Jackie Torres
Donna Umali
Mabel Valdiviezo
Deon Van Rooyen
Diego Velasco
Viviane Vives
Vince Wright
Edward Ybarra
Guillermina Zabala

Director, Short, Experimental
Maria Agui-Carter
Jorge Aguirre
Luis Aira
Russell Alexander-Orozco
Iris Almaraz

Raquel Almazan
Emilia Anguita Huerta
Juliette Carrillo
Marisa Castaneda
Patricia Cunliffe
Carlos de Jesus
Juan C. Garza
Omar Eqequiel Gonzalez
Lou Hernandez
Cristina Ibarra
Margarita Jimeno
Benjamin Lobato
Andrea Melendez
Dora Peña
Mike Racioppo
Arnie Reyes
Alexander Rivas
Maria Teresa Rodriguez
Marise Samitier
Rosario Sotelo
Michael Toribio
Vince Wright

Director, Stage Play
Raquel Almazan
Janis Astor del Valle
Michael Baez
Salvador Benavides
María Berns
Juliette Carrillo
Elvira Carrizal
Susan Claassen
Angel David
Mylo Egipciaco
Verena Faden
Josefina Lopez
Miguel Mas
Jon Mercedes III
Antone Pagán
Elizabeth Peña
Felix Pire
Alexander Rivas
Elaine Romero
Carlos San Miguel
James Stevens-Arce
Jose Luis Valenzuela
Nicole Zepeda

Director, TV Movie
Felix Alcala
Emilia Anguita Huerta
Alfonso Arau

Juliette Carrillo
Oscar Luis Costo
Manny Coto
Patricia Cunliffe
Carlos de Jesus
Leon Ichaso
Betty Kaplan
Jim Mendiola
Ramon Menendez
Jesus Nebot
José Orraca-Brandenberger
Miguel Picker
Mike Racioppo
Gabriela Tagliavini
Marcos Zurinaga

Director, TV Movie, Animated
Phil Roman

Director, TV Series
Jorge Aguirre
Felix Alcala
Maxim Almenas
Emilia Anguita Huerta
Miguel Arteta
Carlos Avila
Norbeto Barba
Maria Bures
Juan Jose Campanella
Salvador Carrasco
Mike & Gibby Cevallos
Alfonso Cuaron
Michael Cuesta
Patricia Cunliffe
Carlos de Jesus
Jaime Escallon
Errol Falcon
Joao Fernandes
Rodrigo Garcia
A.P. Gonzalez
Elmo Lugo
Juan Mandelbaum
Chuck Martinez
Ricardo Mendez Matta
Linda Mendoza
Joe Menendez
Ramon Menendez
Sylvia Morales
Gregory Nava
Jesus Nebot
Andres Nicolini
José Orraca-Brandenberger

Antonio Pelaez
Elizabeth Peña
Tony Plana
Mike Racioppo
Joe Ramirez
Diana Rico
James P. Rodriguez
Nancy Savoca
Luis Soto
Jesús Salvador Treviño
Luis Valdez
Camilo Vila
Vince Wright
Alex Zacarias
Del Zamora

Director, TV Series, Animated
Rafael Andreu
Emilia Anguita Huerta
Patricia Cunliffe
Sergio Guerrero
Phil Roman
Rafael Rosado

Director, TV Special
Frank Borres
Carlos de Jesus
Jaime Escallon
Zetna Fuentes
Benjamin Lobato
Elmo Lugo
Juan Mandelbaum
Antonio Pelaez
Miguel Picker
Mike Racioppo
Joe Ramirez
Alex Zacarias

Director/Producer, EPK
Russell Alexander-Orozco
Natalia Almada
Emilia Anguita Huerta
Maria Piedad Bonilla
Roger Castillo
Mike & Gibby Cevallos
Rene Simon Cruz
Juan Carlos (JC) Duran
Kevin Estrada
Rami Frankl
Zetna Fuentes
Lisa Garibay
Lucas Guerra

Jesus Nebot
Antonio Ogaz
Gabriela Quiros
Vince Wright

Director of Photography
Damian Acevedo
Alejandro Agresti
Felix Alcala
Natalia Almada
Iris Almaraz
Michael Baez
Almudena Carracedo
Elvira Carrizal
Roger Castillo
Chuy Chavez
Claudio Chea
Richard Crudo
Lucia Diaz
Jesus "Chuy" Elizondo
Joao Fernandes
Rodrigo Garcia
William Garcia
David Gonzalez
Victor Gonzalez
Fernando Herrera
Arthur Lopez
Emmanuel Lubezki
John Montoya
Guillermo Navarro
Edwin Pagan
Xavier Perez Grobet
Paulina Porter
Mike Racioppo
James P. Rodriguez
Sylvie Rokab
Juan Ruiz Anchía
Dalia Tapia
Diego Velasco
Aram Velazquez
Reynaldo Villalobos
Alex Wolfe
Vince Wright

Distributor
Roman Alvarado
Vanessa Arteaga
Jose Gonzalez
Alex Mendoza
Gustavo Nieto-Roa
Julio Noriega
Horacio Oyhanarte

Anthony Perez
Danny Rodriguez
Michael Toribio
Luis Villanueva

Editor
Luis Aira
Magdalena Albizu
Natalia Almada
Iris Almaraz
Rafael Andreu
Frank Aragon
Edward Luis Arguelles
Janis Astor del Valle
Michael Baez
Salvador Benavides
Gabriela Bohm
Carlos Bolado
Margarita Borda
Laura Cardona
Almudena Carracedo
Salvador Carrasco
José Casado
Carlos Castañeda
Marisa Castaneda
Roger Castillo
David Cortez
Rene Simon Cruz
Rafael del Toro
Alfonso Espinosa
Kevin Estrada
Verena Faden
Sebastian Feldman
Isabel Galvan
Manuel Ray Garcia
Juan C. Garza
Michael Gavino
Jeff Gipson
Sonia Gonzalez
Maureen Gosling
Phillip V. Guerra
Kristy Guevara-Flanagan
Carla Gutierrez
Matthew Handal
Fernando Herrera
Soledad Herrera
Cristina Kotz Cornejo
Deborah Kravitz
Joseph LaMorte
Gloria LaMorte Herrera
Elmo Lugo
Ignacio Manubens
Marta Masferrer

Rick Ramirez
Ana Ramos
Lise Ramos
Angel Rivera
Carolina Rodriguez
Richard Rodriguez
Sonia Rosario
Gustavo Sagastume
Richard Saiz
Carlos Sanchez
Ralph Sanchez
Gail Silva
Antonio Sosa
Herta Suarez
Jeff Valdez
Jerry Velasco
Luis Villanueva

Executive Producer
Sergio Aguero
Jorge Aguirre
Alejandro Amenabar
Elizabeth Avellan
Carlos Avila
David Chavez
Kaye Cruz
Carlos de Jesus
Moctesuma Esparza
Anna Felix
Evy Ledesma Galán
Hector Galán
Kathryn F. Galán
Nely Galán
Andy Garcia
Alejandro Gonzalez Iñarritu
Erika O. Grediaga
Dennis Leoni
Elmo Lugo
Barbara Martinez-Jitner
Jon Mercedes III
Scott Montoya
Gregory Nava
Lionel Pasamonte
Santiago Pozo
Jorge Reyes
Isabel Rivera
Danny Rodriguez
Robert Rodriguez
Phil Roman
Cristina Saralegui
Rick Telles
Frida Torresblanco
David C. Valdes

Jeff Valdez
Marcos Zurinaga

Graphic Designer
Samuel Cordoba
Patricia Cunliffe
Lucas Guerra
Alex Mendoza
Joe Miraglilo
Mike Racioppo
Leo Reyes
Alexander Rivas
Stephen Sariñana-Lampson
Samantha Smith
Aram Velazquez

Line Producer
Victor Albarran
Patricia Cunliffe
Alicia Flores
Rosa Gonzalez
Laura Greenlee
Evangeline Griego
Soledad Herrera
José Carlos Mangual
Nellie Medina
Kaaren F. Ochoa
Antonio Ogaz
Edwin Pagan
Ramon Ricard
Alicia Rivera Frankl
Frida Torresblanco
Vince Wright
Raquel Yepes

Manager
Marvin Acuña
Marilyn R. Atlas
Ivan de Paz
Ron del Rio
Miguel Herrera
Jon Mercedes III
Omar Meza
Santiago Pozo
Xaviar C. Salinas
Matt Wolf

Marketing/Fundraising Consultant
Lucas Guerra
Brenda Herrera
Kathy Im

Angela Martinez
Jon Mercedes III
Lourdes Ortega
Sandra Perez
Carlos San Miguel
Michael Toribio
Benjamin N. Torres
Kirk Whisler

Media Advocate
Bonnie Abaunza
Lucero Arellano
Eddie T. Arnold
Kirk Cabezas
Claudia Flores
Consuelo Flores
Helen Hernandez
Brenda Herrera
Mary Lampe
Marcie Longoria
Cynthia Lopez
Andrea Melendez
Lisa Navarrete
Alex Nogales
Dr. Chon Noriega
Edwin Pagan
Louis E. Perego Moreno
Sandra Perez
Angel Rivera
Alex Rodriguez
Richard Rodriguez
Gail Silva
Herta Suarez
Jerry Velasco
Alex Zacarias

Novelist
Eric Garcia
Carolina Garcia-Aguilera

Postproduction Supervisor
Elmo Lugo
Faith Radle
Nestor N. Rodriguez
Irene Sosa
Astrid M. Vega

Producer, Commercial
Luis Aira
Evelyn Badia
Maria Bures
Deborah Calla

Félix Leo Campos
Carlos Castañeda
Maria Chavez
Armando Guareño
Fernando Herrera
Soledad Herrera
Diana Lesmez
Arthur Lopez
Elmo Lugo
Juan Mandelbaum
José Carlos Mangual
Nellie Medina
Maria Meloni
Antonio Ogaz
Jose Luis Partida
Emily Perez
Begonya Plaza
Ginny Wolnowics
Vince Wright
Raquel Yepes
Alex Zacarias

Producer, Documentary
Maria Agui-Carter
Magdalena Albizu
Russell Alexander-Orozco
Natalia Almada
Patricia Alvarado-Nuñez
Louis Alvarez
Claudia Amaya
Emilia Anguita Huerta
José Araujo
Luis Argueta
Evelyn Badia
Trina Bardusco
Marta Bautis
Jellybean Benitez
Nelson Betancourt
Gabriela Bohm
Angelo Bolanos
Margarita Borda
Frank Borres
Maria Bures
Deborah Calla
Félix Leo Campos
Almudena Carracedo
Carlos Castañeda
Roger Castillo
Pedro Celedon
Maria Elena Chavez
Barbara Guadalupe Bustillos
  Cogswell
Alex D. Cortez

Maria Elena Cortinas
Rene Simon Cruz
Patricia Cunliffe
Carlos de Jesus
Nonny de la Peña
Nancy de los Santos
Alberto Dominguez
Mario Dubovoy
Alfonso Espinosa
Paul Espinosa
Natatcha Estebanez
Hector Galán
Isabel Galvan
Lisa Garibay
Polita Glynn
A.P. Gonzalez
Jackie Gonzalez-Carlos
Maureen Gosling
Evangeline Griego
Armando Guareño
Phillip V. Guerra
Kristy Guevara-Flanagan
Jason Gurvitz
Matthew Handal
Rudy Hernandez, Jr.
Catherine Herrera
Fernando Herrera
Cristina Ibarra
Bill Jersey
Lillian Jiménez
Mercedes Jimenez-Ramirez
Karen Johnson
Joseph LaMorte
Gloria LaMorte Herrera
Frances Lausell
Rick Leal
Diana Lesmez
Adam Lopez
Cynthia Lopez
Elmo Lugo
Yuri Makino
Juan Mandelbaum
Alma Martinez
Marta Masferrer
Bienvenida Matias
Eren McGinnis
Nellie Medina
Andrea Melendez
Rafael Merino
Melissa Montero
John Montoya
Tomas Aceves Mournian
Gregory Nava

Frances Negron-Muntaner
Gustavo Nieto-Roa
Antonio Ogaz
Edward James Olmos
José Orraca-Brandenberger
Louis E. Perego Moreno
Marilyn Perez
Patrick Perez
Lourdes Portillo
Santiago Pozo
Anayansi Prado
Ernesto Quintero
Gabriela Quiros
Mike Racioppo
Faith Radle
Daniela Ramirez
Mario Ramirez
Diana Rico
Alex Rivera
Felix Rodriguez
Maria Teresa Rodriguez
Phillip Rodriguez
Sylvie Rokab
Fernanda Rossi
Bernardo Ruiz
Ray Santisteban
Stephen Sariñana-Lampson
Irene Sosa
Gustavo Stebner
Rick Tejada-Flores
Raymond Telles
Joseph Tovares
Ela Troyano
Pepe Urquijo
Dawn Valadez
John Valadez
Maria Valdez
Laura Varela
Rosadel Varela
Adolfo Vargas
Ligiah Villalobos
Alex Wolfe
Vince Wright
Raquel Yepes
Alex Zacarias
Marcos Zurinaga

**Producer,
Documentary Short**
Maria Agui-Carter
Russell Alexander-Orozco
Patricia Alvarado-Nuñez
Louis Alvarez

Emilia Anguita Huerta
Edward Luis Arguelles
Janis Astor del Valle
Trina Bardusco
Marta Bautis
Jellybean Benitez
Frank Borres
Carlos Castañeda
Maria Elena Chavez
Patricia Cunliffe
Carlos de Jesus
Mario Dubovoy
Paul Espinosa
Hector Galán
Polita Glynn
A.P. Gonzalez
Maureen Gosling
Kristy Guevara-Flanagan
Carla Gutierrez
Matthew Handal
Mary Harder
Rudy Hernandez, Jr.
Margarita Jimeno
Frances Lausell
Rick Leal
Elmo Lugo
Juan Mandelbaum
Alma Martinez
Marta Masferrer
Eren McGinnis
Rafael Merino
Tomas Aceves Mournian
Antone Pagán
Marilyn Perez
Patrick Perez
Lourdes Portillo
Anayansi Prado
Gabriela Quiros
Mike Racioppo
Faith Radle
Daniela Ramirez
Alex Rivera
Maria Teresa Rodriguez
Sylvie Rokab
Fernanda Rossi
Ray Santisteban
Dalia Tapia
Rick Tejada-Flores
Raymond Telles
Joseph Tovares
Ela Troyano
Dawn Valadez
John Valadez

Laura Varela
Rosadel Varela
Adolfo Vargas
Ligiah Villalobos
Vince Wright

Producer, DVD
Maria Agui-Carter
Maria Piedad Bonilla
David Cortez
Rene Simon Cruz
Rami Frankl
Jackie Gonzalez-Carlos
Maureen Gosling
Elmo Lugo
Juan Mandelbaum
Lisandro Perez-Rey
Mike Racioppo
Stephen Sariñana-Lampson

Producer, Educational/Industrial
Maria Agui-Carter
Russell Alexander-Orozco
Evelyn Badia
Maria Piedad Bonilla
Margarita Borda
Maria Bures
Carlos Castañeda
Roger Castillo
Patricia Cunliffe
Alfonso Espinosa
Elmo Lugo
Juan Mandelbaum
José Carlos Mangual
Angela Martinez
Jesus Nebot
Antonio Ogaz
Marilyn Perez
Lisandro Perez-Rey
Mike Racioppo
Maria Teresa Rodriguez
Fernando Ruiz
Dalia Tapia
Fabiola Torres
Dawn Valadez
Laura Varela
Vince Wright
Alex Zacarias

Producer, Feature
Marvin Acuña
Alejandro Agresti
Maria Agui-Carter
Alejandro Amenabar
Olga Arana
Alfonso Arau
Sergio Arau
José Araujo
Luis Argueta
Yareli Arizmendi
Ishmael Arredondo Henriquez
Isaac Artenstein
Marilyn R. Atlas
Elizabeth Avellan
Mario Avila
José Bayona
Jellybean Benitez
Cynthia Buchanan
Alberto Caballero
Carolyn Caldera
Deborah Calla
Ivan Cevallos
Alex D. Cortez
Rene Simon Cruz
Michael Cuesta
Tania Cypriano
Victor de Jesus
Mario F. de la Vega
Ivan de Paz
Alfredo de Villa
Guillermo del Toro
Moctesuma Esparza
Cari Esta-Albert
Natatcha Estebanez
Kathryn F. Galán
Erick C. Garcia
Lisa Garibay
Victor Gonzalez
Erika O. Grediaga
Sergio Guerrero
Jason Gurvitz
Christy Haubegger
Salma Hayek
Judy Hecht-Dumontet
Margarita Jimeno
Karen Johnson
Judi Jordan
Frances Lausell
John Leguizamo
Diana Lesmez
Luis Llosa
Rick Lombardo

Joseph D. Peters
David Portorreal
Carolina Posse
Henry K. Priest
Ernesto Quintero
Arnie Reyes
Alexander Rivas
Jorge Rodriguez
Maria Teresa Rodriguez
Nestor N. Rodriguez
Elaine Romero
Rogelio & Rachel Salinas
Carlos San Miguel
James Stevens-Arce
Dalia Tapia
Pablo Toledo
Fabiola Torres
Pepe Urquijo
Maria Valdez
Deon Van Rooyen
Tontxi Vazquez
Ginny Wolnowics
Vince Wright
Raquel Yepes

Producer, Stage Play

Raquel Almazan
Janis Astor del Valle
Michael Baez
José Bayona
María Berns
Juliette Carrillo
Tonantzin Esparza
Evelina Fernandez
Zetna Fuentes
Josefina Lopez
Miguel Mas
Richard Montoya
Antone Pagán
Ivonne Pérez Montijo
Ernesto Quintero
Carlos San Miguel
James Stevens-Arce
Jackie Torres
Jose Luis Valenzuela

Producer, TV Movie

Marilyn R. Atlas
Jellybean Benitez
Natalie Chaidez
Oscar Luis Costo
Carlos de Jesus

Ivan de Paz
Moctesuma Esparza
Phil Esparza
Cari Esta-Albert
Tery Lopez
Omar Meza
Kimberly Myers
José Orraca-Brandenberger
Sonia Rosario
Luis Soto

Producer, TV Series

Jorge Aguirre
Maxim Almenas
Carlos Avila
Jellybean Benitez
Maria Bures
Paul F. Cajero
Laura Castañeda
Mike & Gibby Cevallos
Natalie Chaidez
Manny Coto
Tania Cypriano
Carlos de Jesus
Juan Carlos (JC) Duran
Moctesuma Esparza
Dolly Josette Espinal
Natatcha Estebanez
Errol Falcon
Cris (Cristóbal) Franco
Nely Galán
Gia Galligani
Hector Gonzalez
Phillip V. Guerra
James Lima
Rick Lombardo
Gilda Longoria
Tery Lopez
Elmo Lugo
Juan Mandelbaum
Luis Mandoki
Barbara Martinez-Jitner
Joey Medina
Maria Meloni
Joe Menendez
Sylvia Morales
Peter Murrieta
Gregory Nava
Bill Nieves
Lorenzo O'Brien
José Orraca-Brandenberger
Lionel Pasamonte
Antonio Pelaez

Laura Pelaez
Maria Perez Brown
Lisandro Perez-Rey
Joe Ramirez
Leo Reyes
Diana Rico
Isabel Rivera
Jose Rivera
James P. Rodriguez
Lupe Rodriguez-Haas
Phil Roman
Robert G. Rose
Ray Santisteban
Manny Santos
Luis Soto
Gustavo Stebner
Dalia Tapia
Rick Telles
Joseph Tovares
Jeff Valdez
Vince Wright
Alex Zacarias

Producer, TV Series, Animated

Rafael Andreu
Phil Roman

Producer, TV Special

Frank Borres
David Chavez
Carlos de Jesus
Juan Carlos (JC) Duran
Cris (Cristóbal) Franco
Gia Galligani
Diana E. Gonzales
Gilda Longoria
Elmo Lugo
Juan Mandelbaum
Marta Masferrer
Eren McGinnis
Joey Medina
Nellie Medina
Lionel Pasamonte
Paul Rodriguez
Jeff Valdez
Yvette Yates

Production Accountant

Alicia Rivera Frankl

Production Assistant
Barbara Guadalupe Bustillos Cogswell
Keyla Echevarria
Carlos Espinoza
Mariana Garbagnati
Mary Harder
Sandra Hernández
Yvan Iturriaga
Margarita Jimeno
Benjamin Lopez
Rachel Pineda
Mike Racioppo
Jorge Rodriguez
Lupe Rodriguez-Haas
Fabiola Torres
Rosadel Varela
Astrid M. Vega
Vince Wright
Nicole Zepeda

Production Consultant
Maria Bozzi
Diana E. Gonzales
Laura Greenlee
Scott Kardel
Octavio Marin
Mike Racioppo
Alicia Rivera Frankl
Ethan Van Thillo

Production Coordinator
Maria Piedad Bonilla
Maria Elena Chavez
Valintino Costa
Patricia Cunliffe
Isabel Galvan
Fernando Herrera
Melissa Levine
Benjamin Lopez
Tery Lopez
Maria Meloni
Jose Manuel Murillo
Mike Racioppo
Guiomar Romero
Manny Saldivar
Carlos San Miguel
Benjamin N. Torres
Ethan Van Thillo
Raquel Yepes
Alex Zacarias

Production Designer/ Art Director
Magdalena Albizu
Elizabeth Calienes
Samuel Cordoba
Joleen Koehly
Lawrence D. Melendez
Mike Racioppo
Thomas Zamora
Nicole Zepeda

Production Facilities & Services
Rafael Andreu
Victoria Arias-Fraasa
Rami Frankl
Michelle Guanca
Shelli Hall
Francisco Hernandez
Richard Martinez
Dan Medina
Jon Mercedes III
Joe Miraglilo
Sergio Molina
Alex Moreno
Annie Perez
Cesar Peschiera
Anna M. Poore-Cordova
Margarita Ramon
Paul Rodriguez
Frances Tobler
Roselly A. Torres-Rojas

Production Manager
Leslie Arcia
Paul F. Cajero
Maria Chavez
Sergio Coronado
Victor de Jesus
Gilda Longoria
Octavio Marin
Maria Meloni
Richard A. Murray Jr.
Kaaren F. Ochoa
David Portorreal
Alicia Rivera Frankl
Veronica Sanchez
Ginny Wolnowics
Edward Ybarra
Raquel Yepes

Promotion/Event Producer
Jaime Angulo
Shawna Baca
Maria Piedad Bonilla
Félix Leo Campos
Juan Carlos (JC) Duran
Jeff Gipson
Lucas Guerra
Claudine "Playful" Guerrero
Bel Hernandez
Peggy Hernandez
Brenda Herrera
Andy Lebron
Melissa Levine
Benjamin Lopez
Elmo Lugo
Antonio Ogaz
Carolina Posse
Henry K. Priest
Mike Racioppo
Lupe Rodriguez-Haas
Manny Saldivar
Carlos San Miguel
Benjamin N. Torres

Publicist
Frank Barron
Kirk Cabezas
Dan del Campo
Norma Flores
Jon Mercedes III
Lourdes Ortega
Gigi Otero
Alex Rodriguez
Benjamin N. Torres

Researcher
Edward Luis Arguelles
Daniel Bernardi
Maria Piedad Bonilla
David Cortez
Patricia Cunliffe
Mariana Garbagnati
Erick C. Garcia
Michelle Guanca
Sandra Hernández
Gary Keller
Rick Leal
Melissa Levine
Alma Martinez
Andrea Melendez
Danilo Rodriguez

Abel Salas
Carlos San Miguel
Fabiola Torres
Roselly A. Torres-Rojas

Script Supervisor
Evelyn Badia
Maria Meloni
Aurora Sarabia
Nicole Zepeda

Sound
Joe Basquez
Kaye Cruz
Jeff Gipson
Andres Nicolini
Daniel Somarriba

Special/Visual Effects
Sebastian Feldman
Gary Michael Gutierrez

Storyboard Artist
Felipe Galindo
Rafael Rosado

Stunt Man
Carlos San Miguel

Supervising Producer
Melissa Levine
Antonio Ogaz
Sonia Rosario
Carlos San Miguel

Talk Show Host
Magi Avila
Mylo Egipciaco
Cris (Cristóbal) Franco
Elmo Lugo
Jesus Nebot
Jonisha Rios
Cristina Saralegui

Web Developer
Joe Basquez
Samuel Cordoba
Kaye Cruz
Nicole Mattei
Joe Miraglilo
Rachel Pineda

Mike Racioppo
Victoria Regina
Stephen Sariñana-Lampson
Samantha Smith
Benjamin N. Torres

Writer, Award Shows
Russell Alexander-Orozco
David Chavez
Cris (Cristóbal) Franco
Dan Guerrero
Elmo Lugo
Lionel Pasamonte
Jerry Velasco

Writer, Commercial
Luis Aira
Patricia Cunliffe
Sergio Guerrero
Gloria LaMorte Herrera
Elmo Lugo
Jesus Nebot
Henry K. Priest
Carlos San Miguel
Astrid M. Vega
Diego Velasco
Vlamyr Vizcaya
Vince Wright

Writer, Documentary
Maria Agui-Carter
Russell Alexander-Orozco
Emilia Anguita Huerta
José Araujo
Luis Argueta
Gabriela Bohm
Margarita Borda
Maria Bures
Roger Castillo
Joaquin Chavez
Maria Elena Chavez
Patricia Cunliffe
Nonny de la Peña
Nancy de los Santos
Mylo Egipciaco
Lisa Garibay
Jason Gurvitz
Matthew Handal
Mary Harder
Cristina Ibarra
Rick Leal
Elmo Lugo

Juan Mandelbaum
Alma Martinez
Nellie Medina
Andrea Melendez
Tomas Aceves Mournian
Peter Murrieta
Jesus Nebot
Antonio Pelaez
Louis E. Perego Moreno
Marilyn Perez
Patrick Perez
Lisandro Perez-Rey
Begonya Plaza
Anayansi Prado
Gabriela Quiros
Mario Ramirez
Diana Rico
Fernanda Rossi
Martin Salinas
Rick Tejada-Flores
Raymond Telles
Joseph Tovares
Ela Troyano
Dawn Valadez
John Valadez
Adolfo Vargas
Ligiah Villalobos

Writer, Documentary Short
Iris Almaraz
Emilia Anguita Huerta
Edward Luis Arguelles
Marisa Castaneda
Maria Elena Chavez
Barbara Guadalupe Bustillos
  Cogswell
Patricia Cunliffe
Matthew Handal
Mary Harder
Rick Leal
Elmo Lugo
Juan Mandelbaum
Alma Martinez
Andrea Melendez
Tomas Aceves Mournian
Andres Nicolini
Louis E. Perego Moreno
Marilyn Perez
Patrick Perez
Lisandro Perez-Rey
Anayansi Prado
Gabriela Quiros
Fernanda Rossi

Martin Salinas
Rick Tejada-Flores
Raymond Telles
Joseph Tovares
Ela Troyano
Dawn Valadez
John Valadez
Adolfo Vargas
Ligiah Villalobos
Vince Wright

Writer, Edutainment
Luis Aira
Iris Almaraz
Maxim Almenas
Emilia Anguita Huerta
Margarita Borda
Roger Castillo
Mylo Egipciaco
Verena Faden
Cris (Cristóbal) Franco
Cristina Ibarra
Elmo Lugo
Jesus Nebot
Marilyn Perez
Patrick Perez
Lisandro Perez-Rey
Stephanie Saint Sanchez
Fabiola Torres
Vince Wright

Writer, Experimental
Raquel Almazan
Edward Luis Arguelles
Marisa Castaneda
Roger Castillo
Patricia Cunliffe
Ana Marie de la Peña Portela
Andrea Melendez
Patrick Perez
Vince Wright

Writer, Feature
Ricardo Acuña
Alejandro Agresti
Jorge Aguirre
Luis Aira
Russell Alexander-Orozco
Raquel Almazan
Alejandro Amenabar
Emilia Anguita Huerta
Frank Aragon

Sergio Arau
José Araujo
Edward Luis Arguelles
Luis Argueta
Yareli Arizmendi
Ishmael Arredondo Henriquez
Guillermo Arriaga
Miguel Arteta
Mario Avila
Michael Baez
José Bayona
Vera Blasi
Carlos Bolado
Juan Jose Campanella
Juliette Carrillo
Elvira Carrizal
Mike & Gibby Cevallos
Ernie Contreras
Rosemary Contreras
Rene Simon Cruz
Patricia Cunliffe
Angel David
Victor de Jesus
Mario F. de la Vega
Nancy de los Santos
Guillermo del Toro
Mylo Egipciaco
Katrina Elias
Jaime Escallon
Maria Escobedo
Alfonso Espinosa
Evelina Fernandez
Cris (Cristóbal) Franco
John Carlos Frey
Rodrigo Garcia
Georgina Garcia Riedel
Lisa Garibay
Michael Gavino
Julieta Gonzalez
Sonia Gonzalez
Alejandro Gonzalez Iñarritu
Erika O. Grediaga
Sergio Guerrero
Jason Gurvitz
Lou Hernandez
Fernando Herrera
Cristina Ibarra
Leon Ichaso
Benjamin Lobato
Benjamin Lopez
Jessica Lopez
Josefina Lopez
Ignacio Manubens

Cheech Marin
Barbara Martinez-Jitner
Miguel Mas
Marta Masferrer
Joey Medina
Nellie Medina
Jim Mendiola
Joe Menendez
Ramon Menendez
Jon Mercedes III
Nestor Miranda
Sylvia Morales
Michael Narvaez
Gregory Nava
Frank Nuñez
Javier Olivera
José Orraca-Brandenberger
Antonio Pelaez
Jack Perez
Patrick Perez
Ivonne Pérez Montijo
Lisandro Perez-Rey
Erin Ploss-Campoamor
Henry K. Priest
Franc Reyes
Jorge Reyes
Jose Rivera
Baldemar Rodriguez
Jorge Rodriguez
Robert Rodriguez
Lupe Rodriguez-Haas
Elaine Romero
Marconi Salazar
Martin Salinas
Rogelio & Rachel Salinas
Walter Salles
Marise Samitier
Carlos San Miguel
Nancy Savoca
Adam Schlachter
Gustavo Stebner
James Stevens-Arce
Gabriela Tagliavini
Dalia Tapia
Miguel Tejada-Flores
Pablo Toledo
Fina Torres
Jackie Torres
Oskar Toruno
Jesús Salvador Treviño
Ela Troyano
Leslie Valdes
Jeff Valdez

Rosie Vargas Goldberg
Diego Velasco
Ligiah Villalobos
Viviane Vives
Vlamyr Vizcaya
Edward Ybarra
Marcos Zurinaga

Writer, Game Show
Cris (Cristóbal) Franco
Jon Mercedes III

Writer, Magazine Articles
Belinda Acosta
Maria Piedad Bonilla
Kirk Cabezas
Michael Caro
Laura Castañeda
Barbara Guadalupe Bustillos
  Cogswell
Patricia Cunliffe
Mylo Egipciaco
Cris (Cristóbal) Franco
Bel Hernandez
Brenda Herrera
Robert Leach
Jessica Lopez
Angela Martinez
Sandra Perez
Lisandro Perez-Rey
Diana Rico
Elaine Romero
Carlos San Miguel
Cristina Saralegui
James Stevens-Arce
Kirk Whisler

Writer, Short
Jorge Aguirre
Luis Aira
Iris Almaraz
Cruz Angeles
Emilia Anguita Huerta
Sergio Arau
Edward Luis Arguelles
Yareli Arizmendi
Ishmael Arredondo Henriquez
Guillermo Arriaga
Janis Astor del Valle
Mario Avila
Shawna Baca
Evelyn Badia

Michael Baez
Salvador Benavides
María Berns
Juan Caceres
Julissa Carmona
Juliette Carrillo
Elvira Carrizal
Marisa Castaneda
Joaquin Chavez
Ana Marie de la Peña Portela
Perla de Leon
Nelson Denis
Mylo Egipciaco
Jaime Escallon
Verena Faden
Cris (Cristóbal) Franco
Isabel Galvan
Georgina Garcia Riedel
Lisa Garibay
Michael Gavino
Omar Eqequiel Gonzalez
Erika O. Grediaga
Jason Gurvitz
Mary Harder
Lou Hernandez
Fernando Herrera
Betty Kaplan
Joseph LaMorte
Gloria LaMorte Herrera
Benjamin Lobato
Julian Londono
Adam Lopez
Benjamin Lopez
Ignacio Manubens
Jesus Martinez
Miguel Mas
Marta Masferrer
Alonso Mayo
Jim Mendiola
Jon Mercedes III
Elisha Miranda
Andres Nicolini
Frank Nuñez
Antone Pagán
Edwin Pagan
Ivonne Pérez Montijo
Joseph D. Peters
Erin Ploss-Campoamor
David Portorreal
Arnie Reyes
Ruperto Reyes
Diana Rico
Alexander Rivas

Jorge Rodriguez
Lupe Rodriguez-Haas
Elaine Romero
Nicole Sacker
Stephanie Saint Sanchez
Marise Samitier
Carlos San Miguel
Aurora Sarabia
Adam Schlachter
Patricio Serna
James Stevens-Arce
Pablo Toledo
Leslie Valdes
Deon Van Rooyen
Diego Velasco
Vince Wright
Edward Ybarra
Del Zamora
Nicole Zepeda

Writer, Stage Play
Raquel Almazan
Janis Astor del Valle
Michael Baez
José Bayona
María Berns
Juliette Carrillo
Elvira Carrizal
Angel David
Mylo Egipciaco
Katrina Elias
Verena Faden
Evelina Fernandez
Cris (Cristóbal) Franco
Anne Garcia-Romero
Michael Gavino
Marina González-Palmier
Benjamin Lobato
Tomas Aceves Mournian
Antone Pagán
Ivonne Pérez Montijo
Felix Pire
Ruperto Reyes
Alexander Rivas
Elaine Romero
Carlos San Miguel
James Stevens-Arce
Leslie Valdes

351

Writer, TV Movie
Emilia Anguita Huerta
Alfonso Arau
Natalie Chaidez
Ernie Contreras
Nancy de los Santos
Maria Escobedo
Diego Gutierrez
Leon Ichaso
Betty Kaplan
Dennis Leoni
Luis Llosa
Josefina Lopez
Jim Mendiola
Ramon Menendez
Gregory Nava
José Orraca-Brandenberger
Jose Rivera
Jeff Valdez
Ligiah Villalobos

Writer, TV Series
Jorge Aguirre
Luis Aira
Maxim Almenas
Carlos Avila
Juan Jose Campanella
Laura Castañeda
Mike & Gibby Cevallos
Natalie Chaidez
Barbara Guadalupe Bustillos
   Cogswell
Ernie Contreras
Rosemary Contreras

Victor de Jesus
Nonny de la Peña
Nancy de los Santos
Jaime Escallon
Maria Escobedo
Dolly Josette Espinal
Alfonso Espinosa
Natatcha Estebanez
Cris (Cristóbal) Franco
Rodrigo Garcia
A.P. Gonzalez
Erika O. Grediaga
Phillip V. Guerra
Diego Gutierrez
Fernando Herrera
Dennis Leoni
Luisa Leschin
Josefina Lopez
Barbara Martinez-Jitner
Joey Medina
Nellie Medina
Joe Menendez
Ramon Menendez
Jon Mercedes III
Peter Murrieta
Gregory Nava
Javier Olivera
José Orraca-Brandenberger
Antonio Pelaez
Maria Perez Brown
Joe Ramirez
Jorge Reyes
Diana Rico
Jose Rivera

James P. Rodriguez
James Stevens-Arce
Leslie Valdes
Jeff Valdez
Luis Valdez
Ligiah Villalobos
Vince Wright
Del Zamora

Writer, TV Series, Animated
Jorge Aguirre
Rafael Andreu
Barbara Guadalupe Bustillos
   Cogswell
Ernie Contreras
Rosemary Contreras
Sergio Guerrero
Jessica Lopez
Ashley Mendoza
Maria Perez Brown
Phil Roman
Leslie Valdes
Ligiah Villalobos

Writer, TV Special
Nonny de la Peña
Cris (Cristóbal) Franco
Zetna Fuentes
John Leguizamo
Antonio Pelaez
Jeff Valdez
Astrid M. Vega

National Association of Latino Independent Producers

index by
state

355

Fernando Herrera
Mike Higuera
Lena Hyde
Leon Ichaso
Jorge Insua
Arturo Interian
Yvan Iturriaga
Raymundo Jacquez
Bill Jersey
Judi Jordan
Otavio Juliano
Betty Kaplan
Robert Kubilos
Carlos R. Lara
Chris Lemos
Dennis Leoni
Luisa Leschin
Diana Lesmez
Melissa Levine
David Levinson
Anna Leyva
Josef Manuel Liles
James Lima
Paul Lima
Matias Lira
Ruth Livier
Efrain Logreira
Rick Lombardo
Adam Lopez
Angel Dean Lopez
George Lopez
Jessica Lopez
Tania Lopez
Tery Lopez
Lalo Lopez Alcaraz
Roberto Lovato
Carrie Lozano
Monica Lozano
Emmanuel Lubezki
Fred Lugo
Azucena Maldonado
Luis Mandoki
José Carlos Mangual
Pancho Mansfield
Ignacio Manubens
Billy Marchese
Poli Marichal
Cheech Marin
Octavio Marin
Carmen Marron
Ivy Martin
Alma Martinez
Beatriz "Vivi" Martinez
Benito Martinez
Chuck Martinez
Gerardo Vicente Martinez
Johnnie Martinez
José Martinez, Jr.
Barbara Martinez-Jitner

Miguel Mas
Alonso Mayo
Sara Mayorga
Agustin Medina
Dan Medina
Daniel Medina
Hugo Medina
Joey Medina
Louis Medina
Joey Mendez
Ricardo Mendez Matta
Jim Mendiola
Alex Mendoza
Edy Mendoza
Linda Mendoza
Joe Menendez
Ramon Menendez
Jon Mercedes III
Humberto L. Meza
Jean Meza
Leonardo Meza
Omar Meza
Oralia Michel
Nestor Miranda
Lilia Molina
Julie Monroy
Ricardo Montalban
John Montoya
Richard Montoya
Scott Montoya
Danny Mora
Rosalinda Morales
Sylvia Morales
Alex Moreno
Mylene Moreno
Bob Morones
Tomas Aceves Mournian
Maria Muñoz
Robert Muñoz
Summer Joy Muñoz-Main
Jose Manuel Murillo
Maria Murillo
Joaquin Murrieta
Kimberly Myers
Mateo-Erique Nagassi
Monica Nanez
Gerardo Naranjo
Gregory Nava
Guillermo Navarro
Jesus Nebot
Nestor Nieves
Alex Nogales
Dr. Chon Noriega
Emanuel Nuñez
Frank Nuñez
Lorenzo O'Brien
Antonio Ogaz
Paul Ohnersorgen
Francisco Olea

Jorge Oliver
Javier Olivera
Edward James Olmos
Andrew Orci
Delia Orjuela
Paulette Orona
Roberta Orona-Cordova
Lourdes Ortega
David Ortiz
Luis Ortiz
Yazmin Ortiz
Gissele Ospina
Gigi Otero
Nelly Otsu
Horacio Oyhanarte
Carolina Paiz
Lawrence Palomo
Robert Parada
George Parra
Eric Partida
Lionel Pasamonte
Carlos Pelayo
Jaime Pelayo
Elizabeth Peña
Sandra Peña
Steven Peña
Jeff Penichet
Juaquin Perea
Sylvia Perel
Rene Pereyra
Anthony Perez
Dianna Pérez
Emily Perez
Leo Perez
Patrick Perez
Paul Perez
Robert Perez
Rosana Perez
Ivonne Pérez Montijo
Quincy Perkins
Ted Perkins-Lopez
Cesar Peschiera
Joseph D. Peters
Carlos F. Pinero
Jorge Pinos
Felix Pire
Tony Plana
Erin Ploss-Campoamor
Anna M. Poore-Cordova
Paulina Porter
Lourdes Portillo
David Portorreal
Mitchell Posada
Santiago Pozo
Francesca Prada
Anayansi Prado
Henry K. Priest
Freddie Prinze Jr.
Pablo Proenza

Paulina Plazas
Diana Rios

Florida
Carlos Abascal
Stephen Acevedo
John Acosta
Diane Almodovar
Rafael Andreu
Emilia Anguita Huerta
Jaime Angulo
Alfonso Arambula
Leslie Arcia
Nelson Betancourt
Jorge Bonamino
Margarita Borda
Pablo Bressan
Maria Bures
Maria Chavez
Vanessa Dalama
Christian de la Fe
Alfredo de Villa
Zulma del Toro
Andrew Delaplaine
Mario Dubovoy
Manuel Elgarresta
Verena Faden
Errol Falcon
George E. Fernandez
Esteban Galarce
William Garcia
Carolina Garcia-Aguilera
Melba Gasque
Michael Gavino
Mauricio Gerson
Sergio Giral
Polita Glynn
David Gonzalez
Maritza Guimet
Lou Hernandez
Rudy Hernandez, Jr.
Adriana Ibanez
Andy Kleinman
Joleen Koehly
Duba Leibell
Luis Llosa
Alfredo Lopez-Brignoni
Madeleine Lopez-Silvero
Daniel Lucio
Elmo Lugo
Grace Machado
Phillipe Martinez
Stephanie Martinez
Madeline Mazzaira
James McNamara
Louis Mejia
Luis Mejia

Maria Meloni
Elisa Menendez
Rick Michaels
Rhonda L. Mitrani
Gustavo Nieto-Roa
Julio Noriega
Mercedes Palomo
Rey Parla
Luis Peraza
Annie Perez
Lisandro Perez-Rey
Luis Perez-Tolon
Giugliana Pessagno
Ximena Ponce
Raul Puig
Alexander Rivas
Jesus "Chuchi" Rivero
Carolina Rodriguez
Roy M. Rodriguez-Padron
Sylvie Rokab
Carla Sanchez
Milton Santiago
Cristina Saralegui
Guillermo Sauceda
Orlando Sosa
Astrid M. Vega
Aram Velazquez
Luis Villanueva
Raquel Ybes
Raquel Yepes
Juan Carlos Zaldivar

Georgia
Roberto Arevalo
Rudy Beserra

Illinois
Juan Frausto
Carolina Gaete
Olga Gonzales
Kathy Im
Robert Leach
Juan Jose Lopez
Elsa Madrigal
Jesus Martinez
Carolina Posse
Erica Rangel
Ricardo Rios
Diana Romero
Sonia Rosario
Stephanie Saint Sanchez
Dalia Tapia
Pepe Vargas
Rosie Vargas Goldberg

Kansas
David Chavez
Sarah Chavez

Kentucky
Eren McGinnis

Maine
Roberto Mendoza

Maryland
Daniel Perez

Massachusetts
Maria Agui-Carter
Patricia Alvarado-Nuñez
Blanca Bonilla
Josefina Bonilla-Ruiz
Evelyn Brito
Natatcha Estebanez
Digna Gerena
Magdalena Gomez
Lucas Guerra
Cristina Kotz Cornejo
Juan Mandelbaum
Susie Potter
Veronica Robles
Fernando Ruiz
Joseph Tovares

Michigan
Deborah de la Torre
Irma Gonzalez

New Jersey
Maxim Almenas
Angelo Bolanos
Ezequiel Colon-Rivera
Juan M. Dominguez
Edgar Endress
Lisa Marie Fabrega
Maria Gonzalez
Brian F. Grabski
Wilfredo Hernandez Jr.
Roberto Herrero
Mercedes Jimenez-Ramirez
Umesh Krishnan
Roberto Lopez
Vanessa Macedo
Nicole Mattei
Pepper Negron
Victor Rosa
Jinny Sample
Irene Sosa
Carolina Sotola
William Tucker

Milcha Sanchez Scott
Carlos Sandoval
Sinnel Sandoval
Manny Santos
Joan Shigekawa
Gustavo Stebner
Yamila Sterling
Candido Tirado
Michael Toribio
Roselly A. Torres-Rojas
Frida Torresblanco
Ela Troyano
Susana Tubert
John Valadez
Myra Varadi
Rosadel Varela
Yvette Vega
Vlamyr Vizcaya
Cheryl Williams
Alex Wolfe
Craig Young
Tony Zertuche
Pedro Zurita

Ohio
Rafael Rosado

Oklahoma
Mario Avila

Pennsylvania
Michael B. Case
Javier Gonzalez
Juvencio Gonzalez
Carla P. Morales
Christina "Herricane" Morales
Richard A. Murray Jr.
Maria Teresa Rodriguez
Gustavo Sagastume

Puerto Rico
Jorge Luis Aquino Calo
Maria Bird-Pico
Ricardo Cardona-Marty
Ileana Ciena
Gloribel Delgado
Alexon Duprey
Sonia Fritz
Ana Maria Garcia
Joe D. Gonzalez
Frances Lausell
Paco López
Elba Luis Lugo
Juan Marquez
Alex Matos
Von Marie Mendez

Danny Nieves
José Orraca-Brandenberger
Ivan Ortiz
Ingrid Ramirez
Raul Rios-Diaz
Roberto Jose Sanchez-Santos
Alex Santiago
Antonio J. Sifre Seín
James Stevens-Arce
Emmanuel Vargas-Ocasio
Carlos Anibal Vazquez
Laura Velez
Miguel Villafañe

Rhode Island
Victor Ramos

South Carolina
Joseph Delgado

Texas
Martin Acevedo
Belinda Acosta
Gustavo Aguilar
Felix Alcala
Elizabeth Avellan
Marcos Baraibar
Ruben Barrera
Joe Basquez
María Berns
Bette Brown
Georgia Brown-Quiñones
Cynthia Buchanan
Nora Cadena
Carlos Castañeda
Roger Castillo
Carol Chavez
Federico Chavez Blanco
George Cisneros
Dolores Colunga-Stawitz
Carlos Corral
Kaye Cruz
Ana Marie de la Peña Portela
Guillermo del Toro
Karina Duque
Benny Flores
Korina Flores
Evy Ledesma Galán
Hector Galán
Kristin Elise Gamez
Naiti Gamez
Albert Garcia
Eric Garcia
Jose Jesus JJ Garcia
Manuel Ray Garcia
Mario Garza

Lydia Garza-Marines
Jeff Gipson
Luis Guerra
Phillip V. Guerra
Johnathan Gwyn
Mary Harder
Melchor B. Hawkins
Roger Hernandez
Sharon Hernandez
Veronica R. Hernandez
Mita Hernandez-Gosdin
Jacob Herrera
George Iniguez
Karen Johnson
Mary Lampe
Rick Leal
Claudia Loewenstein
Julian Londono
Gilda Longoria
Marcie Longoria
Jesse Lujan
Angelica Mata
Drew Mayer-Oakes
Armando Medrano
Nick Medrano
Andrea Melendez
Joe Miraglilo
Chris Navarro
Arturo Parra
Jose Luis Partida
Dora Peña
Chris Perez
Veronica Potter
Travis R. Rendon
Victora Rene
Arnie Reyes
Leo Reyes
Rose Reyes
Ruperto Reyes
Baldemar Rodriguez
Grisel Rodriguez
James P. Rodriguez
Luis Rodriguez
Robert Rodriguez
Lydia Rousey
Ralph Salazar
Rogelio & Rachel Salinas
Valerie Samaniego-Finch
Ray Santisteban
John Scheiber
Samantha Smith
Olga Talavera de Magana
Mike Tolleson
David M. Torres
Marta Valadez
Lupe Valdez
Deon Van Rooyen
Laura Varela
Raymond Villareal

index by state

OUR SUPPORTERS

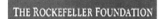

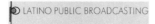

DATA COLLECTION FORM

Dear NALIP members and friends,

We hope you enjoy the **Latino Media Resource Guide**™ and find it beneficial. Please help us make this book a powerful tool by updating and providing us with your most current credit and contact information on the questionnaire below. In addition to this invaluable book, NALIP brings to our community a state-of-the-art intranet site at http://my.nalip.info. This communication tool gives NALIP members and chapters their own website, email address, searchable directory, chat rooms, job boards and much more! You can even update all your information online! Employers can find you, members can contact you, and we can continue emailing you *Latinos in the Industry* and other important opportunities for your projects and careers.

First Name_____ Last Name _____

Title/Position_____

Company_____

Address_____

City _____ State _____

Zip Code_____ Country_____

Phone 1 _____ Phone 2 _____

Cell Phone _____ Fax _____

Email _____ Website_____

What is your primary job in the industry? (e.g. Writer, Producer, Editor, D.P., Agent, Executive, Publicist, etc.):

_____

Please list produced titles where you received that/those credit(s). Include year, distributor or production company, and type of project (e.g. feature, tv movie, documentary, short, etc.). Use back of form if needed.

_____

_____

_____

_____

_____

Are you a member of any of the following organizations?

❏ NALIP   ❏ AIVF   ❏ DGA   ❏ IFP   ❏ SAG   ❏ WIF
           ❏ ASC   ❏ IDA   ❏ PGA   ❏ WGA   ❏ Other_____

REPRESENTATION:

Agency _____ Contact_____

Phone _____ Email _____

Manager _____ Contact_____

Phone _____ Email _____

Publicist_____ Contact_____

Phone _____ Email _____

Attorney _____ Contact_____

Phone _____ Email _____

Please mail completed form to NALIP/LMRG, P.O. Box 1247, Santa Monica, CA 90406, or email to LMRG@nalip.info or fax to 310.395.8811. Thank you.